Managing an Information Security and Privacy Awareness and Training Program

Second Edition

Managing an Information Security and Privacy Awareness and Training Program

Second Edition

REBECCA HEROLD

CRC Press
Taylor & Francis Group
Boca Raton London New York

CRC Press is an imprint of the
Taylor & Francis Group, an **informa** business
AN AUERBACH BOOK

Cover design by Noah Herold.

CRC Press
Taylor & Francis Group
6000 Broken Sound Parkway NW, Suite 300
Boca Raton, FL 33487-2742

© 2011 by Taylor and Francis Group, LLC
CRC Press is an imprint of Taylor & Francis Group, an Informa business

No claim to original U.S. Government works

Printed in the United States of America on acid-free paper
10 9 8 7 6 5 4 3 2 1

International Standard Book Number: 978-1-4398-1545-8 (Hardback)

Library of Congress Cataloging-in-Publication Data

Herold, Rebecca.
    Managing an information security and privacy awareness and training program / Rebecca Herold. -- 2nd ed.
        p. cm.
    Includes bibliographical references and index.
    ISBN 978-1-4398-1545-8 (alk. paper)
    1. Computer security--Management. 2. Data protection--Management. I. Title.

QA76.9.A25H46 2010
658.4'78--dc22   2010000151

Visit the Taylor & Francis Web site at
http://www.taylorandfrancis.com

and the CRC Press Web site at
http://www.crcpress.com

To my two beautiful boys, Noah Theodore and Heath Xavier.
They are the very best things I have brought into the world.

To my husband, Tom, who for many years has shouldered most of the
work in the house, in addition to all his farm business work, to give me the
ability to run my business and write. I am eternally grateful to him.

To my father, Harold Walker Flint, who spent his life as a professional
educator, in addition to serving in the U.S. Navy in World War II and farming.
He lost a hard-fought battle with cancer in January, 2010. I miss him.

To my mother, Mary Ann Flint, who was the most wonderful,
caring and kind person I've ever known. She encouraged me
from a very young age to write and do whatever I wanted to do;
I miss her a lot. She left this world far too young in 1996.

Contents

Foreword

For the past 30 or so years that I have been closely involved in information security, security awareness training has been the most valuable yet the most overlooked and underfunded mechanism for improving the implementation of information security. This, unfortunately, is true for both public and private sectors—not because it isn't recognized as important, but because it isn't seen as the "silver bullet" that everyone seeks to solve security problems overnight.

In retrospect, it may, in fact, be that silver bullet because information security is now realized by many experts to be more of a people problem than a technical one. Of course, there are many technical devices that are necessary to obtain and maintain appropriate controls, but these are used by or used to control people. Because security awareness training is not as glamorous or unique as the newest technical system, it does not get the respect it deserves and often rests on the back burner of implementation priority.

This book is remarkable because it covers in detail all the facets of providing effective security awareness training. One of the early chapters deals with the question of why this is important. This chapter is key because for training to be effective, the organization has to believe that it is necessary. Management from top to bottom must know the several drivers behind the need for awareness. The more obvious ones deal with the need to comply with federal and state legislation, as well as the requirement to ensure the privacy of personal information. A whole chapter is devoted to the issues of legal and regulatory compliance. Failure to address these requirements can result in heavy fines and potential time behind bars for executives. The need for awareness training is also related to the problem of compliance with organization policy. It is difficult to hold people accountable for policies and procedures that they don't fully understand.

Once an organization establishes, and its people understand, its policies and procedures for providing appropriate information security, it is faced with the immediate problem of how to get people to comply. There must be some significant incentive that provides employees with the desire to focus on compliance. We have attempted the "big stick method" of involving auditors and their very effective comments, findings, and recommendations—the terrible weapons that user groups universally dread and dislike—as well as threats of punishment, and these have limited success. A better method—that of including security responsibilities in job descriptions and encouraging compliance by performance appraisal evaluations—is described in detail.

Now, having laid the foundation for training and awareness, we arrive at the major hurdle—getting started. The standard project management tools and methods come into play here. But first, it is important to peruse the chapter dealing with common mistakes that organizations are apt to make. The chapter covering this is interesting and provides a number of items for consideration.

Then, we move onto getting started; obviously, defining goals and mission is a big first step. Identifying specific needs based on what is already being accomplished is next. All of this and more are thoroughly discussed.

Related to getting started is the need to identify the training and awareness methods that are best suited for your organization. The book provides complete guidance on how to accomplish this, in addition to discussing how to fit the various topics to the different audiences involved.

Everyone needs some basic understanding, such as how to cope with social engineering, while specific groups need performance-oriented instruction, such as incident response procedures.

Not to be ignored is the need to obtain executive level support and sponsorship. Without this, it will be extremely difficult, if not impossible, to achieve success because your training and awareness project will be ongoing and expensive in terms of people's time and organization funding.

Executive support is essential to obtain the required funding; therefore, preparing a budget that will be accepted is critical. You can find proven methods for creating your budget in this book. Many useful ideas are presented.

You will notice that considerable space in the book focuses on the design and development of your training program. Many considerations are involved and all are covered thoroughly. Design and development must be created to fit your particular organization culture and needs. The final chapter provides several articles that demonstrate the use of the guidance from previous chapters. These articles are descriptive of successfully implemented training and awareness programs from both the public and private sectors. Here you will learn the proverbial "tricks of the trade."

The 22 appendices will prove to be extremely useful because they provide a plethora of forms, examples, and samples. This means that you won't need to develop your own and get tied into that waste of valuable time called "reinventing the wheel."

Finally, I can, without reservation, recommend use of this book to any organization faced with the need to develop a successful training and awareness program. It surely provides everything you need to know to create a real winner.

Hal Tipton

Preface

Everybody hates information security and the constraints it imposes on work performance and convenience. So how do you make people aware of security and train them in safeguard requirements and practices and provide the motivation to make them effective? Rebecca Herold has the answers in her definitive book on everything everybody needs to know about how to impart security awareness, training, and motivation. Motivation has been missing from the information security lexicon until Herold put it there in most thorough and effective ways, especially in the most important Chapter 4 of her book. She demonstrates that security must become a part of job performance rather than being in conflict with job performance. You can't achieve more than superficial and cosmetic security in any organization until you have achieved motivation to make security awareness and training effective. Hal Tipton also expresses this in his fine Foreword to this complete exposition on security awareness and training.

The power of this book also lies in applying real education theory, methods, and practice to teaching security awareness and training. I am particularly pleased when experts in other fields, such as Herold in education, become specialists in information security to bring other relevant disciplines to bear on security. However, this book contains more than just Rebecca's ideas. Chapter 19 has 10 quoted short authoritative articles from other experts in awareness training.

I have never seen a more thorough and extensive justification for security awareness than in Chapters 2 and 3. She covers most of the legislation and regulations governing the need for awareness, at least applicable in the United States. After reading this book, there is no question about the necessary and important roles of security awareness, training, and motivation.

In Chapter 9, she clearly separates awareness and training with the statement, "Awareness is typically the 'what' component of your education strategy; training is typically the 'how' component." And she continues thoroughly to provide 250 awareness materials and methods (Chapter 14), 42 tips to trainers (Chapter 16), and 22 appendices with sample forms, slide presentations, and checklists, of course content. However, there is no detailed awareness and training content. You have to get that from the many sources available such as the International Organization for Standardization/International Electrotechnical Commission (ISO/IEC) and from your own culture, environment, policies, standards, and guidelines. But everything else that you need that I can think of is in this book that every chief privacy officer, chief information security officer, and security trainer should have open and in use on their desks, not just on the shelf.

Donn B. Parker, CISSP

About the Author

Rebecca Herold, CIPP, CISM, CISA, CISSP, FLMI, is an information privacy, security, and compliance consultant, author, and instructor who has provided assistance, advice, services, tools, and products to organizations in a wide range of industries during the past two decades. Rebecca is a widely recognized and respected information security, privacy, and compliance expert. Some of her awards and recognitions include

- Being named one of the "Best Privacy Advisers in the World" multiple times in recent years by *Computerworld* magazine.
- Being named one of the "Top 59 Influencers in IT Security" for 2007 by *IT Security* magazine.
- Having her blog named one of the "Top 50 Internet Security Blogs" by the Daily Netizen in 2008.
- Having the information security program she created for the Principal Financial Group, where she worked for 12 years, receive the 1998 Computer Security Institute (CSI) Outstanding Information Security Program of the Year Award.

Rebecca was one of the first, and possibly the very first, practitioners to be responsible for both information security and privacy within a large organization, in 1994 in a multinational insurance and financial organization. In 2008 Rebecca helped the European Network and Information Security Agency (ENISA) to create their well-received "Obtaining Support and Funding from Senior Management," which used much of her "Managing an Information Security and Privacy Awareness and Training Program" information. In 2009, Rebecca was asked to participate in the National Institute of Standards and Technology (NIST) Smart Grid standards committee, and to lead the Privacy Impact Assessment (PIA) activity, the very first performed in the electric utilities industry. Rebecca recently launched the Compliance Helper service (http://www.ComplianceHelper.com) to help healthcare organizations and their business associates meet their Health Insurance Portability and Accountability Act (HIPAA), Health Information Technology for Economic and Clinical Health Act (HITECH), and other information security and privacy compliance and risk mitigation requirements.

Rebecca assists organizations of all sizes and industries throughout the world with their information privacy, security, and regulatory compliance programs, content development, and strategy development and implementation through a large variety of tools and services. She offers a range of standard and customized 1- and 2-day workshops including one addressing how individuals across disciplines can work together to most effectively ensure privacy and regulatory compliance while efficiently implementing security controls. Rebecca is also an adjunct professor for the Norwich University Master of Science in Information Assurance (MSIA) program.

Rebecca has written 14 books to date, over 20 chapters for other books, has published over 200 articles in a wide range of publications, and has released over a dozen podcasts. She has created customized 1- and 2-day training for the specific needs of many different organizations. She is the creator and editor of the "Protecting Information" multimedia security and awareness quarterly publication (http://www.privacyguidance.com/piqa_newsletter.html), an effective training event (http://www.privacyguidance.com/security_search.html), and is releasing a series of information security and privacy training modules in 2009.

Rebecca serves on the advisory boards for Alvenda (an ecommerce technology company), Subroshare (a subrogation technology tools company), and Wombat Security Technologies (an online information security training company), was invited to be on the prestigious Institute of Electrical and Electronics Engineers (IEEE) ISTAS10 Program Committee, and is on the Norwich University *Journal of Information Assurance* Board of Review. Additionally, she has served as a board and council member of various other organizations, such as MaxMD and I'dCheck. She is also currently participating in the NIST standards committee to help create information security and privacy standards and practices for the U.S. Smart Grid. Rebecca also is often invited to participate in unique activities, such as serving as a preliminary judge for the 2009 American Business Awards.

Rebecca is frequently interviewed and quoted in diverse publications such as *IAPP Privacy Advisor, BNA Privacy & Security Law Report, Wired, Popular Science, CUinfosecurity, Bankinfosecurity, SearchWinIT, Consumer Financial Services Law Report, Computerworld, hcPro Briefings on HIPAA, SC Magazine, SearchSecurity, Information Security, Business 2.0, Disaster Resource Guide, The Boston Herald, Pharmaceutical Formulation and Quality, IT Business Edge, Fortifying Network Security, IT Architect, CIO Strategy Center, Physicians Weekly, IEEE's Intelligent Systems, Cutter IT Journal, Health Information Compliance Insider, Baseline, Western Michigan Business Review,* and others, including several radio interviews and broadcasts including on MyTechnologyLawyer.com, the "Privacy Piracy" California radio broadcast, and the "Michigan Technology News" radio broadcast.

Prior to owning her own business, Rebecca was Vice President–Privacy Services and internal Chief Privacy Officer at DelCreo, Inc. for 2 years. Prior to DelCreo, she served as Chief Privacy Officer and Senior Security Architect, QinetiQ Trusted Information Management, Inc. (Q-TIM), where she worked since the inception of the company as Securus in November 2001. Prior to joining Q-TIM, Rebecca was the Global Security Practice Central Region Security Subject Matter Expert for 2 years at Netigy (which became ThruPoint in September 2001). Prior to joining Netigy, Rebecca was Senior Systems Security Consultant at Principal Financial Group (PFG).

Rebecca began her career at PFG as a Customer Information Control System (CICS) systems analyst, and moved into an IT auditor position. It was at the recommendation of one of her audits that the information protection department was created, and she was asked to help build the department and functions. Her efforts helped PFG to be awarded the CSI Outstanding Information Security Program of the Year Award in 1998. Prior to working for PFG, Rebecca taught secondary school math and computer education in Missouri.

With a BS in math and computer science from Central Missouri State University in Warrensburg, and an MA in computer science and education from the University of Northern Iowa in Cedar Falls, Rebecca is a certified information systems security professional (CISSP), a certified information systems auditor (CISA), a certified information systems manager (CISM), a certified information privacy professional (CIPP), and a fellow of the Life Management Institute (FLMI). Rebecca has been a member of the Information Systems Audit and Control Association (ISACA) since 1990 and has held all board positions throughout her membership in the Iowa chapter. Rebecca is a charter member of the Iowa Infragard chapter that was formed in 2000, and a member of the International Association of Privacy Professionals (IAPP). She is also a member of ACM and of IEEE. Rebecca is currently on the Review Board for the Norwich University *Journal of Information Assurance* and serves on the Advisory Boards of Alvenda, Inc; Wombat Security Technologies; and Claim Catcher. In the past, Rebecca served as a member of the Advisory Board for I'dCheck, LLC and the Advisory Board for MaxMD.

Frequently invited to speak at conferences and seminars, and having created and delivered training workshops on behalf of CSI, ISACA, the Information Systems Security Association (ISSA), IAPP, Carnegie Melon, and the University of California, Berkeley, and customized training for a wide range of organizations, Rebecca has given presentations at internationally attended conferences and seminars since the early 1990s.

Introduction

When planning for a year, plant corn. When planning for a decade, plant trees. When planning for life, train and educate people.

—Chinese proverb

Education is the most powerful weapon which you can use to change the world.

—Nelson Mandela

Genius without education is like silver in the mine.

—Benjamin Franklin

Information security, and privacy training and awareness, were hot topics when I wrote the first edition of this book in 2004, and they are hotter issues today. As the need for education becomes more apparent, the number of training and awareness vendors has grown exponentially. Some of their offerings are very good, and others are very bad. In speaking with many security and privacy practitioners over the years, I have heard common themes regarding training and awareness: Where do I start? How do I plan for my program? How do I get funding? Where can I find good materials? How do I know that is effective?

I have also found a great lack of adult learning methodology or research to back much of the offerings for information security and awareness education. Education should be based upon sound adult learning research and incorporated into an education program for information security and privacy practitioners. Education should be tailored to the needs of the organization and the targeted learners.

As time goes on, and more and more information security incidents and privacy breaches occur, I continue to hear otherwise smart people say silly and completely wrong statements about the need for (or lack of) information security and privacy training and awareness!

In almost every information security incident and privacy breach, humans were ultimately the cause, sometimes because of malicious intent, but more often through lack of knowledge and awareness or mistakes or omissions made, often because security and privacy were not in mind. Even when malicious intent was involved, it typically exploited human security unawareness in some way.

Computer systems and applications must be built with more robust and more transparent security capabilities than are currently found. However, you cannot create a computer technology so secure that no training is necessary for those using the computers. It's like saying you can build a car so secure that you don't need to teach people how to drive safely. Who wants to be on the road with those folks? And, anyway, when it comes to effective information security and privacy protection, effective and regular information security, privacy training, and ongoing awareness communications is absolutely necessary at all levels throughout the enterprise. Systems and applications will not be built with these safeguards without educating those building them.

And, besides being smart and wise by providing effective regular training and ongoing awareness communications to help prevent information security incidents and privacy breaches, it is also a requirement in most data protection laws and regulations to provide such education. That is one thing our government leaders have recognized and generally have been careful to require within numerous laws and regulations.

Providing effective information security and privacy training and awareness is one of the most cost-effective and results-effective practices that businesses can do to keep their information assets safe.

Business leaders, if technology-specific vendors tell you that training is a waste of time and money, it is likely they want to put their hands in your pockets, much deeper than any education investment would be, to sell you a system or application that is ten to hundreds of times the cost of any education program you could put in place.

I wrote this book to provide a starting point and an all-in-one resource for information security and privacy education practitioners. I incorporated much of the information and knowledge I obtained while working on my MA in computer science and education as applicable to providing education to adult learners. Additionally, I included the same type of information that I have used and found helpful over the years when creating awareness and training programs. I included many pointers to other resources where you can get more specialized information. My goal was to provide a more comprehensive resource of everything involved with managing an information security and privacy training and awareness program than I had been able to find—a reference for practitioners to go to when implementing any part of their education program and get ideas that will help them be successful with their own program. I hope you feel I came close to meeting this goal.

I have included examples and tools for a very wide range of businesses and organizations. I do not expect that there will be any one organization that will be able to use every single idea or suggestion within this book. However, I hope this serves as a type of "cookbook" for your education efforts where you can pick and choose, sift and sort, and identify all the ingredients for what will become your most successful education program menu.

There is much misinformation being sold and circulated about information security and privacy education. There are many products being offered for training and awareness that are not based upon a sound educational foundation. Hopefully, this book will help you to identify those products that will be effective from those that were just thrown together in the hope of making a quick buck.

I do not expect that this book will be read cover to cover, front to back. Of course, if you want to read it this way, that would be spectacular! I structured the book to go from the inception of an information security and privacy education program through development, implementation, and delivery, all the way to evaluation, and then added a cornucopia of appendices. I hope my readers will use this as a reference book to flip through and find whatever they need to help with their education efforts—tools, tips, worksheets, case studies, ideas, resources, and research on regulatory requirements for education of which practitioners must be aware.

The first 18 chapters of this book contain many lists, recommendations, plans, tools, ideas, and research for you to incorporate into your education program. Chapter 19 contains some excellent examples of real education experiences and case studies for information security education. Because Chapter 19 focuses primarily upon information security, I am putting a little more emphasis on privacy examples throughout the other chapters in the book to try and achieve a balance between security and privacy. You can modify as necessary for your particular organization. Twenty-two appendices are provided to serve as examples and give additional information for specific training and awareness issues.

Information security and privacy training and awareness programs are important. Knowledge can, and should, be used as a basis for competitive strategy. When personnel learn more about the business, what business requires with regard to security and privacy, and what is expected of them when performing business activities, you will be more assured not only of security and privacy success but also of business success. You can have the most well-written information security and privacy policies and procedures in the world, but if your personnel do not know them, understand them, or implement them within their own job responsibilities and activities, then you will not have effective security or privacy. The more personnel know about information security and privacy issues, requirements and impacts, the more you will be assured of success with implementing security, and awareness measures, complying with applicable regulations, and having business success with information security and privacy goals.

The success of any awareness and training program depends on using a thoughtful, systematic approach for delivering effective awareness activities and instructional sessions to your target audiences. Several types of approaches are presented for practitioners to consider and modify to make most effective within their environment.

Effective training and awareness methods will enhance human performance and lead to accomplishing learning and understanding goals. An employee's ability to perform his job is limited by a lack of knowledge or skill. A person's ability to secure your organization's information and processing systems is limited by a lack of knowledge of what is necessary to preserve privacy and establish security, and a lack of skills necessary to successfully secure the information as appropriate for each situation.

Thank you in advance for indulging me my quotes, anecdotes, and stories. As with most learners, I find I can relate to concepts easier when I can put them in a different perspective and connect them to events that happen in nature or in real-life relationships. Also, I find some quotes to be thought provoking, putting a concept into a slightly different perspective, so I hope you enjoy reading the quotes I've chosen that relate to each of the chapter topics.

I want you to be successful and to use this book to help you achieve that success. I hope you find this to be a valuable asset in obtaining your professional, work-related, and education-related goals.

Rebecca Herold

Chapter 1

Brief History of Corporate Information Security and Privacy Awareness and Training

Learning is not compulsory but neither is survival.

—W. Edwards Deming

It is worthwhile to take a brief look at workplace training and awareness history. I am certainly not going to go into great detail here; there are many very good books that cover this history quite thoroughly. However, to give you a high-level overview of where training and awareness started and how far it has come in recent years, I want to provide a historical perspective.

Once Upon a Time ...

Of course, apprenticeships and guilds, both of which are types of professional training associations, have been around for thousands of years. Apprenticeships are reported as early as 1800 B.C.*

---

* Robert L. Craig. The history of training, in *The ASTD Training and Development Handbook*, 4th edition, McGraw-Hill, New York, 1996, p. 4.

It is an interesting topic but let us start a little more recently, though, around the 1880s in the United States, when there was a general shift from a primarily agricultural economy to a primarily industrial economy. Apprenticeships became quite popular at this time as the method of choice for what could be considered corporate teaching or training. Around 1900 to 1910, mass production started to become popular, and management became a recognized profession. Frank and Lillian Gilbreth promoted time-management methods, and a move was made toward providing systematic training to improve efficiency, based on job activities. Around the 1940s, education and training were designed to create a formal management structure, using the methods of leaders such as B.F. Skinner and his automated teaching machine.

Starting around 1960, individualized learning emerged. Around the 1980s, there was another shift, and many consider this time to represent a shift from an industrial to an information economy. PCs started being used widely. And then, around the 1990s, the concept of organizational training and education started to revolve around how to perform tasks and how to view job responsibilities and activities. The Internet has had a huge impact on organizational behavior. During the dot.com boom, many business considerations were put on hold (often including fiscal common sense) so that large infrastructures could be built. It seemed during this time, within many organizations, that information security and privacy and awareness training were put on hold as well. People are now dependent on electronic mail and Web sites to do business. Return on investment (ROI), in general, and ROI specific to information security and privacy, as well as online learning became very hot topics into the 2000s.

Preindustrial age businesses relied heavily on having a high degree of specialized labor, with a relatively small workforce. For example, the shoemaker would select and train his apprentice, beginning with the simplest tasks and graduating to the more complex cobbling tasks. The apprentice–master relationship would be a long one, based on a lifetime employee model. With the rise of the Industrial Revolution, the size of the workforce increased through such inventions as the steam engine and rudimentary automation techniques. The separation of labor drove employers to train more than one employee at a time. As corporations grew larger and became more complex, the applicability of one-on-one training, except for the most targeted or specialized training, became inadequate; therefore, companies started to develop formalized training.

This took the form of lectures led by company (or outside) experts in a classroom setting at company locations. Instructor-led training, in which one instructor would train many employees, became the method of choice. This model has remained essentially the same since the invention of the steam engine, whereas the content has certainly become optimized to the particular needs of work teams.

Welcome to the Information Age

The Internet really became a significant information dissemination medium only in the late 1990s. Some credit this development with giving birth to what is known as the "information age." With the information age came new challenges in managing

Exhibit 1   Example of How Businesses Educate Customers with YouTube.*

and leveraging the tremendous rise in intellectual property, and customer and internal corporate information.

While educational services have remained essentially the same, the face of business has changed significantly. On the global front, companies are wrestling with issues such as multi-language and in-country support. In the Old Economy, businesses were able to get by with generic corporate learning programs for a large, stable workforce. In the New Economy, this approach is costly, time consuming, and unrealistic due to the specialized job responsibilities and regulatory requirements, and it no longer fits the business model, which is aimed at sustaining the company's competitive advantage.

Training and awareness are no longer considered internal functions only. Now, you must also consider how to make your customers aware of important issues, such as security and privacy, which are related to their using your organization's services and purchasing your products. Organizations increasingly find themselves liable for breaches that occur as a result of their customers' poor security practices if they have not made their customers aware of what they should do to protect their information.

You now have responsibilities to pass on information as required by multiple regulatory requirements and communicate information to demonstrate due diligence, in addition to setting expectations for your services and products. Organizations are now using electronic educational methods, aside from employee awareness and training, as part of their marketing strategy to reach channel partners, end users, and consumers. Web 2.0 tools, such as videos on YouTube™ (see Exhibit 1) and

---

* Accessed on June 2, 2009, from http://www.youtube.com/watch?v=h7LtTH-pVUk&feature= channel_page.

Exhibit 2 Example of How Businesses Educate Customers with Instant Presenter Webcasts.*

webcasts using such tools as Instant Presenter (see Exhibit 2), also called social media, can also be used effectively for information security and privacy education. Customers have many more choices regarding where to make their purchases. If they are unhappy with how your company handles security and privacy issues, they can easily take their business to a competitor that handles those issues to their satisfaction. It is not only a competitive advantage, but a marketing differentiator, to provide good information security and privacy education to not only your personnel, but also your consumers and customers.

Information Security and Privacy Education

With regard to information security and privacy-specific awareness and training, the privacy training issue emerged in the late 1990s and early 2000s as more and more privacy regulations and laws were being passed.

Information security, however, began to be addressed by organizations such as the Computer Security Institute (CSI) in 1974 and the MIS Training Institute organization in 1978. Professional organizations, such as the Institute for Internal Auditors (IIA; established in 1941), the Information Systems Audit and Control Association

---

* Accessed on June 2, 2009, from http://www.instantpresenter.com/Web-Conferencing-Solutions/ WebcastandWebinarSolutions.aspx.

(ISACA; started as the EDPAA in 1967), Association for Computing Machinery (ACM; started in 1947), the Information Systems Security Association (ISSA; started in 1984), and the International Association of Privacy Professionals (IAPP; started in 2000) have promoted awareness and sponsored training events since their inceptions, through local, regional, national, international, and publication activities.

Current Challenges Bring Changes in Professional Education

The constantly increasing demands of the global economy, in tandem with the rapidly spreading information technologies and quickly growing numbers of regulatory and legal requirements for how information must be handled and processed, will continue to change the way organizations operate. Information is being stored and accessed in more widely dispersed, and often poorly secured, locations than ever before. Human lack of knowledge, mistakes, and malicious intent are overwhelmingly the cause of most information security incidents and privacy breaches.

These factors increase the need for both better awareness and training activities in general and for improved understanding of security and privacy issues in particular. The need to constantly learn about these changes, and to update policies and processes, make the importance of information security and privacy training and awareness more significant than ever before.

Professionals responsible for ensuring information security and privacy awareness and training now need to work with many models of individual and organizational learning, and identify the method that works best for each identified target audience. Classroom training and instructor-led instruction will still be necessary, but in many instances these traditional methods can and will be effectively replaced by other technology-based instruction methods. It is safe to state that as the need for personnel to truly understand corporate information security and privacy issues increases, the educational focus will shift from the instructors (and the instruction they impart) to the personnel, as learners who need to understand corporate-risk issues to effectively meet their job responsibilities and assume accountability for their activities. The methods of professional education and delivery are now more diverse than they ever have been in history.

Chapter 2

Why Training and Awareness Are Important

It's all to do with the training: You can do a lot if you're properly trained.

—**Queen Elizabeth II**

Education is not the filling of a pail, but the lighting of a fire.

—**W.B. Yeats**

Creating an information security and privacy awareness and training program is not a simple task. It is often a frustrating task. It is often a challenging task. And many times, unfortunately, it is often a thankless task. However, providing your personnel with the security and privacy information they need, and ensuring they understand and follow the requirements, is an important component of your organization's business success. If your personnel do not know or understand how to maintain confidentiality of information, or how to secure it appropriately, not only do you risk having one of your most valuable business assets (information) mishandled, inappropriately used, or obtained by unauthorized persons, but you also risk being in noncompliance of a growing number of laws and regulations that require certain types of information security and privacy awareness and training activities. You also risk damaging another valuable asset, corporate reputation. Information security and privacy education are important for many reasons, including the following.

Regulatory Requirements Compliance

There are an increasing number of laws and regulations that require some forms of training and awareness activities to occur within the organizations over which they have jurisdiction. Factors under the U.S. Federal Sentencing Guidelines that impact the severity of the judgments include the following:

- How frequently and how well does the organization communicate its policies to personnel?
- Are personnel getting effectively trained and receiving awareness?
- What methods does the organization use for such communications?
- Does the organization verify that the desired results from training occur?
- Does the organization update the education program to improve communications and to get the right message out to personnel?
- Does the training cover ethical work practices?
- Is there ongoing compliance and ethics dialogue between staff and management?
- Is management getting the same educational messages as the staff?

According to the Department of Justice, in 1995, 111 organizational defendants were sentenced under the guidelines, with 83 cases receiving associated fines. By 2001, the number of organizational defendants sentenced rose to 238, with 137 getting fines and 49 getting both fines and restitution:

- Average fine: $2.2 million.
- Average restitution awarded: $3.3 million.
- Of those sentenced, 90 had no compliance program.

From 2005 to 2006 there were 217 organizational defendants, and only three of the organizations were found to have an effective compliance program in place as required by the guidelines. The existence of what the courts consider as effective compliance programs is more important, and carries more weight in sentencing judgments, than they ever have before. And they are getting more important as more regulations and laws are put into effect. Along with this increased scrutiny of compliance programs, and the training and awareness activities that are necessary within it, it is likely that the numbers of fines and penalties will increase.

A regulatory education program should

- address your company's interpretation of applicable security and privacy laws and regulations,
- support the activities your organization takes to mitigate risk and ensure that security and privacy are based on the results of a baseline assessment, and support your company's policies.

Customer Trust and Satisfaction

Respect for customer security and privacy is one of the most important issues facing your company today. The public is getting sick and tired of reading about privacy breaches every day in the newspaper headlines, and they want to know that your company is doing everything reasonable and responsible to safeguard their personally identifiable information (PII), as well as all other types of personal information.

To gain and keep both customer and employee trust, your company must exercise good judgment in the collection, use, and protection of PII. Not only do you need to provide training and awareness of this to your personnel, but you also need to keep your customers (with whom you already have a business relationship) and consumers (with whom you would like to have a business relationship, and who may have provided some information to you) informed regarding what you are doing to protect their privacy and ensure the security of their information through various awareness messages.

These topics will be discussed in more detail in Chapter 10, but I will list a few specific items here to be sure you include them in your training and awareness program, because they can have such a big impact on how consumers and customers view your organization, and on how much trust and satisfaction will result from your educational efforts. The goal is to provide training and awareness that will result in

- your company adequately protecting each customer's PII from inappropriate exposure or sharing;
- giving your customers the opportunity to indicate their contact preferences at the point where their PII is collected;
- personnel's understanding that senior management is serious about protecting customer's PII, and that personnel who do not comply with security and privacy policies could face serious consequences, including termination;
- customer PII not being used for any purpose that was not disclosed to the customer at the time of collection;
- customers being able to opt out of any touchpoint or service (such as a newsletter subscription or Web site), and ensuring that your personnel know the appropriate processes that must be in place to honor the decision;
- ensuring you give customers information about what you are doing to protect their PII, how it will be used, and knowing how to allow them to choose whether to be included in your marketing databases;
- all your company e-mail communications being opt-in, with very few approved exceptions for administrative contact. Mobile phone marketing and third-party data sharing should also be restricted to opt-in. Postal and phone communications are typically opt-out, but it is a good leading practice to also make these opt-in;
- protecting your customer PII by contract (written agreement) and compliance audits.

All workers (employee and contract) and companies directly involved in the handling of your company's customer PII should receive targeted security and privacy training before being entrusted with customer information, with refresher training every year, or more often, based on the nature of your business and the potential impact on your business if PII is not handled correctly. They should also receive ongoing awareness communications to reinforce security and privacy issues and requirements and help to embed such practices within their daily work activities.

You should provide training and awareness to ensure that all your organization's activities comply with your privacy policy, as well as with local laws and regulations. Your security and privacy messages must communicate that

■ your company is obligated to fulfill the privacy expectations that it has communicated,
■ your personnel must know the customer privacy principles,
■ your personnel must incorporate the principles into their daily job responsibilities and tasks,
■ your personnel face sanctions, including possible termination, for not complying with security and privacy policies.

Compliance with Published Policies

Organizations are obligated to comply with their own information security and privacy policies. If compliance is not enforced, such policies are basically worthless!

So, organizations need to educate personnel about their information security and privacy roles and responsibilities, especially in support of published policies, standards, and procedures. Awareness and training should be designed to support compliance with security and privacy policies. Executive management acts as role models for personnel, and their actions heavily influence the level of employee awareness and policy compliance.

Senior management should clearly and visibly support, encourage, and show commitment to information security and privacy training and awareness activities. Training and awareness activities should include a review of the policies, and address issues and topics such as those discussed later in this book.

If possible within your organization, implement a procedure to obtain a signed information security and privacy awareness agreement at the times you deliver the training, to document and demonstrate that training and awareness activities are occurring, that the personnel acknowledge understanding, and that the education efforts are ongoing.

Due Diligence

In general, due diligence is providing demonstrated assurance that management is ensuring adequate protection of corporate assets, such as information, and compliance with legal and contractual obligations. This is a powerful motivator for implementing a training and awareness program.

Key provisions of the U.S. Federal Sentencing Guidelines and recent amendments include establishing an effective compliance program and exercising due diligence in the prevention and detection of criminal conduct. Any organization with some type of compliance requirement (basically all public entities, given the Sarbanes–Oxley Act of 2002) is directly impacted by the guidelines. One way such due diligence is demonstrated is through an effective, executive-supported, information security and privacy education program.

The organizational sentencing guidelines motivate organizations to create a program to reduce and, ideally, eliminate criminal conduct by implementing an effective ethics and compliance program that includes compliance with all applicable laws. The updates to the sentencing criteria incorporate leading practices that have been referenced and identified in such regulations as the Sarbanes–Oxley Act (SOX), the Health Insurance Portability and Accountability Act (HIPAA), the Gramm–Leach–Bliley Act (GLBA), the Red Flags Rule, the Health Information Technology for Economic and Clinical Health Act (HITECH), and other internationally recognized standards. The 2004 updates are contained in guidelines (at §8B2.1, as discussed later in this chapter) and elaborate on the need for organizations to more rigorously demonstrate responsibility and demonstrate executive leadership.

To have a program that effectively conforms to the guidelines, an organization must demonstrate that it exercises due diligence in meeting compliance requirements and also promotes "an organizational culture that encourages ethical conduct and a commitment to compliance with the law." It is important to note that the guidelines describe functional requirements, and it does not matter if an organization calls the program a compliance program, an ethics program, or some other name. It is the actions and activities of the program that are reviewed if a due diligence and sentencing situation arises. At a high level, the following are the organizational requirements described in the updated guidelines:

- Develop and implement standards and procedures to prevent and detect criminal conduct.
- Assign responsibility and ensure adequate resources at all levels, and authority for the program.
- Perform personnel screening as applicable (in accordance with laws, regulations, and labor union requirements) and as related to program goals and the responsibilities of the staff involved.
- Ensure adequate and effective awareness and training at all levels of the organization.
- Ensure auditing, monitoring, and evaluating activities occur to verify program effectiveness.
- Implement internal reporting systems that ensure nonretaliatory reaction.

- Provide incentives and enforce discipline to promote compliance.
- Consistently take reasonable steps to respond to violations and prevent similar violations from occurring.

The motivation behind these updated guidelines seems to be to ensure that if an organization is found guilty of a federal offense, the leader will face stiff sentences and civil penalties unless proof is provided of having a stringent, well-communicated compliance program. This should drive organizations to make ongoing, continuously communicated compliance programs, including awareness and training components, a priority.

The 2004 U.S. Federal Sentencing Guidelines state:*

§8B2.1. Effective Compliance and Ethics Program

(a) To have an effective compliance and ethics program, for purposes of subsection (f) of §8C2.5 (Culpability Score) and subsection (c)(1) of §8D1.4 (Recommended Conditions of Probation Organizations), an organization shall—
   (1) exercise due diligence to prevent and detect criminal conduct; and
   (2) otherwise promote an organizational culture that encourages ethical conduct and a commitment to compliance with the law.

   Such a compliance and ethics program shall be reasonably designed, implemented, and enforced so that the program is generally effective in preventing and detecting criminal conduct.

   The failure to prevent or detect the instant offense does not necessarily mean that the program is not generally effective in preventing and detecting criminal conduct.
(b) Due diligence and the promotion of an organizational culture that encourages ethical conduct and a commitment to compliance with the law within the meaning of subsection (a) minimally require the following:
   (1) The organization shall establish standards and procedures to prevent and detect criminal conduct.
   (2) (A) The organization's governing authority shall be knowledgeable about the content and operation of the compliance and ethics program and shall exercise reasonable oversight with respect to the implementation and effectiveness of the compliance and ethics program.
      (B) High-level personnel of the organization shall ensure that the organization has an effective compliance and ethics program, as described in this guideline. Specific individual(s) within high-level personnel shall be assigned overall responsibility for the compliance and ethics program.

---

* United States Sentencing Commission, Sentencing Guidelines for United States Courts, http://www.ussc.gov/FEDREG/05_04_notice.pdf.

(C) Specific individual(s) within the organization shall be delegated day-to-day operational responsibility for the compliance and ethics program. Individual(s) with operational responsibility shall report periodically to high-level personnel and, as appropriate, to the governing authority, or an appropriate subgroup of the governing authority, on the effectiveness of the compliance and ethics program. To carry out such operational responsibility, such individual(s) shall be given adequate resources, appropriate authority, and direct access to the governing authority or an appropriate subgroup of the governing authority.

(3) The organization shall use reasonable efforts not to include within the substantial authority personnel of the organization any individual whom the organization knew, or should have known through the exercise of due diligence, has engaged in illegal activities or other conduct inconsistent with an effective compliance and ethics program.

(4) (A) The organization shall take reasonable steps to communicate periodically and in a practical manner its standards and procedures, and other aspects of the compliance and ethics program, to the individuals referred to in subdivision (B) by conducting effective training programs and otherwise disseminating information appropriate to such individuals' respective roles and responsibilities.

(B) The individuals referred to in subdivision (A) are the members of the governing authority, high-level personnel, substantial authority personnel, the organization's employees, and, as appropriate, the organization's agents.

(5) The organization shall take reasonable steps —

(A) to ensure that the organization's compliance and ethics program is followed, including monitoring and auditing to detect criminal conduct;

(B) to evaluate periodically the effectiveness of the organization's compliance and ethics program; and

(C) to have and publicize a system, which may include mechanisms that allow for anonymity or confidentiality, whereby the organization's employees and agents may report or seek guidance regarding potential or actual criminal conduct without fear of retaliation.

(6) The organization's compliance and ethics program shall be promoted and enforced consistently throughout the organization through

(A) appropriate incentives to perform in accordance with the compliance and ethics program; and

(B) appropriate disciplinary measures for engaging in criminal conduct and for failing to take reasonable steps to prevent or detect criminal conduct.

(7) After criminal conduct has been detected, the organization shall take reasonable steps to respond appropriately to the criminal conduct and to prevent further similar criminal conduct, including making any necessary

modifications to the organization's compliance and ethics program. (c) In implementing subsection (b), the organization shall periodically assess the risk of criminal conduct and shall take appropriate steps to design, implement, or modify each requirement set forth in subsection (b) to reduce the risk of criminal conduct identified through this process.

It is not enough to simply write and publish information security and privacy policies and procedures. Organizational leaders must now have a good understanding of the policies and the program, support them, and provide oversight as reasonable for the organization. This reflects a significant shift in the responsibilities of compliance and ethics programs from positions such as the compliance officer and/or committee to the highest levels of management. The guidelines require that executive leaders support and participate in implementing the program. To accomplish this, an effective ongoing information privacy, security, and compliance education program must be in place.

Every compliance plan, including information security and privacy, must include continuing involvement of the highest level of organizational management in its design and implementation. Compliance will then become part of the daily responsibilities of upper management. Requirements for effective training and awareness now extend not only to personnel and business partners and associates but also to the highest levels of management, and must be ongoing.

When considering due diligence, it follows that a standard of due care must be observed. Quite simply, this means that organizational leaders have a duty to ensure the implementation of information security and privacy even if they are not aware of the specific legal requirements. If leaders do not ensure that actions are taken to reasonably secure information and ensure privacy, and as a result others experience damages, it is possible both the organization and the leaders could face legal action for negligence. This certainly should motivate leaders to invest time, resources, and personnel in establishing an ongoing, effective, well-documented information security and privacy awareness and training program.

Corporate Reputation

Reputation is another critical organizational business success asset. Without a good reputation, customers leave, sales drop, and revenue shrinks.

Reputation must be managed well. A component of managing a good reputation is ensuring that personnel and business partners follow the right information security and privacy precautions to lessen the risk of compromising personal information; such incidents will likely lead to some very unfavorable news reports and media attention. Corporate social responsibility (CSR) is another way to manage reputation risks more effectively, by building trust and legitimacy with your key customers, consumers, and stakeholders. Many recent news reports and various studies* reveal that most organizational chief executives believe that corporate reputation is more important now than ever before. Organizations are now taking reputation seriously into consideration when devising business strategy. Some of the activities for which they are devoting resources to help ensure good reputation include

- determining the impact of corporate policies and providing advice to business leaders on how corporate strategies and policies influence reputation;
- identifying risks and opportunities that can affect corporate reputation negatively or positively, such as information security and privacy practices;
- identifying target audiences of consumers by following the analysis of current and desired perceptions and assisting in the definition and articulation of key information security and privacy messages;
- developing government relations at multinational, national, state, and local levels to more easily facilitate compliance with mandates;
- preparing security and privacy awareness programs to raise the company's profile with the public;
- developing media strategies, customer relations, and internal communications programs to ensure consistency of information security and privacy messages that may be communicated by personnel;
- establishing and maintaining a high standard of security, privacy, and crisis management within the organization, and providing training to security and privacy crisis management and media communications groups.

There are many issues that impact corporate reputation that can be addressed through effective ongoing information security and privacy training and awareness activities. Some of these include

- customer complaints,
- competitor messages and internal messages related to competitors,
- customer satisfaction levels with your organization's security and privacy practices,
- providing for customers with special needs and requests,
- number of legal noncompliance reports regarding security and privacy,
- perceived strength of posted security and privacy policies,
- marketing through what is considered as spam,
- number of staff grievances,
- upheld cases of corrupt or unprofessional behavior,
- number of reported security and privacy incidents,
- staff turnover related to training and communications,
- value of training and development provided to staff,
- perception measures of the company by its personnel,

---

* For example, as reported in Corporate Reputation Watch 2003, the annual survey of chief executives conducted by Hill & Knowlton in partnership with Korn/Ferry International.

- existence of confidential grievance procedures for workers,
- percentage of suppliers and partners audited for security and privacy compliance,
- proportion of suppliers and partners meeting security and privacy norms,
- perception of the company's performance on the security and privacy fronts by consumers worldwide,
- proportion of company's managers meeting the company's standards on security and privacy within their area of operation,
- perception of the company's performance on the security and privacy fronts by its employees,
- perception of the company's performance on the security and privacy fronts by the local community,
- dealing with activist groups, especially militant groups, opposed to the organization.

According to www.csreurope.org, over 100 empirical studies published between 1972 and 2000 have analyzed the relationship between what respondents considered to be socially responsible conduct of organizations and their financial performance, which included how the organizations handled the security and privacy of their customer PII. Sixty-eight percent of the results in the studies exhibit a positive relationship between organizations' public reputation and perceived social performance and their financial performance. More recent studies continue to support these findings:

- Ernst & Young (E&Y) 2009 Global Risks Survey: Reputation risks, ranked 22nd in the 2008 E&Y global risks report, rose dramatically to number 10 in the 2009 report. The impact of the financial crises, including information security incidents and privacy breaches, were factors in this ranking.*
- According to the Corporate Reputation Watch 2006 from PR firm Hill & Knowlton, 90% of financial analysts believe that companies which fail to adequately look after nonfinancial aspects of reputation, including such areas as information security and privacy, will suffer financially.†

Accountability

Most personnel understand that if their performance is being measured for certain activities, then they had better do them efficiently because those measures can impact their career with the company in some way. If an organization reports information security and privacy compliance and connects it with personnel

---

* Accessed on June 1, 2009 from http://www.ey.com/Global/assets.nsf/International/2009_business_risk_report/$file/2009_business_risk_report.pdf.
† Lisa Valentine, Talk is not cheap, *ABA Banking Journal* 99.12, 2007.

performance, then personnel understand their accountability more clearly and are even more likely to comply.

Accountability now has more impact on a company and corporate personnel than ever before. There are a growing number of legal actions in which the victims of inadequate information security and privacy practices are filing suits against organizations that were not necessarily the perpetrators of an incident, but whose systems and poor practices contributed to allowing the incident to occur. For example, there have been instances involving denial-of-service (DoS) attacks in which lawsuits have been filed against Internet service providers (ISPs) whose networks were used by hackers to launch attacks.* The effect of such legal actions is to make organizations and people with poor information security and privacy practices accountable for the misuse of their network. Such shifts in accountability start moving the enforcement of policy away from management toward individuals and are also being supported by new regulations and U.S. government moves, such as requiring federal agencies to increase personnel accountability for breaches and requiring security to become standard in all networking and computing products. These moves are publicly supported, such as when Daryl White, then chief information officer for the U.S. Department of the Interior, was reported to have said in 2002 with regard to information security, "You can't hold firewalls and intrusion detection systems accountable. You can only hold people accountable."†

To achieve accountability, the information security and privacy training and awareness program must be well organized, support business goals, and must be clearly supported by executive leaders to ensure participation. The regulations and sentencing-guideline updates discussed earlier require organizations to make their personnel accountable for their business activities, and training and awareness are ways in which this accountability can be established.

Also consider implementing the use of awareness acknowledgments to further increase awareness and accountability for information security and privacy. Your organization should expect all employees, officers, contractors, and business partners to comply with privacy, security, and the acceptable use of policies, and protect your organization's information and systems assets. Obtaining signed acknowledgments documents your organization's efforts and due care to ensure that all personnel are given the information they need to perform their job responsibilities in a manner that protects information and network resources, and therefore these

---

* For example, in 1999, a class action lawsuit was filed against Pacific Bell, including an allegation for "negligence for inadequately protecting its customers against unauthorized Internet intrusions and failure to inform that the digital subscriber line (DSL) connections were not secure." As another example, an ISP located in the United Kingdom brought an action against Nike.com, charging Nike.com to be negligent in selecting a low level of security when registering its domain name, which resulted in the ISP's server being overloaded after the Nike.com domain name was hijacked.

† Dan Verton, Federal Agency Faces Judicial Ultimatum, *Computerworld*, April 8, 2002, http://www.computerworld.com.

documents may be considered facilitators for your awareness and training efforts. Such documented acknowledgments could also provide valuable support for any sanctions you need to administer for policy noncompliance.

See Exhibit 1 for an illustrative acknowledgment agreement to help you get started with designing one that will befit your organization's requirements and environment.

Exhibit 1 Personal Information Privacy and Security Plan

<table>
<tr><td>

Company X Annual Personal Information Privacy and Security Plan

Date:
Employee Name:
Department & Location:
Reviewing Manager:

1. Types of Confidential Information Handled
   a. _____ Customer information
   b. _____ Employee information
   c. _____ Trade Secrets
   d. _____ Other
2. Home & Mobile Computer Profile (Complete if using for business purposes)
   a. Computer make and type (if a laptop is used, describe the type of locking mechanism used):
   b. Home ISP: AOL_____ WorldNet_____ MSN_____ Earthlink_____ Other_____
   c. Access type: Dial-up_____ DSL_____ Cable modem_____
   d. Home network (if applicable): Ethernet_____ Token Ring_____ Wireless_____
   e. Home protection profile (Please describe methodologies or technology used at home to protect computers and networks.)
       i.   Antivirus software (vendor, version):
       ii. Personal firewall (vendor, version):
       iii. Other:
3. Annual security plan goals (List training to be taken, preventative measures to be undertaken in the upcoming year, planned awareness activity participation, presentations and/or articles to create, and so on.)
4. I agree that this accurately represents my use of corporate computer resources. In addition, I have read and understood the corporate information security and privacy policies.

   Employee Signature   _____

   Manager Signature   _____

5. This section to be completed by supervisor: From annual security and privacy audit, describe any security violations or compliance issues:
   a. Number of times passwords were manually reset:
   b. Number of violations of Web access policies (if any):
   c. Indicate any involvement of employee in any audit issues:
   d. Changes in employee access profile or security clearance:

</td></tr>
</table>

Chapter 3

Legal and Regulatory Requirements for Training and Awareness

Teaching should be such that what is offered is perceived as a valuable gift and not as a hard duty.

—Albert Einstein

I enjoy walking through my hay fields in late August. The grasshoppers are large and numerous in the late summer heat and dryness. They all hop out of the way like green popping corn as I walk through the knee-high grass. I have a great feeling of control over the grasshoppers' movements; I can direct when they hop and where they hop, and they seem to follow my wishes, based upon my actions. However, if I pause and look back, I will see them all hopping right back to where they were, continuing on their original path and doing what they were doing before, only temporarily interrupted by my influence. I really did not have the effect that I appeared to have had initially on these seemingly amenable creatures. Without my constant intervention and revisiting, they will always go right back to what they were doing before I disturbed their pastoral dining.

This parallels the typical effects of a security and privacy awareness and training program. It may appear that you are in control of the education efforts. However, if you do not remain diligent in your efforts and constantly reevaluate your effectiveness and modify your activities accordingly, it is likely the "grasshoppers" in your organization would have hopped back to their old, familiar ways.

Awareness and Training Needs

Awareness and training are important activities and key components of an effective information security and privacy program. In fact, many regulations require awareness and training as part of compliance. Currently, the most commonly discussed regulations are the Health Insurance Portability and Accountability Act (HIPAA), the Sarbanes–Oxley Act (SOX), and the Gramm–Leach–Bliley Act (GLBA). However, personnel education has been a requirement under other guidelines and regulations for several years. For instance, the Federal Sentencing Guidelines enacted in 1991, used to determine fines and restitution for convictions, have seven requirements, one of which is for executive management to educate and effectively communicate to their employees the proper business practices with which they must comply. Issues that impact the severity of the judgments, along with accompanying sentences, were discussed in Chapter 2.

Much has been written about the need for security and privacy education through effective awareness and training activities. A regulatory education program should address your organization's interpretation of applicable security and privacy laws and regulations, as well as supporting the activities your organization would take to mitigate risk and ensure security and privacy.

Executives must understand not only their own organization's training and awareness requirements, but also the related requirements and legal considerations of their business partners, subsidiaries, and parent company. Information security and privacy leaders must also consider the training and awareness requirements of applicable international laws and regulations. It is vital for organizations to evaluate, and to reevaluate, the effectiveness of these education programs. I have seen too many organizations spend considerable time and money to launch awareness and training programs only to let them then wane, wither, and die on the vine because they did nothing beyond the big implementation; they failed to put forth the effort and activities necessary to evaluate, update, and modify their programs to make them truly effective.

> He who dares to teach must never cease to learn.
>
> **—Richard Henry Dann**

You must spend time not only on creating awareness and training programs, but also on evaluating the effectiveness of your security and privacy education efforts. You'll find that as you make improvements based on your evaluations, your training methods will become more effective. See Chapter 18 for a discussion of evaluation methods.

Legal Considerations

Always consult your legal counsel before making decisions regarding information security and privacy, especially the education program activities. It is important to have knowledge of the legal ramifications and requirements for training and awareness activities. The legalities of information security and privacy risks and managing legal compliance with applicable laws and regulations are a growing concern for managers, lawyers, and human resources (HR) personnel. A plethora of international, federal, and state laws govern how personnel and individuals with access to personal and confidential information must be trained.

Consequences of inadequate training span a wide spectrum, from regulatory penalties and fines all the way to lawsuits, for failure to show due diligence in the training of employees and establishment of an environment that clearly has a standard of due care that is known to all personnel. There are generally three ways in which an organization may legally establish the duty to train and make personnel aware:

- In certain industries, there may be a minimum standard of due care that applies to organizational training and awareness programs. The standard of due care is considered the level of activity and conduct expected of similarly trained professionals within similar organizations or industries, for example, in the healthcare and financial fields. This chapter lists some of the specific laws and regulations.
- A statute or a regulatory requirement may establish a standard of due care that governs a specific type of information or specific type of industry. For example, the Children's Online Privacy Protection Act (COPPA) governs specifically how information must be handled and controlled, establishing a standard of due care regarding that information. Such expected standards of due care, often in combination with an organization's policies and published promises, can result in judicial decisions beyond applicable regulatory fines and penalties.
- An organization's own policies, procedures, and other practices can establish a standard of due care, especially when the organization clearly exceeds any applicable minimum regulatory or statutory requirements. Exceeding requirements can certainly help to draw more customers, establish a better public perception, and increase business competitiveness by showing your concern about security and privacy, which is possibly greater than your competitors'. However, keep in mind that by doing so, you may establish a new, higher standard of due care for your organization with which you must comply. This higher standard could be considered within any potential and related legal action within which your organization is involved.

Patricia S. Eyres provides good summaries of legal liabilities in a number of different articles and chapters she has authored.* She identifies and discusses, at a high level, five primary areas that include

1. Noncompliance with statutory required training;
2. Civil actions resulting from inadequate or no training or negligence in training;
3. Training related to personnel claims or workers' compensation;

---

* For example, see *Training and the Law: The ASTD Training and Development Handbook*, 4th edition, edited by Robert L. Craig, McGraw-Hill, New York, 1996.

4. Inadequate training for special needs, such as for people with English as a second language or disabled personnel;
5. Discrimination in the opportunities to receive training or in the way training and awareness is offered.

A few more miscellaneous legal considerations to keep in mind when creating and offering your information security and privacy awareness and training materials and activities are to

- provide equal opportunities for training and awareness activities to all members of your target groups to avoid disparate treatment discrimination. Ensure that the ways in which you offer your training and awareness activities are in compliance with any applicable remedial and affirmative action programs and requirements;
- accommodate the special needs for training and awareness of the members of your target groups;
- incorporate diversity into your information security and privacy education programs to parallel other diversity programs within your organization. For example, in multinational organizations, include examples from multiple geographic locations, not just from one country;
- carefully review the content of your education materials to ensure statements are not, or cannot be, considered racially, religiously, or gender biased. Discuss this with your HR and law departments to get their opinions;
- ensure that the content of your education program, as well as how it is delivered, does not lend itself to being interpreted as sexual harassment. The opinions of your HR and law departments must be sought;
- ensure that your chosen training methodologies or requirements do not lend themselves to creating potential liability for sexual harassment suits, discrimination, etc. Seek the advice of your HR and law departments.

Copyright Considerations

It is becoming common to see requests in e-mails and on Web sites for copies of information security and privacy materials that can be used for education efforts. Keep in mind when you are looking for such freebies that the information you seek may very well be covered by copyright protection. When people put in many hours of hard work to create a good instructional or awareness document or product, it is a great disservice to take their information without any acknowledgment or compensation.

If you find something you believe would be a great awareness document or that would enhance your training, be sure to get permission for its use, and provide attribution to the creator as applicable to the situation. Unauthorized use of information and materials may create an avenue for a copyright infringement claim. Such remedies can be civil or criminal.

Check with your legal counsel before reusing materials and information for your educational efforts. In general, keep the following points in mind:

- You need to obtain permission to use a copyrighted work.
- Usually, such permission must be in writing.
- Situations for which the creator's permission must be obtained include
  - when the work is not in the public domain,
  - when the intended use goes beyond what is considered the bounds of fair use.

In general, under the bounds of fair use, you can make limited use of a work without written permission as long as proper acknowledgment is given to its creator. Confirm your understanding, and obtain counsel for your specific situation, when using other people's materials and work.

Specific Regulatory Education Requirements

As mentioned earlier, there are a growing number of laws and regulations that include requirements for the covered entities to provide some type of information security and/or privacy awareness and training to not only their personnel, but also in some instances to their customers and consumers.

This is not an exhaustive list, but these laws and regulations include the following:

- The Health Insurance Portability and Accountability Act (HIPAA)
- The Health Information technology for Economic and Clinical Health Act (HITECH)
- 21 CFR Part 11 (Electronic Records/Electronic Signatures)
- The Bank Protection Act (12 CFR Chapter V §568)
- The Computer Security Act
- The Computer Fraud and Abuse Act (CFAA)
- The Privacy Act (Applies to U.S. Government Agencies)
- The Freedom of Information Act (FOIA)
- The Fair Credit Reporting Act (FCRA)
- The Red Flags Rule
- The Federal Information Security Management Act (FISMA)
- 5 U.S.C. §930.301 for Federal Offices (Office of Personnel Management [OPM] Security Awareness and Training Regulations)
- Appendix III to OMB Circular No. A-130*
- The Digital Millennium Copyright Act (DMCA)
- The Gramm–Leach–Bliley Act (GLBA)
- Department of Transportation DOT HM-232

---

* http://www.whitehouse.gov/omb/circulars/a130/a130appendix_iii.html.

- The Sarbanes–Oxley Act (SOX)
- 1980 Organization for Economic Cooperation and Development (OECD) Privacy Guidelines, January 2003 Guidance*
- Title IV Section 406—Code of Ethics for Senior Financial Officers
- The U.S. Chemical Sector Cyber Security Program
- The Federal Energy Regulatory Commission (FERC) Cyber Security Standard
- Regulation (EC) No. 460/2004 of the European Parliament and of the Council
- Canada's Personal Information Protection and Electronic Documents Act (PIPEDA)

The following text presents the specific training and awareness requirements as they are stated or described within some of these laws and regulations. Some details not specific to education, training, or awareness have been omitted for brevity.

The Health Insurance Portability and Accountability Act (HIPAA)

As stated in the Privacy Rule: § 164.530 (b)(1):

> A covered entity must train all members of its workforce on the policies and procedures with respect to protected health information required by this subpart, as necessary and appropriate for the members of the workforce to carry out their function within the covered entity.

As stated in the Security Rule §164.308(a)(5)(i):

> Implement a security awareness and training program for all members of its workforce (including management). Implement:
> (A)   Security reminders (addressable)
> (B)   Protection from malicious software (addressable)
> (C)   Log-in monitoring (addressable)
> (D)   Password management (addressable)

The Health Information Technology for Economic and Clinical Health Act (HITECH)

This regulation requires the following training and awareness activities:

> SEC. 3011.
>   (a)
>   (3) Training on and dissemination of information on best practices to integrate health information technology, including electronic health records, into a provider's delivery of care, consistent with best practices learned from the Health Information Technology Research Center developed

---

* This is not a law or a regulation, but is the basis of many privacy laws throughout the world.

under section 3012(b), including community health centers receiving assistance under section 330, covered entities under section 340B, and providers participating in one or more of the programs under titles XVIII, XIX, and XXI of the Social Security Act (relating to Medicare, Medicaid, and the State Children's Health Insurance Program).

(c) (3)

(F) integration of health information technology, including electronic health records, into the initial and ongoing training of health professionals and others in the healthcare industry that would be instrumental to improving the quality of healthcare through the smooth and accurate electronic use and exchange of health information.

(e) (3) train personnel in the use of such technology;

SEC. 3016.

(c) PRIORITY. In providing assistance under subsection (a), the Secretary shall give preference to the following:

(1) Existing education and training programs.

SEC. 4201.

(a)

(2) by inserting after subsection (s) the folllowing new subsection:

(t)(1) (A) to Medicaid providers described in paragraph (2)(A) not in excess of 85 percent of net average allowable costs (as defined in paragraph (3)(E)) for certified EHR [electronic health records] technology (and support services including maintenance and training that is for, or is necessary for the adoption and operation of, such technology) with respect to such providers;

(6) Payments described in paragraph (1) are not in accordance with this subsection unless the following requirements are met:

(ii) Amounts described in clause (i) may also be paid to an entity promoting the adoption of certified EHR technology, as designated by the State, if participation in such a payment arrangement is voluntary for the eligible professional involved and if such entity does not retain more than 5 percent of such payments for costs not related to certified EHR technology (and support services including maintenance and training) that is for, or is necessary for the operation of, such technology.

21 CFR Part 11 (Electronic Records/Electronic Signatures)

As stated in Sec. 11.10 Controls for closed systems:

i) Determination that persons who develop, maintain, or use electronic record/ electronic signature systems have the education, training, and experience to perform their assigned tasks.

j) The establishment of, and adherence to, written policies that hold individuals accountable and responsible for actions initiated under their electronic signatures, to deter record and signature falsification.

Bank Protection Act (12 CFR Chapter V §568)

This act requires, in general, that covered entities

- adopt appropriate security procedures;
- establish and implement appropriate administrative, technical, and physical safeguards to protect the security, confidentiality, and integrity of customer information;
- designate a security officer;
- provide to officers and employees initial and periodic training in their responsibilities under the security program.

The Computer Security Act

This act requires the following training and awareness activities:

- Sec. 2(b) (4) Mandatory periodic training for all persons.
- Sec. 3(a)(2) (5) Guidelines for training employees in security awareness and accepted security practice and (6) develop validation procedures to evaluate the effectiveness.
- Sec. 3(b) (4) Assist in developing regulations pertaining to training.
- Sec. 5(a) Mandatory periodic training in computer security awareness and accepted computer security practice.
- Training must be designed to enhance employees' awareness of the threats to, and vulnerability of, computer systems and to encourage the use of improved computer security practices.
- Must issue regulations prescribing the procedures and scope of the training to be provided and the manner in which such training is to be carried out.

For more information on this topic, see http://security.isu.edu/pdf/opmplcy.pdf.

The Computer Fraud and Abuse Act (CFAA)

This act requires the following training and awareness activities:

Sec. 1030. Fraud and related activity in connection with computers
Whoever knowingly accesses a protected computer without authorization or exceeding authorization and uses the access for injury, advantage of a foreign government, commits fraud or extortion, destroys information, sends confidential information (e.g., passwords) obtained in unauthorized manner, etc.

One court has interpreted the CFAA as providing an additional cause of action in favor of employers who may suffer the loss of trade secret information, or any other negative impact, at the hands of disloyal employees. To enforce this act, employees must be made aware of related policies.

The Privacy Act (Applies to U.S. Government Agencies)

This act requires the following training and awareness activities:

(e) Agency requirements. Each agency that maintains a system of records shall—
    (9) Establish rules of conduct for persons involved in the design, development, operation, or maintenance of any system of records, or in maintaining any record, and instruct each such person with respect to such rules and the requirements of this section, including any other rules and procedures adopted pursuant to this section and the penalties for noncompliance;

(f) Agency rules. To carry out the provisions of this section, each agency that maintains a system of records shall promulgate rules, in accordance with the requirements (including general notice) which shall—
    (1) Establish procedures whereby an individual can be notified in response to his request if any system of records named by the individual contains a record pertaining to him.

The Freedom of Information Act (FOIA)

This act requires the following training and awareness activities:

(4)(A)(i) Each agency must promulgate regulations, pursuant to notice and receipt of public comment, specifying the schedule of fees applicable to the processing of requests under this section and establishing procedures and guidelines for determining when such fees should be waived or reduced.

(E)(i) Each agency shall promulgate regulations, pursuant to notice and receipt of public comment, providing for expedited processing of requests for records.

The Fair Credit Reporting Act (FCRA)

This regulation requires the following training and awareness activities:

§ 610. Conditions and form of disclosure to consumers [15 U.S.C. § 1681h]
(c) Trained personnel. Any consumer reporting agency shall provide trained personnel to explain to the consumer any information furnished to him pursuant to section 609 [§ 1681g] of this title.

The Red Flags Rule

This regulation requires the following training and awareness activities:

Subpart J—Identity Theft Red Flags
§ 41.90 Duties regarding the detection, prevention, and mitigation of identity theft.
  (e) Administration of the Program. Each financial institution or creditor that is required to implement a Program must provide for the continued administration of the Program and must:
  (3) Train staff, as necessary, to effectively implement the Program;
§ 222.90 Duties regarding the detection, prevention, and mitigation of identity theft.
  (e) Administration of the Program. Each financial institution or creditor that is required to implement a Program must provide for the continued administration of the Program and must:
  (3) Train staff, as necessary, to effectively implement the Program
§ 334.90 Duties regarding the detection, prevention, and mitigation of identity theft.
  (e) Administration of the Program. Each financial institution or creditor that is required to implement a Program must provide for the continued administration of the Program and must:
  (3) Train staff, as necessary, to effectively implement the Program;
§ 571.90 Duties regarding the detection, prevention, and mitigation of identity theft.
  (e) Administration of the Program. Each financial institution or creditor that is required to implement a Program must provide for the continued administration of the Program and must:
  (3) Train staff, as necessary, to effectively implement the Program;
§ 717.90 Duties regarding the detection, prevention, and mitigation of identity theft.
  (e) Administration of the Program. Each federal credit union that is required to implement a Program must provide for the continued administration of the Program and must:
  (3) Train staff, as necessary, to effectively implement the Program;
§ 681.2 Duties regarding the detection, prevention, and mitigation of identity theft.
  (e) Administration of the Program. Each financial institution or creditor that is required to implement a Program must provide for the continued administration of the Program and must:
  (3) Train staff, as necessary, to effectively implement the Program;

The Federal Information Security Management Act (FISMA)

This act requires the following training and awareness activities:

Sec. 3544
    (a) In general, the head of each agency shall —
        (4) Ensure that the agency has trained personnel sufficient to assist the agency in complying with the requirements of this subchapter and related policies, procedures, standards, and guidelines.
    (b) Develop, document, and implement an agency-wide information security program, approved by the Director under section 3543(a)(5), to provide information security for the information and information systems that support the operations and assets of the agency, including those provided or managed by another agency, contractor, or other source, that includes —
        (4) Establishing security awareness training to inform personnel, including contractors and other users of information systems that support the operations and assets of the agency, of —
            (A) Determining information security risks associated with their activities; and
            (B) Knowing their responsibilities in complying with agency policies and procedures designed to reduce these risks.

5 U.S.C. §930.301 for Federal Offices (Office of Personnel Management [OPM] Security Awareness and Training Regulations)

This act requires the following training and awareness activities:

Sec. 930.301 Information systems security awareness training program.
Each Executive Agency must develop a plan for federal information systems security awareness and training and
    (a)   Identify employees with significant information security responsibilities and provide role-specific training in accordance with National Institute of Standards and Technology (NIST) standards and guidance available on the NIST Web site, http://csrc.nist.gov/publications/nistpubs/, as follows:
        (1) All users of federal information systems must be exposed to security awareness materials at least annually. Users of federal information systems include employees, contractors, students, guest researchers, visitors, and others who may need access to federal information systems and applications.

(2) Executives must receive training in information security basics and policy level training in security planning and management.

(3) Program and functional managers must receive training in information security basics; management and implementation level training in security planning and system/application security management; and management and implementation level training in system/application life cycle management, risk management, and contingency planning.

(4) Chief information officers (CIOs), IT security program managers, auditors, and other security-oriented personnel (e.g., system and network administrators, and system/application security officers) must receive training in information security basics and broad training in security planning, system and application security management, system/application life cycle management, risk management, and contingency planning.

(5) IT function management and operations personnel must receive training in information security basics; management and implementation level training in security planning and system/application security management; and management and implementation level training in system/application life cycle management, risk management, and contingency planning.

(b) Provide the federal information systems security awareness material/exposure outlined in NIST guidance on IT security awareness and training to all new employees before allowing them access to the systems.

(c) Provide information systems security refresher training for agency employees as frequently as determined necessary by the agency, based on the sensitivity of the information that the employees use or process.

(d) Provide training whenever there is a significant change in the agency information system environment or procedures or when an employee enters a new position that requires additional role-specific training.

Appendix III to OMB Circular No. A-130

This act requires the following training and awareness activities:

A. Requirements

3. Automated Information Security Programs. Agencies shall implement and maintain a program to assure that adequate security is provided for all agency information collected, processed, transmitted, stored, or disseminated in general support systems and major applications.

Each agency's program shall implement policies, standards, and procedures which are consistent with government-wide policies, standards, and procedures issued by the Office of Management and Budget, the Department of Commerce, the General Services Administration and the Office of Personnel Management (OPM). Different or more stringent requirements for securing national security information should be incorporated into agency programs as required by appropriate national security directives. At a minimum, agency programs shall include the following controls in their general support systems and major applications:

a. Controls for general support systems.

    2) b) Training. Ensure that all individuals are appropriately trained in how to fulfill their security responsibilities before allowing them access to the system. Such training shall assure that employees are versed in the rules of the system, be consistent with guidance issued by NIST and OPM, and apprise them about available assistance and technical security products and techniques. Behavior consistent with the rules of the system and periodic refresher training shall be required for continued access to the system.

b. Controls for Major Applications.

    2) b) Specialized Training. Before allowing individuals access to the application, ensure that all individuals receive specialized training focused on their responsibilities and the application rules. This may be in addition to the training required for access to a system. Such training may vary from a notification at the time of access (e.g., for members of the public using an information retrieval application) to formal training (e.g., for an employee that works with a high-risk application).

4. Assignment of Responsibilities

a. Department of Commerce. The Secretary of Commerce shall:

    2) Review and update guidelines for training in computer security awareness and accepted computer security practice, with assistance from OPM.

b. Office of Personnel Management. The Director of the Office of Personnel Management shall:

    1) Assure that its regulations concerning computer security training for federal civilian employees are effective.

    2) Assist the Department of Commerce in updating and maintaining guidelines for training in computer security awareness and accepted computer security practice.

The Digital Millennium Copyright Act (DMCA)

This act requires the following training and awareness activities:

Section 512 (e)

(C) The institution provides to all users of its system or network informational materials that accurately describe, and promote compliance with, the laws of the United States relating to copyright.

The Gramm–Leach–Bliley Act (GLBA)

This act requires the following training and awareness activities:

Safeguards Rule § 314.4
  (a) Designate an employee or employees to coordinate your information security program.
  (b) Identify reasonably foreseeable internal and external risks to the security, confidentiality, and integrity of customer information that could result in the unauthorized disclosure, misuse, alteration, destruction or other compromise of such information, including a risk assessment including:
       (1) Employee training and management

Department of Transportation DOT HM-232

This act requires the following training and awareness activities:

- Security Awareness Training Requirement (49 CFR Section 172.704(a)(4))
  Each HAZMAT [hazardous materials] employee must receive training.
- Security Plans Requirement (49 CFR Part 172 new Subpart I)
  Each hazardous materials shipper and each hazardous materials transporter must develop and adhere to a Security Plan.
- In-Depth Security Training Requirement (49 CFR Section 172.704(a)(5))
  Each HAZMAT employee of a shipper/carrier required to have a Security Plan in accordance with Part 172 Subpart I, must be trained concerning the Security Plan and its implementation.

The Sarbanes–Oxley Act (SOX)

This act requires the following training and awareness activities:

Title III Section 302 (a)(4)
  (A) Establishing and maintaining internal controls;
  (B) Designed internal controls to ensure material information is made known to officers

SEC references compliance activities to relate to Section 404 of COBIT (Control Objectives for Information Technology):

DS 7.2 Delivery of Training and Education
Appoint trainers and organize training sessions on a timely basis. Registration attendance and performance evaluations should be recorded.

Title IV Section 406—Code of Ethics for Senior Financial Officers

The SEC guidance is as follows:

> Although codes of ethics typically are designed to promote high standards of ethical conduct, they also generally seek to instruct those to whom they apply as to improper or illegal conduct or activity and to prohibit such conduct or activity.

The U.S Chemical Sector Cyber Security Program

This program requires the following training and awareness activities:

> 5.15 Staff Training and Security Awareness
> Effective cyber security training and security awareness programs should provide each employee with the information necessary to identify, review and remediate control exposures.

The Federal Energy Regulatory Commission (FERC) Cyber Security Standard

This standard requires the following training and awareness activities:

> CIP-004-1: Personnel & Training Energy/Infrastructure
> R1. Awareness—The Responsible Entity shall establish, maintain, and document a security awareness program.
> The program shall include security awareness reinforcement on at least a quarterly basis.

1980 Organization for Economic Cooperation and Development (OECD) Privacy Guidelines, January 2003 Guidance

These guidelines advise all organizations world wide to do the following training and awareness activities.

> 4) The promotion of user education and awareness about online privacy and the means of protecting privacy through:
> ■ Fostering effective education and information for organizations and individual users about online privacy protection issues and solutions, including privacy enhancing technologies.
> ■ Further providing online resources for raising awareness about privacy regulations and best practices.

- Raising awareness among individual users for them to better understand the technology and the privacy implications of transactions and interactions on the internet.
- Supporting academic work to analyze in more detail how to efficiently persuade organizations and individual users to use an effective complementary mix of online privacy protection solutions.

Regulation (EC) No. 460/2004 of the European Parliament and of the Council

This regulation supports the European Union Data Protection Directive, and requires that the council provide training and awareness activities as follows:

(14) Ensuring confidence in networks and information systems requires that individuals, businesses and public administrations are sufficiently informed, educated and trained in the field of network and information security. Public authorities have a role in increasing awareness by informing the general public, small and medium-sized enterprises, corporate companies, public administrations, schools and universities. These measures need to be further developed. An increased information exchange between Member States will facilitate such awareness raising actions. The Agency should provide advice on best practices in awareness-raising, training and courses.

Canada's Personal Information Protection and Electronic Documents Act (PIPEDA)

This act requires the following training and awareness activities:

Section 4.1.4:
Organizations shall implement policies and practices to give effect to the principles, including

(a) Implementing procedures to protect personal information;
(b) Establishing procedures to receive and respond to complaints and inquiries;
(c) Training staff and communicating to staff information about the organization's policies and practices; and
(d) Developing information to explain the organization's policies and procedures.

Chapter 4

Incorporating Training and Awareness into Job Responsibilities and Appraisals

Knowledge is power.

—**Francis Bacon**

Every organization struggles to have personnel follow good information security and privacy practices. Generally, this is because most personnel do not like to jump through the perceived hoops that good security and privacy often require, and there is usually no motivation for them to perform security and privacy activities and no consequences to face when they do not comply with the organization's information privacy, security, and compliance rules.

In numerous discussions with conference and training attendees, the common reasons employees give for not complying with security and privacy requirements include

- pressure to be productive; meeting deadlines is more critical to their job success and job preservation than complying with security and privacy requirements that negatively impact their productivity;
- having to obey managers (for fear of falling into disfavor) who tell them to do something against privacy or security requirements.

It is safe to say that most personnel have difficulties performing all the tasks they are expected to accomplish each day. Most want to make their work easier by finding shortcuts. One of the easiest shortcuts is to go around security and privacy; technology as implemented in most organizations makes this fairly simple and seemingly nonidentifiable. Who is going to find out if an individual "loaned" his or her password to a coworker when he or she could not get to the office and needed to get an important message sent on his or her behalf? And, is it not tempting to save time by not making a regular backup of laptop and handheld computer files and e-mail? Or think of the time saved if they do not bother to apply those operating system (OS) patches that seem to be released almost daily? These and other actions truly do save some time, and most personnel are willing to gamble that something unfortunate will not happen to them anyway.

Information security and privacy professionals must effectively, and often, communicate the impact of information privacy, security, and personnel activities. Executives must clearly and visibly support policies and practices on information security and privacy. Organizations are almost completely dependent upon technology to secure information because they cannot confidently expect that personnel are going to follow information security and privacy rules just because it is the right thing to do. Personnel must be motivated, and management must actively enforce information security and privacy requirements.

Motivational Factors

Information security and privacy must become integrated with job performance and the appraisal process. Personnel become motivated to actively support information security and privacy initiatives when they know that their job advancement, compensation, and benefits will be impacted. If this does not exist, then an organization is ultimately destined to depend only upon technology for information security assurance. The International Organization for Standardization/International Electrotechnical Commission (ISO/IEC) 27001 supports this position by addressing the need for documented security responsibilities within Section 6.1.3, titled "Allocation of information security responsibilities." This internationally accepted set of standards advises organizations to document the security requirements within job responsibility descriptions, including general as well as specific information asset protection requirements, processes, and activities.

Privacy and security in most nonmilitary organizations are typically considered a secondary objective for business success, resulting in security and privacy compliance being an afterthought. Organizational motives for information security and privacy must support primary business objectives.

For example, information security and privacy activities are necessary to

■ comply with applicable laws and regulations,
■ demonstrate due diligence,

- help prevent loss and thus increase profit,
- protect from liabilities related to security negligence,
- enhance and support customer and public reputation.

Donn Parker has discussed motivation for security compliance at length over the years through his publications* and presentations. In general, he observes in his writings that the circumstances and incidents that effectively increase motivation for security and privacy compliance include

- a desire to remain employed;
- experiencing a privacy or security attack or privacy or security incident;
- meeting security and privacy requirements during compliance reviews;
- implementing unmanned, transparent, automatic, and effective safeguards that work without degrading system performance or slowing business processing;
- making the most private and secure way the most convenient way;
- being rewarded and punished for security and privacy activities relative to the rewards and penalties corresponding to job responsibilities.

The sixth motivator is the most controllable and also the most powerful.

Rewards and penalties are traditional job performance motivators in business and should be used for motivating personnel to maintain privacy and security. Rewards for information security and privacy can include

- job advancement,
- praise and recognition,
- financial remuneration (often in the form of specific bonuses for exemplary behavior and/or performance),
- prizes for outstanding security performance.

Motivation is the key to effective security and privacy to protect against people who are already motivated to attack networks or misuse information, to ensure care is taken to be thorough in creating new systems and applications so that they do not contain flaws that lead to security and privacy incidents, and to ensure all legal and contractual requirements for security and privacy are addressed. Personnel must be at least as equally motivated to secure networks and information. Privacy and security motivation must not only be part of any awareness and training program, but also play a role in the job performance and appraisal process. Parker also lists the following possible motivators for information security and privacy:

- Career advancement and recognition
- Law and regulatory compliance

---

* For example, see his book, *Fighting Computer Crime: A New Framework for Protecting Information*, published by John Wiley & Sons, New York, 1998.

- Anticipation and receipt of rewards
- Fear and experience of penalties
- Ethical, honest, social, and good business convictions
- Personal loss experience
- The loss experiences of others
- Gratefulness to the employer and dedication to the profession
- Protection of personal investment and employers' reputation
- Competitive desire to excel beyond peers
- Expediency and convenience

Here are just a few suggestions for possible prizes:

- A "casual day" or "jeans day" whenever the employees choose
- A book about making backups or some other information security and/or privacy topic
- Additional vacation time
- Balloons with security and/or privacy sayings
- Balloons with your information security and/or privacy mascot printed on them
- Bonuses
- Bookmarks with privacy and/or security sayings
- Books related to business and success
- Box of blank CDs or DVDs, with your security and privacy mascot affixed on it if possible
- Calendar with privacy or security sayings
- Coffee mug with security and privacy mascot
- Coupon for a discount or free meal to your cafeteria or a local eatery
- DVD with a movie with information security and/or privacy issues included (see Appendix S)
- Electronics equipment, such as storage drives or digital voice recorders
- Feature articles in company publications
- Free lunch
- Gift card to a book store
- Gift card to Best Buy, Target, Walmart, etc.
- Gift certificates to any store in the area or online that your personnel would like
- Half-day of vacation
- Lunch with the CIO, CEO, or other executive leader
- Memo pads, preferably with your security and privacy mascot
- Monitor mirror to stay aware of who is in the work area
- MP3 player
- Paid vacation trips

- Personal degausser
- Personal diary or journal
- Personal shredder
- Photo with the CEO
- Posters that show good security and privacy practices
- Promotions
- Raises
- Recognition plaques and trophies
- Screen savers with the security and privacy mascot or office security and privacy scenes
- Shredding scissors
- Special car-parking privileges
- Stick-on labels with the security and privacy mascot for books, folders, and so on
- Tickets to a local live concert, ball game, or other event
- T-shirt with a security or privacy slogan, scene, or mascot
- TVs for break rooms
- USB thumb drive with encryption capabilities

You are limited only by your own imagination!

Penalties and sanctions, on the other hand, can include the following actions:

- Dismissal
- Demotion
- Loss of benefits, perks, or remuneration
- Leave without pay
- Department reassignment
- Legal action
- Internally posting names of personnel in noncompliance with policies

Always discuss any of the motivators, prizes, penalties, and sanctions with the human resources (HR) and legal departments, and labor union representatives prior to implementation. See Appendix K for a questionnaire to send to your contacts prior to discussions. Include the answers within your education inventory details, and keep track of the progress made as intended plans are incorporated into the appraisal process. It is important to ensure that plans are in compliance with existing laws, contracts, and policies, and also to guarantee that the information security department has the support of the unions and the legal and HR departments.

Motivation through Job Appraisals and Responsibilities

There are at least five ways in which personnel can be motivated to participate in information security and privacy education activities as well as comply with policies and procedures. Consider the following, and you may think of others.

1. *Include security and privacy as specific objectives in job descriptions.*
   Work with management to develop the objectives and do what labor unions and laws allow. Job descriptions should include specific security assignments to avoid endangering assets, to adhere to policy, and to protect and make employees accountable for your organization's information assets. Implement this for members of the organization whose job description requirements include handling customer and other private information, using the network, and working with other security- and privacy-related elements.

2. *Periodically require personnel, including third parties such as consultants and contractors, to sign a security and privacy agreement that supports your organizational policies and standards.*
   Consider requiring employees to sign a security and privacy agreement upon initial employment and subsequently on an annual basis. This ensures personnel and third parties have reviewed the policies and understand that they will be held accountable.

3. *Establish security and privacy as specific objectives within the scheduled periodic performance appraisals.*
   Ensure that your plans are implemented with the support of your management and the applicable unions. This motivator should be implemented for all employees whose job description includes information privacy and/or security responsibilities or activities. Annual job appraisals should include specific evaluations and discussions of the employees' support for and practice of security, including references to any exemplary efforts, to violations, and to endangering information.

4. *Obtain support from executive management to commit to explicitly reviewing the security and privacy performance of all managers.*
   Your managers are role models for those who report to them. It is vital that all levels of personnel be aware that everyone within their organization, no matter at what level, is responsible and accountable for following security and privacy requirements.

5. *Implement security and privacy program rewards and penalties that are clearly supported by the management.*
   Establish rewards and penalties at appropriate levels to support business and to address appropriate levels of risk. Remember, you cannot eliminate 100% of all security and privacy risks; you must implement security and privacy to address applicable regulatory and legal requirements, to effectively protect

your information assets and the privacy of your confidential information, and to ensure that the security and privacy cures are not more costly or burdensome than the ailments.

Methods of Security and Privacy Objectives Assessments

Incorporating information security and privacy responsibilities into job descriptions, employment agreements, and policy awareness acknowledgments increases accountability and motivation for personnel to know and follow security and privacy requirements. Business unit managers can communicate general and specific privacy security roles and responsibilities for the personnel with their job descriptions. All employees, officers, and contractors should be held accountable for compliance with privacy, security, and acceptable use policies and to protect the institution's information and network assets. Job descriptions for security personnel should detail the systems and processes they will protect and the control processes for which they are responsible. Job descriptions for personnel whose primary job responsibilities are not strictly information security and privacy but who handle the organization's information or maintain the network should include specific directives regarding their responsibilities for maintaining security and privacy as they relate to their job function. All contractors and consultant contracts should include information security and privacy responsibilities and consider tying financial rewards or penalties based on compliance with the listed responsibilities and requirements.

In 2002, PentaSafe Security Technologies (since acquired by NetIQ) conducted a survey of more than 1000 employees in over 350 companies that revealed that 70% of the companies failed to follow up the employees who had not signed off on the corporate security policy. I have not been able to find any more recent studies, but based on my discussions with a large number of information security and privacy practitioners and business leaders I believe the percentage has not improved.

Organizations must seek to move information security and privacy responsibilities to both management and employees. Follow-up is critical to ensuring that responsibilities are understood and addressed. A very effective way to do this is to include information security and privacy activities and responsibilities as a part of the job appraisal process. There are generally two methods for incorporating information security and privacy into the job evaluation process:

■ Evaluating performance against specific predefined security and privacy objectives
■ Considering general security and privacy activities within job performance as a whole

Performance against Specific Privacy and Security Objectives

For the greatest success in creating workable objectives, involve employees and managers in determining appropriate assessment procedures to help achieve fairness and objectivity. Consider creating a joint group of management, information security and privacy experts, and employees to identify performance levels and factors. The information security and privacy area should facilitate identifying the information security and privacy activities to include within the performance appraisal procedures.

Always try to base the security and privacy performance assessment items on specific tasks and achievements to make the appraisal as objective as possible and not just based on someone's opinion. Establish procedures so that managers and personnel work together each year to set security and privacy objectives, and then at the yearly performance appraisal they can determine the extent to which the objectives were met. (A nice effect of this is a good security- and privacy-awareness-raising exercise.) Results from the appraisal discussion will determine the overall security and privacy performance level in relation to predetermined standards, which can then be linked to an appraisal-related pay (ARP) award if appropriate for your organization.

Types of information security and privacy performance objectives to consider including within-your-job performance appraisals include

- participation in an annual security and privacy promotion week;
- exemplary daily clean desk practices;
- no infractions found during security and privacy reviews;
- promoting security to team members by writing memos, giving presentations, etc.;
- reading security newsletters at the online information security and privacy intranet site;
- participating in information security and privacy training;
- notifying team members of newly discovered security risks and how to address them;
- viewing information security videos. Be careful to choose good ones; there are many bad ones out there. Select the video to match your audience. See Appendix S for some ideas;
- participation in information security and privacy contests.

You can expand upon this idea by including performance-related criteria, measures, and details about the personnel's current use of information and computers: the security they use, how and where they use computers, and so on. This could be followed nicely with role-based access and authentication controls. An advantage of this approach is that it helps to ensure employee understanding of security and privacy responsibilities and information access rights as they relate to job requirements, resulting in increased awareness and assigned accountability.

The following types of elements could be added to the performance criteria for a manager to track:

- Personnel information access levels and authorizations (public, proprietary, confidential, top secret, etc.)
- Date of last change for personnel authorizations
- Type of authorization capabilities (read, write, update, delete, etc.)
- Special privileges (production update, override authorization, etc.)
- System administration capabilities and level access, if any (supervisor, operator, analyst)
- Development of additional security and privacy skills, privacy and security certification
- Changes in information and network access levels (for example, when personnel get assigned new responsibilities and no longer perform some activities, the access that is no longer necessary for the new role should be removed as soon as possible)
- Start and stop dates of access credentials, as well as the results of audits of those credentials
- Personnel security and privacy access rules, authorization levels, and record of compliance with the rules

The results from the appraisal can be fed into the methods for incorporating information security and privacy into the job evaluation process discussed earlier. These plans need to be updated on an annual basis, and the various items in the plan updated as both the employee's usage and the technology changes. However, once the process gets started, documenting the changes becomes a routine part of the employee's duties.

Using Appraisal Results

Managers should be responsible for determining their personnel's performance and the extent to which the security and privacy objectives are met. Based on this, a rating can be applied using a consistent and common standard of performance. For example, a simple, basic standard may look like the following:

- *Very good*—A very high level of security and privacy performance has been met; identified security and privacy objectives were consistently achieved.
- *Good*—A satisfactory performance meeting all or nearly all security and privacy objectives.
- *Less than satisfactory*—The sufficient security and privacy objectives were not met; the individual needs to improve skills or effort, or both.
- *Wholly unsatisfactory*—The basic requirements of the job have not been met, and little or no progress has been made toward the identified security and privacy objectives.

When implementing these security and privacy objectives, the managers doing the appraisals must use common business sense. Some of the objectives may be met, but others may not as a result of circumstances beyond the personnel's control. Managers must conduct regular reviews with personnel to consider if security objectives need revision for unforeseen circumstances, for example, implementation of new systems based on economic situations, and so on. It is a very good idea to create guidelines for managers to follow to perform these types of appraisals, and obtain joint training for appraising personnel from HR and information privacy and security departments.

Considering Security and Privacy within Job Performance as a Whole

In considering security and privacy within job performance, begin from a job description, then break down the main features of the job and examine against an agreed and predetermined set of security- and privacy-related performance factors and standards. The security and privacy factors and standards will vary with the nature of the job, but some, such as workstation security, are often common to all personnel. Consider personnel performance under the chosen factors and around three to six performance standards. The methods used to guide appraisers will vary between organizations, but definitions are often provided both for the factors and for the standards.

Some of the factors may include

- privacy and security knowledge and demonstrated competence,
- forward privacy and security planning,
- privacy and security communications,
- privacy and security compliance,
- privacy and security problem solving,
- privacy and security training and awareness activities.

Another example of security and privacy standards to use when assessing security performance standards is

- *Exceptional*—The individual maintains a level of information security and privacy quality well in excess of the requirements of the job and position.
- *Highly effective*—The individual consistently achieves all the information security and privacy requirements related to his or her job responsibilities.
- *Effective*—The individual achieves the requirements of job-required information security and privacy but sometimes needs guidance to reach this level.
- *Less than effective*—The individual fails to meet the information security and privacy requirements of the job, and weaknesses need to be identified and addressed.
- *Unacceptable*—The individual's demonstration of information security and privacy activities and compliance is unacceptable.

A variation of this method adds a rating matrix to the procedure to incorporate point scoring for each factor against set performance standards. Exhibit 1 provides a sample rating matrix based specifically on information security activities. Something similar could be used for privacy and for a combination of security and privacy. The factors can be weighted to reflect the varying degrees of importance attached to the different security factors based on the job position. Appraisers award points to each employee, and the final points tally is converted into whatever percentage of ARP is appropriate. This is based on similar rating matrices HR departments have used for several years, but specifically pulls in security and privacy activities.

Exhibit 1   Example of Security Factors Rating Matrix

Factor	Unacceptable	Less than Effective	Effective	Highly Effective	Exceptional	Score
Security training attendance	0	2	5	10	15	
Use of malicious code-prevention software	0	4	8	12	15	
Fewest reported audit security issues	0	6	12	18	25	
Greatest number of continuous days without lost-time security incident	0	3	7	11	15	
Security suggestion implemented	0	3	7	11	15	
Points						
ARP percentage						

It is rare to have an ARP higher than 10%. This method is relatively easy to design and implement, whether or not some method of weighting is included, but has the disadvantage of relying on subjective judgments of the appraisers.

Another variation is to combine narrative and comments about the person being appraised with the points-scoring system. For example, award points in a range from 0 to 10 and provide guidelines to help appraisers minimize subjectivity in determining performance. The guidelines will help the appraiser determine the points to award, in addition to discussing the employee's performance. For example, the narrative for the person being reviewed may read something as follows, "Alec implemented a new training and awareness program and was able to determine that unusual network traffic is malicious." It is left to the appraiser to determine a point value based on the activities listed. There still is some subjectivity involved, but it is minimized if the guidelines clearly detail the types of activities to document, award points based on the values suggested within the guidelines, etc. It is simple to operate but has the disadvantage of not including weightings against the factors. This disadvantage can be offset by assigning a weight of importance for each accomplishment or failure within the guidelines.

The two methods of assessment (performance against objectives and whole job performance) do not need to be mutually exclusive. Organizations can supplement objective setting with the whole job method to arrive at an approach to make use of the advantages of both methods.

Whatever method is used, the next step is relating the overall security and privacy performance assessment to a reward payment.

Paying for Performance

To take into account existing pay and appraisal systems and the need to meet differing objectives, there are a number of possible approaches for introducing ARP. The methods will be uniquely suited to your organization.

Organizations can reward security and privacy performance, as assessed during an appraisal, using the many different methods listed earlier. As an example, common salary-based methods can be used, such as one of the following:

- A preset percentage of pay added to the pay amount, depending on the information security and privacy performance standards reached by the employee
- Pay amount tied to an incremental scale with movement up the scale depending on above-average performance

Additional Percentage Element Added to Pay

Under this method, and subject to their level of performance, personnel would receive an extra percentage element added to their pay in a range from, for example, 0% to 10%, depending on their performance level. A sample is shown in the table in Exhibit 2.

Exhibit 2   Example of ARP Percentage

Rating	ARP Percentage Element
Excellent	10
Good	7.5
Satisfactory	5
Fair	2.5
Poor	0

Either of the columns given in the table can be modified to suit your organization. The rating descriptions can be changed, or the corresponding values raised or lowered with regard to the importance of information security and privacy within each of the positions being appraised and as appropriate to the corresponding job responsibilities. However, with HR methods in general, it is unusual for ARP awards to exceed 10% of salary. For personnel new to a job or still in training, the appraisal and ARP methods may be designed to give the manager the opportunity to place an employee under a special category, for example, "needs further training."

The assessment may be treated as the equivalent of a "fair" assessment, and the employee can then receive an appropriate increase in pay.

Controlling the Amount and Distribution of the Awards

The key factor in determining eligibility and the amount of ARP is the pay philosophy of your organization. It is unlikely that you will achieve any motivational effect if only a small percentage of eligible personnel can receive an information privacy and security ARP; the remaining personnel may be discouraged. If becoming eligible is seen as success, ineligibility will likely be seen as failure. The demotivational effect of not receiving anything requires serious consideration when you are designing the ARP method. Ideally, you should have a long and thorough discussion with your HR and law departments as well as any labor union leaders about this method, including brainstorming on the positives and negatives of its usage.

The procedures that organizations adopt for allocating the ARP budget vary; it depends on your organization's existing payment system and the proposed design of the method. You may want to assure employees that the overall value of the ARP budget would be greater than if the existing pay structure was boosted purely by a general increase. This way, they will see the additional value of including security and privacy as a component of the appraisal process. Some organizations choose to make lump-sum payments to employees to ensure the smooth introduction of ARP. For example, the first year the ARP is given, all employees would receive the same amount as the others within their department. The differentiators would be taken into consideration during subsequent appraisal periods.

Some organizations prefer to allocate a limited amount of money to managers, who in turn award ARP among their personnel following a predetermined formula. This approach has some advantages:

- It reflects cash limits for possible awards.
- It provides a way to crosscheck managers' opinions of personnel, for example, to make sure the managers are giving the awards consistent with the rest of the other factors within the personnel appraisal.
- It encourages managerial consensus of personnel performance. Often, the managers within a department meet together to determine the awards to make to each personnel, and the award values are determined by a consensus of the managers.

However, some organizations, and possibly yours, may feel that this method contradicts the ideal of a method of payment designed to encourage each employee so that security and privacy performance are raised to a level that results in an additional award. For example, if each member of a manager's team was rated excellent, then due to the limited ARP funds allocated, the manager would have to pay each employee less money than if there was only one employee in the group who rated excellent. Thus, the employees would be given less than the justified increases because they would in effect be "punished" because they work in a group with many high-rated personnel. The assessment procedure may also be seen as secondary to financial considerations.

In such a forced distribution, the proportion of employees to be allocated to each overall assessment category might be as indicated in Exhibit 3.

Using this method, managers would be expected to produce assessments mirroring these percentages. This approach has the benefit of keeping costs within known limits, and is a safeguard against both extreme assessments at each end of the scale and the inclination of managers to bunch ratings around the average point. However, it assumes that the actual distribution of performance standards naturally follows these percentages.

In effect, it might force managers to downgrade assessments. It is particularly inappropriate for small groups, teams, or departments of employees because it would force

Exhibit 3   Forced Distribution Percentages

Exceptional	5
Highly effective	20
Effective	60
Less than effective	15
Unacceptable	0

personnel who are doing equally well with security and privacy efforts to receive differing awards. Organizations should use this method only when it fits and should be prepared to set more flexible guidelines for the distribution of ARP, based on true security and privacy performance if they find that this forced percentage will not be equitable.

Applying Security and Privacy ARP to Certain Groups of Employees

During the preparatory stage of an ARP method, your organization should consider how to apply payment conditions to particular groups of employees. Some appraisal schemes may already include guidelines that can be extended to the ARP method. Others may need to be reviewed. You need to have a clear understanding about the following groups so that the scheme is fair and credible. These decisions should be made following consultation with the HR and legal departments and, where appropriate, negotiation with applicable employee and labor union representatives:

- Information security and privacy staff
- Compliance personnel
- Systems administrators
- New personnel and trainees
- Temporary employees and contract workers
- Recent or pending promotions
- Transfers and terminations
- Maternity/paternity/adoption/parental, and authorized sick leave
- Part-time workers
- Trade union officials and members
- International personnel (taking into consideration applicable employment and privacy laws)
- Other groups that handle customer or confidential information, or who have responsibilities for systems and applications maintenance

Individual Security and Privacy Plans

Consider incorporating an individual security and privacy plan into each employee's annual performance appraisal. Such a plan can address the basic core issues of security and privacy, in addition to any unique issues for the job position. It does not need to be highly technical. The goal is to focus on aspects of the personnel's routine activities that can reduce security and privacy risks for your organization. The items to be measured should include the need to track compliance at a technical level, but you also need to include other activities, such as participation in information security and privacy awareness activities and training. Do not just rely on the employee making a plan and then automatically complying.

You will need to ensure that the managers know the plans, and verify compliance with the plans just prior to the appraisal. The management must use the details of the individual plans to verify participation and success. For example, based on the plan, some of the ways in which the management can verify the individual plans might include using the following:

- Training-attendance logs to ensure the employee participated in the training identified in the program
- Password-cracking programs to measure the strength of the passwords used by the employees
- Awareness activity participation evidence such as e-mails, posters, contests, subscriptions to mailing lists, and so on
- Remote connection and log-in tracking reports to determine the number of times the user tried to log in remotely and succeeded or failed
- Results of network security audits and vulnerability assessments
- Results of privacy impact assessments
- Results of after-hour work area security and privacy walkthrough reviews
- Presentations or articles on privacy or security that the individual has published internally or externally

By creating such plans, personnel should be able to relate more closely to security and privacy issues and broaden their focus on how the issues relate to not only their job success, but also the success of the business.

By making each person accountable for creating and following a personal security and privacy plan, each will have a stake in security and privacy compliance and in practicing safe computing within the organization.

A nice side effect will be that personnel will also become more knowledgeable about the effect of their actions on security and privacy in general.

Implementing the Individual Plan

So, how can you include individual security and privacy plans in the job appraisal process? The following provides a basic instruction list for you to start with and modify as necessary for your organization:

- Train personnel on how to write an information security and privacy plan.
- Prior to the annual performance appraisal, require every employee to create a personal information security and privacy plan.

- Design a plan suited to your organization's information security and privacy policies that includes requirements for such issues as privacy policies, remote access policies, password policies, secure computing guidelines, etc.
- Each individual should create the plan detailing his or her personal information usage profile accompanied by his or her plans to help ensure the security and privacy of computing resources and corporate information for the upcoming year. Items could include such activities as
  - using personal firewalls in mobile computing devices,
  - attending specific training sessions,
  - making a presentation to the team or department on a privacy or security topic,
  - participating in an organization-wide awareness event,
  - regularly updating antivirus software on remote computing devices.
- Annually certify the individual's plan. This can be an important document if the individual is ever suspected of a violation or other security- or privacy-related incident during the year.
- The individual's manager should review the plan with the individual and provide a signature indicating approval of the plan.
- Give a copy of the plan to the individual for his or her files and keep the original with the individual's employee or HR files.

An accompanying benefit of these plans is that they provide a way to help the information security and privacy area to check compliance within each of the business units and departments.

Enforcing the Individual Plan

To successfully include individual security and privacy plans into the performance appraisal process, consider using the following plan and modify to meet your organization's environment:

1. Communications must be given to personnel so that they know that their job performance and compensation are now linked to their personal plans.
2. All personnel should develop their own plans.
3. The effectiveness of both the individual plans and the appraisal process should be measured and centrally managed.
4. Human resources, law department, applicable labor unions, and executive management should provide documented approval of the approach. They should be willing to do this because this approach provides evidence that an information security and privacy compliance method has been implemented and supported by organizational leaders.

5. Internal audit should use the plans created, and portions of the resulting appraisals that are specifically related to security and privacy, without infringing upon the employee's privacy, as ways to measure accountability.
6. Information privacy and security job functions will have a procedure to demonstrate compliance, find compliance gaps, and determine how to meet compliance for the gaps based on individual activities and evaluations.
7. In the event of a failure to execute the plan, sanctions and disciplinary action must be taken to demonstrate the program's importance. This has the effect of moving responsibility for security and privacy to the actual personnel who handle information and must comply with policies to ensure information security and privacy assurance.

Individual security and privacy plans should have all the components that describe the employee's access rules, authorization levels, and record of compliance with the rules. This would be much more specific and would require more time for the manager to review and assess. The manager would need to review violations, audit logs, and document any violations that occurred during the planning period.

An advantage of this approach is that it helps to ensure employee understanding of security and privacy responsibilities and information access rights as they relate to job requirements, resulting in increased awareness and assigned accountability.

Challenges

As with anything worthwhile, you may face some challenges when incorporating security and privacy considerations into the job appraisal process. Think about these problems and be prepared to address them as appropriate within your organization. Here are a few possible challenges:

■ Be aware of the distribution of the ratings, particularly excellent ratings, based on sex, ethnicity, race, religion, and other factors related to discrimination. Discuss these possibilities with your HR and law departments to find the best ways to implement the appraisal process without having these characteristics possibly being linked to the rating.
■ Be prepared for some personnel who demand or complain that they deserve a higher rating or bigger bonus than others in the same role or with the same security and privacy responsibilities. For example, Windows system administrators may demand that they deserve a higher rating and bigger bonus than another coworker who administers a different system because it is harder to secure a Windows system.

- Know your economic environment. If your organization has to reduce spending, and the ARP payments are subsequently cut or reduced, it will send the message that information security and privacy are not important.
- Anticipate that managers may demand proof that rewarding good security and privacy behavior has made systems and information more secure, before they agree to ARP payments. There is, of course, no solid proof for this, but do your homework to gather information that provides inferences linking improved security and privacy with motivation to personnel through such means as ARP payments.

Chapter 5

Common Corporate Education Mistakes

The only real mistake is the one from which we learn nothing.

—John Powell

The mediocre teacher tells. The good teacher explains. The superior teacher demonstrates. The great teacher inspires.

—William Arthur Ward

I like to run around my lake next to the hay field. Not only is it good exercise, it also gives me some good thinking time. As I run, I hear the constant croaking of the bullfrog and the intermittent but regular chirps of the leopard frog. When I'm close to the water, the sandpipers start squeaking at me from where they stand and continue until I leave the water's edge. There are three red-winged blackbird nests right next to my running path. When I approach each, the parent birds start screaming at me and flying around me, trying to distract me from their nest. As soon as I am a little distance away, they stop their tirade. These are four different creatures with four different and distinct ways of communicating. The bullfrog constantly drones with his loud message, the leopard frogs emphasize their chirping message regularly, the sandpipers start sounding their warnings when I approach, and consistently squeak while I am in their area. The red-winged blackbirds scream only when I am very close.

They remind me of how organizations perform their awareness and training activities: The frogs sing out to anyone within earshot, such as many organizations do who send awareness messages for anyone to read or notice. The blackbirds targeted their messages specifically at me, much like training efforts that are targeted at specific groups. As with most organizations, these messages are basically the same, regardless of who might be within hearing range. Indiscriminate announcements are bound to be ineffective with some types of passersby. This consistent and unvarying type of communicating is often the same move that organizations make when it comes to information security and privacy training and awareness activities; they send the same messages in the same way to widely diverse groups of audiences. This is just one of the mistakes organizations make when launching training and awareness programs.

The following text describes several of the mistakes that organizations make when implementing education programs—mistakes you should strive to avoid.

Throwing Education Together Too Quickly

Many organizations try to put together information security and privacy training and awareness quickly just to meet either an auditor's or regulator's requirements or to try to quickly and easily comply with a regulatory or legal requirement deadlines. Such training and awareness is rarely effective.

Do not toss together your program without thought. Some real-life practitioner experiences described in Chapter 19 will give you some pointers and ideas for putting together a program within a limited period of time, while also taking into consideration all the elements of a good education program.

Not Fitting the Environment

Many organizations do not build the education program around the business environment. They purchase a ready-made training module and a trailer load of awareness materials, or they copy the awareness and training program for a specific topic from another organization, but do not take the time to modify the materials to fit with their own unique business environment. Do not try to introduce a ready-made program or another organization's education program into your organizational environment without modification and customization. If the content does not fit your business environment, training and awareness will be ineffective and viewed as a waste of time.

Not Addressing Applicable Legal and Regulatory Requirements

When organizations put together information security and privacy education programs without researching or taking into consideration the regulatory requirements for such education, large gaps in their education efforts result. Training and awareness requirements applicable to your organization must be researched.

No Leadership Support

Executive leaders often do not clearly or visibly support education efforts. This is one of the most common reasons that training programs fail. If personnel do not think that executive leaders support training and awareness efforts, then they will probably not be motivated to participate. Executive sponsorship and support are necessary for a successful information security and privacy education program. You must get your executive leaders to sponsor and promote your education efforts.

Budget Mismanagement or No Budget

Many organizations labor under the misconception that training and awareness activities take little expertise, little preparation, little resources, or a combination of all of these. They do not carry out an education impact analysis to determine education needs and then establish a budget. Plan adequately for education then obtain appropriate budget. See Chapter 12 for a discussion on budget and funding.

Using Unmodified Education Materials

Organizations are often unrealistically optimistic that information security and privacy training and awareness efforts can be fulfilled using off-the-shelf materials without any modification or tailoring. This leads to ineffective training and awareness, along with frustration of the trainers and the learners, with the use of inappropriate materials. This will ultimately damage your education efforts. Always ensure materials are modified as appropriate to meet your organization's unique education requirements.

Information Overload

Organizations often try to dump a huge amount of information into a learner's brain in a short period of time. Many studies indicate, however, that people can only take in and comprehend, or remember, five to nine items, or chunks, of information at any one time.*

Also, if you cover too much material at once, learners might feel as though they are having massive amounts of material unrealistically piled upon them. This will likely make your learners resentful and not want to learn. Break up your training and awareness messages and sessions into chunks that can be successfully absorbed by your learners.

---

* Stolovitch, H.D., and Keeps, E.J., *Telling Ain't Training*, ASTD Press, Alexandria, VA, 2002, p. 23.

No Consideration for the Learner

Organizations often create training programs from the viewpoint of the person presenting. Instead, training and awareness should focus on the learner. Be sure to create training curriculum and awareness activities with which the learner can relate and can easily apply to his or her job responsibilities.

Poor Trainers

Organizations often choose subject matter experts (SMEs) to deliver the training.

However, just because someone is an expert on a topic does not mean that he or she will also be a good instructor. SMEs often do not see a topic with the same perspective as a person who has no knowledge on the subject. If the SME has no background or knowledge about what it takes to be an effective instructor, then the SME, even with the best of intentions, will likely not be successful in getting the message across.

Ensure that the trainers you use are not only knowledgeable about the topic but are also experienced in effective training methods.

Information Dumping

Content developers and trainers often mistakenly believe that telling is teaching. Trainers and training-content developers must realize that different people learn in different ways. There are many people who do not learn well by just listening or by just reading. You must consider your target audiences and deliver training in different ways to accommodate your audience's learning styles. Methods of delivering training are discussed later in this book. Do not just dump information on your audience; provide training and awareness using methods with which they can relate, understand, and absorb.

No Motivation for Education

There is often no motivation for participants to learn the information security topic and, sometimes, even no motivation for attending training.

Organizations must provide motivation for personnel to know and understand information security and privacy issues. The issue of motivation is discussed later in the book, as well as in Chapter 4. Motivate your personnel to participate in information security and privacy awareness and training activities. Tell learners why the security and privacy issues the topics cover are in place and how they directly impact their jobs.

Inadequate Planning

Organizations often do not plan well for awareness and training events.

Information security and privacy training are usually scheduled at the same time as another big training event within the organization or during a time that conflicts with the target audience's own deadlines, products releases, and so on. Also, inadequate planning can lead to missing resources during training events, inadequate materials for awareness activities, and a hodgepodge of other problems that will negatively impact your education efforts. Be aware of everything going on within your organization and know everything you need, right down to the minutest detail. Plan well for education delivery and success. Many planning tools are provided in this book.

Not Evaluating the Effectiveness of Education

Chapter 18 goes into detail about methods for evaluating the effectiveness of education efforts. If you continue to give poor or ineffective training, your program will not be successful. You must evaluate the effectiveness of your program and make changes as necessary.

Using Inappropriate or Politically Incorrect Language

Chapters 13 and 14 discuss the various issues related to creating training content and awareness materials that will not offend your learners and to discuss issues in such a way that will not be inappropriate within your business environment or within each of the geographic locations where you are providing the education.

Chapter 6

Getting Started

What is the first business of one who studies .... To part with self-conceit. For it is impossible for anyone to begin to learn what he thinks he already knows.

—Epictetus (Greek Philosopher)

I have had my solutions for a long time, but I do not yet know how I am to arrive at them.

—Karl Friedrich Gauss

Before diving right into building your information security and privacy awareness and training program, take into account the current general training and awareness environment within your organization, unless you want to spend a lot of time reinventing the wheel or building unnecessary wheels.

Determine Your Organization's Environment, Goals, and Mission

First, make sure you really know and understand your organization's environment, goals, and mission. Every non-revenue-generating initiative, such as an information security and privacy education program, must support the organization to justify funding such an education program.

To help you do this, determine the answers to these questions:

- What products and services does your organization offer?
- Where are your customers located?
- Where are your business partners located?
- In which geographic areas are your organization's facilities located?
- What are your organization's goals for this year, and the coming 10 years?
- What is your organization's mission?
- What kind of reputation does your organization have?
- Does your organization use logos, trademarks, or mascots?
- What are the major business risks that your organization faces?

Identify Key Contacts

As the second step, identify key contacts with whom you should meet; discuss your thoughts, ideas, and activities; and with whom you can form alliances. The more partnering you can find throughout the organization, the easier (comparatively) your job will be. Check with the people filling the following positions to discuss what training and awareness programs they are currently implementing or have planned, and discuss how you can work together:

- Information technology management
- Privacy officer
- Security officer
- Human resources (HR) management
- Physical security
- Legal counsel
- Compliance officers
- Corporate training
- Systems and applications owners
- IT support personnel
- Customer care/service
- Marketing management
- Internal audit
- Risk officers
- Public relations

Here are some sample questions to help you get started in planning your interviews with the contacts and obtaining an understanding of their expectations from your education program:

- Executive leaders
  - What expectations do you have from the training participants?
  - What results do you need to see to determine if an education program is successful?

- Will you visibly support the education efforts?
- What delivery channels will you support for our education efforts within the organization?
- What funding will you provide for the education program?
- What should people be doing to contribute to achieving strategic objectives? How can you demonstrate support for ensuring that personnel learn what is needed to get the job done? How can we assist in that? What funding is available to influence security and privacy activity transfer?
- What problems or opportunities exist that we can influence with information security and privacy training?
- What organizational measures need to be influenced by security and privacy education programs?
- What information security and privacy education activities must the organization perform to comply with regulations and laws?
- Which laws and regulations affect the organization?

■ Education contacts and middle-level managers
- What are your preferences (time, location, day, etc.) for your personnel to attend or participate in education programs?
- What level of information security and privacy learning do you expect to see after participation in training?
- How much time can you allocate for personnel to participate in education activities and formal training?
- What do you expect your personnel to be able to do after attending the training program?
- How can you become involved before and after the training to make this happen?
- If your people apply what they learn, how will it benefit the organization?
- What are the other factors that can influence the results you want?
- What deficiencies do you see in the current training and awareness program?

■ Learning participants
- What is important to you as you participate in the information security and privacy programs?
- What do you expect to get out of the training experience?
- What do you need to learn with regard to information security and privacy?
- How will this benefit you?
- How would you like to learn? Which learning methods work best for you?
- What do you need to be able to do with regard to information security and privacy within your job? How can we best help you learn to do that?
- What enablers need to be in place to help you do these things?
- How do you think the organization will benefit from your increased information security and privacy knowledge and skills?

- What problems related to security and privacy, for example, not being informed of changes to systems, not being informed of security and privacy law requirements, etc., do you encounter while performing your job?
- In which security and privacy topics do you need training?

Review Current Training Activities

The third step consists of reviewing the current training activities going on within your organization. The contacts you just made should be able to give you a good description of almost everything that is going on related to training within your organization. Consider any type of training in all the departments. Some of these will likely include

- new-employee orientation,
- systems administration training,
- management training,
- customer service training,
- diversity training,
- supervisor development,
- sales and marketing training,
- computer skills training,
- executive development,
- facilities and physical-security training,
- ethics training,
- call center staff training.

Review Current Awareness Activities

The fourth step consists of reviewing the current awareness capabilities and activities. As with training, consider all types of awareness activities going on throughout the company. See if you can tie your information security and privacy messages in with these already-established awareness activities. Common types of awareness activities that may currently occur within your organization include

- corporate e-mail and awareness intranet Web sites,
- corporate newsletters,
- paycheck enclosures,
- externally published magazines,
- corporate magazines,
- posters,
- cafeteria table tents,
- facility video monitors,
- streaming audio and video,

- facility intercom messages,
- lunchtime presentations,
- auditorium presentations.

I provide a very long list of possible awareness activities in Chapter 14.

Conduct a Needs Assessment

At the fifth step, you are ready to perform an information security and privacy awareness and training needs assessment. The results of the needs assessment will help you plan your training and awareness road map, in addition to providing justification for having the program, and for requesting a budget based on the discovered needs.

Why should one take all the time and trouble to do a needs assessment? In order to

- determine if information security and privacy training and awareness programs are needed. In most organizations it is needed, but an assessment will demonstrate the need;
- determine where there are gaps in information security and privacy requirements that can be impacted by training and awareness;
- determine the information security and privacy content and scope of your training and awareness efforts;
- determine the desired outcome from your training and awareness efforts;
- create a baseline that can be used as a basis for measuring the success of your efforts, as well as the impact of your efforts on the organization's security and privacy activities and compliance;
- gain support of the management by involving them in the process, and to develop awareness and training that directly address their specific needs.

Involve the key contacts in your assessment. When performing the assessment, you will want to discover certain things from people who fill different roles. Specifically, you will want to determine if

1. Management and legal leaders visibly support the awareness and training efforts; they know and understand the laws and regulations that require training and awareness activities; they understand that they need to fully support information security and privacy efforts to ensure compliance by personnel;
2. Information security staff and management are prepared to be the experts available for consultation by organizational members; they must understand that they are the role models and have a role as an information security and privacy leader, fully comply with information security and privacy directives, and ensure that others comply as well;
3. To comply with requirements, systems owners have a thorough understanding of security and privacy policies, standards, and other requirements, and

truly understand how to implement security and privacy controls within the systems they manage;

4. Systems administrators and other IT support personnel are aware of their significant role in security computer systems and networks; typically, they have a very high degree of authorization and authority for the support operations. Such personnel must thoroughly understand the importance and impact their activities have upon security, and must clearly understand the corporate information security and privacy requirements. Additionally, as custodians of the systems, they must stay up to date with the latest systems vulnerabilities and security patches;

5. Computer operations managers need specific security awareness and training related to the systems for which they are responsible and also on how to best secure and control access to your organization's computing equipment;

6. Systems users need specific training and awareness about the risks involved with using the organization's network, the impact such risks can have on the business, and what their role is in securing the network;

7. Direct reports to managers provide them with the necessary information regarding security and privacy. If the target group for education is management, a good source of information can come from the people who report directly to them. Direct reports can provide insights and feedback about the information security and privacy skills and issues that managers and supervisors can improve upon;

8. Coworkers and peers are aware of each other's security and privacy practices. Performing a 360-degree feedback exercise is a popular assessment process in many organizations. When you speak with or get information from your target group's coworkers, you can obtain valuable insight about the information security and privacy issues that need to be improved to have a positive impact on business processes and the team work environment in general;

9. HR has records and documents, and also is the centralized repository for complaints, incidents, grievance, violations, and other events, especially as they relate to security and privacy;

10. Vendors can provide some enlightening qualitative information and give you a feel of their perceptions about your organization's information security and privacy practices. Also, see if they can give you some good ideas about industry information security and privacy training and awareness standards and practices;

11. Internal and external customers can provide information about their perception of your organization's security and privacy practices. Surveys can be useful in obtaining feedback from customers to provide quantitative information that can review information security and privacy deficiencies or problems, or gaps between the documented, promised behavior and the actual behavior;

12. Information security and privacy incidents and breaches have occurred as a result of not handling customer information, or dealing with customers, appropriately;

13. Competitors can provide insight into security and privacy issues. You may review published competitor information and keep track of published incidents in news reports. You can see where your organization is on the road to similar information security and privacy incidents or noncompliance actions by learning from others;

14. Those responsible for information security and privacy are aware of the latest and evolving risks. Information security and privacy experts and observers need to keep up with the latest risks and controls. By speaking with the experts, you can learn current trends in protecting information, current trends in incidents, emerging technologies and regulations of which you need to be aware, etc. You can identify experts through security and privacy organizations, trade publications, books, conferences, seminars, etc.

Here is one high-level method for conducting an information security and privacy training and awareness needs assessment:

■ Identify the information security and privacy problems or needs.
  – What is your organizational context? Look at your organization's vision statements, mission, goals, and values as they relate to information security and privacy.
  – Identify security and privacy problems or needs. State in dollar terms if possible, such as potential fines or penalties. What is the problem costing your organization? Or, what could it cost? What are the major risks to your organization?
  – Determine the specific information security and privacy objectives that your training and awareness program must address. Your objective should document the desired performance, behavior, or outcome, and it should be something that is measurable, observable, feasible, and something that can be corrected.
■ Determine how to design your needs analysis.
  – Determine your criteria for selecting a method. Consider using several types of techniques and tools, such as surveys, questionnaires, interviews, direct observation, documents review, etc.
  – Look at the advantages and disadvantages of your methods. Choose the method most appropriate to your situation and the topic at hand. Consider the cost, time to perform, resources available, number of people involved, disruption to the workplace, confidentiality, complexity, knowledge necessary, reliability, participant involvement, etc.
■ Collect information using one of the potential methods, or a combination of many of them. A few of these include
  – interviews,
  – questionnaires,
  – proficiency tests,

- attitude surveys,
- incident reports,
- recent audit findings,
- regulatory compliance reviews,
- job descriptions,
- sample work output and documents,
- HR and proficiency tests,
- turnover and termination statistics and records,
- fraud reports and investigations,
- help desk problem statistics,
- training evaluations,
- awareness feedback forms,
- suggestion box contributions,
- documented complaints,
- performance appraisals and reviews as allowed by HR and law departments,
- employee manuals and handbooks,
- training participation statistics,
- reviews of existing documents (such as awareness and training material, schedules, attendee lists, etc.),
- work area observations performed during the workday and at night after everyone has gone home,
- existing awareness and training metrics,
- security plans for systems and applications,
- systems inventories and application user ID databases access controls,
- event analyses (such as malicious code, denial of service attacks, spam, Web site defacements, etc.),
- patch-management practices.

■ Analyze the information.
- Perform qualitative analysis. This includes such methods as individual or group interviews, open-ended questionnaires, observation, etc. Sort your information into common categories. Try to quantify as much as possible without injecting much of your own interpretation (see Chapter 18 for ideas about surveys).
- Perform quantitative analysis. This includes such methods as statistics, observations, tests, etc. Perform a simple statistical analysis; look at your numbers in terms of means (averages), modes (the most commonly occurring number or item), and medians (the middle value or item).
- Identify solutions and recommendations. Clarify and define the discovered problems. Then, identify the type of training and awareness indicated by your analysis. What you choose should directly address the identified issues. It is at this point that you should add your personal opinions and perceptions about the problems and risks that have been identified. Your collected data will provide verification.

- Prioritize your training and awareness activities. Consider target groups, topics, regulatory requirements, scheduled compliance reviews, upcoming organizational activities, and other factors.
■ Provide feedback.
  - Write the report. Design your action plan and strategy based on your analysis. Document your conclusions and recommendations. Present the information in a clear and succinct format, followed by your summaries and recommendations. Consider constructing the report in the following way:
    • Executive summary/overview
    • Description of your assessment process
    • Summary of findings
    • Preliminary conclusions
    • Recommendations
    • Potential barriers
■ Make presentations. Present your report in person, if at all possible. Give your decision makers the opportunity to ask you questions, and also listen to their reactions. This is your chance to sell your ideas and your program.
■ Set the next steps to address findings. After submitting your report and making your presentation, ask your key decision makers to give you feedback, and ask them for their help in reaching your goals. It is possible that they may immediately approve your proposal. However, you will likely be asked to go back and get more information, identify more possible solutions, or do some more digging. Do not let that discourage you; it is a common part of the process in all organizations. When your proposal has been approved, you should create a road map for the design, development, and delivery of your information security and privacy training and awareness program.

Needs assessments can be very detailed and cost much money and time. National Institute of Standards and Technology (NIST) Special Publication 800-50 provides a comprehensive, detailed description of the needs assessment they created for federal offices to use as a guideline for complying with Federal Information Security Management Act (FISMA). Realistically, few organizations can afford to do comprehensive, detailed needs assessment. A good alternative is to perform an abbreviated form of needs assessment.

Following the approval of your program, consider doing another type of needs assessment prior to your training and awareness sessions; with the needs of your target audience in mind, fine-tune your delivery methods and content so that those needs are better met, and you ultimately obtain better results for your program. Besides the questions provided earlier, Appendix O contains sample pretraining and awareness questionnaire you can send to your target audience before you have finalized the development of your training and awareness content.

Create Your Road Map

Now that you have identified your needs and obtained executive approval and support, create your information security and privacy awareness and training road map. Consider creating something similar to the following.

Sample Information Privacy and Security Awareness and Training Road Map

1. Identify and assign roles.
   a. Organization-wide information privacy and security executive champion/sponsor.
   b. Information privacy and security training and awareness leader.
   c. Information privacy and security training and awareness support personnel.
   d. Business unit (BU) and regional privacy managers/sponsors/champions.
   e. BU and regional information privacy and security contacts.
   f. Third-party information privacy and security contacts.
2. Determine training and awareness needs.
   a. Interviews (see Appendix I for sample interview questions, along with the questions earlier in this chapter).
   b. Surveys.
   c. Site inspections.
   d. Document reviews.
3. Obtain sponsorship.
   a. Contact appropriate executive sponsor.
   b. Provide a master implementation plan that serves as a blueprint for your program.
   c. Create a communications plan focused on sending key messages to the audiences affected by each of the activities.
   d. Include sponsor's name on communications.
4. Create and update training and awareness materials.
   a. Computer-based training (CBT).
   b. Group activities.
   c. Classroom training.
   d. Messages and memos.
   e. Signs and posters.
   f. Other chosen training and awareness delivery methods (see Chapter 9).
5. Establish deployment schedule.
   a. Pilot-group vetting:
      i. Send explanatory message to subject matter experts (SMEs) and representatives from target groups (pilot group).
      ii. Obtain information from SMEs for incorporating into content.

      iii. SMEs and representatives review and provide feedback and evaluation of content.

      iv. Update training and awareness materials as necessary.

  b. Roll out content to targeted groups:

      i. Identify group members.

      ii. Send communications to the group members asking them for participation.

      iii. Follow-up to ensure participation.

  c. Ongoing activities:

      i. Perform training and awareness as indicated by event or situation triggers (described later).

      ii. Update material based on feedback and organizational changes.

6. Training and awareness delivery:

  a. Write announcement memo.

      i. The first announcement should outline your company and BU security and privacy awareness and training strategy. You should always let personnel know what they can expect with regard to training and awareness requirements before you start rolling out one activity at a time. This will help to ensure that they participate in more than just the first activity. See Appendices A and E for sample announcement memo and voice message.

      ii. The subsequent communications should include the following components:

        A. What is expected of the employee/partner receiving the communication?

        B. Why should personnel participate in education activities, and what are the benefits to the employee and the organization?

        C. When must the recipient perform the requested actions?

        D. How does the action relate to the recipient's job performance and responsibilities?

        E. Who sponsors the action (such as the privacy sponsor executive)?

        F. Whom to contact for further information?

  b. Notify security and privacy sponsor and champions.

      i. Explain purpose for the training and awareness action.

      ii. Reconfirm the use of their name on the communications.

7. Evaluate effectiveness of efforts and update appropriately. See Chapter 18 for more information about evaluations.

Event and Situation Triggers

Awareness activities and training sessions will be necessary in most organizations when the following events or situations occur:

- After posting a new or updated Web site privacy policy
- After updating existing security or privacy policies

- When bringing in contracted or outsourced personnel prior to, or at, project start
- Following extortion attempts
- During and following acquisitions, mergers, and divestitures
- Launching new products
- Launching new systems
- Resolving major security or privacy incidents
- Implementing new Internet applications and e-commerce
- Providing initial general awareness to all your company personnel
- Providing initial in-depth awareness to target groups
- When layoffs are planned
- During new-employee orientation soon after start
- When new executive management come on board
- Opening new facilities
- When new laws and regulations applicable to your organization are passed
- When launching new marketing campaigns
- Prior to new-technology implementation
- For ongoing awareness for all groups each month, or even each week, during the year
- When the organization is in the news for a privacy or security issue or breach
- During and following physical threats, such as from protestors or disgruntled customers or employees
- Following recent privacy or security incidents
- During security and privacy days
- Providing specialized awareness when information security or privacy policies or procedures change
- Providing third-party awareness following contract updates and when initiating new contracts
- When updating policies, procedures, standards, and guidelines
- When releasing new security or privacy policies
- When new technologies, such as Twitter, second-life online sites, social networking sites, and other Web 2.0 and Web 3.0 technologies start being used by the public, which includes your workers

Elements of an Effective Education Program

You should always keep in mind that there are four critical steps in the life cycle of a security and privacy awareness and training program:

1. Program design:
   - Conduct a needs assessment.
   - Develop and get approval for the awareness and training strategy.
   - Identify implementation tasks to be performed in support of established security and privacy education goals.

2. Material development:
   - Identify available awareness and training sources.
   - Identify target groups.
   - Set scope.
   - Create content outline.
   - Develop training material.
3. Program implementation:
   - Communication and rollout of the awareness and training program.
   - Delivery of awareness and training material (Web-based, distance learning, video, on-site, etc.).
4. Post-implementation:
   - Keep the program current.
   - Monitor and measure its effectiveness.
   - Use feedback methods (surveys, focus groups, benchmarking, etc.).

Your security and privacy awareness and training should include the following:

- An education budget that accounts for the communications, planning, and implementation activities that is proportionate to this piece of the total amount of the regulatory compliance and education budget
- A timeline indicating target dates for all phases of the awareness and training program
- Procedures and tools for measuring the overall effectiveness of the security and privacy awareness activities and training sessions
- Identification of integration points and implementation windows to effectively coordinate the awareness and education practices within the overall security and privacy compliance plan
- A strategy to integrate the training and awareness processes throughout all your company departments and teams to help ensure a successful security and privacy training and awareness program
- Execution of a training and awareness risk assessment to identify training and awareness compliance gaps and form the baseline to use for measuring future compliance success
- A description of the tactical objectives of the training and awareness program
- Policies and procedures to mitigate risk and ensure ongoing compliance with security and privacy requirements and regulations

See Chapter 5 for common mistakes to avoid when creating and implementing your education program.

Chapter 7

Establish a Baseline

We learn more by looking for the answer to a question and not finding it than we do from learning the answer itself.

—Lloyd Alexander

During your planning and assessment of needs, you gathered much information. Use this information to create a baseline for your organization with regard to effectiveness and quality of information security and awareness activities and materials. Do some evaluation planning to be able to specify in detail what your training and awareness evaluation activities will include. Your evaluation planning should also specify and document how success with your education program will be measured. You will use the data collected from the needs assessment. This will help you focus on the measures of success and outcomes when you design and create your training and awareness activities. Without this focus, your training and awareness focus could go off track and be developed only with a vague expectation and objective of learning and not where learning is necessary or in tying this learning to job responsibilities. Your baseline measurements represent the starting line with which you can compare improvements and measure various components of your training and awareness program.

You may have defined your learning objectives within your needs assessment. You may have established some measures for the objectives as well.

Look at your needs assessment and use that information when establishing your baseline measurements. The results of some training and awareness activities are fairly easy to observe and evaluate. However, results of most will be less obvious and hard to measure. To help with this, think about the baseline information you are using as hard data or soft data.

Hard Data

Think of hard data as improvement measurements or bases for improvement measurements. Such measurements should be undisputed facts and easily accumulated. This data is the most valued because it is objective, and it is easier to assign a monetary value.

Exhibit 1 lists examples of some typical hard data that you can use as baseline measurements for your information security and privacy education program.

Exhibit 1   Examples of Information Security and Privacy Hard Data

Topic	Metrics	Needs Assessment Findings	Baseline <Date> Numbers	Checkup <Date> Numbers
RESULTS	Number of viruses stopped			
	Number of spam messages filtered			
	Number of systems patches applied			
	Number of personnel certified			
	Number of forms processed			
	Number of accounts created			
COSTS	Security software variances			
	Security budget variances			
	Fixed security and privacy costs			
	Costs of security incidents			
	Costs of privacy incidents			

Exhibit 1   (continued)

Topic	Metrics	Needs Assessment Findings	Baseline <Date> Numbers	Checkup <Date> Numbers
	Cost per person for firewalls			
TIME	Network downtime from security incidents			
	Time spent addressing viruses			
	Time spent tracking network break-in			
	Time spent patching software with security fixes			
QUALITY	Number of customer privacy complaints successfully resolved			
	Number of security incidents			
	Number of privacy incidents			

Soft Data

Sometimes you will have issues, topics, and situations on which there will be no hard data available for you to use. Soft data will be more useful in some situations. It is more difficult to collect and analyze, but it can reveal some very useful information that may enhance your education program. Soft data is usually subjective, based on behavior, but is difficult to directly measure and quantify. It is difficult to assign dollar values to, and is seen as less credible as a performance measure (see Exhibit 2).

Determining where your organization is currently at with regard to information security and privacy awareness and training adequacy will not only help you to

Exhibit 2   Examples of Information Security and Privacy Soft Data

Topic	Metrics	Needs Assessment Findings	Baseline <Date> Numbers or Ratings	Checkup <Date> Numbers or Ratings
WORK	Violations of security policies			
	Violations of privacy policies			
	Number of communication breakdowns			
	Misuse of systems			
	Established unauthorized wireless access points			
	Grievances related to security and/or privacy			
	Job satisfaction of information security staff			
	Job satisfaction of information privacy staff			

Exhibit 2 (continued)

Topic	Metrics	Needs Assessment Findings	Baseline <Date> Numbers or Ratings	Checkup <Date> Numbers or Ratings
	Information security and/or privacy personnel turnover			
	Number of posted passwords			
	Number of unsecured, logged-in workstations			
FEELINGS and ATTITUDES	Reactions (favorable or unfavorable) to information privacy efforts			
	Reactions (favorable or unfavorable) to information security efforts			
	Attitude changes about information security and privacy			
	Perceived changes in information security and/or privacy performance			

(continued)

Exhibit 2 (continued)

Topic	Metrics	Needs Assessment Findings	Baseline <Date> Numbers or Ratings	Checkup <Date> Numbers or Ratings
	Increased confidence in organization's security and privacy efforts			
SKILLS	Information security and/or privacy decisions made			
	Information security and/or privacy problems solved			
	Information security and/or privacy incidents avoided			
	Information security and/or privacy complaints resolved			
DEVELOPMENT and ADVANCEMENT	Number of information security and/or privacy training sessions attended			
	Number of information security and/or privacy publications regularly read			

Exhibit 2 (continued)

Topic	Metrics	Needs Assessment Findings	Baseline <Date> Numbers or Ratings	Checkup <Date> Numbers or Ratings
	Performance appraisals with information security and privacy considerations			
INITIATIVES	Implementation of new information security or privacy ideas			
	Successful completion of security or privacy projects			
	Number of suggestions submitted to the information security and/or privacy department			
	Number of suggestions implemented			
	Setting information security and privacy goals and objectives			

Exhibit 3 Privacy and Security Education Inventory Worksheet

Training and Awareness Inventory

Company Name:

Inventory Date:

Type of Education: (for example, *Information Security, Information Privacy*, etc.)

Information Security Training

Topic Description	Been Given? Y/N	Baseline Measurement? Y/N	Exec Support? Y/N	Goals	Target Group	Group Size	Delivery Method (e.g., CBT, Classroom, Webinar, Video, etc.)	Next Delivery Date	Local, National, or International?	Notes
<add more rows as necessary>										

Information Security Awareness

Topic Description	Been Given? Y/N	Baseline Measurement? Y/N	Exec Support? Y/N	Goals	Target Group	Group Size	Delivery Method (e.g., Poster, Web Site, Newsletter, Presentation, Contest, etc.)	Next Delivery Date	Local, National, or International?	Notes
<add more rows as necessary>										

(continued)

Exhibit 3   (continued)

	Job Appraisal Process:								
1	How often are job appraisals performed?								
2	Who performs job appraisals?								
3	What items are consistent for all personnel appraisals?								
4	What impact do appraisals have on personnel job success (e.g., promotions, raises, demotions, terminations, etc.)?								
5	When are job appraisals performed? At the same time each year for all personnel?								
6	What global issues do you need to consider? In what countries do you have personnel?								
7	Do you have any restrictions with regard to the job appraisal process in other countries that are different from the United States? These could be organizational restrictions, or regulatory and legal restrictions.								
8	Do you need to make training and awareness available in different languages? This could impact how you can incorporate into the job appraisal process depending on how widely you can deploy your set of training and awareness curriculum.								

Exhibit 4 Baseline Worksheet

Information Privacy and Security Awareness and Training Offering Baseline Worksheet
Reviewer Name: **Review Date:**
Training or Awareness Activity Name:
Delivery Method:
List existing activities, communications, and history for this education offering:
What objectives have been successful or completed?
What are the strengths in the current offering?
What are the weaknesses in the current offering?
Have the appropriate people been participating?
How many people have been asked to participate?
How many actually participated?
Why the discrepancy? (Takes too long? Not supported by management? Not localized? Not clearly applicable to business? Etc.)

(continued)

Exhibit 4 **(continued)**

Do training and awareness support business goals? If so, how? If not, why?
Which trainers had the most success with this offering?
Which participants were most successful or satisfied with the offering?
Is the offering message and language localized where possible or necessary? (e.g., Spanish, French, German, Japanese, Cantonese, Korean, and so on)
How is the offering marketed?
List 3–7 major points made to the participants during the training or awareness.
Are training or awareness methods and efforts appropriate for the specific business needs? If yes, how? If not, why?
What percentage of the target group has received this training or awareness offering to date?
Were evaluation forms obtained for the training or awareness efforts? If so, what were the ratings?

gain buy-in and support for your program, but it will also provide a baseline against which you can measure your success or your shortcomings. Use your baseline data to help you prioritize your education efforts. The baseline can also become part of an education contract you develop with your key contacts to help them understand your education program and to see easily and quickly where you are at with program progress in relation to the situation when you started.

If you already have an inventory of all the documents and training and awareness activities that exist within your organization, review it closely. If you do not, then it is a good idea to create one. By having an inventory of everything related to information security and privacy, you will be better able to identify gaps for specific areas and topics, and to answer any audit or regulatory questions regarding your organization's information security and privacy initiatives and activities. Create an inventory that best meets your business style and organization needs.

Exhibit 3, shown earlier in this chapter, is one example for you to consider and use as a model. A similar version is presented in Appendix J. See Chapter 9 for a detailed discussion of methods that you can use to fill in the Delivery Method columns.

Note that in Exhibit 3 there is a section for information regarding job appraisal. As part of establishing a baseline, do not forget to include documenting the ways personnel are made accountable for participating in education activities. Accountability is an effective, but often overlooked, key to ensuring a successful information privacy and security program.

Review all your organization's polices, procedures, standards, guidelines, and other communications that address information privacy and security compliance. Identify what can be updated and what must be created. Create any necessary documents, forms, and plans to support your goals. For each of the education offerings you include in the inventory, document the current state of success or challenges. Use a worksheet similar to the one in Exhibit 4 shown earlier in this chapter, to record your baseline status for each.

Chapter 8

Get Executive Support and Sponsorship

Management is doing things right; leadership is doing the right things.

—Peter F. Drucker

Executive management must support your information security and privacy training and awareness efforts for them to be successful. Not only must they provide financial support to effectively develop the program, but they must also provide visible support to demonstrate to the workforce the importance and necessity of your efforts. Create an information security and privacy education project plan that includes your objectives for awareness and training, and include estimates for necessary personnel, materials, time schedules, and any other associated costs (such as videos, manuals, and so on). Ask the management to provide funds to support the organization's training and awareness compliance requirements. If you do not perceive support from senior management, it is likely you will encounter passive resistance from a significant percentage of personnel. They may not attend training for which they were scheduled, may ignore your requests to read and acknowledge policies and procedures, may ignore awareness activities, or may blatantly violate policies and procedures. It is important to prevent this by having executive management clearly communicate the importance of everyone's participation prior to your training and awareness rollout.

You will find some executives who already believe that information security and privacy education is an important endeavor and will be only too willing to financially support training efforts. However, a larger proportion will probably believe that such efforts should not be allocated much, if any, budget and that personnel should learn about security and privacy issues as part of performing their job responsibilities. It is crucial to the success of your education program to first and foremost convince executive management that information security and privacy is valuable and an essential part of doing successful business.

You may find it helpful to bring in information security and privacy training professionals from outside to support and communicate the need for information security and privacy education. Such professionals can also help you to determine how to implement an education program to meet your business needs, help to determine immediate education needs, and provide guidance based on their previous experiences and best practices. It is a fact in most companies that executive management will often pay closer attention to the experiences of an outside expert than to what their own personnel indicate are important company needs.

Executive Security and Privacy Training and Awareness Strategy Briefing

Schedule a briefing with executives well ahead of your planned awareness and training deliveries to communicate your goals, and ask for their visible support. A few high-level pointers for the briefing are as follows:

■ Keep it simple and succinct.
■ Keep it nontechnical.
■ Use a peer-led roundtable discussion format.
■ Demonstrate value.
■ Discuss budget needs and strategy.
■ Focus on the executive's responsibilities. For example, when speaking to the CIO, speak about business aspects of information.
■ Ask for sponsorship and support before leaving the meeting.

To help emphasize the importance of an information security and privacy education program, and to persuade executive management to invest in and visibly support the program efforts, make the following points when communicating to executives to get their support:

■ Explain how a security or privacy incident could potentially impact business. A sample scenario is described later in this chapter.
■ Emphasize legal and regulatory requirements for education. Use the information from Chapter 2.
■ Explain how training helps retain employees. It is a common misconception that training personnel will cause them to leave and use the acquired knowledge at another company. There are a few such employees. However,

studies* show that personnel who receive what they feel is adequate training and awareness to do their job responsibilities to the best of their abilities are more likely to be satisfied with their employer and stay with the company.

■ Find an executive who will be an advocate for your efforts with the other executives. This ally should be able to speak positively about education efforts and needs in communications and conversations with the other executives when you are not around and should keep the issue alive and in mind.

■ When describing your education program, clearly show how it reflects and supports the business goals and needs. You must be able to describe succinctly and clearly the benefits of your program. This means you must know and understand the current state of information security and privacy education, areas where weaknesses exist, and how to address these weaknesses.

■ Have a clear strategy to describe how you will market the education program to personnel. Be ready for this question; some savvy executives will not want to invest in a program if they do not believe you have adequately thought about and prepared how to make it successful. You will need to demonstrate and describe how the education program will support all job function needs of personnel.

■ Know how much funding to ask for and justify the amount you are requesting. If you know you will not be able to get the maximum, start by asking what you know is realistic. Do your best to make these initial activities successful, and use these successes to ask for more support and resources. The management is more likely to support and dedicate resources to your education program if you have shown, even in a small way, that you can be, and have been, successful. See Chapter 12 for information about budgeting and funding.

■ Anticipate executive management's objections prior to your meeting. Speak with others who have tried to implement similar or parallel programs. What are the issues and problems that may be presented? What do they like or not like in education programs? Have they had bad experiences with similar programs in the past? Use the answers, and develop information in your presentation that will address these challenges.

■ Always include, when possible and feasible, the management's ideas in your program. They will have more ownership in the program, and they will, of course, think the program has been vastly improved by their inputs.

■ Some executives like to be given alternatives. Present what you want, as well as, perhaps, a scaled-down less expensive but adequate alternative, and let the executive choose. Even if you win the scaled-down alternative, it is much better than what you had before the meeting. Also, the executive may be willing to spend more money after the program is successful.

---

* One, for example, includes the Rewards of Work 2000: What Do Employees Value at Work, a survey of the American workforce, conducted by Sibson & Company. This survey identified training and development as one of the most important factors in retaining personnel. The ASTD has conducted studies with similar findings.

Communicate Program Roles

During your executive briefing, clearly communicate the roles you will need to successfully implement your strategy. There will be different roles for different organizations based on size, industry, location, regulatory requirements, etc. However, some of these roles will include

- Business unit (BU) security and privacy managers:
  - Design BU deployment strategy
  - Define and document the associated company regional–country–BU deployment model
  - Serve as content specialization resources
- Security and privacy advocates (see examples in Appendix D):
  - Form the communication and implementation link between the corporate security and privacy office and field employees
  - Serve as the first point of contact for BU personnel security and privacy questions and advice
  - Ensure personnel awareness and training activities
- Regional security and privacy managers:
  - Deploy core and functional modules
  - Communicate security and privacy issues for their region
  - Serve as content experts on legal, regulatory, and country-specific issues
- Workforce management:
  - Visibly and actively support security and privacy awareness and training activities
  - Ensure staff participation in security and privacy education activities
- Executive security and privacy champions (see examples in Appendix D):
  - Provide local executive sponsorship for their business unit
  - Promote and support security and privacy implementation strategy
  - Support security and privacy advocates network

Education Program Success Indicators

It is common for executives to want to know what the success indicators will be for your program before they give their support and funding. Think carefully about this as it relates to your organization, and be ready to list what you define as your organization's information security and privacy education program success indicators. We discuss evaluating effectiveness in detail in Chapter 18. However, at a high level, these will include some or all of the following:

- Number of customer complaints regarding security and privacy decline
- Improved audit and risk assessment reports
- Less network downtime as a result of malicious code and break-ins

- Sufficient funding to implement the proposed and approved education program
- Appropriate management support and organizational placement to enable effective program implementation
- Visible support of awareness through posters, communications, etc., within 100% (or whatever percentage is reasonable for your organization) of departments
- High percentage (e.g., 97%) of participation for training events
- Personnel performance appraisals incorporate information security and privacy education requirements
- Level of attendance at briefings and awareness events
- Participation in security and privacy contests and other participation events

Demonstrate Importance

Demonstrate the importance of information security and privacy to the executives in your organization. The management relates to economic impact and how business can be affected. When seeking to get sponsorship, consider developing and presenting an executive paper to your executive management that they can immediately relate to from a business perspective. Consider including the following components, as they are applicable to your organization, in the executive paper.

Provide Examples of Security- and Privacy-Impacting Events

Addressing security and privacy concerns, implementing enterprise security, and ensuring compliance with applicable security and privacy laws are significant to achieving uninterrupted business processing, demonstrating due diligence, and minimizing risks due to noncompliance. If unprepared, a privacy or security breach could result in significant business downtime and monetary loss, negatively impact an organization's reputation, generate legal fines and penalties, possibly result in costly civil suits, and negatively impact customer satisfaction and loyalty.

Your presentation should provide examples of some recent internal incidents or attacks, and incidents that have occurred in other organizations, particularly those in your industry. The examples given in the rest of this chapter would be ideal to use within your presentation.

Demonstrate How Security and Privacy Incidents Are Increasing

Do a little research and dig up statistics to support the need to have an effective information security and privacy program. Especially effective are statistics that reveal the trend for information security and privacy incidents to continue to rise. For example:

- From the Federal Trade Commission (FTC): Occurrences of identity theft continue to rise
  - In 2001: 86,212
  - In 2003: 214,905
  - In 2008: 313,982
- From the Anti-Phishing Working Group (APWG): The number of phishing attacks is quickly growing
  - November 2003: 28 reported unique attacks
  - April 2004: 1,125 reported unique attacks
  - October 2008: 34,758 reported unique attacks

Demonstrate How Information Security and Privacy Is a Core Business Issue

As awareness of privacy, security, and related issues grows, organizations must treat security and privacy as core business issues or find themselves at a disadvantage in the marketplace. Customers are increasingly inclined to seek to do business with organizations that can give them control over their personal information. Information security and privacy are becoming essential to maintain a competitive edge, profitability, legal compliance, and commercial image, and to meet a standard of due care. A study by the Ponemon Institute reported on December 15, 2008,* that in polling over 6400 adult U.S. consumers, the top ten trusted companies for privacy in the United States were American Express, eBay, IBM, Amazon, Johnson & Johnson, Hewlett Packard (HP), U.S. Postal Service, Procter and Gamble, Apple, Nationwide, Charles Schwab, and USAA.

The study revealed that the importance consumers place upon privacy and the sense of control they have over their PII is of critical importance. As stated in this study:

- **Importance of privacy continues to rise.** Seventy-three percent of consumers said the protection of their personal privacy is "important" or "very important," up from 69 percent in 2006.
- **Consumers feel they are losing control of personal information.** Only 45 percent of consumers feel they have control over their personal information, down from 56 percent in 2006.
- **Identity theft is top of mind.** Sixty-two percent of consumers believe that identity theft most saliently affects their perceptions about a company's privacy, while 53 percent named data breach notification and 42 percent cited annoying background chatter in a public venue. Only 18 percent of consumers cited social networking abuse as a factor.

---

* Accessed on June 1, 2009 from http://truste.org/about/press_release/12_15_08.php.

Businesses, including your organization's competitors, are becoming acutely aware of the trend to address privacy and use privacy assurances as a differentiator for keeping and obtaining new customers. A clear example of this is HP. In 2003, HP awarded the first HP Privacy Innovation Award at the PrivacyCon conference to "recognize worldwide leadership in privacy protection and practices." The Chief Information Office of the Province of Alberta, Canada, and eBay received the 2003 awards. It is reported that HP plans to make this an annual award.

Another indicator of the trend to promote and implement privacy assurances is the undeniable statistics that show privacy breaches continue to increase, and continue to cost businesses more and more. For example, in February 2009, the Ponemon Institute released the results of a different study, the annual *U.S. Cost of Data Breach Study** funded by PGP, which revealed that privacy breaches cost business more than ever before. According to the study, privacy breaches cost U.S. companies $202 per breach of customer records in 2008, compared to $197 in 2007. The largest cost to businesses was loss of customers.

The annual *U.S. Cost of Data Breach Study* tracked many cost factors, including expensive costs to detect, escalate, notify, and respond, in addition to legal, investigative, and administrative expenses; customer losses; opportunity losses; reputation management; and costs associated with customer support such as information hotlines and credit monitoring subscriptions. Other findings included the following:

- Average total per-incident costs in 2008 were $6.65 million, compared to an average per-incident cost of $6.3 million in 2007.
- Healthcare and financial services companies experienced the highest churn rate—6.5% and 5.5%, respectively, on a total average of 3.6%, which reflect the sensitivity of the data collected and the customer expectation that information will be protected.
- Third-party organizations accounted for more than 44% of all cases in the 2008 study and are also the most costly form of data breaches due to additional investigation and consulting fees.
- More than 84% of 2008 cases involved organizations that had had more than one data breach in 2008—meaning that companies are becoming more experienced in managing breaches over time.
- More than 88% of all cases in this year's study involved insider negligence.
- More than half of the respondents believe that training and awareness programs assist in preventing future breaches and 44% have expanded their use of encryption.
- The most significant cost decrease was seen in activities relating to post breach response, which indicates that organizations are becoming more cost-effective in managing data breaches.

---

* Accessed on June 1, 2009 from http://www.pgp.com/insight/newsroom/press_releases/2008_annual_study_cost_of_data_breach.html.

Communicate the Increasing Security and Privacy Threats and Breaches

Increasingly, organizations and their information systems and networks face information security and privacy threats from a wide range of sources such as identity theft, mistakes, lack of knowledge, inappropriate business practices, computer-assisted fraud, network attacks, sabotage, vandalism, and fire or flood, to name a few. Privacy and security risks such as e-mail schemes, identity theft, fraud, medical identity theft, and so on, have become more common, more ambitious, and increasingly sophisticated. Additionally, the number of security- and privacy-related laws and regulations continues to proliferate at exponential rates throughout the world.

Dependence on information systems, application services, personnel knowledge, mobile computers, and mobile storage devices means that organizations are more vulnerable to information security and privacy threats. The interconnecting of public and private networks, the trend toward distributed computing, connections to business partners and third parties, and sharing of information resources increase the difficulty of achieving adequate and acceptable information protection and access control. Keeping up with the large number of laws requiring security and privacy activities can be overwhelming if there is not one person, or area, responsible for knowing, understanding, and addressing the related requirements. Monitoring the laws is necessary to ensure compliance and to prevent being fined or undergoing legal action as a result of noncompliance.

Someone needs to ensure that the appropriate and applicable personnel get the information they need to comply with the laws. Organizations have been significantly impacted by security and privacy breaches. See Appendix S for some possible resources that you can use to find statistics and events to support your case to executives. The following are just a few examples of the incidents and suits that have occurred and impacted businesses:

- April 1, 2010: The FTC fined Civic Development Group LLC, CDG Management LLC and owners Scott Posch and David Keezer $18.8 million, plus they must surrender their pricey Picasso paintings, luxury cars and guitar collection, for their telephone fundraising activities which duped consumers about their donations to police and firefighters. The civil penalty was the biggest ever to date in an FTC consumer protection case. The telemarketers misled consumers by telling them the telemarketers worked directly for the charities for which they were calling and that "100 percent" of consumers' donations would go to charity. Only about 10 to 15 percent of donations went to charity.
- January 13, 2010: Connecticut Attorney General Richard Blumenthal sued Health Net of Connecticut, Inc. for not securing patient records and financial information involving 446,000 individuals endangered by a security breach. The lack of security violated HIPAA requirements.

- February 18, 2009: CVS Caremark received a $2.25 million fine, plus 20 years of ongoing reporting and regular independent audits, from the FTC for HIPAA violations—for failing to take reasonable and appropriate security measures to protect the sensitive financial and medical information of its customers and employees for poor disposal practices at their more than 6300 retail outlets. See more at http://www.ftc.gov/opa/2009/02/cvs.shtm.
- December 17, 2007: The FTC fined the American United Mortgage Company a $50,000 civil penalty plus 10 years of ongoing activities and regular independent audits for tossing PII into dumpsters, thus violating the Fair and Accurate Credit Transactions Act (FACTA), the Fair Credit Reporting Act, the Gramm–Leach–Bliley Act (GLBA), and the FTC Act.
- January 30, 2007: The U.S. FTC and Department of Justice jointly announced a $465,000 penalty against TJ Web Productions for violating the Controlling the Assault on Non-Solicited Pornography and Marketing Act (CAN–SPAM). This is one of seven companies that were charged in July 2005 with violating CAN-SPAM by sending sexually explicit e-mail. Settlements with five of the operations have resulted in civil penalties totaling $1.624 million. In addition to the fine, for which the owners are personally responsible and could lose their property, or worse, if not paid, TJ Web Productions must submit several different types of documents over the next 5 years to the FTC to demonstrate their compliance and existence of appropriate procedures to support compliance.
- September 7, 2006: Puget Sound Energy (PSE), Washington state's largest electricity and natural gas utility, with over 1 million customers in 11 western Washington counties, was ordered to pay a total of $995,000 in fines for selling their customer information to marketing companies over a 5-year period. The Washington Utilities and Transportation Commission (Commission) charged that PSE had permitted improper access to consumer information more than 18,000 times, in violation of the Commission's rules.
- September 7, 2006: Xanga.com was ordered to pay the largest-to-date civil penalty of $1 million for violating the Children's Online Privacy Protection Act (COPPA). Xanga did not obtain permission from parents to use children's information, and they did not contact parents to get permission, prior to using children's information. Not obtaining parental permission has been part of all the many penalities that have been applied under COPPA to data.

Security- and Privacy-Related Laws Impact Business

The number of laws and regulations that govern how personal information must be handled continues to grow worldwide. For example, the European Union (EU) Data Protection Directive 95/46/EC impacts the activities of any office located outside the EU that receives, from an entity in the EU, any information considered as personal information. These restrictions result from the 1995 EU Data Protection

Directive 95/46/EC that provides detailed procedures regarding the treatment of personal data and requires each of the EU member states to enact national legislation to conform to those requirements.

Organizations (and their employees handling personal information) doing business in EU countries must understand and comply with these requirements and laws.

As another example, California SB 1386 became law on July 1, 2003, and requires all companies that do business in California, or maintain information about California residents in computerized formats, to promptly notify, through one of four possible ways, each of their California customers in the event a security breach occurs that involves improper access to the resident's unencrypted personally identifiable information (PII). SB 1386 authorizes any person injured by a violation of this statute to institute civil action to recover damages. The statute also authorizes mandates against businesses that violate or propose to violate it. Hence, a court may force a business to disclose a breach and possibly discontinue business until evidence is provided that the breach has been addressed. In addition to legal and monetary penalties, additional impact resulting from a security breach and SB 1386-noncompliance is negative publicity and lost business.

Since SB 1386 was enacted, there have been, as of April 15, 2010, 48 additional U.S. state and territory breach notice laws that went into effect, as listed in Exhibit 1. Organizations that have been impacted by these breach notice laws, generally all organizations within the United States, must ensure they have dedicated human and financial resources to comply with the laws so they can react efficiently, effectively, and quickly following security incidents and resulting privacy breaches.

The Financial Impact of Privacy on Business*

A privacy or security breach could significantly impact your organization's business just as it impacted the previously discussed organizations. A breach could potentially cost hundreds of thousands to millions of dollars in human resources, communications, and materials expenses in addition to negative publicity, lost business, and legal counsel costs. Give your executives an idea about how it could affect your organization financially by providing a scenario showing the impact of an incident.

When creating a scenario, consider that your security can be breached in a number of ways. The impact of an information security incident and associated privacy breach will likely be far greater than you would anticipate. Not only will the loss of sensitive or critical business information directly affect your competitiveness and cash flow, it could also damage your reputation and have a long-term detrimental effect. It can take your organization years to establish a good reputation and build an image as a trustworthy and reliable business, but a security incident

---

* This section includes much of the information from Chapter 1 of my e-book, *Understanding Data Protection from Four Critical Perspectives*; Rebecca Herold; Realtime Publishers; 2009; http://nexus.realtimepublishers.com/sgudp.php.

Exhibit 1   U.S. State and Territory Laws as of April 15, 2010

U.S. State and Territories Breach Notification Laws as of April 15, 2010	Effective Dates
1. Alaska HB 65	7/1/09
2. Arizona SB 1338	12/31/06
3. Arkansas SB 1167	8/12/05
4. California SB 1386 and AB 1298	7/1/03 and 1/1/08
5. Colorado HB 1119	9/1/06
6. Connecticut SB 650	1/1/06
7. Delaware HB 116	6/28/05
8. District of Columbia § 28-3852	7/1/07
9. Florida HB 481	7/1/05
10. Georgia SB 230	5/5/05
11. Hawaii SB 2290	1/1/07
12. Idaho SB 1374	7/1/06
13. Illinois HB 1633	1/1/06
14. Indiana HB 1101	7/1/06
15. Iowa SF 2308	7/1/08
16. Kansas SB 196	7/1/06
17. Louisiana SB 205	1/1/06
18. Maine LD 1671	1/31/06
19. Maryland HB 208 and SB 194	1/1/08
20. Massachusetts HB 4144	2/3/08
21. Michigan SB 309	6/29/07
22. Minnesota HF 2121	1/1/06
23. Mississippi HB 583	7/1/11
24. Missouri HB 62	8/28/09
25. Montana HB 732	3/1/06
26. Nebraska LB 876	4/6/06
27. Nevada SB 347	1/1/06 [10/1/08 for encryption]

(continued)

Exhibit 1 (continued)

U.S. State and Territories Breach Notification Laws as of March 22, 2009	Effective Dates
28. New Hampshire HB 1660	1/1/07
29. New Jersey A4001	1/1/06
30. New York S 3492, S 5827, and AB 4254	12/7/05
31. North Carolina SB 1048	12/1/05
32. North Dakota SB 2251	6/1/05
33. Ohio HB 104	2/17/06
34. Oklahoma HB 2357	6/08/06
35. Oregon SB 583	10/1/07
36. Pennsylvania SB 712	6/20/06
37. Puerto Rico HB 1184, Law 111	6/2006
38. Rhode Island HB 6191	3/1/06
39. South Carolina SB 453, Act 190	12/31/08
40. Tennessee HB 2170	7/1/05
41. Texas SB 122	9/1/05
42. Utah SB 69	1/1/07
43. Vermont SB 284	1/1/07
44. Virgin Islands VI Code § 2209	10/17/05
45. Virginia SB 307, Chapter 566	3/11/08
46. Washington SB 6043	7/24/05
47. West Virginia SB 340	6/6/08
48. Wisconsin SB 164	3/31/06
49. Wyoming SF 53	7/1/07

can destroy the reputation and customer trust in a matter of hours or even minutes. When privacy breaches occur

- customer trust is lost,
- customers are lost,
- brand value decreases,
- breach response activities result in significant costs to the business,
- time involved for breach response will go for years,
- penalties and sanctions could reach into the millions of dollars.

Addressing privacy concerns, implementing enterprise security, and ensuring compliance with applicable privacy laws are significant for achieving uninterrupted business processing, demonstrating due diligence, and minimizing risks due to noncompliance. Losing millions of dollars as a result of a breach could significant damage a business, or even result it its demise.

According to a 2009 Ponemon Institute study, the average cost to an organization where a breach of PII occurred in 2008 was $202 per compromised record, up 2.5% from $197 per record in 2007. Consider how these costs can be broken down according to specific breach response activities.

As an example, let us examine how a breach could impact a hypothetical business, Company X, for a file containing unencrypted PII for 10,000 customers. Exhibit 2 provides, at a high level, an example of some of the activities and associated conservatively estimated costs and times in total personnel man-hours that would have a financial and human resource impact to the organization.

So, in this case, the breach cost the company an average of $386 per client record. Add to these costs a wide variety of unanticipated costs. Although these numbers are significant, there are even more financial impacts than those shown that are associated with information security incidents and privacy breaches. Throughout my research over the past couple of decades, I have identified at least 50 different types of financial impacts that can be involved with a breach, as I have documented within my Privacy Breach Impact Calculator within my Privacy Management Toolkit.

Case Studies

It often helps to consider some actual incidents to see how information security incident and privacy breaches can impact businesses and customers. Consider the following two incidents and consider how similar situations would impact your business.

Cost of Responding to Breaches

Maine's Bureau of Financial Institutions, a division of the Department of Professional and Financial Regulation, conducted a survey* at the direction of the

---

* See the full "Maine Data Breach Study" report at http://www.maine.gov/pfr/financialinstitutions/reports/pdf/DataBreachStudy.pdf.

Exhibit 2 Privacy Incident Business Impact Example*

Breach Impact Components	Hours/Cost
Time (in man-hours) to determine and confirm the files within which a breach of PII occurred	40
Time to determine all the individuals impacted	40
Time to collect contact information for impacted customers	60
Time to write and mail letters to notify customers of the breach	60
Time to create and update a Web page containing information about the breach	48
Time to answer customer questions about the breach	500
Total Man-Hours	**748**
Average Cost per Man-Hour Cost (include all HR benefit considerations)	$200
Total Man-Hour Costs	**$149,600**
Customer Credit Monitoring	
Annual cost per individual for credit monitoring	$100
Number of years to monitor	3
Total Monitoring Cost for 10,000 Individuals	**$3,000,000**
Potential Legal Damages	
Fines and fees for applicable laws	$250,000
Number of individuals bringing civil suit	500
Award per individual	$500
Total civil suit award	$250,000
Total Legal Damages	**$500,000**

---

* I provide an abbreviated version of the Privacy Breach Impact Calculator at http://www
.informationshield.com/privacybreachcalc.html to allow business leaders to provide numbers
to see the potential impact of a breach as it would impact their own organizations.

Exhibit 2 (continued)

Breach Impact Components	Hours/Cost
Lost Customer Revenue Impact	
Number of customers lost as result of breach	1000
Value per customer	$200
Total Lost Customer Value	**$200,000**
Estimated Cost of Breach Response Materials	
Letter paper and envelopes	$1000
Postage ($0.44 × 10,000 individuals)	$4400
Total Materials Cost	**$5400**
TOTAL BREACH COSTS	**$3,855,000**

Source: The Privacy Management Toolkit, Rebecca Herold, Information Shield, 2005.

state legislature that revealed the costs of Maine's banks and credit unions when responding to breaches. Here are a few of the findings:

- 95% of the 75 responding financial institutions (50 credit unions and 25 banks) were affected by one or more of 20 data breaches identified in the survey.
- The cost of investigating all of the data breach incidents was $269,900, or 12.6% of total breach response costs in all categories.
- Providing notice to individuals of all the data breaches cost respondents a total of $304,500, or 14.2% of total breach response costs.
- Reissuing credit and debit cards to affected customers cost nearly $1.2 million, representing 54.3% of the total breach response costs.
- Undefined "other" costs totaled $68,800, or 3.2% of total costs for the survey respondents.
- The total cost of covering fraudulent purchases and transfers was $336,100, or 15.7% of total breach response costs.
- A little more than one-third (25) of the institutions that reported breaches reported unauthorized or fraudulent transfers as a result of the breaches.

Of the 75 survey respondents, 71 reported being affected by a data breach since January 1, 2007, and incurring expenses reported at $2.1 million. As documented in the report, "The Hannaford breach had the largest impact, affecting the most institutions (71), the highest number of affected account holders (243,599), and had the largest dollar cost ($1.6 million)."

In this survey, the cost of reissuing credit cards was significant because of the large numbers of individuals impacted. Collectively for the 71 impacted institutions, 246,479 cards had to be reissued.

It is interesting to note that the majority of the financial institutions responded that they first learned of each breach through the compromised account management system (CAMS) alerts that they receive. A CAMS alert is an e-mail sent out by a card issuer, such as Visa, after it has verified that an account compromise potentially has occurred. They did not hear about it from their business partners, nor did they have any internal processes in place to identify the breach activities themselves.

This example provides insights into the complexities of privacy breach response and how many costs can be accumulated by the impacted organizations. It also demonstrates that when breaches occur within business partners, such as TJX and Hannaford, it can have significant detrimental and costly impacts another organizations. Your business partners' breaches can have significant costly impacts on your organization.

ATM Break-In

On November 8, 2008, more than 130 ATMs in 49 cities throughout the world were hit by a group of apparently well-organized cyber criminals during a 30 minute period. The ATMs were all part of the RBS Worldpay system. The company put out a press release about this gigantic breach on December 23, 2008. The hackers somehow got into the application code and removed the daily withdrawal limits on the ATM cards. They stole $9 million dollars through 100 cards during that 30 minute period.

Even if your organization does not have ATM systems, the concepts involved apply to all types of networks. Consider the following:

- How were the hackers able to lift the limits? Does your organization have controls in place to prevent such hacks?
- What security controls should have been in place to prevent such a hack? Do you have enough security controls in place around your business applications?
- What controls were in place to protect the customer information? What controls are in place to protect your organization's customer information?
- What types of intrusion detection systems (IDSs) could help detect such an attempt to break into a system? Are you using IDS within your own organization?
- What types of audit logs should be generated on systems? Do you have sufficient audit logs generated for your own business applications?

It is worth noting that all these are activities also support the Red Flags Rule* requirements to have protections in place to prevent such types of fraudulent activity.

---

* The Red Flags Rule was created as a result of the Fair and Accurate Credit Transactions (FACT) Act of 2003. This rule requires financial institutions and creditors with covered accounts to have identity theft prevention programs and supporting processes in place to identify, detect, and respond to patterns, practices, or specific activities that could indicate identity theft.

Lose Clear Text PII, Get a Fine

The U.S. Department of Health and Human Services (HHS) applied the very first HIPAA noncompliance sanction on July 17, 2008, against Seattle-based Providence Health & Services (Providence).* On several occasions between September 2005 and March 2006, backup tapes, optical disks, and laptops, all containing unencrypted electronic protected health information (PHI), were removed from the Providence premises and were left unattended. The media and laptops were subsequently lost or stolen, compromising the PHI of over 386,000 Providence patients. HHS received over 30 complaints about the stolen tapes and disks, submitted after Providence informed patients of the theft, as required by multiple state notification laws. Providence also had reported the stolen media to HHS. Under the sanction, Providence agreed to pay $100,000 and implement a detailed corrective action plan to ensure that it will appropriately safeguard identifiable electronic patient information against theft or loss.

The fact is that any type of PII that moves, either through networks or via the legs of individuals carrying mobile computers and storage devices, is at much greater risk of having bad things happen to it than the PII stored more securely on centralized servers deep within the layers of network security defenses within your corporate network. Business leaders must ensure that all types of mobile PII are strongly safeguarded. To demonstrate your due diligence for this PII protection, regardless of your industry, ask your information security and privacy officers the following questions:

■ What kind of PII does your organization collect, manage, and store?
■ Where is all this PII stored?
■ What safeguards are protecting the PII?
■ Is mobile PII encrypted to most effectively protect it?

Key Business Leader Information Protection Responsibilities

Virtually every organization today obtains and maintains information in many different ways using an ever-growing number of technologies. These expanded quantities of information and technologies bring not only new business opportunities but also increased business risks. As a result, business leaders have many more information protection responsibilities than ever before. A few of these include the following:

■ Being in compliance with growing numbers of regulatory and legal requirements and emerging legal issues. More data protection laws exist worldwide than ever before, and more will be implemented. Business executives are ultimately responsible for ensuring that their organizations are in compliance.

---

* This first HHS sanction is in addition to the October 2006 agreement Providence made with the Oregon Department of Justice to pay $95,764 to the Department of Justice Consumer Protection and Education Revolving Account for these same personal data theft incidents.

- Demonstrating due diligence and standard of due care for information protection and sufficiently supporting and funding information security programs.
- Providing visible and strong sponsorship of information security and privacy initiatives.
- Addressing the growing personnel demands to use new technologies while at work, not only for business purposes but also for personal activities such as e-mail, instant messaging, blogging, tweeting, and using other social media sites.
- Ensuring the existence, awareness, and consistent support throughout the enterprise of information security policies and supporting procedures by endorsing regular training and ongoing awareness communications and activities.
- Understanding the business impact of not protecting data and taking responsibility for ensuring appropriate safeguards exist throughout the enterprise.
- Staying up-to-date with new and emerging information protection challenges.

Business leaders must make it a point to do what is necessary to instill a culture of information security and privacy throughout the enterprise to protect business information assets as well as meet legal, regulatory, and industry standards and contractual requirements.

Provide Visible Support for Information Security and Privacy Initiatives

The most important ingredient for information protection success within business is having clearly visible, strong, and consistent executive management support. Over the years, I have seen a consistent common denominator within organizations that have successful information security, privacy, and compliance programs. They have visibly strong and consistent management support. Every organization I have seen without such support has had ineffective information assurance programs, resulting in ineffective privacy preservation, and their information assurance professionals then face great challenges and frustrations in not being able to be effective in their efforts.

This observation is validated through many studies. For example, consider a report released in late October 2006 sponsored by the International Information Systems Security Certification Consortium (ISC*2) and conducted by the International Data Corporation (IDC). The study obtained feedback from 4016 information security professionals located in 100 countries. The most critical factor identified by these professionals for having a secure enterprise with effective information security policies and processes was having clear management support of their efforts. This emphasis on the importance of management support for information security also supports the need for management support of privacy initiatives.

Chapter 9

Identify Training and Awareness Methods

Before you become too entranced with gorgeous gadgets and mesmer-izing video displays, let me remind you that information is not knowl-edge, knowledge is not wisdom, and wisdom is not foresight. Each grows out of the other, and we need them all.

—**Arthur C. Clarke**

You don't understand anything until you learn it more than one way.

—**Marvin Minsky**

Adult Learning

Malcolm Knowles,[*] one of the foremost authorities on adult learning, did considerable research on the most effective adult learning methods. He found that adult learning should follow four basic principles discussed in the next four sections. With this in mind, you need to consider the types of training and awareness methods you may choose to best meet education goals.

Readiness

Your training content should show the participants that the training will show them how to solve or avoid a problem, provide a chance for advancement or increased

---

[*] Malcolm S. Knowles, *Informal Adult Education*, Association Press, Chicago, 1950.

status within the organization, and result in professional advancement or personal growth. To do this, you need to focus on the learners' needs and be able to answer one basic question each participant has: "What's in this training session for me?"

Sample Scenario

The group of participants comprises UNIX administrators. They are not happy to be in training, they have much work to do, and they believe that they already know everything there is to know about security. The topic of the training is configuring a CISCO firewall router. Present them with the scenario of an active-network intruder attack. Ask them to demonstrate how they would react and what they would do.

Experience

Remember that your participants are coming into your training with prior experiences and knowledge, which will influence what they think about the training content. Some of this existing experience and knowledge will facilitate their learning, but keep in mind that it can also inhibit their learning as well. The more you consider the experience of your participants, the more effective the learning outcome. With this in mind, be aware of the following points:

- If you treat your participants as though they have little or no experience when they really do, then you will probably insult them and lose their interest. Acknowledge that participants have experience, perhaps different from the topic, yet no less valuable.
- Help participants contribute not only to their own learning, but also to the learning of others.
- Always remember that previous experiences can create a resistance to learning something new for similar topics.
- Check the backgrounds, aptitudes, attitudes, prerequisite skills, culture, and other related experiences of your participants. This will help ensure you do not aim your training either too high or too low.
- Use familiar language, examples, and references without being patronizing.
  - If you are covering a topic in which the participants have had bad experiences, let them know you are going into uncomfortable and possibly negative territory. This will demonstrate your empathy for their past experiences and help to diffuse any resistance they may have. It may also help prevent the situation from recurring.
- Ask participants to share their examples and experiences. Not only will this make your session more interesting, you will also likely learn something new and useful.

Sample Scenario

In a training session with customer service personnel, ask which of the participants have had the experience of speaking to an irate customer with a complaint about a privacy or security issue. Ask how they handled the situation, what they learned from the experience, and what they would do differently if they had the chance to go through the experience again.

Autonomy

Adults will acquire knowledge and understand best if they are able to take charge of their own learning. Involve your participants. Allow them to contribute and actively participate. Provide instruction in a way that allows your participants to make their own decisions regarding the information you are giving them. Always treat your participants as the capable intelligent people they are; show your participants respect, and they will feel more in control of their own learning. Consider the following:

- Build many opportunities for participation into your training. Use exercises, hands-on exercises, case studies, games, discussions, brainstorming, etc. Such activities are discussed in detail in Chapter 13 and Chapter 16.
- Create your training so that participants have many opportunities to share their experiences, ideas, examples, and suggestions. The more they are allowed to contribute, the more they will feel ownership of their learning. Also, the participation will help the learners to stay focused and pay attention.
- Reward and encourage independent ideas and innovations. This will prompt your participants to learn in ways that will enhance their learning experience.

Sample Scenario

In a training session with law department personnel and compliance officers, hold a brainstorming session to ask all the possible ways in which the participants can try to keep up to date with all the new and emerging information security and privacy-related laws and requirements. List all the ideas on a flip chart. Copy and distribute to participants following the class.

Action

The participants want to use the training you give them to improve or alter their job performance. For them to buy into your training session, you need to focus immediately on the goals of learning within the session. You must show them how they will be able to take and put into action what you give them as soon as they go back to their jobs; otherwise, you will see their interest and attention decrease.

Sample Scenario

You have a training session filled with systems administrators. The topic is patch management. Cover the procedures and organizational expectations with the participants. Provide printed copies of the procedures for the participants to take with them. Review scenarios related to patch management. Consider dividing into teams and having a competition modeled on *Jeopardy!* or *Concentration*, covering all aspects of patch management.

Training Delivery Methods

Educating with formal training is generally for those within the organization whose roles require special knowledge and following specific policies and procedures for addressing information security and privacy issues and events. Training is focused on providing knowledge, skills, and abilities specific to a person's job responsibilities and roles. Training is a targeted, interactive event requiring the participant's full attention to benefit.

The size of your training groups may vary greatly. Large organizations may have as many as 50 personnel in a classroom-setting training session. However, for the most effective training, it is best to try to keep the number to 25 or less in this type of face-to-face training to promote the most interaction and also to help reduce side discussions and maintain attention. Another good option for training, especially for the initial all-employee sessions, is using a computer-based training (CBT) method, an online interactive method (such as a "Webinar"), or a conference call training session. The most effective delivery method will largely depend on your target audience and the topic. Budget may also be an issue. Do not purchase an inexpensive, poor-quality option for a delivery method just to stay within budget. If you cannot afford quality, then choose an effective delivery method you can afford. Chapter 16 discusses delivering the training in detail primarily for in-person training, but many of the concepts can be carried into the other methods as well. The following are some methods for you to consider:

Activity-Based Group Learning Activities

Engaging departments or groups as teams within learning activities, to encourage them to discuss information security and privacy risks as they relate to their own areas, and then talk about how to reduce or eliminate those risks, is one of the most effective learning activities.

I originally used this type of learning exercise with over 130 teams within a company's organization, located at multiple geographic locations. Teams had a week to fill out their answer sheets with all of the security infractions and risks they could identify on the learning poster I provided without knowing how many risks there actually were. Nearly 100% of teams actively participated in this exercise, and the response was unconditionally enthusiastic. Several of the teams had fun with their "infraction" answers (for example, "a man wearing a plaid jacket with mismatched striped pants"). Others delved so deeply into the exercise that they identified additional security problems not even purposefully planned into the poster!

The results and benefits were impressive. They included the following:

- Teams were actively engaged in thinking critically about the vast range of information security issues within a business.
- Participants talked with their coworkers about the situations, engaging in friendly debate about whether each identified situation should actually be a risk.
- Staff began talking with their managers about their own related situations, thus bringing potential issues to the forefront.
- Many units updated their departmental procedures after realizing some of the situations presented were similar to risks in their own areas.
- Employees began talking in the cafeteria, hallways, gym, and meeting rooms about information security and privacy issues during passing conversations.
- The information security intranet Web site started getting an influx of hits—levels never seen before.
- The information security area began receiving additional calls and e-mails about potential security issues.
- Many of the areas left the poster hanging in their area for months—even years—following the exercise, facilitating ongoing awareness.

See more about this type of training at my Web site, http://www.privacyguidance.com/security_search.html.

General Lectures: Small- to Medium-Size Groups

Lectures can be effective, if the topic is right, and if the length of the lecture is right. Because of the limited amount of information, most people can take in at any one time, lectures are generally most effective if they last from 10 to 20 minutes. Any longer, and the learners will likely lose interest after they have reached their information overload limit. This amount of time works well for lunchtime training or during the day to keep work interruption to a minimum. Use lectures when there are just a few important, basic points you want to get across to your learners. Consider using a lecture for hitting upon current and critical topics in which you want to be able to personally discuss the issues and be able to gauge by the learners' reactions the areas where you may need to expand upon or explain more. Some audiences who are good candidates for lectures include

- Departmental members
- Team members
- Management
- Board members

Auditorium Presentations to Large Groups

Inviting guest speakers and presenters to your organization can be a very good way to communicate a message to a very large group and make it a special event. Such an event can be structured as a training session or as an awareness event. It all depends on whether the presentation topic is specific to one of your training goals, and you want to see the behavior of the participating learners changed as a result, or if you just want to raise awareness of a certain topic. However, a training session generally lends itself well to some learning goals and objectives. Giving such presentations is especially good for special information security–related days (see Appendix M for a list of designated privacy- and security-related days).

Choosing a guest speaker who is a known authority on the topic is a good way to pull your learners into listening to the topic at hand. Consider inviting not only well-known information security and privacy experts but also

- politicians;
- local or national celebrities;
- law enforcement representatives;
- security or privacy experts from other companies;
- speakers from the National Security Agency (NSA) or the U.S. Department of Defense (DoD), including military. They may be able to demonstrate nonclassified spy gadgets to whet the audience's appetite for the topic. Although some of the devices might not be relevant to the organization (small cameras and privacy), the devices will make the talk entertaining.

Good candidates for such training are

- large groups,
- all employees,
- visitors from satellite offices.

Classroom

Classroom training can be a very effective way to ensure that learners truly grasp the concepts and become proficient in the topics being covered. The keys to successful classroom training include a well-planned instruction experience, including effective content and clear goals, and a great instructor who knows how to engage the learners as well as effectively and accurately communicate the topic details. Too often, organizations try to quickly throw together a training class, with little or no thought about the training goals, audience, or topic, and ultimately end up with a disappointing session as well as disappointed participants.

The following are good to consider for training target groups who need to practice or participate in doing activities or procedures, or who potentially need much interaction and contact with the instructor:

- Call center and customer care
- Systems administrators
- Marketing and sales
- Human resources
- Public relations

Computer-Based Training (CBT) Modules

Because of the popularity of using CBT instruction, I want to go into a little more detail with this topic than some of the other topics. There are many different types of CBT modules, and many different potential costs involved. Developing your own modules and hiring your own staff can be quite an expensive venture, but may result in a module of very high quality and completely unique to your organization. If your training needs can be met using a more generic course for a common information security or privacy topic, though, you can probably obtain a very good off-the-shelf course for a fraction of the cost. For something in between, you can consider purchasing off-the-shelf material and then either modifying it yourself in-house or hiring a training-content specialist to modify it to meet your organization's needs.

Probably the best reasons for using CBTs are that they allow learners to control their training schedules; facilitate easier distance learning, allow using technology to effectively address varying systems and times availability requirements, and allow for a way to centrally and automatically track learner participation and success with such training. They are also a good consideration when training will occur in a bilingual environment or in non-English-speaking countries.

There are a growing number of information security and privacy CBT vendors. The range of quality of what is available is very wide. Be sure to review any off-the-shelf modules closely to ensure they are of high quality, coincide closely with the message you want to communicate, and can be easily used by your personnel. Also review closely the features offered by the CBT modules. Good modules should include a way to track and measure progress and achievement.

When considering an off-the-shelf CBT, always review a sample of the course, determine if adult instructional experts were used to create the course, and ensure that the vendor will provide, support, and modify the CBT to best suit your organization's training needs. Consider using something similar to Exhibit 1, which is based on what a security officer at a large financial organization used when considering different information security and privacy training CBT vendors.

There are three basic types of CBTs.

Exhibit 1   Security Awareness Vendors: Competitive Marketing Analysis

eLearning Vendor	Joe Doe
Competitive Market Analysis	Info Security Policy &
Est.: 05/29/09	Practices
Rev.: 06/12/09	

Objective: Create a Web-based exam with 5 topics @ 10 minutes each. Total seat time of 1 hour. Use internal SMEs.

eLearning Firms	Miscellaneous	Staffing Team	Number of Business Days	Fixed Bid	Hourly Rate
Vendor A (contracted for the Learning Management System [LMS]) http://www .vendora.com	Teleconference Three phases: Analysis, Design, Development	4–5	20–30 days	$25,000– $28,000	$85– 135
Vendor B http://www .vendorb.com/	Provided input: New 60 minute course based on existing course, using Company X SMEs	4	23	$15,000 (checking to determine add'l costs)	$100–$250
Vendor C http://www .vendorc.com	Teleconference	5	60 days	$20,000– $45,000	$250
Vendor D http://www .vendord.com/	Engaged with, since 1998, 5 versions of the application.	3–4	30 days	$50,000– $60,000	$200
Vendor E http://www .vendore.com/	Teleconference Three phases: Analysis, Modelization, and Production	3	30–50 days	$30,000– $50,000	$70– $170

Exhibit 1 (continued)

Vendor F http://www .vendorf.com/	6/7/02 Teleconference*	1–3	15	$175,000[a] ($5 per user) or $65,500	$95–$175
Vendor G http://www .vendorg.com	3/1/02 Completed Web request for information.	No information yet			
Vendor H http://www .vendorh.com/	3/1/02 Completed Web request for information.	No information yet			

[a] May be most useful if a firm does have the time, or staff expertise/SME to create content. Also, probably better for larger firms where cost can be spread over a large audience (e.g., 35,000 users/$50,000 cost = $0.70 cost per user).

Entertaining

You will sometimes see these referred to as "sizzle" CBTs. These types of modules focus on giving learners a fun experience and on making them comfortable with using technology to learn. This is a pretty good idea; however, watch out for modules that use flash, bells, and whistles and have little educational value for your learner. Often, the content is presented primarily or solely in the form of a game, using cartoons, questionable competitions, and often very poor humor. It has been noted[†] that many people start these types of CBTs but very few finish them. The people taking the module often remember the activities and that it was fun, but usually they do not remember content or messages. In fact, many organizations looking at such modules have considered these types of modules more as marketing schemes than true teaching tools. Review the details of the module carefully and the company selling it. Is a marketing company one of the developers? Do the developers have a background in instructional development?

---

* Pending another estimate based on their hours input to provide only code. They usually provide the host-based environment, usability testing, and help desk support.

[†] Piskurich, Beckschi, and Hall, Selecting off-the-shelf courseware and suppliers: CD-ROM, LN and Web, *The ASTD Handbook of Training Design and Delivery*, 2000, p. 180.

Subject Matter–Focused

This type of CBT is virtually the opposite of the entertainment-style modules in that it focuses almost exclusively on presenting content over everything else. This type of module is based on a few assumptions, such as that the learner can read, the learner will remember and comprehend, and that the learner will know how to use the information later.

What can easily happen with this type of CBT if not constructed properly is that the learner will become overwhelmed with all the information presented. Organizations often purchase these types of modules because they want to get all the content possible for their money and hope that it will serve a second purpose, such as a delivery method for the organization's information security policies. However, when you make your buying decision, you need to remember that if the interaction of the module is not effective, the course will be very boring, and that the typical learner will not retain much of the information presented. Also, be aware that these types of modules may be constructed on more of a typical child-in-school-learning model instead of an adult learning model. By this, I mean that the information is pushed to the learner and does not allow for interaction, treating the learner, instead, as a passive recipient. Be sure that any subject matter courseware you create or consider purchasing actually engages your learner and does not just offload information.

Skills-Based

The primary goal of a skills-based CBT should be to provide performance-based training. The CBT should give just the right amount of knowledge and information to improve learners' skills and close any skills gaps for the topic being covered, thus improving their job performance. The CBT should be constructed in such a way that the learner can take what is learned and apply it to real-life situations right after training.

The type of feedback you should hope to hear after learners have taken this type of CBT is something similar to, "What I learned is what I need to know to do my job better. Now I know how to apply this to my daily job responsibilities." When employing this type of CBT, success will depend on the design of the instruction and how the training is deployed. Both factors must be given attention, not just one or the other. Critical for this type of training is getting the right training topic and information to the right audience.

Using some type of testing is one measurement for the effectiveness of this type of training. Pretesting can establish the learner's current knowledge and capabilities and can easily be incorporated into a CBT. Pretesting can also be used within a well-constructed CBT to adjust the instruction presented to focus specifically on the skills and knowledge where the learner has gaps. Then, following the CBT, a concluding test can reveal how much the learner has succeeded in closing those gaps, and also provide one type of evidence of the learner's skill in the topic.

CBT Audiences

The use of CBTs should be considered for training and instructing skills such as configuring firewalls, resetting passwords, explaining the organization's privacy practices, etc., in addition to communicating policies, procedures, and standards to employees. Some of the personnel who are good candidates for CBTs include

- systems administrators,
- marketing personnel,
- sales personnel,
- compliance officers,
- law department personnel,
- HR staff.

Remote Access Labs

Performing training through remote access labs can be quite effective for providing personnel in highly decentralized offices an opportunity to obtain hands-on training when they cannot easily travel to another location for the training. An instructor can administer these types of training sessions live via conference call or satellite hookup. The live activities can occur through remote connections such as virtual private networks (VPNs), or learners can be provided with workbooks and given directions for accessing the remote lab and perform the training according to their own schedule and availability.

Good candidates for such training are

- systems administrators,
- applications programmers,
- help desk operators.

Satellite or Fiber-Optic Long-Distance Learning

As mentioned earlier, a good complement to the remote access lab is satellite or fiber-optic long-distance learning. It is also a very nice option on its own. You still need to have such instruction well planned and carefully constructed, keeping in mind that this type of delivery does not typically allow for two-way interaction in and of itself. You will need to identify the materials you need to use in conjunction with this type of training. Most likely, you will need comprehensive workbooks for the topic that are designed to make this style of training as interactive as possible. Also, satellite instructors must be well prepared and be aware of the fact that there are learners listening and watching whom they cannot see. They will not be able to get the immediate feedback regarding the learners' reactions and their questions. What helps address this is to have remote site facilitators available to relay questions through a centralized communication path to the instructor, and to assist with the evaluation and feedback process.

Good candidates for such training are

- remote office personnel,
- third-party partners,
- subsidiary personnel in remote locations.

Web-Based Interactive Training (such as Webinars)

This type of distance delivery uses computers to either provide the training live with an instructor or through a type of application services provider (ASP) to allow learners to take the training at times that are convenient for them. Typically, this type of learning is less expensive than satellite or fiber-optics-based distance learning. And, depending on how it is constructed, it can allow for much more interaction. The key to success, as with the other methods, is careful design of the instructional material and goals. Additional elements include control mechanisms: Will the training be multi-participant, two-way interactive, or something else? Will all the learners' systems be able to satisfy the technical requirements? And, if it is to be a live facilitated session, is the instructor well prepared?

Good candidates for such training are

- information security department personnel,
- HR department personnel,
- legal department personnel,
- IT staff,
- help desk staff,
- marketers.

Audio Instruction

Audio instruction can be provided on a variety of media such as CDs, cassettes, over the network via streaming audio, and from any one of the great podcasts available that you can download to MP3 players. The cost of producing training on audio is often much less than with other types of user-controlled training methods. Targeted learners can listen to audio training in a wider range of situations than with other types of methods. For instance, if your target listeners travel frequently, providing audio training is a great opportunity for them to listen while on a plane or in airports and trains. Workbooks can be created to accompany and complement the audio messages and to increase learner interaction. Audio is very good for providing training that includes building interpersonal skills and for covering case studies or narratives of examples.

Good candidates for such training are

- managers,
- sales and marketing staff,
- executives,
- legal staff,
- generally all personnel.

Video and DVD

Videos and DVDs (I'll refer to both as videos) work well for groups of any size and also provide a fairly easy way to allow learners to check out the training and take them home or to another location, and view them whenever their schedule allows. Or better yet, to provide via your corporate Web site, or even from YouTube, to view from anywhere.

Well-produced and well-constructed videos can be amazingly effective. However, a drawback of videos is that there is typically no learner interaction (some DVDs allow for this), and some learners may have a tendency, depending on where they watch the video, to fall asleep. The cost relative to other training methods for a ready-made video used to be moderate but now organizations, and individuals, can produce their own video quite easily and quite inexpensively. For a large, highly dispersed organization, a custom-made, in-house-produced video can be very effective in that it can be created specifically for the organization and include organization leaders within the video talking directly to the learners.

Good candidates for such training are

- remote office personnel,
- personnel with nonstandard work hours,
- personnel who travel frequently,
- personnel whose job responsibilities do not allow for them to participate in training during the workday,
- generally all personnel.

Workbooks

Workbooks for adult education are commonly considered as anything from handouts to manuals. Workbooks typically provide information for later reference and, unlike other printed resources, they are reader interactive. Workbooks can offer the learner ways to interact through exercises such as filling in blanks with correct terminology and resolving complex situations or problems. The learner will be utilizing portions of the brain that are often not used for typical classroom learning. Workbooks can be very simple to very complex and can range from very inexpensive, hole-punched, stapled photocopies to slickly produced, elaborately bound, and custom-printed publications. Workbooks offer good interactivity and provide credibility for the topic covered, in addition to serving as a lasting reference. However, some learners are not successful with dependence on the amount of reading required.

Good candidates for such training are

- regulatory compliance officers,
- HR personnel,
- managers,
- customer service personnel.

On-the-Job (OTJ)

On-the-job training is one of the oldest methods of business training, harking back to the days of apprenticeships. It is often most commonly thought of for craft-related jobs, but OTJ training also lends itself well to technical skills training. Forms of OTJ training include mentoring and role model programs. In general, OTJ takes place when a skilled or experienced person discusses and demonstrates the skills and knowledge needed to discharge job responsibilities to an unskilled and inexperienced person while both are actively working. Of course, informal OTJ takes place in all organizations. However, you can also consider implementing a formal OTJ program for positions that require repetition or practice in performing certain activities such as customer call center functions or systems administrator network monitoring. Important success factors for OTJ include the following:

- Identifying the skills and knowledge necessary for successfully performing job responsibilities
- Creating performance objectives and measures
- Designing and creating supporting training materials
- Choosing OTJ trainers who have in-depth knowledge and experience, who want to serve as a trainer, and who have themselves received training for effective training and communication skills and methods
- Providing the training on noncritical or development systems

The following materials can greatly improve the success of OTJ training:

- Trainer's guide
- Lesson plans

- Job aids
- Checklists
- Examples
- Demonstrations
- Questions and answers to use during OTJ training

Good candidates for such training are

- call center staff,
- systems administrators,
- incident response team members,
- business continuity planning personnel,
- virus response team members.

Conference Calls

Conducting training and awareness through conference calls can be a good option for highly dispersed target group members. It provides a good way to promote interaction among the participants. It is great for brainstorming sessions and, augmented with slides, can provide a good way to give more lecture-style presentations. Conference calls are most successful when an agenda is communicated to all participants ahead of time. Having training facilitators at each location also will enhance the success of the training. When designing such training, keep the following in mind:

- Be sure to have the participants in locations without background noise.
- Have video monitors, flip charts, and fax machines available at each of these locations.
- Provide objectives for the training to the participants.
- Provide workbooks and guides to the participants, as applicable.
- Ask speakers to identify themselves before speaking.
- Expect that there will be a little dead air time as people think about their responses.
- Ensure that the conference call phone number and password are distributed securely. Otherwise, it could be easy for unauthorized personnel to listen in on the calls.
- Discourage using cell phones for the calls. Besides possible poor cell coverage, it is easy to be distracted when driving, etc.

Good candidates for such training are

- field office personnel,
- mobile workers,
- brokers and agents,
- business partners.

Outsourced Training and Awareness with Professional Educational Services

Probably the most important consideration for going outside your organization to get help with training or awareness is the lack of competency and availability of qualified personnel within your own organization. If you do not have people who are experienced and able to be effective educators internally or if they do not have the time to provide these services, then going to an outside education vendor is definitely something to consider. The following should be contemplated when considering outsourcing:

- Consider what the costs would be to produce the training in-house and compare with the costs you are quoted from outsourcing vendors. Internal costs are often underestimated because all time, materials, facilities, and human resource costs are often not considered. This will help you determine if the vendor is giving you a reasonable quote.
- Research the background and credibility of the vendor you are considering. What is their adult education background and expertise? Are their past customers happy with them?
- Determine what specifically you need to have outsourced. What is the range of outsourcing options? What are the benefits? What are the risks?
- Be sure to detail, within your contract and service level agreement (SLA), the scope of the work, the timelines, how to resolve any conflicts that emerge, the quality control process, etc.

Good candidates for such training are

- all employees,
- targeted training groups,
- targeted awareness groups,
- executives. (Some trainers specialize in executive training. Also, it would be advantageous to have someone who is not in the executives' chain of command, to provide them with security and privacy guidance.)

Education Provided by Professional Societies

Professional organizations and societies often provide their members training and awareness opportunities as a service, as well as to preserve, advance, and enhance the reputation of the profession. Such educational opportunities are often provided during monthly meetings, special training workshops, and at regularly scheduled conferences and seminars. Attending such training is a good way for the personnel responsible for the topics covered by the profession to obtain insights from others and receive typically low- or no-cost but quality training. It is also a good way for your certified professionals, such as certified information systems managers (CISMs), certified information systems auditors (CISAs), certified information systems security professionals (CISSPs), certified protection professionals (CPPs,) certified information privacy professionals (CIPPs), and so on, to obtain the continuing professional education (CPE) credits they need to maintain certification.

Good candidates for such training are

- information security personnel,
- internal audit personnel,
- systems administrators,
- business continuity personnel,
- facilities security personnel.

Government-Sponsored Training

There are a number of U.S. government–sponsored organizations that support and provide training and awareness opportunities that your organization can consider in your education strategy. A few sample organizations follow:

- Federal Information Systems Security Educators' Association (FISSEA): http://csrc.nist.gov/organizations/fissea/index.html
- National Institute of Standards and Technology (NIST) Computer Security Division Events: http://csrc.nist.gov/events/index.html
- NIST Regional Information Security Workshops: http://csrc.nist.gov/securebiz/
- NIST Information Security and Privacy Advisory Board: http://csrc.nist.gov/ispab/index.html
- Federal Computer Security Program Managers' Forum: http://csrc.nist.gov/organizations/cspmf.html
- Infragard chapter events: http://www.infragard.net/library/combating_cyber-crime.htm

Good candidates for such training are

- government officers,
- information security officers,
- privacy officers,
- compliance officers,
- physical-security officers,
- business continuity and disaster recovery officers.

Awareness Methods

Educating with awareness methods is not training. In contrast to training, awareness can occur at the same time everywhere and on a continuous basis. Information security and privacy awareness activities promote ongoing compliance. Likewise, ongoing compliance helps ongoing awareness. As business models change, so do compliance needs and awareness activities.

Awareness is typically the "what" component of your education strategy; training is typically the "how" component. To make awareness activities effective, you must know your audience. Awareness audiences are very broad; they include everyone within the organization and all those third parties who do work for, or on behalf of, the organization.

The awareness audience has diverse experiences, backgrounds, and job responsibilities. The awareness goal at the decision-making level is to convince the audience that information security and privacy risk reduction is achievable. Awareness goals at the end-user level are generally to help them

- understand information security and privacy risks and the actions to reduce them,
- create a demand for risk reduction.

Awareness must not be boring. The following is a list of 15 ways to make awareness interesting:

1. Use analogies.
2. Use recent, significant, real-world examples and news events.
3. Explain the importance of your message.
4. Use scenarios and multifaceted situations (e.g., What would you do if … ?).
5. Use graphics.
6. Use photos and videos.
7. Make it interactive.
8. Make it memorable … use humor, shock, and wit.
9. Make it personal … show how it relates to your audience, especially to their personal lives, such as preventing identity theft.
10. Make it fresh … tie it to something current.
11. Provide practical, "job-ready" information.
12. Use known people in examples … celebrities, sports figures, etc.
13. Use animation.
14. Recognize employees who have done an outstanding job.
15. Use games and challenges.

Awareness activities are different from training activities. The objectives for delivering information security and privacy awareness are similar to training options. However, there are some very important differences between training and awareness activities. The options and methods for awareness activities are typically much different from the more formal and structured training. Awareness activities should

- occur on an ongoing basis;
- use a wide range of delivery methods;

- catch the attention of the target audience;
- be less formal than training;
- take less time than training;
- be even more creative, memorable, and fun than how you may have your training sessions planned;
- reinforce the lessons learned during formal training;
- be the foundation for preparing for the first level of training for various target topics.

An awareness program must remain current. As information security and privacy regulations change and, subsequently, information security and security and privacy policies and procedures, personnel must be notified. Establish a method to deliver immediate information and updates when necessary. Perhaps new information is sent as the first alert item personnel see when logging into the network for the day. The awareness messages and methods must also be simple. The purpose is to get messages and ideas out to personnel quickly and easily. They must not be confusing or convoluted, which will dissuade personnel from reading them, and eventually they will not pay any attention at all to the messages. Make it easy for personnel to get information security and security and privacy information, and make the information easy to understand.

Think of positive, fun, exciting, and motivating methods that will give employees the message and keep the information security and privacy issues in their mind as they perform their daily job responsibilities. The success of an awareness program is measured by its ability to reach all personnel using a variety of techniques. Examples of awareness materials and methods are discussed in Chapter 14.

Chapter 10

Awareness and Training Topics and Audiences

The fish only knows that it lives in the water after it is already on the river bank. Without our awareness of another world out there it would never occur to us to change.

—Source Unknown

I do not teach, I relate.

—Michel de Montaigne

The goal of this chapter is quite simple: to provide you with a list of possible topics and the corresponding audiences for the information security and privacy issues that impact your organization. Through discussions with many organizations, I find that those responsible for the awareness and training programs are often overwhelmed by the amount of information they have to deliver to their personnel. Often they try to deliver all information in one session or message. Remember, people can absorb only bite-sized chunks of information at a time. You should keep your messages and training sessions manageable for learner comprehension and efficiency. Identify target groups that need more detailed and in-depth information.

The topics covered in this chapter are taken from multiple sources, including the International Organization for Standardization/International Electrotechnical Commission 27001 domains, the Organization for Economic Cooperation and Development (OECD) security and privacy principles, the Control Objectives for Information and related Technology (COBIT) and the Committee of Sponsoring Organizations of the Treadway Commission (COSO) frameworks, and the National

Institute of Standards and Technology (NIST) guidelines for information security awareness and training topics for U.S. federal offices. Standards and principles are covered at the end of this chapter. Additionally, other topics are included that may not be specifically identified within these sources, but are important to address within a security and privacy program. When creating your program, first identify the target groups to whom you need to deliver training and awareness.

Target Groups

Training content for target groups (see Exhibit 1) must be specialized based on specific issues that they must understand and with which they must comply. Not only is this a good idea pedagogically, it is also a requirement under some laws and regulations (see

Exhibit 1   Target Group Examples

Role	Target Groups	Definitions
R1	Customer Privacy Advocates	Communication and implementation link between the information privacy office and business unit personnel
R2	Information Security Advocates	Communication and implementation link between the information security office and business unit personnel
R3	Executive Management and Privacy/Security Champions	Executive management and privacy/security champions; local executive sponsorship of security and privacy efforts
R4	Mid-Level Managers	Managers throughout your organization responsible for overseeing personnel activities and performing performance appraisals
R5	Personnel Working on Behalf of Your Organization	Contractors, consultants, and others who perform work on behalf of your company or within your company, and whose daily work is managed by your company
R6	Information Technology (IT) Personnel	IT architects, programmers, systems designers, administrators, and so on
R7	Systems Administrators	Personnel responsible for the settings and security of network servers and security systems
R8	Marketers	Marketing and product/services promotion personnel and customer relationship management personnel

Exhibit 1 (continued)

	Target Groups	*Definitions*
R9	Sales Representatives	Personnel who sell your organization's products or services directly to consumers and customers
R10	Research and Development	Researchers and developers who create applications and processes; includes both business planners as well as IT architects and programmers
R11	Internal Audit	Auditors and others responsible for ensuring compliance with policies and practices
R12	Physical Security	Personnel responsible for security of the facilities and physical properties
R13	Public Relations	Personnel responsible for speaking with news media and responding to questions about your organization
R14	All Employees	All your organization's personnel
R15	New Employees	All your organization's new employees
R16	Legal and Human Resources (HR)	Legal and HR staff who must stay aware of security and privacy laws, regulations, and corporate issues related to security and privacy compliance
R17	Third Parties	Suppliers, partners, and third parties contracted to perform work for your company, but whose own employers (business partners) manage their work
R18	Customer Services and Call Centers	Call center, customer care staff, and any other personnel who communicate directly with customers and consumers
R19	Physicians and Medical Providers	On-site medical care providers directly employed or contracted by your organization
R20	Trainers	Personnel responsible for training delivery and development for a wide range of training topics

Chapter 3 for more information about this). The course content must be matched to job responsibilities and roles to be most effective. Exhibit 1 contains examples of groups, as shown in the second column, that can be targeted for specialized security and privacy training and awareness. These will need to be modified to meet your organization's needs. The first column is provided to create a shorter reference to each of these groups.

Topics

Identify the topics related to information privacy, security, and regulatory compliance that are critical for the success of your business, and the target audiences for each of the topics. Then, develop training content and awareness activities for the identified topics and corresponding audiences.

The following is a laundry list of potential topics, applicable to most organizations, for you to consider and add to your list if applicable. This is not meant to be an exhaustive list, and there are likely some significant topics missing for your particular organization, industry, locality, or environment. However, this should give you a good start to identifying your awareness and training topics. Accompanying each topic are some of the types of information to be included in your communications and training.

1. Information Security and Privacy Policies and Procedures

All personnel and third parties who handle or access your organization's information, in any form, should be given training and awareness with regard to their responsibilities and as required by your organization's policies and procedures. Policies and procedures cannot be effective if they are not communicated. Some of the information you should consider communicating include the following:

- Overview of your organization's policies.
- Overview of your organization's standards.
- Overview of your organization's procedures.
- Overview of your organization's guidelines.
- How they all fit together.
- Targeting specific policies to specific groups. (For example, training for identity verification policies should be targeted to all groups that have direct communications with customers, such as customer service centers, sales staff, and so on.)

2. Information Security and Privacy Framework and Architecture

Information communicated could include the following:

- The information security and privacy management framework for your organization
- Those responsible for supporting the framework

- Related roles and responsibilities
- Definitions for the personally identifiable information (PII) used within your organization

3. Security of Third-Party Access

Information communicated could include the following:

- How to maintain the security of organizational IT facilities and information assets accessed by nonorganizational third parties
- Identification of risks from third-party connections
- Security requirements to include within third-party contracts

4. Security and Privacy for Outsourced Services

Information communicated could include the following conditions:

- The security of information should be maintained even when the responsibility for the processing has been outsourced to another organization.
- Include the security requirements of the information in contracts between the owners and the outsourced organization.

5. Information Classification and Controls

Information communicated could include the following:

- How to establish appropriate accountability for organizational assets
- Security classifications used to prioritize protection of information assets
- Establishing controls appropriate for each type of information classification
- How classification supports data protection and privacy laws compliance
- Regulatory and legal requirements for classification applicable to your organization
- Handling and disposal instructions
- Labeling guidelines

6. Security and Privacy in Job Definitions and Performance Appraisals

Information communicated could include the following tasks:

- Addressing security and privacy during the recruitment stage
- Safeguarding employment applications, including information for those who were not hired
- Including security and privacy within job descriptions and contracts
- Monitoring security and privacy during personnel employment
- Including security and privacy responsibilities within employee job descriptions
- Including security and privacy responsibilities within employee performance appraisals

7. Security Incident and Privacy Breach Response

Information communicated could include the following:

- How to communicate incidents affecting privacy or security as quickly as possible through appropriate management channels
- Reporting forms and procedures for security and privacy incidents
- Reporting forms and procedures for security and privacy weaknesses
- Reporting software malfunctions
- Lessons to learn from incidents
- Your organization's sanctions and disciplinary processes related to incidents
- Responding to alerts and incidents from outside organizations such as the Computer Emergency Response Team (CERT) advisories and law enforcement

8. Physical Security

Communications could include information about the following:

- Secured areas within your organization
- Physical security perimeter procedures and mechanisms
- Physical entry controls
- Security of offices, rooms, and facilities
- Working in secure areas
- Security for isolated delivery and loading areas

9. Computing Equipment Security

Information communicated could include details on the following:

- Physically protecting computing equipment from security threats and environmental hazards
- Equipment location and protection
- Power supplies
- Cabling security
- Equipment maintenance
- Security of off-premises equipment
- Secure disposal or reuse of equipment

10. Work Area Security and Privacy

Information communicated could include the following:

- How to protect information and information processing facilities from disclosure to, or modification by, unauthorized persons, or theft
- Controls that should be in place to minimize loss or damage

- Clear desk and clear screen policies
- Procedures for removal of property

11. Operational Procedures and Responsibilities

Information communicated could include the following:

- Established responsibilities and procedures for the management and operation of all computers and networks
- Documented operating procedures
- Operational change control procedures and requirements
- Incident management procedures
- Segregation of duties
- Separation of development and operational production facilities
- External facilities management

12. Systems Planning and Acceptance

Information communicated could include the following:

- Advance planning and preparation requirements to ensure the availability of adequate capacity and resources
- Capacity planning tools and procedures
- Systems acceptance procedures
- Support level agreements (SLAs)

13. Protecting against Malicious Software

Information communicated could include the following:

- How to apply precautions to prevent and detect the introduction of malicious software
- Approved solutions to safeguard the integrity of software and data
- Controls against malicious software
- Procedures for suspected malicious code (such as with e-mail)
- Protecting against malicious software when using social networking sites, instant messaging, texting, Twittering, and other Web 2.0 and Web 3.0 technologies
- Procedures for detected and confirmed malicious code

14. Backups and Logging

Information communicated could include the following:

- Procedures for making backup copies of data
- Procedures for logging events and faults
- Monitoring the equipment environment and when appropriate

- Operator logs
- Fault logging
- Procedure to periodically test effectiveness of backups

15. Network Security and Privacy Controls

Information communicated could include the following tasks:

- Managing the security of computer networks that span organizational boundaries
- Safeguarding information and protecting the supporting infrastructure
- Maintaining network security and privacy controls
- Testing the effectiveness of network security and privacy controls, for example, periodically testing backups
- Building security and privacy controls into the network at every access point

16. Media Handling and Security

Information communicated could include the following:

- How to control and physically protect computer media, documents, input/output data, and system documentation to prevent theft, damage to assets, and interruptions to business activities
- Management of removable computer media
- Disposal of media
- Information-handling procedures
- Security of system documentation

17. Exchanging Information and Software between Organizations

Information communicated could include the following:

- How to control exchange of data and software between organizations to prevent loss, modification, or misuse of data
- Data and software exchange agreements
- Security of media in transit
- Electronic commerce security
- Security of electronic messages
- Security of electronic office systems
- Publicly available systems
- Newsgroups and instant messaging rules and guidelines
- Other forms of information exchange

18. Business Requirements for Systems Access Control

Information communicated could include the following:

- Control of access to computer services and data on the basis of business requirements
- Policies for information dissemination and entitlement
- Access control policy

19. IT User Access Management

Information communicated could include the following:

- Formal procedures to control allocation of access rights to IT systems and services
- User registration
- Privilege management
- User password management
- Review of user access rights
- Procedures to remove inactive IDs and IDs that are no longer needed

20. Information and Systems User Responsibilities

Information communicated could include the following:

- Security procedures and the correct use of IT facilities to support your organization's security policy in the normal course of work
- Ways to minimize security and privacy risks
- Password use
- Unattended user equipment
- User responsibility to report any suspected security and privacy incidents
- Acceptable use of systems

21. Network Access Control

Information communicated could include the following:

- Control of connections to network services to ensure that connected users or computer services do not compromise the security of any other networked services
- Limited services

- Enforced path
- User authentication
- Node authentication
- Remote diagnostic port protection
- Network segregation
- Network connection control
- Network routing control
- Security in network services

22. Operating Systems Access Control

Information communicated could include how to limit access to computers through the use of the following:

- Automatic terminal identification
- Terminal log-on procedures
- User IDs
- Password management
- A duress alarm
- Terminal time-out
- Limited connection time
- Smart cards
- Biometrics

23. Application Access Control

Information communicated could include the following:

- Logical access controls to protect application systems and data from unauthorized access
- Information access restriction
- Sensitive system isolation
- Access control to program source libraries

24. Monitoring Systems Access and Use

Information communicated could include the following:

- Monitoring systems to ensure conformity with access policy and standards
- Monitoring systems to detect unauthorized activities
- Monitoring systems to determine the effectiveness of security measures adopted
- Event logging
- Clock synchronization

- Centralized log storage and protection
- Log file entries standards

25. Mobile and Remote Computing

Information communicated could include the following:

- Examination of the risks of mobile computing and teleworking
- Application of appropriate protection to the equipment or site
- Theft or loss
- Passwords
- File access
- Viruses and other malicious software
- Unauthorized network access
- Wireless concerns
- Network bandwidth
- Device retrieval
- Device disposal
- Personal device ownership
- Policies and procedures

26. Security and Privacy Requirements of Systems

Information communicated could include the following tasks:

- Ensuring security and privacy are built into IT systems, from the beginning of the systems development process and addressed throughout the lifecycle
- Identifying, justifying, accepting, and documenting security and privacy requirements definition stage of all IT system development projects
- Security and privacy requirements analysis and specification procedures

27. Security and Privacy in Application Systems

Information communicated could include the following:

- Security controls that conform to commonly accepted industry standards of good security practice
- Design of security and privacy for applications systems to prevent loss, modification, or misuse of user data
- Input data validation
- Control of internal processing
- Message authentication to protect the integrity of network traffic, and verify the identity of the traffic's originator
- Output data validation

- Secure application coding standards and techniques in addition to input/output validation
- Application testing procedures

28. Cryptographic Controls

Information communicated could include the following:

- Use of cryptographic systems and techniques to protect the confidentiality, authenticity, or integrity of information, and to protect information that is considered at risk
- Policy on the use of cryptographic controls
- Encryption algorithms and organization standards
- Digital signatures
- Non-repudiation services
- Key management

29. System Files Security

Information communicated could include the following:

- Responsibility for controlling access to application system files to ensure that IT projects and support activities are conducted securely
- Control of operational software
- Protection of system test data
- Access control to program source library
- Use of public domain, freeware, and shareware
- Policies concerning copyrights

30. Security and Privacy in Development and Support Environments

Information communicated could include the following:

- How to strictly control project and support environments to maintain the security of application system software and data
- How to change control procedures
- Technical review of operating system changes
- Restrictions on changes to software packages
- How to prevent covert channels and Trojan code

31. Security for Outsourced Services

Information communicated could include the following:

- Performing security and privacy program reviews of outsourced vendors
- Outsourced software development requirements and procedures
- Protecting intellectual property
- Preinstallation testing
- Not using production data for testing
- Regulatory and legal security and privacy requirements for outsourcing
- Outsourcing policies that indicate what services may and may not be outsourced
- Security and privacy requirements to include within outsourcing contracts

32. Business Continuity Planning

Information communicated could include the following:

- Business continuity plan availability to counteract interruptions to business activities
- Business continuity management process
- Business continuity and impact analysis
- Writing and implementation of continuity plans
- Business continuity planning framework
- Testing, maintenance, and reassessment of business continuity plans

33. Information Security and Privacy Laws, Regulations, and Standards

Information communicated could include the following tasks:

- Identifying the laws, regulations, and standards that apply to your organization
- Communicating the requirements, as they apply to your organization, to the appropriate personnel and third parties
- Identifying all relevant requirements for each IT system

34. Personal Information Privacy

Information communicated could include the following tasks:

- Discussing applications that process personal data and how they must comply with the applicable data protection legislation
- Describing how to obtain and process personal data honestly and lawfully
- Discussing requirements to hold personal data only for specified and lawful purposes

- Protecting personal data from use or disclosure in any way incompatible with its intended purpose
- Ensuring personal data is adequate and relevant, and not excessive in relation to its intended purpose
- Ensuring personal data is accurate and, where necessary, kept current
- Ensuring personal data is kept only as long as necessary for its intended purpose
- Informing persons that their personal data is being maintained
- Informing persons that they are entitled to access their personal data
- Informing persons that they may have their personal data corrected or erased
- Taking appropriate security measures to protect personal data from unauthorized access, alteration, disclosure or destruction, and to prevent accidental loss or destruction
- Following appropriate procedures if private information is inappropriately or accidentally disclosed

35. Collection of Electronic Evidence

Information communicated could include the following:

- Determination of when an action against a person involves the law
- The rules for evidence for admissibility, quality, and completeness
- Organizational roles and responsibilities

36. Security and Privacy Compliance Reviews and Audits

Information communicated could include the following:

- Compliance review schedules
- Purpose of reviews, to ensure compliance of IT systems with organizational security policies and standards
- Technical compliance checking, including testing the effectiveness of technical controls
- Compliance with security and privacy policies

37. Systems Audit Controls and Tools

Information communicated could include the following:

- Controls to safeguard operational systems and audit tools during system audits
- Minimization of interference to and from the system audit process
- Protection of the integrity of, and preventing the misuse of, audit tools
- Other protection requirements for system audit tools

■ Secure storage of audit reports
■ Access to audit reports
■ Audit occurrence policies (for example, those that must occur annually, triggers for audits, and so on)

38. Security and Privacy Tools

Information communicated could include the following:

■ Identification of the security and privacy tools used within your organization
■ Appropriate and correct ways to use security and privacy tools
■ Some tools you may want to include covering include, but are not limited to, the following:
  − PETs (privacy enhancing technologies)
    • Encryption
    • Steganography
    • P3P (Platform for Privacy Preferences Project)
    • Access control systems
    • Privacy seals for Web sites
    • Blind signatures
    • Digital signatures
    • Biometrics
    • Firewalls
    • Spam filters
    • Cookie cutters and bug zappers
    • HTML filters
    • Pseudonymous and anonymous systems, such as communication anonymizers
    • Trusted sender stamps
    • EPAL (enterprise privacy authorization language)
  − Privacy threatening technologies (generally were not created to invade privacy, but can be used to do so)
    • Cookies
    • Log files
    • Web bugs/Web gifs/web beacons/clear gifs
    • Filtering and monitoring
    • Spyware
    • Spam and phishing
    • "Always online" Web-phones with audio and video capabilities
    • Grid networks and cloud computing
    • Blogs and microblogs (such as Twitter)
    • Instant messaging
    • Peer to peer

- Active content and client-based scripting
- Surveillance technologies
- Trojans

39. Customer and Consumer Interactions (Customer Relationship Management)

Information communicated could include the following:

- How to ensure appropriate access
- Customer contact when privacy policy changes
- Opt-in and opt-out
- Effective communication when customers complain
- Coordinating customer privacy requests
- Customer information retention
- Online payments
- Storage issues
- Marketers
- Privacy inhibiting technologies
- Identity verification
- Secondary use of data
- Effective resourcing and response to customer calls and correspondence

40. Asset Management Security and Privacy Issues

Information communicated could include the following:

- Tracking computing devices and software
- Disposal of storage media and computers
- Retrieval of information and storage devices
- Inventorying data on storage devices and computers

41. Electronic Commerce

Information communicated could include the following:

- Applications security and privacy
- Use of encryption
- Non-repudiation
- Security testing issues
- Penetration versus vulnerability testing

42. Social Engineering

Information communicated could include the following:

- Common social engineering methods
- Common targets for social engineering
- Verification of the identity of requestors
- Recognition of possible social engineering attacks
- Procedures for responding to potential social engineering attempts
- How information classification helps defeat social engineering attempts
- Organizational documents social engineering perpetrators like to use
- Physical security requirements that help prevent social engineering
- Preventing social engineering through voice mail and other voice communications
- The impact of social engineering on the training participants
- Response to suspected social engineering attacks

43. Data and Records Retention

Information communicated could include the following:

- Procedures
- Security controls
- Off-site storage
- Responsibilities
- Information classification to determine retention requirements
- Legal requirements for certain types of information
- On-site storage
- Destruction of information at end of retention period
- Organizational contacts

44. Third Party and Partners

Information communicated could include the following:

- Security and privacy requirements to include within contracts and agreements
- Business associate agreements
- Downstream liability issues
- Partner facilities locations and restrictions
- Impact of outsourcing to locations outside the country

45. Cross-Border Data Flow

Information communicated could include the following:

- Laws covering cross-border data flow of personal information
- Ways in which information flows across country borders
- Procedures for sending information across borders
- Whom to contact for more information

46. Due Diligence

Information communicated could include the following:

- Description of due diligence
- How due diligence impacts the organization
- Legal requirements for due diligence
- Ways in which the organization demonstrates due diligence
- Organizational responsibilities for due diligence

47. PII, PHI, NPPI, and Other Information

Information communicated could include the following tasks:

- Defining personally identifiable information (PII) and the related regulations and laws
- Defining protected health information (PHI) and the related regulations and laws
- Defining nonpublic personal information (NPPI, sometimes NPI) and the related regulations and laws
- Describing other types of personal information
- Reviewing controls necessary for personal information
- Roles and responsibilities

48. E-Mail Security and Privacy

Information communicated could include the following:

- Policies and procedures
- Security and privacy tools
- Hoaxes
- Malicious code and attachments
- Spoofing identities
- Spamming
- Encryption

49. Identity Verification

Information communicated could include the following:

- Organizational policies and procedures
- Items to use for verification
- Effective communication with callers and other types of requestors

50. Ethics

Information communicated could include the following:

- Definition of ethical behavior
- How information handling and technology relate to corporate ethics
- Ethics and the law
- Computing ethics
- Information-handling ethics

51. Policies

Information communicated could include the following:

- The importance of policies
- Executive support of policies
- Policy responsibilities
- Policy ownership
- Sanctions
- Updates
- Exceptions
- Whom to contact for questions
- Reference information

52. Procedures

Information communicated could include the following:

- Definition of purpose of procedures
- Who is responsible for following procedures
- Procedure ownership
- Documentation

53. Information Classification

Information communicated could include the following:

- Classification categories
- Controls
- Labeling
- Regulatory requirements
- Procedures
- Responsibilities

54. Fraud Identification and Prevention

Information communicated could include the following:

- Definition of fraud
- Prevalence of fraud
- Laws and regulations
- Regulatory and legal requirements for training
- Penalties and fines
- Due diligence in fraud prevention
- Roles and responsibilities
- Fraud indicators
- Procedures for reporting suspected fraud

55. Incident Response

Information communicated could include the following:

- Definition of a privacy incident and security incident
- Roles and responsibilities
- Timelines
- Procedures
- Documentation
- Testing the incident response plans
- Preparation
- Detection
- Containment
- Eradication
- Recovery
- Follow-up
- Reporting
- Improvement of security and privacy based on lessons learned from the incident

56. OECD Privacy Principles

Information communicated could include the following:

- Overview of OECD
- Countries with laws built around the principles
- Accountability
- Identification of purposes
- Consent
- Limiting collection
- Limiting use, disclosure, and retention
- Accuracy
- Safeguards
- Openness
- Individual access
- Challenging compliance

57. Web Site Privacy Policies

Information communicated could include the following:

- Purpose of the policy
- Supporting procedures
- Roles and responsibilities
- Answers to customer and consumer questions about the policy
- Policy updates

58. Customer Privacy Communications

Information communicated could include the following:

- Response to customer privacy concerns and complaints
- Procedures
- Documentation
- Whom to contact
- No-contact lists

59. Exiting Personnel Security and Privacy

Information communicated could include the following:

- Roles and responsibilities
- Information to return to individual

- Access controls
- Retrieval of computing devices and information
- Nondisclosure agreements for exiting personnel
- Checklists for managers

60. Information Disposal

Information communicated could include the following:

- How to securely dispose of confidential and sensitive printed information
- How to irreversibly delete information from electronic storage
- How to securely dispose of computers when sending them out of the business
- How to securely dispose of electronic storage media

Mapping Topics to Roles and Target Groups

Now that you have identified your target audiences and roles, in addition to the topics for which you need to communicate information security and privacy policies, procedures, issues, and other business information, you are ready to match the roles within the target audiences to the corresponding topics with which they work when fulfilling their business responsibilities. Based on this, and taking into account your own unique business environment, you may determine from the sample mapping table of topics shown in Exhibit 2 the course content that should be given to additional groups, or to different groups altogether.

The roles are taken from the table earlier in this chapter (Exhibit 1). Some of the roles are not represented simply because of space restrictions on this page; be sure you include all your roles and target audiences when you are planning your awareness and training messages.

You do not necessarily have to have a separate course for each of these topics; you need to ensure that each indicated group receives training and is made aware of the relevant topic. Multiple topics may be included in one class or awareness communication if they are small enough to not overwhelm the learner.

Standards and Principles

Currently there are several standards used worldwide for information security and privacy risk mitigation. Because it is a growing trend to create policies and procedures around these standards, it is also becoming a popular training trend to teach appropriate personnel the information security and privacy responsibilities associated with these standards and all the requirements within.

Besides providing guidance for information security and privacy management and activities, some of the most noted and used standards also include some explicit requirements for information security and privacy awareness and training activities.

Exhibit 2 Roles to Topic Mapping Example

Security and Privacy Topic	Roles											
	R1	R2	R3	R4	R5	R6	R8	R9	R10	R14	R15	R18
Workstation Security										X	X	
Web Site Privacy Policies			X		X	X	X	X	X	X		
Customer Privacy Communications	X		X		X		X	X		X		X
E-Mail Security and Privacy			X	X	X	X	X	X		X	X	X
Privacy Laws and Regulations	X		X				X	X				
Social Engineering		X		X	X	X		X	X	X		X
Third Party and Partner Security and Privacy				X	X			X				
Identity Verification	X					X		X				X
Technical Security Mechanisms		X				X	X		X			

Included here are only a few, to serve as examples of the type of detailed directives within these awareness and training standards. As you can see, they are typically very general in their directives. It makes it that much more important for organizations to determine the types of education efforts they need to make, not only to demonstrate due diligence, but also to show that they are following a widely accepted standard.

OECD

The Organization for Economic Cooperation and Development (OECD) is made up of 30 member countries sharing a commitment to democratic government and market economy, with active relationships with over 70 other countries and societies. The OECD covers 200 diverse topics, including information communications and technology, which include principles for security and privacy. The OECD internationally recognized norms, known as fair information practices (FIPs), outline secure and responsible information-handling practices. Over 100 countries worldwide use these FIPs as the basis for their existing or proposed privacy laws and commerce requirements and as guidelines for handling PII. These are commonly referred to as the 10 international privacy principles.

These principles serve as a good basis to examine, at a high level, compliance with many different worldwide privacy laws simultaneously and to identify issues needing more research. The principles cover the following areas:

- Accountability
- Identifying purposes
- Consent
- Limiting collection
- Limiting use, disclosure, and retention
- Accuracy
- Safeguards
- Openness
- Individual access
- Challenging compliance

The OECD also provides guidelines for information systems and network security. They recognize the importance of information security education within organizations, as demonstrated by the following excerpts:

2002 OECD Guidelines for the Security of Information Systems and Networks; Principle 1:

Awareness: Participants should be aware of the need for security of information systems and networks and what they can do to enhance security.

Awareness of the risks and available safeguards is the first line of defense for the security of information systems and networks. Information systems and networks can be affected by both internal and external risks. Participants should understand that security failures may significantly harm systems and networks under their control. They should also be aware of the potential harm to others arising from interconnectivity and interdependency. Participants should be aware of the configuration of, and available updates for, their system, its place within networks, good practices that they can implement to enhance security, and the needs of other participants.

2001 OECD Guidelines on the Protection of Privacy and Transborder Flows of Personal Data:

… promote user education and awareness about online privacy issues and the means at their disposal for protecting privacy on global networks.

ISO/IEC 27001

The International Organization for Standardization/International Electrotechnical Commission (ISO/IEC) 27001 is a standard that sets the requirements for an information security management system. The requirements "help identify, manage, and minimize the range of threats to which information is regularly subjected."

The ISO/IEC 27001 Information Security Standard is published in two parts:

- *ISO/IEC 27001 Code of Practice for Information Security Management*
- *ISO/IEC 27002 Specification for Information Security Management*

The standard is written as a list of guiding notes and recommendations. The standard topics are incorporated into the list of possible education topics found within this chapter. The following is an excerpt from ISO/IEC 27002* that specifically discuss the need for information security education:

8.2.2 Information security awareness, education, and training

Control

All employees of the organization and, where relevant, contractors and third party users should receive appropriate awareness training and regular updates in organizational policies and procedures, as relevant for their job function.

Implementation Guidance

Awareness training should commence with a formal induction process designed to introduce the organization's security policies and expectations before access to information or services is granted.

Ongoing training should include security requirements, legal responsibilities and business controls, as well as training in the correct use of information processing facilities e.g. log-on procedure, use of software packages and information on the disciplinary process (see 8.2.3).

Other Information

The security awareness, education, and training activities should be suitable and relevant to the person's role, responsibilities and skills, and should include information on known threats, who to contact for further security advice and the proper channels for reporting information security incidents (see also 13.1).

Training to enhance awareness is intended to allow individuals to recognize information security problems and incidents, and respond according to the needs of their work role.

---

* You can purchase the full set of standards online at http://www.sriregistrar.com/A55AEB/ sricorporat eweb.nsf/layoutC/974 EF12F7E9942868625 71DC00743CE6? Opendocument &key=Standards&g clid=COCHldne_Z oC FQ3yDAodtlirdw.

NIST

Public Law 100-235, titled The Computer Security Act of 1987, mandated NIST and the Office of Personnel Management (OPM) to create guidance on computer security awareness and training based on functional organizational roles. Guidance was produced in the form of a NIST Special Publication 800-16 titled *Information Technology Security Training Requirements: A Role- and Performance-Based Model.** The learning continuum modeled in this guidance provides the relationship between awareness, training, and education.

A brief excerpt from page iii of this 188-page document describes the intent of the publication:

The key to addressing people factors or competencies is awareness, training, and education. Certainly the need for government wide attention to this area of IT security has never been greater, so issuance of this publication, *Information Technology Security Training Requirements: A Role- and Performance-Based Model* (Training Requirements) is especially timely. This document has been designed as a "living handbook" to have the longest useful life possible as the foundation of and structure for "do-able" training by federal agencies.

COBIT

COBIT serves as a framework of generally applicable information systems (IS) security and control practices for information technology control. The report can be ordered from Information Systems Audit and Control Association (ISACA)[†] by phone or mail. The COBIT framework strives to help the management benchmark the security and control practices of IT environments, allows users of IT services to be assured that adequate security and control exists, and allows auditors to confirm their opinions on internal control and to advise on IT security and control matters. The primary motivation for ISACA to provide the framework was to enable the development of clear policy and good practices for IT control throughout the industry worldwide. The following are some brief excerpts from COBIT specifically addressing the need for awareness and training:

---

* You can download the document from http://csrc.nist.gov/publications/nistpubs/800-16/ 800-16.pdf.
† See http://www.isaca.org.

6.11 Communication of IT Security Awareness

Control Objective

An IT security awareness program should communicate the IT security policy to each IT user and assure a complete understanding of the importance of IT security. It should convey the message that IT security is to the benefit of the organization, all its employees, and that everybody is responsible for it. The IT security awareness programme should be supported by, and represent, the view of management.

7.4 Personnel Training

Control Objective

Management should ensure that employees are provided with orientation upon hiring and with on-going training to maintain their knowledge, skills, abilities and security awareness to the level required to perform effectively. Education and training programs conducted to effectively raise the technical and management skill levels of personnel should be reviewed regularly.

The Committee of Sponsoring Organizations of the Treadway Commission (COSO) Enterprise Risk Management Framework

The COSO framework* describes the meaning of "internal control" and its components. It also provides criteria against which control systems can be evaluated. The report serves as an aid for management, auditors, and other risk professionals to guide how to report and document internal controls and also provides materials that can be used for evaluation. The two major goals of COSO are to establish a common definition of internal control that can be used by many diverse organizations as well as to provide a standard for organizations to use to assess their control systems and identify ways to improve them.

The COSO report includes over 20 references to training and education. The following is an excerpt on page 39 that addresses this topic:

Adequate Training—Management supports employees by providing access to the tools and training needed to perform their financial reporting roles.

---

* You can purchase the full framework, and get the Executive Summary free, from http://www.coso.org/ERM-I ntegratedFra mework.htm.

Generally Accepted Privacy Principles

The American Institute of Certified Public Accountants (AICPA) and the Canadian Institute of Chartered Accountants (CICA) formed the AICPA/CICA Privacy Task Force, which developed the Generally Accepted Privacy Principles (GAPP)* to help organizations design and implement sound privacy practices and policies. They provide a "business version" as well as a "practitioner's version." Both versions include numerous directives for providing information security and privacy training to personnel.

---

* You can download the document from http://infotech.aicpa.org/Resources/Privacy/Generally+Accepted+Privacy+Principles/.

Chapter 11

Define Your Message

Many attempts to communicate are nullified by saying too much.

—Robert Greenleaf

The great successful men of the world have used their imaginations, they think ahead and create their mental picture, and then go to work materializing that picture in all its details, filling in here, adding a little there, altering this a bit and that bit, but steadily building, steadily building.

—Robert Collier

Now that you have chosen your topics and your target audiences, you are ready to define your training and awareness messages. For each topic, you should go into the details of what you want to cover within the training and awareness communications, and document the issues you need to review within your organization.

You will find that you have common themes across multiple education topics. By identifying the common themes, you will save development time by creating the details of the common themes and then using the applicable details within each of the appropriate topics. This will also help to ensure consistency of your messages across multiple training sessions. Use your organization's policies and standards to help define messages directly applicable to your organization. Also, augmenting the messages by using standards such as the International Organization for Standardization/International Electrotechnical Commission (ISO/IEC) 27001, National Institute of Standards and Technology (NIST), Organization for Economic Cooperation and Development (OECD) principles, and others will provide tremendous assistance in identifying all issues without leaving gaps. Also look at the requirements for certifications such as the following to identify detailed messages as applicable to your specific topics:

- Certified Information Systems Manager (CISM)
- Certified Information Systems Security Professional (CISSP)
- Certified Information Privacy Professional (CIPP)
- Certified Information Systems Auditor (CISA)

Refer to *NIST Special Publication 800-16* for further ideas.

The remaining sections in this chapter provide illustrative outlines and lists to help you define, refine, and list the issues within some of these common themes and associated messages to be incorporated, as applicable, into your identified training and awareness topics. Depending on your style and preference, you may want to write very descriptive sentences to guide you or just list the items to ensure they are covered. Both of these types of outlining are combined here to be used as a model for creating your own library of common theme messages. You will need to add the issues and elements that are applicable to your industry, environment, and regulatory requirements. All themes and topics are not covered here; doing so would be a completely separate book. This is provided only as a guide to get you started. Consider labeling each of your statements to indicate whether you want to convey the message through training (T), awareness (A), or both.

Customer Privacy

Training and awareness communications should include, as appropriate for the target audiences and delivery methods, information and direction for the following:

- Respect for customer privacy is one of the most important issues facing the organization today. Your customers are very aware of privacy, and there are many legal and regulatory requirements for addressing privacy.
- To gain and keep customer trust, the organization must exercise good judgment in the collection, use, and protection of personally identifiable information (PII).
- The organization must protect each customer's PII from inappropriate exposure or sharing.
- Customers must have the opportunity to state their contact preferences at the point where their PII is collected.
- Customer PII must not be used for any purpose that was not disclosed to the customer at the time of collection.
- Customers must be able to opt-out from any touch-point or service (such as a newsletter subscription or Web site); appropriate processes must be in place to honor the opt-out.

- When considering a new program or activity, give notice (tell customers what you're doing) and choice (let them decide whether to be included); these must be ensured.
- With very few approved exceptions for administrative contact, all organization e-mail communications should be opt-in. Mobile phone, texting and instant messaging marketing, and third-party data sharing should also be restricted to opt-in.
- Postal and phone communications should ideally be opt-in, but most are opt-out (suppress all "no's" before initiating contact).
- Customer PII must be protected by contract (written agreement) and compliance audits.
- All workers (employee and contract) or third-party personnel who directly handle or impact the handling of the organization's customer PII must take the organization's privacy training before handling customer information, with refresher training every 1 or 2 years, as appropriate to your organization, and whenever privacy-impacting changes occur.
- All organizational activities must comply with the organization's privacy policy as well as local laws and regulations.
- The organization is obligated to fulfill the privacy expectations that have been communicated to customers and consumers.
- Organizational personnel must know and follow the customer privacy principles.
- Organizational personnel must incorporate the principles into their daily job responsibilities and tasks.
- When collecting PII directly from individuals, they should be informed about the purposes for which the information is collected and how the organization uses the PII, the types of third parties to which the organization discloses that information, and the choices and means, if any, the organization offers individuals for limiting the use and disclosure of their PII.
- Clear and apparent notice should be provided when individuals are first asked to provide PII to the organization, or as soon as practicable thereafter, and in any event before the organization uses the information for a purpose other than that for which it was originally collected.
- The organization may disclose PII if required to do so by law or to protect and defend the rights or property of the organization. (Discuss with your law department whether you should create procedures to notify PII owners when their information is turned over to law enforcement.)
- There are situations when PII is transmitted to third parties for legitimate business purposes, including to provide compensation or fringe benefits for personnel, or to satisfy country-specific government reporting requirements.
- Third parties, acting as agents for the organization, to whom PII is transferred will be required to either subscribe to the safe harbor principles or enter into a written

agreement with the organization requiring the third party to provide at least the same level of privacy protection as is required by the relevant principles.

■ Upon request, the organization will grant individuals reasonable access to their applicable PII. In addition, the organization will take reasonable steps to permit individuals to correct, amend, or delete information that is demonstrated to be inaccurate or incomplete.

■ The organization will take reasonable precautions, including security procedures, technology, etc., to protect PII in its possession from loss, misuse, and unauthorized access, disclosure, alteration, and destruction.

■ The organization limits access to PII and data to those persons within the organization, or as agents of the organization, that have a specific business purpose for maintaining and processing the PII.

Laws and Regulations

Training and awareness communications should include, as appropriate for the target audiences and delivery methods, the following:

■ Identification of the major legal and policy issues related to information as a resource in the organization as well as in economic and social life. Determine the laws that apply to handling information in general.

■ Definitions of information communication, knowledge production, knowledge utilization, technology transfer, etc., as they relate to laws, regulations, and policies.

■ Descriptions of the major factors affecting the development of information policies.

■ Descriptions and identifications of the relationships between domestic and international information and telecommunication policies, laws, and regulations.

■ Descriptions of the information policy process.
   – Legal policy models: classical, incremental, others
   – Policy instruments: traditions, norms, and cultural patterns

■ Discussions and definitions of economic measures and considerations as they relate to security and privacy.

■ Discussions of laws, regulations, and consent decrees.
   – The security and privacy laws, regulations, standards, and guidelines for all countries where you have offices, employees, customers, and business partners
   – Treaties and international agreements
   – Applicable country, U.S. federal, state, local, and international law and regulations affecting information production, ownership, and transmission.

■ Discussions of judicial decisions and how they impact the organization's business decisions and considerations regarding information handling, security, and privacy.

- Discussion of trends affecting the development of information policies related to security and privacy.
  - Growth of the service sector of the industrial economies and its dependence on information resources and processes
  - Changes in the domestic and international telecommunications regulatory systems
  - Expansion in the number and size of computer networks at the national and at the international level
  - The need to determine the value and ownership of information as a commodity in terms of its public, private, and commercial use
- Discussion and detailing of national and international information policy issues.
  - Government-regulated markets versus competitive markets that do not have many, or any, regulations addressing information handling
  - Current policies for security and privacy of information systems
  - Privacy of personal information in federal, industry, and international records
  - Access to governmental records through edicts such as freedom of information laws and regulations
  - Public and private interface in database marketing and pricing policies
  - Funding of scientific and technical research and the related information
  - Copyrights, patents, trade laws, and international agreements
- Description and detailing of multinational information policies.
  - Cross-border data flow and the conflicting requirements of various nations toward the transnational transfer of data
  - Technology transfer across international borders
  - International regulations, tariffs, and standards
  - The impact of the Internet on cross-border data flow
  - Access to satellite communications
- Discussion of your existing and proposed organization-specific policies and procedures and the legal ramifications of such documents.
- Description of the role of U.S. federal government-wide and organization-specific laws, regulations, policies, guidelines, standards, and procedures in protecting the organization's IT resources.
- Identification of tangible and intangible information resources and assets.
- Reviews of current and emerging social issues that can affect information assets.
- Reviews and discussion of laws and regulations related to social issues affecting security and privacy issues.
- Discussion of the effect of social issues on accomplishment of organizational missions.
- Reviews of social conflicts with the Freedom of Information Act.
- Discussion of public concern for protection of personal information.
- Reviews of legal and liability issues related to security and privacy topics.
  - Laws concerning copyrights for software and documents
  - Organization policies concerning copyrighted software controls

  - Laws concerning privacy of personal information
  - Organization policies and practices for privacy of personal information
  - Laws and regulations related to the organization's business mission
  - Effects of laws, regulations, or policies on the selection of security controls
- Definition, documentation and description of how each information systems and applications owner is responsible for ensuring all the applicable statutory, regulatory, and contractual requirements for the systems and applications.
  - The countries and U.S. states in which the application or system will be used and through which information will flow
  - The information security- and privacy-related laws applicable for each jurisdiction
  - The information and notices given to customers and personnel for applications and systems that collect or process PII
- Reviews and explanations of the specific controls and individual responsibilities necessary to meet the requirements of the identified laws and regulations and how these requirements are defined and documented within your organization.
- Description of the procedures for information systems and applications owners to consult with the organization's legal counsel about the identified laws and regulations and the controls planned to ensure compliance. Explain how legal counsel should thoroughly review the documentation and provide authorization that legal issues are appropriately addressed before moving the system or application to production.
- Description of the organizational procedures for legal counsel to monitor legislative requirements for all countries in which the organization processes or handles information, and describe how they should communicate the security and privacy requirements to applications and systems owners in a timely manner.
- Outline of how the organization's legal counsel should investigate grandfathering provisions of applicable laws and regulations and ensure service contracts are updated appropriately.
- Discussion of how the organization must ensure that information security and privacy controls, as identified within applicable laws and regulations, are implemented by the applicable corresponding deadlines and the impacts of missing the deadlines.

Access Controls

Training and awareness communications with regard to access controls should include, as appropriate for the target audiences and delivery methods, the following steps:

- Discuss and detail identification and authentication methods.
  - Biometrics
  - Passwords

- – Smart cards
- – Tokens
- – Tickets
- – Others as the emerge
■ Discuss and detail single, or reduced, sign-on and identity management methods and related issues.
- – Directory services
- – Kerberos
- – Secure European System for Applications in a Multi-vendor Environment (SESAME)
- – Thin clients
- – Others as they emerge
■ Discuss and describe information access control models and techniques.
- – State machine
- – Bell–LaPadula
- – Biba
- – Clark–Wilson
- – Information flow model
- – Mandatory Access Control (MAC)
- – Role-Based Access Control (RBAC)
- – Restricted interfaces
- – Capability table and Access Control Lists (ACLs)
- – Content-dependent access control
- – Noninterference model
- – Take–Grant model
- – Access control matrix
- – Others as they emerge
■ Discuss methods for access control administration.
- – Assigning and controlling rights and permissions
- – Centralized access control administration
- – Decentralized access control administration
- – Remote Authentication Dial in User Service (RADIUS)
- – Terminal Access Controller Access Control System (TACACS)
- – Diameter access control protocol
- – Others as they emerge
■ Discuss and describe intrusion detection systems and related issues. (Some organizations like to include this topic within access controls, but other organizations find it more effective or appropriate to cover these as a separate topic.)
- – Preventative
- – Detective
- – Corrective controls
- – Network-based
- – Host-based

- Signature-based
- Behavior-based
- IDS shortfalls
- Unauthorized access control and attacks
- Unauthorized disclosure of information
- Emanation security
- Attack types
- Penetration testing to test the IDS

■ Discuss procedures for controlling access to the organization's information and business processes on the basis of business, risk, legal, and security requirements. Discuss how access controls must be implemented based on the organization's information security policies for information dissemination and authorization.

■ Discuss the organization's business requirements for access control and how they should be defined and documented. Describe access control rules and rights for each user or group of users and how they should be clearly stated in an access standard statement for each business process. Review how users and service providers should be given a clear statement of the business requirements accomplished with the access controls.

■ Describe how the organization's business requirements policy and supporting procedures should consider the following issues when establishing access controls.
- Security requirements of individual business applications
- Identification of all information related to the business applications
- Policies for information dissemination and authorization, such as the need to know principle and security levels and classification of information
- Consistency between the access control and information classification policies of different subsets of an organization that may have different systems and networks
- Relevant legislation and any contractual obligations regarding protection of access to data or services
- Standard user access profiles for common categories of jobs that are not related specifically to systems security administration
- Management of access rights in distributed and networked environments that recognize all types of connections available

■ Explain how personnel using the organization information systems should not try to gain unauthorized access to any other information systems or in any way try to damage, alter, or disrupt the operations of these systems. Describe why personnel should not capture or otherwise obtain passwords, encryption keys, or any other access control mechanisms that could permit unauthorized access, and also highlight the accompanying ramifications of doing so.

■ Review how all software installed on multi-user systems, on desktops, or in mobile and external locations should be regulated and approved by the information security and privacy office.

- Describe access controls for mobile computing devices (hand-held computer, laptop, smart phone, etc.) and describe how if they store or process secret, confidential, or mission critical information, then how the system must also utilize a properly maintained version of the organization's approved password-based access control system with strong authentication.
- Describe how personnel who have been authorized to view information classified at a certain sensitivity level must be permitted to access only the information at this level and at less sensitive levels.
- Explain that the organization personnel are not to move the information classified at a certain sensitivity level to a less sensitive level unless this action is a formal part of the approved process.
- Describe how file access control permissions for all networked systems should be set to a default that blocks access by all unauthorized users. Explain how all access to the organization information should be disallowed by default and only explicitly allowed to authorized users.
- Describe the requirements for computer or network user access control systems that are not functioning properly to default to denial of privileges to end users.
- Describe how all organization records for production information system access privileges should be maintained in a centralized database managed by the information security and privacy office.
- Explain how to disallow users from accessing a command interpreter from within an application, especially an application with privileges, in addition to disallowing users from being able to break out of an application to a command line (except possibly to exit the application, depending upon your network and organization).
- Explain how no one, including programmers and other technically oriented personnel, should install trap doors within program and systems code that circumvent the authorized access control mechanisms found in the operating systems or access control packages.
- Explain how personnel should not compromise security mechanisms based on customer requests unless (1) the organization's executive vice president first approves it in writing or (2) the organization is compelled to comply with the requests by law as approved by the organization's legal counsel.
- Detail how if secret, confidential, or mission-critical information is resident on a computer system and if users are permitted to request all or part of this information through online facilities, special access controls approved by the information security and privacy office must be implemented. Describe how the access controls must protect the information so that a series of permissible requests for information cannot reveal information that is otherwise restricted.
- Detail how personnel should not disclose customer or consumer information to third parties unless the originator of the information has provided advance

approval of the disclosure and the receiving party has signed an approved nondisclosure agreement (NDA).

■ Explain how, unless authorized by the management, all requests for information about the organization and the organization's business activities should be referred to the public relations department.

■ Detail the types of requests such as questionnaires, surveys, and newspaper interviews. Explain how this requirement does not apply to publicly available sales and marketing information about the organization's products and services or to customer support calls.

■ Describe why internal systems developers and designers should not create new security protocols, compose new security schemes, develop new encryption algorithms, or create their own proprietary access control or security mechanism. Detail how personnel should use the approved methods and products that have been proven to be secure.

■ Explain why information system privileges that have not been specifically allowed by the information security and privacy office should not be used.

■ Describe how access to organization information should always be authorized by the designated owner of the information and should be limited to only those personnel with a need to access the information to perform job responsibilities.

■ Detail the processes and specifications for business information access control rules and how the following should occur.
  – Differentiating between rules that must always be enforced and rules that are optional or conditional
  – Establishing an "everything is configured as nonauthorized unless expressly permitted" rule instead of the "everything is configured as permitted unless expressly forbidden" rule
  – Changing information labels that are initiated automatically by the information processing facilities and those initiated at the discretion of a user
  – Changing user permissions that are initiated automatically by the information system and those initiated by an administrator
  – Following rules that require administrator or other approval before implementation and those that do not require any approval.

Risk Management

Training and awareness communications should include, as appropriate for the target audiences and delivery methods, the following actions:

■ Describe the organization's risk analysis processes.
  – Identify assets and values
  – Identify threats

- Identify vulnerabilities
- Identify risks
- Describe relationships between threats, vulnerabilities, and risks
- Quantify and qualify the impact of potential risks
- Describe how to perform a cost analysis between impact of risk and cost of controls
■ Discuss ways to manage risk.
  - Discuss possible threats
  - Threats from authorized system users
  - Threats and vulnerabilities from connection to external systems and networks
  - Unauthorized user (hacker) threats
  - Malicious code and virus threats
  - Environment threats
  - Errors and omissions
  - Theft
■ Explain the types of security controls (safeguards and countermeasures) used within the organization and how each addresses risks.
  - Management controls
  - Operational controls
    • Acquisition/development/installation/implementation controls
    • Security awareness and training controls
  - Technical controls
  - How different categories of controls work together
■ Provide examples of information security controls for the protections implemented.
  - Availability protection
  - Integrity protection
  - Confidentiality protection
  - Authenticity protection
  - Disclosure protection
  - Appropriate use protection
  - Destruction protection
  - Added security controls for connecting external systems and networks
■ Describe the organization's business continuity, contingency planning, and disaster recovery processes.
  - How the processes differ
  - Importance of plans to deal with unexpected problems
  - Importance of testing plan and applying lessons learned
■ Discuss the difference between determining acceptable levels of risk and eliminating 100% of risks.
■ Describe the difference between identifying adequate controls and appropriate controls.

- Detail the unique protection requirements of your information networks and systems components.
- Describe how to determine the severity, probability, and extent of potential harm.
- Discuss implementation of cost-effective controls and calculating cost benefits.
- Describe the importance of partnering with all other security groups (physical security, insurance security, internal audit, systems security administrators, etc.) within the organization.
- Describe the importance of internal and external audits, reviews, and evaluations in security decisions.
- Explain why all business areas within the organization should be regularly reviewed to ensure compliance with security policies and standards and to identify risks to the organization information.
- Discuss why risk assessments should be performed by independent reviewers from an area that does not share management with the area being reviewed to ensure objectivity and proper separation of duties.
- Explain why regular reviews of the computer systems and system providers should occur to ensure compliance with security policies and standards and to identify risks within the systems.
- Discuss why information owners should plan regular risk assessments and compliance reviews to ensure only the appropriate personnel have access to their information and to identify new or increased risks.
- Discuss the procedures for performing a regular user access and practices review to ensure compliance with security policies and standards and to identify risks that may exist with the way users handle information.
- Discuss procedures for performing regular management reviews of each business area to ensure management is in compliance with security policies and standards and to ensure management is appropriately communicating and supporting security policies and standards.
- Describe why tests, development and production information, computer systems, and networks should be regularly evaluated to determine the minimum set of controls required to reduce risk to an acceptable level.
- Discuss the procedures for regularly checking and evaluating the organization IT physical facilities to ensure compliance with security implementation standards and identify and address risks.

Chapter 12

Prepare Budget and Obtain Funding

Obstacles are those frightful things you see when you take your eyes off the goal.

—Hannah More

Obtain Traditional Funding if You Can

First, you should obtain executive management support for your program. Chapter 8 discusses in detail how to obtain management support for your information security and privacy awareness and training program. However, it is such a critical component to the success of your program and to get adequate funding that it is worth emphasizing here again.

There are many problems associated with obtaining the funding necessary for information security and privacy programs, particularly for awareness and training. Some of these include the following:

- As technology is being used increasingly in training and awareness programs, the budget necessary to support this technology increases, creating numbers that cannot be approved through traditional means.
- There typically have been no baselines of past training and awareness or measurements to determine the effectiveness of such education activities. Without being able to show efforts that have been, or have the potential to be, effective, it is difficult to get budgets for high-quality, effective education. Instead, those

who approve such budgets often sanction the lowest amount that is sufficient to show that the company is doing something to comply with requirements, but that kind of budget does not really fund quality or effectiveness.

■ Many organizations have spent too much on technologies and services for awareness and training only to find that these did not fit the requirements of their organization, leading many to believe that a big budget is not necessary and only better planning and research are enough. While this may be true to an extent, the effect is often that allotted budgets are insufficient.

■ Usually, training and education budgets are created after all other budgets have been allotted, resulting in such activities getting the limited funds that happen to be still available.

■ Training and awareness budgets are often set by considering just one factor, usually technology. You need to consider all factors to obtain adequate funding, including materials, personnel time, facilities, development costs, and so on.

■ Education funding has typically been underestimated. Many leaders and budget decision makers who have never been involved with creating an awareness and training program assume that such education can be launched without much planning, preparation, time, or resources.

■ Most people do not think outside the box and explore nontraditional potentials for funding training and awareness programs.

■ Funding decisions are sometimes based not on demonstrated needs but instead on company politics, power plays, ego trips, emotions, or faulty assumptions.

■ There is often a failure to spend the time necessary to create a strongly demonstrated business case to present to executives and budget managers.

With your defined awareness and training strategy, you can now determine the funding you will need to successfully implement your plan and reach your goals. It will make your budget goals much easier if you have your executive management and an executive sponsor supporting your efforts (see Chapter 8). If business units are responsible for the funding of your education program, your executive sponsor should clearly present to them the expectations and needs of the program to obtain adequate funding. If the funding is centralized, your executive sponsor should ensure that there are adequate funds to meet all requirements of your education program

There are several different approaches organizations take to budgeting. As part of creating your education strategy and plan, clearly indicate the estimated costs for each component of the plan. See Exhibit 1 for an example of a budget worksheet from which you can build your own budget worksheet. This is also found in Appendix N for easy reference with other worksheets. Consider using budgeting contracts if you have a decentralized funding practice within your organization. Keep the following in mind when applying for a budget:

■ Provide plenty of documentation and information to support funding requirements. Relate your requests to tangible items as much as possible, explain the risks, and put dollar values on incidents and potential fines or penalties including those that have already occurred internally, those that have occurred at other companies, and those that may occur under certain incident scenarios. Too often, budget requests do not include sufficient detail to communicate the true need for the funding.

■ Track losses resulting from all kinds of information security and privacy incidents. Show trends in losses over time. List your security and privacy incidents and their impact on the company, particularly in terms of lost dollars and personnel time. Keep track of all such statistics. Show how awareness and training can impact the trends.

■ Use case studies from other companies and statistics from research organizations to present to your executives and board members. See Chapter 19 for awareness and training case studies and experiences from other organizations.

■ Get to know your organization comptroller, financial officer, and head auditor. Show them the trends you have documented. Ask them to visibly support your funding needs by writing a memo that documents their support of your funding needs or by speaking on your behalf at a budget meeting.

■ Show detailed funding needs and not just a lump-sum amount. Avoid vague and generic labels such as "information security" and "privacy protection." Break it down into the types of activities, personnel, materials, technology, facilities, etc., you need for a successful education program.

■ Use statistics and benchmark studies to show the comparative values and funding for similar efforts at other organizations. For example, Ernst & Young, Deloitte, and Price Waterhouse Coopers all create annual information security survey reports, and they often include budget and funding information for information security programs. Other organizations, such as CSI, SANS, Gartner, Forrester, and others, sometimes perform studies related to information security funding.

Sources for obtaining budget dollars for information security and privacy awareness and training vary greatly from organization to organization. Some possible sources include the following:

■ Percentage of corporate training budget.
■ Percentage of IT budget.
■ Percentage of each business unit's budget based on number of personnel.
■ Allocation of a set amount of dollars per user by role and participation within the education program. (For example, training for dedicated security and privacy personnel would be more costly than training for personnel who do not have responsibilities with security requirements or activities.)
■ Explicit dollar allocations by strategy component based on overall implementation costs.

Exhibit 1 Compute Each of Your Awareness and Training Costs

Awareness/Training Event/Program _____

Date: _____

Education Contact: _____

	TOTAL
Analysis Costs	
Salaries & Employee Benefits—Staff (Number of People x Average Salary x Employee Benefits Costs x Number of Projected Hours on Project)	
Meals, Travel, and Incidental Expenses	
Office Supplies and Expenses	
Printing and Reproduction	
Outside Services—Printing, Consultants, and so on	
Equipment Expense	
Registration Fees	
Other Miscellaneous Expenses	
(A) Total Analysis Cost	
Development Costs	
Salaries & Employee Benefits—Training Staff (Number of People × Average Salary × Employee Benefits Costs × Number of Projected Hours on Project)	
Meals, Travel, and Incidental Expenses	
Office Supplies and Expenses	
Program Materials and Supplies	
Film/Videotape/DVD	
Audio Tapes	

Exhibit 1   (continued)

	TOTAL
35-mm Slides	
CDs/Diskettes	
Overhead Transparencies	
Software	
Artwork	
Poster Boards	
Memo Pads	
Whiteboards	
Pens, Markers, Paint, etc.	
Trinkets, "Chachkas," or other goodies	
Manuals and Materials	
Other	
Printing and Reproduction	
Outside Services—Contract Workers, Consultants, Facilities Rent, and so on	
Equipment Expense	
Registration Fees	
Other Miscellaneous Expenses	
(B) Total Development Cost	
Delivery Costs	
Participant Costs	
Salaries & Employee Benefits—Participants (Number of Participants × Average Salary × Employee Benefits Costs × Number of Hours or Days of Training Time)	
Meals, Travel, and Accommodations (Number of Participants × Average Daily Expenses × Days of Training)	
Participant Replacement Costs	

(*continued*)

Exhibit 1   (continued)

	TOTAL
Lost Production (explain basis)	
Program Materials and Supplies	
Instructor Costs	
Salaries and Benefits	
Meals, Travel, and Incidental Expenses	
Outside Services	
Facility Costs (distance learning, traditional classroom, lab, hotel, conference room, other)	
Facilities Rental	
Facilities Expense Allocation	
Equipment Expense	
Other Miscellaneous Expenses	
(C) Total Delivery Costs	
Evaluation Costs	
Salaries & Employee Benefits — Staff (Number of People × Average Salary × Employee Benefits Cost × Number of Hours on Project)	
Meals, Travel, and Incidental Expenses	
Participants Costs (interviews, focus groups, questionnaires, surveys, online feedback, etc.,)	
Office Supplies and Expenses	
Printing and Reproduction	
Outside Services	
Equipment Expense	
Other Miscellaneous Expenses	
(D) Total Evaluation Costs for Project	
TOTAL PROJECT COSTS (A+B+C+D)	

You will have challenges to successfully implementing your education program without proper funding. Without your needed dollars, your program will likely be perceived as being less important than other, adequately funded programs. You need to think about and plan for the possibility that you will not get sufficient funds to properly support your program. With an insufficient budget, you may have to curtail some of your planned awareness or training activities. You may also have to continue to push and lobby for more funding or find other sources of funding.

Obtain Nontraditional Funding When Necessary

If you have a very supportive executive sponsor and you communicate your budget needs effectively and convincingly, you may get the budget you need. However, if you do not get the budget you need and do not want to, or cannot, eliminate any items from your information security and privacy awareness and training program, you need to consider becoming a little creative and think outside the box.

Such nontraditional funding efforts remind me of my father at his work. Many years ago, he accepted a position as superintendent of a rural school district in Missouri that was deep in the red; it was widely thought that it would be impossible to keep the school going. My father did not follow the traditional ways of thinking about funding. Instead, he spent hundreds of hours poring over all the available state and federal grants and possible sources of money that could be used to save the school district. He analyzed the school budget to see where costs could be cut. As a result, he took advantage of every possible grant, many of which were hidden in the details of obscure regulations and codes, resulting in the bulk of funding. He also found creative ways to accomplish the necessary tasks for much less than traditional costs. For example, he would take me up on the school building roof before each school year to work with him and the janitor to do maintenance and repair work, thereby saving the cost of hiring someone else. At a fraction of the cost of new buses, he purchased, when necessary, perfectly good two- to three-year-old school buses from the neighboring districts that bought new buses each year. He encouraged school groups to hold fund-raisers for the sports, arts, and music programs. Within just a few years, the school district was not only out of the red, but only a very small percentage of the budget was dependent upon the local tax dollars.

We can learn much from other organizations and the manner in which they meet similar funding challenges. Of course, different industries and organizations have unique challenges and requirements for which some creative funding ideas just will not work. However, keep in mind that funding programs is not something new and unique to information security and privacy professionals. You have to follow the budgeting procedures and guidelines for your organization, but you may be pleasantly surprised when you try a less traditional method of funding for your program. It is often very difficult to get funding for information security and privacy; often it is easier to get funds for technology. Try brainstorming a little and consider getting funds from areas you may not have looked at before.

Some of these may be completely unrealistic for some of you because of your organization's environment and politics. Skeptics will likely dismiss some of these ideas outright; I know, because the skeptical side of me tends to do the same. Fortunately, my optimistic side usually wins out, and I go forward to at least consider the possibilities. Keep the following in mind as you think about some less traditional areas of funding. The time you start creating a budget for the coming year is ideal to brainstorm funding options. Include colleagues, peers, and friends, as appropriate, in your brainstorming sessions. Sometimes the best ideas come from those with no preconceived notions or constraints about the topic and from people who are in completely different professions.

Here are some ideas to get you started with brainstorming your funding possibilities. Many of these will probably not be appropriate for your organization, but perhaps they will give rise to other ideas:

- Partner with other training areas such as a corporate training department or personnel training and see if they will share their budget in joint training and awareness efforts. They may already have a great system in place that you can utilize for your own education efforts at a cost significantly lower than that of purchasing a complete system.
- Partner with business units in which education is necessary and share their training funds. A very good area with which to consider partnering is physical security; in my experience, you can usually align information security and privacy training and awareness activities quite well with physical security. Other areas in which you may find good synergy are human resources, corporate compliance, and management services.
- Purchase generic training and awareness materials and modify them in-house instead of having them customized by the vendor. Many, if not most, vendors will first try to sell you customized packages at a much higher rate than that for generic packages and information. There are very few commercial products that are ready to use as-is; organizations should train for their specific policies, standards, procedures, and guidelines, which will be unique.
- Create all your training and awareness materials utilizing the talents, services, and time of your personnel. For example, utilize the help of film hobbyists in the organization to create training and awareness videos. As a bonus, the hobbyists might have very good ideas on how to make the videos more interesting and effective based on their filmmaking experiences.

- Hold fund-raisers. If your organization has no rules or policies against fund-raising, it is worthwhile to take a cue from the numerous youth organizations that have been successfully raising money in this manner for years. You can hold the fund-raiser either internally by involving other departments or externally by involving other organizations. However, you need to be very careful with regard to any external activity. You must check with your public relations and other corporate management staff. This probably works best in not-for-profit or educational organizations.

- Barter for funding. This can apply to bartering with your internal departments as well as with outside third parties. It is likely you have personnel with talent others can use to help them with their objectives; look at what resources those others have that can contribute to your training and education goals. This can be especially true with outside vendors or business partners. However, be sure to discuss with your public relations, legal, and acquisitions areas before doing something like this with outside entities.

- Exchange overtime or vacation time for funding. This is difficult to consider as few, if any, will want to give up their own personal money or vacation time. However, overtime salaries and vacation-related costs make up a significant amount of organizational budgets. Additionally, if managers see you are so dedicated to achieving goals that you are willing to give up your own money and leisure time, they may reconsider and find a way to get you the required funding. Do not count on this, but accept it as a nice surprise if it happens.

- Explore grant opportunities. There are probably many that you are not aware of. For example, the Office of the Privacy Commissioner of Canada (OPC) has been funding privacy research grants, up to $50,000 for any single project, since 2004. In 2008 the OPC gave grants focusing on four priority areas: (1) national security, (2) identity integrity and protection, (3) information technology, and (4) genetic privacy. Check not only with local, state, and federal agencies, but also with universities and research facilities.

- Check with local universities. There are a growing number of universities that have created information security and personal security programs. For example, Iowa State University recently put together a security news electronic newsletter to which anyone can subscribe. This or something similar could be distributed as part of awareness efforts. Also, other potential partnering and sharing opportunities are available with educational institutions at all levels, not just at the university level. Many educational institutions are happy to provide resources such as students, teachers, or materials in exchange for the insights and experiences of business professionals.

- Seek outside help to justify budget needs. Management may listen more attentively to outside sources they view as experts rather than to their own personnel. Discuss with some organizational education or information security and privacy consultants or even check with professional peers who have implemented a program to ask them for their opinion about how much money it would take to fulfill your goals. Consultants will often be happy to visit organizations to provide presentations or attend meetings to discuss training and awareness needs and realistic budgets. Ensure that the consultants you choose are qualified.

■ Closely examine the entire corporate budget and identify items that are not necessary to support business processes or corporate goals. If possible, obtain the detailed budget. Note areas in the budget where you may have scope to reduce costs. This can be a somewhat politically dangerous exercise, but if you do not have people involved who are overly territorial, the company should welcome all ideas about how to make the business run more efficiently while demonstrating security due diligence. Additionally, it is common for some budget items to go to the next budget year by default. You may find some old budget items that are no longer necessary or valid and this may help to clean up the budget in the process. In some, perhaps many, organizations, this may not be realistic. Keep in mind that if you reduce the budgets for other departments, you run the risk of creating training and awareness antagonists that could make your education efforts more challenging and possibly much less effective.

■ Share with and learn from peers. Network with other information security and privacy professionals. Learn how others have their programs funded. See if you can use materials that they have used, being careful to preserve copyright and licensing requirements.

■ Use interns to perform activities. Often you can obtain help from interning students to help perform awareness and training activities and create materials and resources to use within your organization. If you cannot create a formal intern program, consider mentoring students in exchange for having them perform various activities for your program. Schools will generally give such students course credit for such activities.

■ Create an information security and privacy co-op within one of your local chapters of ISACA, Infragard, ISSA, Institute of Internal Auditors (IIA), or a similar professional or special interest group. Many groups maintain a library of resources for their members. See if the group can purchase awareness and training materials and then lend them to members of the co-op to use as necessary.

Final Budget and Funding Thoughts

As with any activity or idea related to supporting your information security and privacy efforts, be sure to discuss with other appropriate areas within your company such as the law department and HR to ensure that you are not violating any copyright, licensing, software, or other applicable contracts, laws, industry standards, or union requirements. Use these discussions also to get them involved in your plans.

Your methods for obtaining funding must be both credible and defensible. If you cannot demonstrate the value of your education program to the funding decision makers to successfully obtain the budget you need, then you need to brainstorm for other places to get that elusive but necessary funding and then look for some not-so-apparent sources of funding.

Chapter 13

Training Design and Development

I never teach my pupils; I only attempt to provide the conditions in which they can learn.

—Albert Einstein

The training session should be designed and the curriculum and content developed based on the learning objectives of the associated target groups. The training delivery method should be based on the best way to achieve your objectives. In choosing a delivery method, consider the learning objectives, the number of learners, and your organization's ability to efficiently deliver the material. Curriculum, content, and development must be designed and created for the topics you have identified to this point, tailored to your target audiences, along with the chosen training methods.

Training Methods

Training methods are described in detail in Chapter 9. However, it is worth mentioning some design and development considerations for the methods you are considering. When determining the best instructional method for your target groups, keep the following in mind:

- *Consider the people within your target group audience.* Consider the audience size, location, experience levels, and time constraints. If the audience is large and geographically dispersed, a technology-based solution, such as Web-based,

CD, satellite learning, or something similar, may work best. I've also developed non-technology–based training packages* that can easily be used for widely dispersed office locations. For small organizations, a classroom or work area learning activity may work best. Consider the language of your learners. In a bilingual environment or in a multinational company, some or all of the content may need to be provided in languages other than the organization's "official language."

■ *Consider the business needs.* If you have a limited budget, then providing an Internet-based online training module, or a non-technology–based training package such as one of those I've developed, may be appropriate. Another good alternative is bringing in an outside instructor with already prepared materials.

■ *Consider the course content.* Some topics are better suited for instructor-led, video, Web-based, or CBT delivery. Some topics, because of their complexity or difficulty, may need to have an accompanying reference guide for the participants to take back to use while they actively apply their learning in their job activities. There are many opinions about what type of method is best. Much depends on your organization. It will be helpful if you can get the advice of training professionals who can assess material and make recommendations. Chapter 9 discusses common training methods.

■ *Consider what kind of learner–instructor interaction is necessary.* Is the course content best presented as self-paced individual instruction or as group instruction? Some topics are best covered with face-to-face and group interaction, whereas others are best suited for individualized instruction. For example, if the goal is just to communicate policies and procedures, a technology-based solution may be the most appropriate. However, if learners need to perform problem-solving activities in a group to reinforce understanding or demonstrate appropriate actions, then a classroom setting, or a cooperative activity performed in groups over a set period of time would be better.

■ *Consider the type of presentations and activities necessary.* If the course content requires learners to fill out forms, using specialized software is probably best; to do role-playing, a classroom setting may be best.

■ *Consider the stability of the class content.* The stability of content is a cost issue. If content will change frequently—for instance, if procedures are expected to change as a result of mergers, acquisitions, or divestitures, or if new software systems are planned—the expense of changing the material needs to be estimated by considering the difficulty, time, and money involved. Some instructional methods can be changed more easily and cost-efficiently than others.

■ *Consider the technology available for training delivery.* This is a critical factor in deciding the instructional strategy. Will all learners have access to the technologies that you require? If doing Web-based training, will all learners have

---

* See all my training packages, tools, and supporting products at http://www.privacyprofessor .com.

access to the intranet or Internet? Do learners have the necessary bandwidth for certain types of multimedia? Also consider the sensitivity of the material. Content falling into the wrong hands can lead to security breaches, depending on the topic. Web-based training should not be used for sensitive content unless you can use strong encryption. Material for some topics may need to be presented in a classroom behind closed doors.

Design and Development

During the design and development phase, you will need to perform the following activities:

- Outline your class content. Clearly identify the three to five key points you want your learners to truly grasp and remember. See Appendix H: Privacy Sample Training Plans for an example of a form you can use to document the above types of issues.
- Divide into manageable instructional units or lessons. Most learners will remember three to five key points in short instructional units much better than if they are given a lot of information in a long instructional unit.
- Determine time requirements for each unit and lesson. Depending on the type of training, try not to go over 15 to 30 minutes for training that does not require the learner to engage and be active.
- Create content based on what personnel need to know to do their job. You should relate why the learning topic is important to the learner in terms they understand.
- Include interactive activities that can be taken back to their job and used immediately.
- Be clear about the actions and activities expected of the learners when performing their jobs.
- Describe the actions that the personnel should perform to demonstrate successfully meeting the objectives being taught.
- Build on existing capabilities and experiences within the group.
- Sequence topics to build new or complex skills on existing ones and to encourage and enhance the learner's motivation for learning the material.
- Use multiple learning methods.

Pitfalls to Avoid

- *Losing track of the learner.* Always stay focused on the learner in all aspects of training-content development. When designing training, it is easy to throw in information that is related to the topic, but that has no impact on the learner.

Likewise, it is easy to overlook something of significance. For example, when training executive leaders in regulatory security and privacy compliance, it may be easy to include interesting information, such as who authored the laws or the technical details for complying with the laws, when your audience may really just need to know the impact to your organization from the law, and the potential penalties and fines.

■ *Not reviewing feedback*. Review feedback from participants very carefully, looking for ways to improve the training. Some organizations have created new and updated training classes using only very few individuals for feedback, and have ignored the feedback from the majority of participants. You need to listen to your learners to ensure that you are meeting their professional security and privacy educational needs.

■ *Not involving the learners early in the development process*. Build the learners' interest and demand by involving them early in the development lifecycle and sustain their involvement throughout the life of the training. This way you also help to ensure the content will be something your learners will relate to and be engaged in learning about.

Design

Exhibit 1 is a sample generic-design road map, fashioned after a number of different design processes promoted by such adult education organizations as the American Society for Training and Development (ASTD),* which you can use as a starting point for your own design process.

Development

Exhibit 2 is a sample generic development road map, also fashioned after a number of different design processes promoted by adult educational organizations, as well as methods taught and promoted within adult education programs in universities. Use this as a starting point for your own development activities.

Choosing Content

The training content for each target group should be based on your information security and privacy policies and the associated standards, together with appropriate business unit practices and guidelines. Additionally, content must support applicable security and privacy laws, regulations, and accepted standards. The following example for privacy training lists the content topics common to some of

---

* http://www.astd.org/astd.

Exhibit 1   Design Process

Step	Action	Collect	Produce
1	Create a training outline for your topic based on the content you want to include, your target audiences, time lengths, baseline information, gap analysis, and other research done to date.	Goals and objectives for the training. Target learner perspectives.	High-level training outline or structure.
2	Expand on your outline by relating the content to your learner performance goals and objectives. Create lesson and course objectives and any necessary learning or job aids. Remember to chunk the information served to the learner in manageable pieces.	Outline and structure for class.	Course objectives; training and job aids; other necessary designs.
3	Break down the information from step 2 into more detail. Create specific objectives. Elaborate upon the topics covered.	Course objectives; training and job aids; other designs.	Detailed content to support the objectives.
4	Perform a quality review of the outline and details created so far to ensure completeness and adequacy of the plan. Validate the outline and structure. Obtain objective feedback from persons not on the development team. Also get feedback from subject matter experts (SMEs) and any type of training review board you have within your organization.	Design deliverables created so far.	Use a review checklist to provide feedback and identify areas for improvement and/or change.
5	Plan to develop all the content to fit the design. Coordinate required activities and identify personnel to perform the activities. Identify the types of evaluation tools within your plan.	Design deliverables collected so far.	Plan for developing and implementing the training, along with an evaluation plan.
6	Obtain approval and sign-off for the design. This will provide documented acknowledgment of your project progress, in addition to validating your design and deliverables.	Design and plans created so far.	Get approval and sign-off from the appropriate oversight entity.

Exhibit 2 Development Process

Step	Action	Collect	Produce
1	Finish your training design document and any identified training or job aids. Incorporate all the information the learners must have. Use applicable examples, analogies, scenarios, and so on. Include a table of contents, glossary, bibliography, and other useful references.	Design document and aids.	Draft of the training content deliverables.
2	Review the deliverables for both accuracy, technical soundness, and instructional appropriateness for the target group. Use development tools, such as a review checklist, to assist with the review process.	Draft of training content deliverables.	Reviewed and updated training content deliverables.
3	Perform a walkthough of the deliverables with the project team and at least one representative from the target group. This will provide practice, validate activities, and refine trainer/facilitator skills. Include your training review board member and SME.	Content deliverables.	Final form of training content and associated documents.
4	Obtain approval and sign-off for the final training content. This will provide documented acknowledgment of your project progress, in addition to validating your deliverables.	Training content and related deliverables.	Get approval and sign-off from the appropriate oversight entity.

the target groups that are described in more detail in Chapter 10 (core content), as well as the content that will need to be specialized for each target group (targeted content).

Core Content

1. Background and definition of privacy
2. Legal requirements
3. Your organization's privacy policy
4. Definition of personally identifiable information (PII) and similar terms

5. Customer privacy protection goals
6. Description of business impact
7. List of terms and definitions
8. Your organization's privacy program

Targeted Content

1. The privacy implications for the targeted group
2. Your organization's privacy fundamentals, rules, policies, standards, procedures, and guidelines applicable to the target group
3. Actions for the target group related to their job responsibilities, interactions with customers, interactions with third-party business partners, and so on
4. Exercises and other practice and reinforcement activities
5. Case studies
6. Review key points
7. Provide tools and checklists to meet privacy goals
8. Resources
9. Summary
10. Questions

For each of these items you will collect information to use within your training content and tools. As an example, Exhibit 3 is the type of content list you may want to include for item 5 in the core content, "Customer privacy protection goals."

Exhibit 3   Sample Content List

Content is based on customer privacy protection goals. Customer privacy training content must include information that supports your company's customer privacy goals and principles, in addition to covering applicable compliance requirements. When creating training curriculum, use the following to guide content development.

Customer Notice and Awareness

Consumers must be notified and/or made aware of your company information practices before any personal information is actually collected from them. These practices must be based on and support the company's customer privacy policy. Content should include instruction covering the following issues:

• General notice and awareness

• Identification of the personal information uses

• Identification of potential recipients of customer information

• Third-party limitations on customer information use

• The nature of the personal information collected

(continued)

Exhibit 3 (continued)

- Steps taken by your company to ensure customer information confidentiality
- Actions the company takes to ensure the integrity and quality of the customer information while in the company's custodial care

Customer Choice and Consent

Consumers must be given the option to decide what personal information collected about them is to be used and whether it may be used for secondary purposes. Content should include instruction covering the following issues:

- Choice of how personal information is used
- Choice of how personal information is shared
- Choice of what personal information is collected and stored

Customer Access and Participation

Define and communicate your goals for allowing or restricting consumer access to a particular site, service, or functionality based on whether or not the consumer provides their personal information. Based upon these goals, you must give consumers the ability to access or correct any personally identifiable information (PII) about them. Content should include instruction covering the following issues:

- Services and products requiring consumer PII
- Services and products where collecting consumer PII is optional
- Providing consumer access to their corresponding PII

Customer Information Integrity and Security

Customer information must be managed to maintain accuracy and security. Your goals should be to define the statements and practices made for maintaining security and integrity that are provided to customers. The messages to customers must not go into too much detail, or you risk compromising security. Content should include instruction covering the following issues:

- Company customer privacy mission statement
- Customer supplied integrity goals
- Use of anonymous PII
- Destroying untimely or sensitive PII
- Managerial measures to protect against loss and the unauthorized access, destruction, use, or disclosure of the PII
- Technical measures to protect against loss and the unauthorized access, destruction, use, or disclosure of PII

Exhibit 3   (continued)

Customer Information Privacy Policy Enforcement
Define and communicate your goals for addressing the mechanisms that are in place to enforce customer information privacy. The company customer privacy policy will indeed become merely suggestive, rather than prescriptive, if this communication does not occur. Describe the ways of working to ensure privacy and general customer privacy guidelines your company must follow. These directives must include both the company requirements as well as the legal and regulatory requirements. Content should include instruction covering the following issues:
• Operational customer privacy protection assurance
• Third-party customer privacy protection assurance
• Impact and redress for failure of customer privacy assurance

When you have created your content list, you are ready to start developing the details of each topic. As an example, Exhibit 4 lists topics and issues to include within the customer privacy training to help accomplish these goals.

Do something similar for each of your targeted training groups to develop your core content and targeted content. To give you a head start, use the following for inspiration.

Exhibit 4   Sample Customer Privacy Topics and Issues

Topics	Issues
Customer and Consumer Monitoring	• Tracking what consumers do on your company sites through means such as cookies. For the consumer's benefit, as when an electronic-commerce application maintains a shopping cart? Or, for your company benefit, either for purely statistical use or for profit by selling the aggregated information to third parties?
	• Monitoring that is incorporated into your company services
	• Monitoring to accumulate statistics
Customer Information Aggregation	• How previously gathered customer information is combined with information from other sources

(*continued*)

Exhibit 4   (continued)

Topics	Issues
Customer Information Storage	• How customer information records are stored in your company systems
	• What customer information is stored in your company systems
	• What security monitoring is in place
	• What audit logs are created
	• Who has access to customer information in storage
Customer Information Transfer	• How customer information is transferred to third parties
	• When and to where is customer information transferred outside your company control
	• When is customer information shared with others
	• Is customer information sold to others
	• What limitations exist for sharing and transferring customer information
Customer Information Collection	• What customer information is collected directly by asking the customer for it
	• What customer information is collected indirectly such as through browsers or network devices
Customer Information Personalization	• When consumers change their personal information, and how
	• When consumers are allowed to customize their information in such locations such as cookies
	• How consumer personalization of Web sites is accomplished
	• How consumer personalization of your company services is accomplished
	• How consumer personalization of advertising, offers, and promotions is accomplished

Exhibit 4 (continued)

Topics	Issues
Customer Contact	• For what purposes your company contacts consumers using their personal information; for assistance, such as validating an address, or something that could be annoying, such as for an unrequested promotion
	• How is customer information used and contact made for security and verification
	• How customer information is used and contact made based on profiling

Job-Specific Content and Topics for Targeted Groups

Here is a laundry list of job-specific content to help you get started with creating your own list of information needs to fit your organizational target groups:

- Security and privacy advocates
  - Roles and responsibilities
  - Applicable laws
  - Privacy administration
  - Security administration
  - Policies, standards, and procedures
  - When to escalate situations
  - Key contacts for questions about laws, policies, incidents, and so on
  - Physical-protection issues
  - Technical-protection issues
  - Sanctions/disciplinary actions
  - Mitigation for privacy incidents, such as following unauthorized disclosure of customer information
- Executive management and security and privacy champions
  - Responsibilities as corporate leaders
  - Recent internal and external security and privacy incidents
  - Applicable laws
    Company security and privacy policies
  - Sanctions/disciplinary actions
  - Key contacts
- Marketing and sales
  - Roles and responsibilities
  - Applicable laws

- Privacy procedures for marketing
- Customer and consumer monitoring
- Customer information aggregation
- Customer information personalization
- Key contacts
- Sanctions/disciplinary actions

■ Customer support and contact
- Roles and responsibilities
- Applicable laws
- Security and privacy procedures for customer and consumer contact
- Dealing with the unexpected
- Key contacts
- Mitigation for customer concerns and complaints
- Sanctions/disciplinary actions

■ Research and development
- Roles and responsibilities
- Information security and privacy policies
- Applications, systems, and privacy implications
- Technical-protection issues
- Security and privacy standards for development and research
- Customer information storage
- Customer contacts
- Sanctions/disciplinary actions
- Key contacts

■ Information technology personnel
- Roles and responsibilities
- Information security and privacy policies
- Applications, systems, and privacy implications
- Technical-protection issues
- Security and privacy standards for systems development
- Customer information storage
- Customer information aggregation
- Customer information transfer
- Customer contacts
- Sanctions/disciplinary actions
- Key contacts

■ Third-party-contracted on-site staff
- Information security and privacy policies
- Information security and privacy procedures
- Applicable laws
- Partner and business-associate expectations
- Customer information transfer

- Customer information storage
- Customer information personalization
- Escalation process
- Key contacts
■ Third parties (consultants, business partners, etc.)
    - Information security and privacy policies
    - Applicable laws
    - Applicable contractual requirements
    - Customer information transfer
    - Customer information storage
    - Customer information personalization
    - Partner and business associate expectations and requirements
    - Key contacts
■ Legal and HR
    - Security and privacy roles and responsibilities
    - Applicable laws
    - Individual rights
    - Security and privacy administration overview
    - Security and privacy incident escalation procedures overview
    - Customer and consumer monitoring
    - Customer contact
    - Key contacts
    - Sanctions/disciplinary actions
    - Mitigation for noncompliance
■ Trainers
    - Security and privacy roles and responsibilities
    - Applicable laws
    - Security and privacy policies
    - Security and privacy procedures
    - Recent internal and external security and privacy incidents
    - Security and privacy administration
    - Security and privacy incident escalation
    - Customer and consumer monitoring
    - Customer information aggregation
    - Customer information storage
    - Customer information transfer
    - Customer information collection
    - Customer information personalization
    - Customer contact
    - Target security and privacy groups
    - Physical-protection issues
    - Technical-protection issues

- Sanctions/disciplinary actions
- Mitigation for risks and incidents
- Key contacts
■ All employees
- Organization security and privacy roles and responsibilities
- Applicable laws
- Company privacy policies
- Company privacy procedures
- Security and privacy incident escalation
- Physical-protection issues
- Technical-protection issues
- Sanctions/disciplinary actions
- Mitigation for noncompliance and incidents
- Key contacts
■ New employees
- Information security and privacy policies
- Applicable laws
- Sanctions/disciplinary actions
- Key contacts

Learning Activities

There are many instructional elements that will be consistent from course to course regardless of the instructional methods used. Most courses will involve content delivery through voice, text, and graphics. To make instruction more effective, you may also incorporate the use of pictures, video, demonstrations, role-playing, simulations, case studies, and interactive exercises where possible and applicable. Using just one type of delivery medium over an extended period of time could easily result in the loss of interest of your learners. Several of these presentation methods will be used in most courses. Remember that it is generally considered most effective for learner understanding to deliver the same message and information multiple times using multiple methods. All your learners have their own unique learning styles, and what works well for one person will not necessarily be effective for the others. Develop your instructional methods based on instructional objectives, course content, delivery options, implementation options, technological capabilities, and the available resources.

Web-based training is often a good alternative for large audiences and to provide an overview of the topic and communicate policies and facts. However, this type of instruction method is often not appropriate for audiences who are learning procedures, or to demonstrate how to act in a specific type of situation in which role-playing is necessary.

Effective security and privacy training is necessary to help you achieve security and privacy compliance. There are many resources freely available on the Internet. Keep in mind that these can be helpful, but that any training needs to be tailored to the organization's own unique environment and needs. To be effective, organizations must take advantage of different types of training methods. Training must support making security and privacy policies and procedures a learned and consistently practiced behavior. Exhibit 5 provides examples of learning activities to incorporate into your training sessions as applicable to the topic, audience, and training method.

Exhibit 5   Examples of Participatory Learning Activities

Activity	Example
Scenario Discussions	• Provide an illustration of a scene where multiple information security and privacy risks are represented and ask the learning participates to work in teams, or individually in small organizations, to identify the risks and then to describe how to mitigate the risks. I have created a series of such activities that you can view at http://www.privacyguidance.com/security_search.html.
	• Show short clips from a video, movie, news program, television show, and so on. Open for discussion as related to the training topic.
	• Have participants read from a script on the topic. Stop at a point within the script, and discuss the reactions of the class, possible solutions, and other issues with the class. You can build scenario scripts based on interviews from your key contacts. Make sure you let them know you would like to do this and get their buy-in; and preserve their anonymity if they so request.
Practice	• Demonstrate how to respond to customer calls asking about how personal information is protected, then have participants practice answering similar questions.
	• Provide encryption devices or computers with encryption software and have participants practice encrypting and decrypting files.
Case Studies	• Provide reality-based cases dealing with different privacy issues. Use recent news related to privacy incidents, or recent incidents within your organization. Have teams identify key problems, issues, solutions, and so on.
	• Provide real information security incident stories and have participant groups identify ways to reduce risks to prevent the incidents from recurring.

(continued)

Exhibit 5 (continued)

Activity	Example
Brainstorming	• Brainstorm as a group ways to verify the identity of callers.
	• Brainstorm good ways to protect mobile computing devices, such as smart phones and laptops, while traveling and staying in hotels.
Role Playing	• Have participants role-play regulators and IT administrators discussing the appropriate control settings on firewalls, why the settings were chosen, and so on.
	• Have participants role-play a customer and a customer representative with the customer expressing concerns about the company's compliance with the posted privacy policy.
Hands On	• Ask participants to execute vulnerability assessment tools on a provided network.
	• Ask participants to write and explain an updated version of the organization's Web site privacy policy.

Training Design Objectives

You should remember that the objectives for designing and developing your information security and privacy training sessions should include the following:

■ Provide a framework that supports your information security and privacy training
■ Arm your personnel with the information necessary to incorporate correct security and privacy actions into their job functions
■ Infuse security and privacy practices into your company's culture
■ Heighten practitioner awareness of security and privacy fundamentals
■ Create a global network of security and privacy advocates
■ Establish a standard for related initiatives, such as other training and awareness programs, within your organization
■ Introduce security and privacy into professional performance criteria
■ Clearly demonstrate the company's commitment to preserving information security and privacy
■ Foster customer relationships built on trust
■ Enable deeper insights into consumer privacy needs, enhancing consumer confidence, and more effectively meeting consumer needs across multiple points of contact with your company, resulting in greater consumer loyalty
■ Provide a competitive edge

- Ensure that everyone within your company knows about new and emerging security and privacy requirements
- Make employees aware of their obligations under the organization's security and privacy policies
- Measure security and privacy awareness levels
- Communicate your company's legal and regulatory security and privacy obligations and impact to the employees
- Obtain visible support from the executive management for security and privacy initiatives
- Comply with regulatory requirements for security and privacy training
- Keep security and privacy in the minds of personnel while they perform daily job tasks

Chapter 14

Awareness Materials Design and Development

Creative thinking may mean simply the realization that there's no particular virtue in doing things the way they have always been done.

—Rudolph Flesch

Contrasting Awareness and Training

Awareness is not the same as training. In contrast to training, awareness can occur at the same time everywhere and on a continuous basis. Information security and privacy awareness activities promote ongoing compliance and keep the issues in the minds of your personnel. Remember that as business models change, so do compliance needs and awareness activities.

Awareness activities are different from training activities. The objectives for ensuring security and privacy awareness are similar to training options. However, there are some very important differences between training and awareness activities. The options and methods for awareness activities are typically much different than the more formal and structured training.

Awareness activities should

- occur on an ongoing basis,
- use a wide range of delivery methods,
- catch the attention of the target audience,
- be less formal than training,
- take less time than training,

- be even more creative and fun than training sessions,
- reinforce the lessons learned during formal training, or act as a forerunner to receiving training.

Awareness is typically the "what" component of your education strategy for influencing behavior and practice; training is typically the "how" component to implement security and privacy. To make awareness activities effective, you should know your audience. Awareness audiences are very broad; they include everyone within your company, all those third parties who do work for or on behalf of your company, and often your customers and consumers. Awareness audiences have diverse experiences, backgrounds, and job responsibilities. The awareness goal, at the decision making level, is to convince the audience that security and privacy risk reduction is achievable, in addition to ensuring that organization leaders are aware of their legal and regulatory obligations. Awareness goals at the end-user level are to

- understand information security and privacy risks within the context of job activities and responsibilities, and know the measures to reduce them;
- create a demand for risk reduction as a result of better understanding risks and legal obligations.

An information security and privacy awareness strategy should be developed and customized, with attention paid to the following:

- Utilizing existing awareness programs, probably with modification to fit your program, wherever possible
- Determining the overall effectiveness of current programs
- Determining current levels of security and privacy awareness knowledge
- Considering the history of security and privacy incidents and how they were resolved
- Estimating risk of security and privacy incidents within identified departments and teams
- Identifying events that lead to security and privacy awareness degradation
- Documenting ongoing activities to reinforce and support continuing security and privacy awareness and diligence in security and privacy compliance
- Outlining timing for awareness activities
- Considering language-based and regional challenges

Make Awareness Interesting

Awareness must not be boring. Here are nine ways to make awareness interesting:

- Use analogies.
- Use recent, significant, real-world examples.

- Explain, in clear and easy-to-understand terms, the importance of the topic being covered.
- Use scenarios and sticky situations (for example, "What would you do if … ?").
- Make it interactive; involve your recipients in the activity.
- Make it memorable (for example, using good humor can make a concept more memorable).
- Consider awareness as "social marketing" and emphasize the importance of security and privacy; get audiences to alter old ideas, understand and accept new ideas, and value their new awareness enough to change attitudes and take positive, effective action to address security and privacy.
- Keep awareness fresh; do not keep reusing the same messages and activities that you've been using over the past year … or years.
- Make awareness messages practical; do not ask the recipients to do more than they are realistically able to do.

Awareness Methods

Think of positive, fun, exciting, and motivating methods that will give employees the message and keep the privacy issues in their mind as they perform their daily job responsibilities. The success of an awareness program is the ability to reach all personnel using a variety of techniques.

Keep in mind that some awareness activities that are very effective for one organization may be completely inappropriate in another organization. You need to use awareness in ways that are acceptable and constructive within your organization.

The following is a list of suggestions to be included in the awareness materials and methods for a wide range of organizations. You may see a suggestion for an awareness event that you think is absolutely ludicrous, but another type of organization may find it quite beneficial. This list will help you brainstorm your own unique and creative awareness activities.

1. Invite guest speakers to give presentations and talks about information security and privacy topics.
2. Obtain a celebrity endorsement of your organization's customer information security and privacy goals; use the endorsement internally and within marketing materials.
3. Host information privacy and/or security awareness days (see Appendix M).
4. Create information security and privacy newsletters to give to your customers and consumers.
5. Create employee information security and privacy newsletters.
6. Create information security and privacy newsletters to give to your consultants, business partners, and contract vendors.
7. Write and publish articles in enterprise-wide newsletters and publications.

8. Maintain intranet Web sites with security and privacy tips and guidance.
9. Display information security and privacy posters: in parking lots, cafeterias, vending areas, meeting rooms, teams locations, restrooms, and so on. Some organizations have indicated increased awareness by posting on the inside of restroom stall doors.
10. Post information security and privacy banners over doorways.
11. Include information security and privacy pamphlets within personnel paycheck envelopes.
12. Send direct mailings of pamphlets or letters to personnel homes.
13. Hold staff and team meeting discussions during a set time each week, month, or quarterly.
14. Host team or department retreats to discuss security and privacy issues.
15. Establish information security and privacy mascots, logos, and/or taglines (see Appendix F).
16. Place attention-grabbing and recurring headlines on the intranet.
17. Host information security and privacy lunch presentations.
18. Hold departmental presentations.
19. Hold organization-wide presentations.
20. Post motivational or catchy slogans on screen savers, browser marquees, and so on.
21. Display a random information security and privacy tip (see http://www .infostruct.net/sectips/ for example of this done with information security tips).
22. Make information security and privacy videotapes and DVDs available in the corporate library. For some ideas, see Appendix S.
23. Hold showings of information security and privacy videotapes or DVDs.
24. Make computer-based awareness quizzes, games, and so on available.
25. Print and distribute brochures and flyers.
26. Distribute tokens, knick-knacks, and other types of promotional items such as the following with short information security and privacy messages.
    - Pens
    - Pencils
    - Key chains
    - Note pads
    - Sticky notes
    - Other types of promotional items
27. Provide information security and privacy stickers for doors and bulletin boards.
28. Publish cartoons and/or other visuals monthly or quarterly in in-house newsletter or specific department notices.
29. Post an information security and privacy thought or advice of the day or week, on bulletin boards, Web sites, and so on.
30. Print and distribute special topical bulletins.
31. Send monthly e-mail notices related to information security and privacy issues.

32. Implement security and privacy banners or pre-logon messages that appear on the computer monitor.
33. Distribute food items with awareness messages. For example, packages of chocolate that have attached labels with sayings like "Maintaining Privacy is Sweet."
34. Ask your cafeteria to create cupcakes with your privacy or security mascot or logo; especially timely to do during international computer security day or some other special, designated privacy or security day or week (see Appendix M).
35. Create special fortune cookies with privacy and awareness logos or slogans inside.
36. Provide a travel first aid kit with an information security and privacy slogan printed on the package, such as "Help ensure healthy information security and privacy."
37. Provide badge holders with an information security or privacy slogan, such as "Protect Privacy" or "Think Private Thoughts."
38. Distribute flashlights with a label similar to "Spotlight information security and privacy."
39. Provide public information security and privacy law information to personnel.
40. Send occasional messages to executives with security and privacy guidance.
41. Provide links to U.S. federal or international information security and privacy reports.
42. Post an information security and privacy reading list (see Appendix S).
43. Post an information security and privacy Web sites list (see Appendix S).
44. Post information-security- and privacy-related templates.
45. Post an information security and privacy glossary (see Appendix T).
46. Send prerecorded voice mails with information security and privacy messages from executives to targeted groups and personnel.
47. Send prerecorded voice mails with information security and privacy messages from executives to all organizational members.
48. Show movies related to and supporting information security and privacy. For example, the James Woods movie *The Billion Dollar Bubble* is a good one to show the need for internal controls to prevent fraud (see Appendix S).
49. Implement browser pop-ups with information security and privacy messages. (Make sure this is something acceptable within your environment and won't annoy your network users more than it helps their awareness.)
50. Post information security and privacy messages within other types of application logons banners that change weekly or monthly.
51. Observe International Computer Security Day activities (November 30).
52. Post instructions to users about how to backup their information from their personal and/or mobile computing devices.
53. Post reminders about business continuity contacts for each department or team.
54. Hold an information security and privacy poster contest.
55. Host demonstrations of security and/or privacy software used by your organization.

56. Pick a privacy or information security policy and publicize it each month, explaining why the policy is needed.
57. Publicize recent news about information security and privacy on an intranet site.
58. Place new information security or privacy tips each week or month within your network logon banner.
59. Have a drawing and give the winners a copy of an information security and/or privacy book.
60. Give an information security and privacy presentation at intern's or children's schools.
61. Recognize an employee each month as being outstanding for his or her information security and privacy practices.
62. Host chat sessions to provide computer users with a basic understanding of computer security.
63. Post an information security and privacy tip list in the computer operations room.
64. Select a computer system on which to perform a risk analysis and communicate the results to the department personnel, indicating how they each can contribute to improve the outcome.
65. Hold a discussion of ethics with computer users.
66. Volunteer to speak about computer security or information privacy at a local computer club or school.
67. Post information on your intranet site about how other organizations recognize International Computer Security Day (November 30), or other designated security and/or privacy days (see Appendix M).
68. Participate in a local computer security or privacy meeting or seminar.
69. Attend a national information security and privacy conference or seminar and report back to coworkers the highlights.
70. Circulate e-mail alerts to appropriate audiences when new information security and privacy laws are enacted.
71. Hold an information security and privacy organization-wide *Jeopardy!* type of contest event.
72. Hold monthly or quarterly drawings and give away security software to personnel to use on their home systems (for example, personal firewalls, antivirus software, and so on).
73. Have an information security and privacy theme for your organization's cafeteria menu.
74. Locate information security and privacy bulletin boards throughout the facilities.
75. Provide laptop users with physical security locks (such as Kensington locks) to protect their devices while traveling.
76. Print and distribute cards to people with handheld computing devices giving tips on how to protect the devices from theft and loss.
77. Implement information security and privacy screensavers.

78. Make online information security and privacy slide presentations available to personnel.
79. Provide personnel and business partners an information security checklist.
80. Provide personnel and business partners an information privacy checklist.
81. Provide an occasional information security or privacy announcement over the loud speaker.
82. Provide mobile and home workers with surge protector strips and uninterruptrible power supply (UPS) devices.
83. Incorporate information security and privacy practices into the job appraisal process.
84. Provide personal privacy self-assessments on cards or posters for personnel.
85. Create an information security and privacy suggestion "box" area on your intranet for ideas on how to improve.
86. Award 4 or 8 hours of vacation time to personnel who are the first to notify the security or privacy area of a significant new security or privacy risk or threat.
87. Change the lyrics to popular songs and tunes with lyrics changed to relate to your information privacy and/or security program. Record, perform, and/or provide lyrics to target groups.
88. Hold an event and offer hot air balloon rides. Put a security and/or privacy message on the balloon.
89. Sponsor community events and activities on behalf of the information privacy and/or security department.
90. Create logos and graphic symbols to represent security and privacy activities.
91. Create stories, fables and myths about security and privacy issues.
92. Hold debates between different departments or teams for information security and privacy issues.
93. Hold brainstorming sessions for miscellaneous security and privacy issues.
94. Post charts, graphs, diagrams, and maps related to information security and privacy on billboards, cafeteria tables, and snack area walls.
95. Sponsor sports teams, reflecting information security or privacy in the team names (for example, the Hacker Hunters).
96. Sponsor sporting events or tournaments, posting banners with the information security and privacy logo at the event.
97. Hold short sessions, at lunch, before work, or during breaks, and select attendees to role-play various types of people involved with information security and privacy. For example, help desk personnel, customers, compliance officers, law enforcement, and so on to determine their understanding of what these roles should do in certain situations.
98. Put on skits and plays with an information privacy or security message at company events; for example, the classic Monty Python "Spam" skit modified to apply to e-mail spam.
99. Hold an information security and privacy fair (like a science fair) and ask representatives from target groups to submit an entry.

100. Take target groups on field trips to other companies with exceptional privacy or security programs, to tour disaster recovery facilities, and so on.
101. Provide hands-on experiments related to information security and privacy in public gathering areas of the company during lunch times or while other events take place nearby. For example, how biometric authentication works, or how to use a smart phone lock.
102. Hold an information security and privacy event during autumn with an autumn theme.
103. Hold an information security and privacy event during winter with a winter theme.
104. Hold an information security and privacy event during spring with a spring theme.
105. Hold an information security and privacy event during summer with a summer theme.
106. Sponsor a golf outing on behalf of the information security and privacy team and label the holes with related terminology.
107. Sponsor a tennis tournament on behalf of the information security and privacy team and award a trophy with the information security and privacy mascot or logo engraved upon it.
108. Sponsor any other type of sports event and place information security and privacy banners or mascot images in strategic locations.
109. Create sunshades for car windshields with the information security and privacy mascot or logo.
110. Create games (board games, card games, and so on) with information security and privacy themes.
111. Give all personnel, or target groups, short monthly information security and privacy quizzes and award small prizes.
112. Create coffee mugs and tea cups with privacy and awareness logos or slogans.
113. Create pop can and bottle coolies with privacy and awareness logos or slogans.
114. Create rulers with privacy or security sayings, such as "measuring security success" or something similar.
115. Create memo wipe boards with privacy and awareness logos or slogans.
116. Create staplers, memo minders, and desk caddies with privacy and awareness logos or slogans.
117. Create trash cans with built-in paper shredders in the top, and privacy and awareness logos or slogans printed on the shredder, or on the side.
118. Create calendars with a daily privacy and awareness reminder, policy, logo, or slogan.
119. Create clocks and paperweights with privacy and awareness logos or slogans.
120. Create computer monitor screen sweeper with privacy and awareness logos or slogans.
121. Create mirrors to attach to the computer monitor or magnetically stick to steel overhead shelves with privacy and awareness logos or slogans.

122. Create monitor toppers with privacy and awareness logos or slogans.
123. Create retractable badge holders or phone cord holders with privacy and awareness logos or slogans.
124. Implement an information security and privacy blog on your intranet to allow for discussion of related issues.
125. Create luggage locks, luggage tags, and key chains with privacy and awareness logos or slogans.
126. Create folding travel mirrors, combs, and brushes with privacy and awareness logos or slogans.
127. Create travel toothbrush holders with privacy and awareness logos or slogans.
128. Create personal care kits, with clippers, tweezers, and so on, with privacy and awareness logos or slogans.
129. Create stress balls, stars, or in the shape of your security and privacy mascot with privacy and awareness logos or slogans.
130. Create tape measures or tool kits with functional screwdrivers and other tools with privacy and awareness logos or slogans.
131. Print "Million Dollar Bills" with privacy and awareness logos or slogans printed on the back of them.
132. Create head bobbers that look like your security and privacy mascot.
133. Create crazy straws with security and privacy logos or slogans attached to the tops of the straws.
134. Create jigsaw puzzles with your security and privacy mascot or logo.
135. Use security and privacy terms to create crossword puzzles, word searches, word scrambles, and other similar activities. See an example crossword puzzle in Appendix V.
136. Create information security and privacy bingo boards to hand out and play during awareness events.
137. Provide a list of information security and privacy mail lists to which your target groups can subscribe to stay up to date with various security and privacy issues. See Appendix S for a partial list of possible mail lists.
138. Give recognition or prizes to personnel who spot and report information security and privacy risks they observe in television programs, movies, books, song lyrics, and other popular entertainment media.
139. Join a professional privacy organization, such as the International Association of Privacy Professionals (IAPP).
140. Join a professional information security organization, such as the Computer Security Institute, the Information Systems Security Association (ISSA), the Information Systems Audit and Control Association (ISACA), and so on.
141. Provide a workshop or demonstration on home security, such as protecting a home from burglary, shredding personal information before putting out with the curbside trash, and so on.
142. Provide a workshop or demonstration on office ergonomics and how to keep information secure while you keep yourself comfortable computing.

143. Provide a workshop on preventing identity theft, protecting children's Internet surfing, and so on.
144. Implement a Twitter-like service on the internal corporate network to put out brief messages throughout the day about information security, privacy and related compliance activities.
145. Create short, 2- to 4-minute, information security podcasts and make available from intranet Web sites.
146. Create short, 2- to 4-minute, privacy podcasts and make available from intranet Web sites.
147. Make instructions available, via intranet Web sites, e-mail messages, and so on, to personnel for how to download the podcasts to MP3 players.
148. Create short videos about current information security topics and post on corporate intranet sites.
149. Create short videos about how personnel can protect their own personally identifiable information and post on intranet Web sites.
150. Create short videos about how to spot social engineering attempts and post on intranet sites.
151. Post the videos that do not contain any confidential information or PII on YouTube and other Internet Web sites, for personnel, business partners, and customers to download.
152. Make instructions available to personnel for how to download videos to their own computers and other types of video players.
153. Create an information security and privacy newsletter and distribute monthly, quarterly, or twice a year.
154. Subscribe to the *Protecting Information* quarterly journal and provide to personnel, business partners, and their families (see http://www.privacyguidance.com) to provide ongoing, effective, awareness communications to your personnel.
155. Use the ideas from the "Awareness Advisor" (comes with the *Protecting Information* subscription) to measure awareness improvements, along with additional new and emerging awareness method.
156. Host a quarterly, biannual or yearly "Meet the Experts" question-and-answer session with the information security and privacy sponsor, privacy officer, and information security officer.
157. Volunteer to provide an information security or privacy presentation at a local elementary or secondary school.
158. Volunteer to provide an information security or privacy presentation at the local parent/teacher's meeting.
159. Provide a guide for personnel to use to backup their data on their home computers.
160. Provide a security and privacy checklist for home and mobile workers.
161. Post a message to your organization's intranet site on January 28 letting your personnel know it is Data Privacy Day (see Appendix M).

162. Offer to give a short talk or presentation at your child's school, your local ISACA, ISSA, Infragard, IAPP, or other professional organization, about privacy.

163. Route a good article about privacy to your personnel, to your friends and family, and/or to your membership organizations. There are many out there to choose from. Just a few of mine you may want to consider include
    - "Herding Grasshoppers: Regulatory Awareness Requirements": This article gives advice on keeping training and awareness programs current and effective, and not letting them "die on the vine" after the programs' initial rollout. (http://www.privacyguidance.com/etraining_awareness.html)
    - "The Eyes Have It": This article discusses the risks of cell phone cameras, contains advice on addressing such risks, and includes URLs of cell phone camera resources. (http://www.privacyguidance.com/etechnology_articles.html)
    - "E-mail Privacy and Security": Your organization scans e-mail for malicious software, but have you considered all important e-mail privacy and security issues? (http://www.privacyguidance.com/etechnology_articles.html)
    - "Quit Bugging Me": Web bugs can be much more invasive than cookies, yet they have not received as much press as I would have expected. (http://www.privacyguidance.com/etechnology_articles.html)
    - "Don't Give Away Privacy!": Have you considered using a degausser before disposing electronic media? This article contains a degaussing FAQ. (http://www.privacyguidance.com/etechnology_articles.html)
    - "Employee Online Privacy": What should you do if you find an unflattering photo of one of your employees on the Internet? Should you fire him or her? I discuss this issue and others regarding the use and trustworthiness of online information about organizations and their employees. (http://www.privacyguidance.com/egeneral_privacy.html)
    - "What Is the Difference between Privacy and Security?": This article covers the relationship between privacy and security and the essential relationship of privacy and security programs. (http://www.privacyguidance.com/egeneral_privacy.html)
    - "Is There Privacy Beyond Death?": Do you have the right to privacy after you die? Should your loved-ones have access to your personal information? (http://www.privacyguidance.com/egeneral_privacy.html)

164. Arrange a lunch-time event, such as a question-and-answer session with executives, about information security and/or privacy at your organization.

165. Give a short presentation about privacy or information security to targeted business units, such as HR or marketing.

166. Show a film about privacy. There are many options to choose from! PBS has shown some great programs on privacy. Check your library, also. It would cost your organization nothing to check out a film for the day to show to your personnel. Also see Appendix S for some ideas.

167. Hold a trivia game about privacy. See Appendix S for some ideas.

168. Arrange an exhibit and provide a table with various privacy tools, such as privacy screen filters, self-encrypting USB drives, etc., and answer questions people may have about them.

169. Make a podcast available to your personnel that discusses privacy in general, or a specific privacy issue. Some of mine that you may want to consider are located at http://www.realtime-itcompliance.com/podcast/.

170. Have a contest for your employees to see which one can identify the most significant employee privacy concern within your organization.

171. Have a contest for your employees to see which one can identify a way in which current procedures put customer and/or employee personally identifiable information (PII) at risk.

172. Have a contest for your employees to see which one can write and submit the most humorous or creative privacy poem, haiku, etc.

173. Have a contest for your employees to see which one can create the best workplace privacy poster.

174. Hold a "Privacy *Jeopardy!*" event in January, or on any of the other special days, weeks, or months listed in Appendix M, during lunchtime, perhaps right outside your cafeteria, and give small prizes or recognitions to the people who correctly answer a privacy-related question.

175. Do a podcast about a privacy incident you were involved with or are concerned about. Share your viewpoints!

176. Download a podcast about a security or privacy topic and play for your personnel from my Web site at http://www.realtime-itcompliance.com/podcast/. Some companies tell me that they have used my podcasts for training and awareness events for their personnel. Here are some I have made available (all on the same Web page; just scroll to see each):
    – Data De-identification and Masking Methods
    – What IT Leaders Need to Know About Using Production Data for Testing
    – Demystifying Privacy Laws: What You Need to Know to Protect Your Business
    – Information Security and Privacy Professionals MUST Work Together to be Successful
    – How to Effectively Address Privacy in Business

177. Film a short video discussing a privacy incident or topic of concern. Here are a few places to get some ideas, which you could also show on Data Privacy Day (January 28) or sometime during that week:
    – Privacy Issues, Photos, and the Internet (http://www.youtube.com/watch?v=-lSkY4X3yNA&feature=related). This is a GREAT one for the marketing folks to watch!
    – Internet Privacy Video (http://www.youtube.com/watch?v=ofEdTMIadus). This is highly informational! However, be aware that it is very loud, and does contain profanity and other expressions that some organizations, or the folks therein, may find offensive.

   - Privacy and Social Networks (http://www.youtube.com/watch?v=X7gWEgHeXcA)
   - Invasion of Privacy (http://www.youtube.com/watch?v=BGrji2bIiG8)
178. Hold an awareness and training event to encourage personnel to discuss and share viewpoints about information security and privacy issues. I've done some very successful training events that had long-term learning benefits; see a package I created to hold such an event, my Privacy Professor Search #1, at http://www.privacyguidance.com/security_search.html
179. Hold a shredding event at your workplace, for your school, in your neighborhood, in your church, or some other location. Work with your local shredding companies; most will be happy to come to a site for such an event and make their shredders and high-power degaussers (for digital storage devices) available for use. See the Document Shredding Organization for more information and possible shredding vendors you can contact. (http://document-shredding.org)
180. Give each of your personnel who are mobile workers a self-encrypting USB drive, such as IronKey, to protect the confidential information they take out of your organization.
181. Hold an "Information Security and Privacy" fair over the lunch time in your organization, and have a booth/table for each of your departments that impacts privacy, including Information Security, Physical Security, Privacy, Legal, Human Resources, Compliance and any others you have. Have knowledgeable representatives from each of these departments answer any questions they get from your personnel about related privacy issues.
182. Invite a privacy or security expert from your area to talk about privacy issues to targeted groups within your organization, or as a type of lunch and learn awareness event.
183. Offer to discuss a privacy topic with one of your local schools, colleges, churches, or other types of nonprofit organizations.
184. Offer to discuss an information security topic with one of your local schools, colleges, churches, or other types of nonprofit organizations.
185. Arrange with a local small- and medium-sized business (SMB) supplies warehouse, such as Costco, Sam's Club, other similar retail wholesalers, to provide a privacy tutorial at their site on Data Privacy Day (January 28) or on each day of that week.
186. Hold a "Privacy Scavenger Hunt" by providing a list of privacy-related situations for personnel to take a photo of *outside* of the work environment and bring in to submit to the information security and/or privacy office.
187. Hold a "Privacy Scavenger Hunt" by providing a list of privacy-related situations for personnel to take a photo of *inside* of the work environment and bring in to submit to the information security and/or privacy office.
188. Hold an "Information Security Scavenger Hunt" by providing a list of information-security–related situations for personnel to take a photo of

outside of the work environment and bring in to submit to the information security and/or privacy office.

189. Hold an "Information Security Scavenger Hunt" by providing a list of privacy-related situations for personnel to take a photo of *inside* of the work environment and bring in to submit to the information security and/or privacy office.

190. Hold a "Privacy Scavenger Hunt" by providing a list of privacy-related items for personnel to find *outside* of the work environment and bring in to submit to the information security and/or privacy office.

191. Hold a "Privacy Scavenger Hunt" by providing a list of privacy-related items for personnel to find *inside* of the work environment and bring in to submit to the information security and/or privacy office.

192. Hold an "Information Security Scavenger Hunt" by providing a list of information security related items for personnel to find *outside* of the work environment and bring in to submit to the information security and/or privacy office.

193. Hold an "Information Security Scavenger Hunt" by providing a list of information-security-related items for personnel to find *inside* of the work environment and bring in to submit to the information security and/or privacy office.

194. Send text messages once a week, once a month, or whenever a significant incident or action has occurred to make personnel aware.

195. Create bookmarks with information security and privacy quotes and/or your privacy and security mascot and make available for personnel to use not only at work, but also for their family members and friends away from work.

196. Establish an internal micro-blog system, similar to Twitter, and send occasional information security, privacy, or compliance messages or "tweets" out for anyone in the company to see.

197. Have a contest to see who can create the most original song dedicated to information security.

198. Have a contest to see who can create the most original song dedicated to privacy.

199. Have a contest to see who can create the best, or most imaginative, information security haiku or other type of poem.

200. Have a contest to see who can create the best, or most imaginative, privacy haiku or other type of poem.

201. Create a poster showing the many areas where information security and privacy overlap in general and post copies throughout your enterprise facilities.

202. Create a poster showing the many areas where information security and privacy overlap with specific regard to your own organization and post copies throughout your enterprise facilities.

203. Have a contest for personnel to create a poster showing the many ways in which privacy and security overlap, then post copies of the top 5, 10, or more throughout your enterprise facilities.

204. Form study groups and provide rooms for those seeking their CISSP, CIPP, CISM, CISA, and other types of professional certifications.

205. Post a daily or weekly information security or privacy tip on your corporate intranet home page.
206. Leave "Posts of Praise" (print messages that contain praise) for people you find who are demonstrating exemplary information security and privacy practices.
207. Create a mind map (see http://www.mindmap.com/) showing your organization's information security and privacy strategy within your business, and put them on posters displayed throughout your enterprise.
208. Put the mind maps mentioned above on your information security and privacy intranet page, on reports, and so on.
209. Create candy bar wrappers with information security and/or privacy messages or themes (similar to the "Congratulations It's A Boy" or "Congratulations It's A Girl" types of wrappers), put onto candy bars, health bars or other types of treats and give to personnel who are demonstrating good security and privacy habits.
210. Designate a "change your password day" and then provide tips for your personnel for how to change all their passwords on that day, including not only their business passwords, but also their cell phone passwords, voicemail passwords, passwords on their personal computers, and so on.
211. Designate a "check your computer day" and then provide tips for your personnel for how to check for a wide range of malware on that day, including not only on their business systems, but also their personal computers.
212. Display a new poster every month, or every other week, in key locations throughout your facilities. There are a very wide range of sites with posters available for downloading or ordering. A few of these are found in Appendix S.
213. Provide a weekly or monthly "Breach of the Week" (or month), and provide an analysis of a recent privacy breach and explain how to prevent a similar breach from happening within your own organization.
214. Go dumpster diving to see how much confidential information you can find throughout your facilities, and then write a report for executive management about your findings.
215. Have a contest for your personnel to go dumpster diving in their neighborhoods, and photograph the risky situations they find. Also give them directions for what to do when they find sensitive information in open and public dumpsters.
216. Hold a "Terminator Day" to educate personnel about how to identify and irreversibly delete all unneeded files from all the many types of computer storage devices and computers.
217. Have a live contest with contestants to see who knows the most about your information security and privacy policies.
218. Perform a privacy impact assessment (PIA) to discover vulnerabilities within your applications, systems and administrative practices. For more information about PIAs, see http://www.privacyguidance.com.

219. Define what "personally identifiable information" means to your organization if you have not already done so.
220. Review your definition of "personally identifiable information" and make sure it is still valid, then update it.
221. Create an inventory of all the personally identifiable information in your organization. If you already have such an inventory review it to make sure it is still valid, and if it is not, update it.
222. Review your computer hardware inventory and update it as necessary. If you do not have one, now is the time to create it!
223. Review your software hardware inventory and update it as necessary. If you do not have one, now is the time to create it!
224. Provide a software and hardware inventory checklist and log sheet to your personnel to take home and make their own inventories.
225. Provide a sample backup and recovery plan to your personnel to use on their own home equipment.
226. Create "You're on Candid Camera" types of videos to show the ways in which people unknowingly put information and privacy at risk, or succumb to social engineering schemes.
227. Run password-cracking software on your network to determine how many bad passwords are found, and then write an article for internal publication about the results, along with a description for why passwords must be strong. Also contact each of the individuals with discovered poor passwords directly to change their passwords immediately following the software run.
228. Perform a security and privacy review of work areas after normal work hours and write a report on how many information security and privacy problems you find, along with notifying the managers for the areas advising them how to fix all the problems found.
229. Do a third-party and business partner security and privacy review.
230. Hold a contest for your personnel to see who can write the best article/essay about a real-life situation, anywhere in the world, that shows how poor privacy protections resulted in ethics violations.
231. Hold a contest in your community for secondary students to write an essay about how information security, privacy, and ethics are interrelated.
232. Create a visual timeline of the history of information security, pointing out key events.
233. Create a visual timeline of the history of privacy concerns and breaches, pointing out key events.
234. Create collectable buttons or pins with information security and/or privacy mascot or slogans on them.
235. Create a deck of playing cards with information security and privacy images and slogans on the backs of the cards.
236. Create a poster showing the top 10 information security concerns for your organization and post copies throughout your facility.

237. Create a poster showing the top 10 privacy concerns for your organization and post copies throughout your facility.
238. Provide copies of the top 10 information security and privacy posters to your business partners to post within their facilities.
239. Create beverage coasters with images of your information security and privacy mascot, or slogan, or tips, to your personnel.
240. Create balloons with your information security and privacy mascot, a slogan, or tips; fill with helium; and hand out to your personnel at awareness activities.
241. Create security and privacy sudoku puzzles for your personnel and/or their family members and friends to do.
242. Communicate to your personnel how they can test their passwords to see how strong they are. One site they can use to do this in an automated way is http://www.securitystats.com/tools/password.asp.
243. Communicate to your personnel how they can test their browser security. One site they can use is http://bcheck.scanit.be/bcheck/. Another is http://www.doxdesk.com/parasite/.
244. Communicate to your personnel how they can test the security of a suspicious file. One site where they can upload a file to be tested is http://virusscan.jotti.org.
245. Communicate to your personnel how they can test their pop-up stoppers. One site they can use is http://www.popuptest.com.
246. Put your information security and privacy mascot, slogan, or tips onto window clings for your personnel to press onto their windows, or to take home and put on their own windows. You can find the window cling material at most craft stores.
247. Post a security- or privacy-related quote from a nonsecurity and nonprivacy person each week. For example, something like, "We will bankrupt ourselves in the vain search for absolute security" by Dwight D. Eisenhower.
248. Test how secure your personnel, or family and friends, are in their e-mail habits. There are many sites that will send the individuals you specify a safe e-mail message that will test for specific security and privacy vulnerabilities. A couple include http://www.gfi.com/emailsecuritytest/ and http://www.jasons-toolbox.com/TestEmail.
249. Test the software you use in your organization for security problems, and tell your personnel how to check the software that they use at home for security and privacy problems. A couple of sites you can use to do this include http://www.fortifysoftware.com/company.htm and http://www.sanctuminc.com/.
250. Hold a "Fact or Fiction?" game event after work, during lunch time, or at some other time when you can get a good attendance. Have a game host ask participants questions about information security or privacy incidents, breaches, and so on, and see if they can correctly answer if the information is "Fact" or "Fiction." Give those answering correctly prizes or points.

Awareness Is Ongoing

It is critical to remember that an awareness program never ends. An effective awareness program must repeat the message multiple times in many ways. The more important the message, the more often it should be repeated using multiple methods. Because it is an ongoing activity, it requires creativity and enthusiasm to maintain the interest of all audience members. The awareness messages must demonstrate that security and privacy are important not only to your organization, but also to each employee, business partner, and customer.

An awareness program must remain current. As security and privacy regulations change, and subsequently security and privacy policies and procedures too, personnel must be notified. Establish a method to deliver immediate information and updates when necessary. Perhaps new information is sent as the first alert item that personnel see when logging into the network for the day. The awareness messages and methods must also be simple. The purpose is to get messages and ideas out to personnel quickly and easily. They should not be confusing or convoluted so as to dissuade personnel from reading them, and eventually not paying attention at all to the messages. Make the information easy to understand.

Developing Awareness Activities and Messages

Awareness messages must support information security and privacy goals. Possible topics to cover in awareness messages and activities include

- General customer privacy policy notice
- Identification of the uses for which your company uses customer information
- Identification of potential recipients of your company's customer information
- Third-party limitations on customer information use
- Types of customer information collected
- Steps taken when collecting customer information to ensure confidentiality, integrity, and quality of the information
- Customer choice for how their information is used
- Customer choice for how their information is shared
- Customer choice for how their information is collected and stored
- Customer information provision requirements
- Customer information optional provisions
- Providing consumer access to their personal information
- Your company's customer information privacy mission statement
- Using anonymous customer information
- Destroying customer information that is no longer needed
- Managerial and procedural measures to protect customer information against loss and unauthorized access, destruction, use, or disclosure

- Technical measures to protect customer information from loss and unauthorized access, destruction, use, or disclosure
- Mechanisms in place to enforce customer information privacy
- Customer information monitoring
- Customer information aggregation
- Customer information storage
- Customer information transfer
- Customer information collection
- Customer information personalization
- Customer contact
- Security policies and procedures
- Security and privacy tools and techniques
- How security helps the organization and its employees
- Why your laptop/notebook/PC, etc., should be protected
- How to anticipate auditor questions and requirements
- Disasters that people think could never happen, but do
- Horror stories of using production information in a test environment
- Horror stories of mixing production and development in the same environment
- What to do if you suspect a security or privacy incident

Plan ahead for the topics to be included in your awareness messages. Create a timetable, such that execution of the awareness materials and activities is simplified. As an example, following are some topics and associated information to include in monthly information security and privacy newsletters.

Monthly Information Security and Privacy Newsletters

- Posted to the privacy intranet site
- Cover topics directly applicable to your company services and job responsibilities
  - Spam (January)
  - International privacy requirements (February)
  - Automatic collection of personal information in your company devices (March)
  - Automatic collection of personal information in your company services (April)
  - Do-not-contact lists and opt-out (May)
  - Customer profiling and customer relationship management (CRM) (June)
  - Communicating with customers in secure ways (July)
  - Identity verification (August)
  - Using social networking sites securely (September)
  - Social engineering, including phishing attempts (October)
  - Secure disposal of information in all forms (November)
  - Information classification and related security requirements (December)

Chapter 15

Communications

If you tell me, I will listen.
If you show me, I will see.
If you let me experience, I will learn.

—Lao Tzu

It will make your life much easier in the long run to create an information security and privacy awareness and training framework and strategy document that clearly records your planned activities for the next 12 (ideally, 24) months. Not only will this help you remain on track as you undertake your education endeavors, but it will also provide you with a document you can use when discussing your plans with others and for ensuring your planned activities do not conflict with other major events within your organization.

Not only should your training and awareness document clearly record the activities and training events, it should also clearly map out your communications plan for ensuring successful participation in the activities. It should identify the success indicators for the projects as well as the planned approaches and sample communications. This will also help you obtain buy-in from your executive sponsors when you demonstrate that you have thoughtfully and carefully taken into consideration all business and timing factors.

Along with your master framework and strategy document, you should create a communications plan and accompanying leadership materials such as sample management memos and leader guides (to help those providing the training), and participant tracking forms to use to track the training and awareness activities.

Here are the steps to take to successfully launch communications about your information security privacy awareness and training program:

1. Identify where you need to improve, update, or create information security and privacy training and awareness.
2. Obtain executive sponsorship.
3. Communicate information security and privacy program overview.
4. Send target groups communications outlining the information security and privacy training and awareness schedules and their participation expectations.

Step 1: Identify Where You Need to Improve, Update, or Create Information Security and Privacy Training and Awareness

The first communication in establishing or updating such a program is to identify areas that work and those that have been overlooked. Assess the program for shortcomings such as ineffective or missing topics. A survey is typically the best way to obtain this type of information from a wide audience. The results of the survey can then be used to effectively plan, update, and implement the program. Chapter 6 and Chapter 7 detail how to get started and setting a baseline. See Appendix A and Appendix E for a suggested memo and voice message to accompany the survey. See Appendix G for a suggested privacy training survey. See Chapter 18 for tips on writing effective surveys.

Step 2: Obtain Executive Sponsorship

To be effective and help ensure high participation, your security and privacy awareness and training program needs to be visibly sponsored and supported by a member of executive management with the ability to influence personnel actions. It is critical to obtain executive sponsorship for your program from a known and respected member of your corporate or business unit executive teams. You should contact your likely sponsors and arrange a meeting. You must be prepared with a succinct, clear, and polished presentation of your plans. Effectively communicate the importance of such activities (see Chapter 8). Appendix L provides a sample executive presentation you can use as the basis for creating and tailoring a presentation to fit your own unique needs.

I cannot emphasize enough the importance of being well prepared in such a meeting to articulate why you need the executive support. You should be prepared to describe the objectives of the program. Be ready to provide facts and describe how the objectives relate to the organization's business. Use Exhibit 1 as a starting point for creating your own objectives as they best fit your organization.

Exhibit 1   Creating Your Own Objectives

Objectives

The objective of the information security and privacy training and awareness program is to provide core communication, content standardization, and training infrastructure in accordance with Company X policies, contractual requirements, industry standards, and country laws and regulations to most effectively enable information security and privacy deployment efforts within Company X offices, regions, countries, and business units.

More specifically, the training and awareness objectives are to:

- Reduce security incidents and privacy breaches as a result of an informed workforce
- Comply with applicable regulatory and legal requirements for privacy education
- Maintain content and version control for information security and privacy training materials
- Identify core and function specific training content and applicable delivery methods
- Track training metrics globally and at the local levels
- Communicate awareness related information and policies, procedures, and standards to corporate and BU areas, such as training offerings, material availability, and so on
- Represent the corporate perspective within the regional and BU deployment efforts
- Motivate change within personnel to improve and ensure information security and awareness

---

Launch Information Security and Privacy Education Communications

Carefully plan your awareness and training deployment prior to execution. A critical factor in the success of this program is to ensure that targeted audiences understand that training and awareness is an ongoing process and not a one-time event. You need to communicate to them the following:

- The mission and goals of the program
- The reasons for participating in the program
- The importance of incorporating security and privacy activities into their job activities
- The components of the program
- A timeline for the training
- The need to participate as part of job requirements

Executive Security and Privacy Training Announcement

When you have obtained executive sponsorship, and have your information security and privacy education plan and materials completed, announce to management and the rest of personnel that they will soon be expected to participate in the training. See Appendix A for a sample memo to issue from the executive customer privacy champion.

Step 3: Communicate Information Security and Privacy Program Overview

After the personnel have received notification from the executive management that an information security and privacy training and awareness initiative has been launched and that they will be expected to participate, your company security and privacy manager should issue a memo outlining the goals and benefits of implementing such a program. See Appendix A for an example of such a memo. The communication should also include a description of the security and privacy advocate roles, along with a list of all the security and privacy advocates within your company. See Appendix D for examples of role definitions. Within a week or two, the advocates should start communicating with their associated areas about security and privacy issues, and training and awareness events. The advocates should work closely with the security and privacy manager to make their plans and launch their communications.

Step 4: Send Target Groups Communications Outlining the Information Security and Privacy Training and Awareness Schedules and Their Participation Expectations

Following the communication from the security and privacy manager, each advocate should send a memo outlining the training schedule and awareness activities planned for the following 12 months to their respective areas.

Training and awareness advocates should additionally work with the security and privacy manager to identify all the personnel within the target groups, and then create memos to send to them indicating the dates for the training and the purpose and goal of each training session.

Plan and Establish Awareness and Training Deployment

Create a detailed deployment plan and communicate your strategy to key contacts and executive sponsors. You can use many different methods to communicate. In addition to the traditional discussion memos, timelines and presentation slides are effective. You may consider creating them as shown in the following subsections.

Deployment Timeline

Use the elements of your education strategy and indicate, on a weekly basis, where you plan to be with each task. You can put this into a project management system for printouts to share among key contacts. Exhibit 2 contains a sample road map similar to the one from Chapter 6.

Exhibit 2   Company X Information Security and Privacy Training and Awareness Strategy

1. Identify and assign roles.
   a. Organization-wide information security and privacy executive champion/sponsor.
   b. Information security and privacy training and awareness leader.
   c. Information security and privacy training and awareness support personnel.
   d. BU and regional security and privacy managers/sponsors/champions.
   e. BU and regional information security and privacy contacts.
   f. Third-party information security and privacy contacts.
2. Determine training and awareness needs.
   a. Interviews (see Appendix I for sample interview questions).
   b. Surveys.
   c. Site inspections.
   d. Document reviews.
3. Obtain sponsorship.
   a. Contact appropriate executive sponsor.
   b. Provide a master implementation plan that serves as a blueprint for your program.
   c. Create a communications plan focused on sending key messages to the audiences affected by each of the activities.
   d. Include sponsor's name on communications
4. Create and/or update training and awareness materials.
   a. Computer-based training (CBTs).
   b. Classroom training.

(continued)

Exhibit 2   (continued)

---

   c. Messages and memos.

   d. Signs and posters.

   e. Other chosen training and awareness delivery methods.

5. Establish deployment schedule.

   a. Pilot group vetting.

      i. Send explanatory message to subject matter experts (SMEs) (pilot group).

      ii. Obtain information from SMEs for incorporating into content.

      iii. SMEs review and provide feedback and evaluation of content.

      iv. Update training and awareness materials as necessary.

   b. Roll out content to targeted groups.

      i. Identify group members.

      ii. Send communications to the group members asking them for participation.

      iii. Follow up to ensure participation.

   c. Ongoing activities.

      i. Perform training and awareness as indicated by triggers (described later).

      ii. Update materials based on feedback and organizational changes.

6. Training and awareness delivery.

   a. Write announcement memo.

      i. The first announcement should outline the full training and awareness strategy. You should always let personnel know what they can expect with regard to training and awareness requirements before you start rolling out one activity at a time. This will help to ensure they participate in more than just the first activity. See Appendix A for a suggested announcement memo.

      ii. The subsequent communications should include the following components:
         (1) WHAT is expected of the employee or partner receiving the communication
         (2) WHEN the recipient must perform the requested actions
         (3) HOW the action relates to the recipient's job performance and responsibilities.
         (4) WHO sponsors the action (for example, the security and privacy sponsor executive)
         (5) WHO to contact for further information

Exhibit 2   (continued)

> (6) WHY the recipient must attend (for example, training and awareness will help reduce risk to the organization, will fulfill certain regulatory requirements, and so on)
>
> b. Notify security and privacy sponsor and champions.
>
> > i. Explain purpose for the training and/or awareness action.
> >
> > ii. Reconfirm the use of their name on the communications.
>
> 7. Evaluate effectiveness of efforts and update appropriately.

Exhibit 3 is a sample resulting timeline based on your road map.

Exhibit 3   Timeline Based on Road Map

Weeks ⇒	1 & 2	3 & 4	5 & 6	7 & 8	9 & 10	11 & 12	13 & 14	15 & 16	17 & 18	19 & 20	21 & 22	23 & 24
Task												
1	X											
2a	X	X										
2b		X										
2c								X				
3	X											
4a	X	X	X	X	X	X	X	X	X			
4b			X	X	X	X	X	X	X	X		
4c	X	X	X	X	X							
4d					X	X	X	X	X	X		
5a		X	X	X	X	X	X	X	X			
5b					X	X	X	X	X	X	X	X
5c					X	X	X	X	X	X	X	X
6ai	X											
6aii		X										
6b	X											
7					X	X	X	X	X	X	X	X

Presentation Slides

Create a presentation to communicate your awareness and training plan and give to target groups, managers, and others who are important to your program's success. A presentation similar to the slides found in Appendix L can be made.

More Ideas

Prepare and motivate your participants for training by getting them interested and communicating the benefits of the training. Chapter 14 lists many different ideas for motivating participants; here are a few more, which may be useful in your particular situation:

- Before announcements, invitations, and notices regarding training are issued, send information about the topic, perhaps recent related news stories, checklists related to addressing topic issues, etc., with payroll checks or other widely circulated mailings. Provide some eye-catching visuals and statistics.
- When sending training announcements, invitations, and notices, include a list of benefits to the participants, their teams, organizations, and even families and friends if the topic is applicable.
- Prior to the training session, send out self-assessment tests or pretests for the participants. Indicate that you will provide a review or explanation of the assessment during the training session.

Communications Checklist

Keep the following in mind when creating your education communications, and include them where appropriate:

- Establish training and awareness schedules and include them in your communications.
- Communicate your program in multiple ways tailored to your target groups such as your executive sponsors, education advocates, targeted participants, business partners, etc.
- Use existing communication paths wherever possible.
- Consider using new technology (satellite transmissions, video tapes, streaming video, online modules, etc.) to add variety, to reach wider audiences, and to take advantage of existing technology communication methods.
- Include key stakeholders within communications.
- Indicate any necessary resources the recipients will need to participate in the training and awareness activities.
- Address international issues within your communications, such as language, customs, etc.

Sample Communication Plan Documents

Create a communication plan for each of your target groups, indicating their responsibilities, as applicable, and an outline for the education goals you have for each of the groups. Exhibit 4 provides a sample of the type of communication you can include to outline each information security and privacy role's responsibilities. Exhibit 5 is a sample communication outlining the CBT training goals. Exhibit 6 is a sample communication outlining the education process for targeted groups. Exhibit 7 is a sample communication outlining, at a high level, the trainer education process.

Exhibit 4   Sample Responsibilities Listing

Information Security and Privacy Responsibilities

Information security and privacy office responsibilities

- Content management for training and awareness.
- Provide and/or ensure the infrastructure for the content.
- Core communications and icon/mascot management.
- Project tracking.
- Management of CBT and outsourced vendors.
- Combined strategies for employee, customer, and information security and privacy office.
- Coordinate all training and awareness activities.

Business unit (BU) and regional information security and privacy champions

- BU deployment strategy.
- Target special needs and groups.
- Define and document the BU deployment model based on organizational model.
- Provide content specialization resources.
- Integrate use of icon/mascot into work areas.
- Track and communicate law and country-specific requirements as applicable to office locations.
- Ensure effective communication within applicable areas.
- Obtain funding from BU executives wherever possible.

Human resources and/or workforce development

- Provide available infrastructure and funding as possible.
- Include within strategy and within events as possible.
- Review education content for appropriateness and sign-off.

Exhibit 5 Sample Communication for CBT Goals

Privacy CBT Training Goals

Goal: To have identified employees take the CBT training.

Who

- Those who handle confidential and customer information
- Contact and customer care centers
- Marketing, e-business, and e-marketing
- Sales (consumer)
- Sales (commercial)

Process

- Communicate CBT messaging to:
  - Business unit leadership
  - Country managers
  - Functional managers
- Localize where possible
- Review issues and comments; where required recommend changes

Issues

- Is the lack of localized versions of the CBT a barrier to sign-up in certain countries?
- Does it take too long to complete (approximately 1 hour)? Can it be shortened?
- Is the sign-up process too complicated?
- Do we need further executive level sponsorship/sign-off to enforce the need to take the CBT?

Exhibit 6 Sample Communication for Targeted Group Education Process

Targeted Training Goals

Goal: To conduct functional group training that is relevant to that function or group.

Who

- Customer care and contact centers
- Marketing, e-business, and e-marketing
- Sales (consumer)

Exhibit 6 (continued)

- Sales (commercial)
- Channels and partner managers

Process

- Work with the security and privacy policy team and training manager to identify groups
- Develop training material tailored to the groups
- Conduct training as required

Issues

- Lack of material
- Lack of resources
- Timing
- Communication to groups that we are available to conduct training

---

Exhibit 7   Sample Communication for the Trainer Education Process

---

Train the Trainer

Goal: To establish a network of "trainers" able to conduct customer privacy training, established in the major customer facing functions.

Who (Departments)

- Marketing communications
- Contact centers
- Corporate training
- CRM

Process

- Identify functions.
- Identify qualified individuals in each.
- Develop training material to train trainers.
- Ensure they have access to training material that is appropriate and effective to train their staff.

(continued)

Exhibit 7 (continued)

Issues
• Identify target training candidates.
• Need training material.
• Partner and vendor training.
• Priorities.
• Identify highest risk groups.
• Scheduling.
• Length of training.

Chapter 16

Deliver In-Person Training

I am always ready to learn although I do not always like being taught.

—**Winston Churchill**

Every act of conscious learning requires the willingness to suffer an injury to one's self-esteem. That is why young children, before they are aware of their own self-importance, learn so easily.

—**Thomas Szasz**

Training is more formal and interactive than an awareness program. The goal of training should be to build specialized skills, to build knowledge in the topic, and to facilitate job responsibility performance and capabilities.

Training should also motivate the participants. The importance of training to help ensure information security has been recognized in recent years as one of the most effective ways to help secure information and protect privacy. In fact, this realization led to the U.S. National Institute of Standards and Technology (NIST) releasing the document SP800-16 in 1998, *IT Security Training Requirements: A Role- and Performance-Based Model*, which provides guidelines for federal agencies to develop their own IT security training programs. It provides a nice structure for nongovernment organizations to use as well, and will be helpful to you in building your security and privacy training program to meet security and privacy-compliance requirements. If you use this as a guide, remember that you will need to modify the curriculum to match your own organization's unique training needs.

Keep in mind that it is the job function and its associated responsibilities that should determine what information security and privacy courses each identified target group needs. An employee may have multiple job responsibilities and may thus need to attend more than one training session. This approach to training, although effective, may be a challenge to implement in some organizations because of time constraints, or unwillingness to acknowledge that training is of such importance.

Other chapters in the book cover technical training methods and delivery. However, providing training in person presents an entirely new dimension of issues to consider. This chapter focuses primarily on in-person training delivery. However, as you read through this chapter, consider how the pointers and suggestions may also be implemented within your CBTs, films, and other more technology-based forms of training delivery.

What to Avoid in Training

Over the years I have heard many people talk about the bad training experiences they have had. Examples of poor experiences from various participants' points of view include, but certainly are not limited to, the following:

- I was not at all interested in the topic; it was boring.
- I do not understand how this stuff applies to me or my job.
- I do not see how I will use any of this information during my work.
- I felt preached at; I could not ask questions.
- Whoa! Way too much information to take in!
- There was no discussion of the topic.
- Why did we not do case studies?
- I really would have liked the opportunity to practice what they were talking about.
- We did exercises, but then the instructor gave no feedback on what we did.
- The class moved way too slow.
- It seemed like there was a lot of time wasted discussing things other than the topic.
- The materials were very poor, very amateurish.
- I cannot realistically use any of this in my job.
- The content was good, but the communication skills of the instructor were very poor.
- I did not understand what they were talking about; I was so confused.
- I did not understand the language or the jargon used.
- I wish they had used examples to demonstrate what they meant.
- The instructor just read off his slides.
- The instructor sounded like she was bored giving the class.
- I did not learn or hear anything new.
- They discussed what we needed to do, but not why we needed to do it.
- The instructor did not listen to me.
- The class was not paced; it seemed like it went way too fast, way too slow, or just went completely off the topic.

- I think the instructor did not really know the topic, and just tried to fake his knowledge.
- It would have been nice if the instructor had at least used something like a flip chart or a whiteboard to write down all the additional points that came out of the discussion.
- The instructor seemed very judgmental.
- The instructor made some very inappropriate and politically incorrect remarks.
- What was the outcome for that training supposed to be?
- The instructor seemed very unhappy or disgusted to be there.

Look these over and structure your training delivery to avoid these mistakes. What leads to these comments? There are many different reasons, and combinations of reasons. A few of these are discussed in the following sections.

Multinational Training Considerations

It would take an entire book to do justice to the topic of multinational training. In fact, there are some good books on this topic; see Appendix T for resources. However, it is important to point out at a high level some considerations for you to keep in mind when providing multinational training:

- Be sensitive to the perceptions of all learners in your session. Be aware that people from different countries and cultures will see the world, and security and privacy issues, from different perspectives.
- Be aware of the assumptions, beliefs, and values of your multinational learners and how they relate to your content.
- Ensure that the training content is modified appropriately to sync with local customs and value systems. Use examples that relate to the local context, and avoid examples that are from cultures foreign to the learners or may not fit with the learners' background.
- Use visuals, graphics, printed words, and pictures wherever possible. Such visuals support and clarify your message for a learner who is not fluent in the language in which you are giving the training.
- Speak at a moderate rate. Check with your learners occasionally to ensure that they understand you if you are speaking a language that is not their first language. It is a good idea, if you feel the learners do not understand you correctly, to ask them to explain back to you something that you just said.
- Be careful when using idioms and slang with a multinational audience and when in an international setting. Even when teaching in a country where the same language is spoken as the instructor's first language, be extra careful to keep in mind there are different dialects; idioms and slang can have very different meanings in different dialects.

- When necessary, find someone local to the learners to be a translator, not only of language, but also of culture. It is good to find a translator who is local so that he or she can best interpret what you are communicating in a manner that makes sense in the cultural perspective.
- Study about the local language and customs to help you to gain perspective and understanding. It is unrealistic to expect that you will become fluent in the language or completely knowledgeable of all the customs. However, it will help you to be empathetic with your learners and understand the difficulties they may be experiencing when trying to learn by listening to a language that is not their first language.
- Observe how local citizens interact with each other. How closely do they stand when talking? Do they have a large or small amount of personal space? Do people touch each other on the arm when speaking? Are colleagues formal or casual with each other?
- Be flexible and open to discussion. Have patience and good listening skills. You must be comfortable enough with your topic that you can make last-minute changes to accommodate the unexpected.
- Avoid mentioning country politics and religion within training content and awareness communications. Politics and religion are some very sensitive topics in many locations throughout the world, and including them will not advance the information security or privacy cause, and will likely inflame certain portions of your learning group.

Delivering Classroom Training

Classroom instructors need to keep the following in mind:

- The classroom instruction should be built around achieving specific learner outcomes. Know what you want the learner to do differently when back at the job. Know what to look for in class to determine if the learner understands the topic and will be able to perform differently, as a result of the training, when back at the job. Determine how to generate learner participation. Choose visuals aids that will help your goals.
- Be very well prepared. Plan carefully and stay learner focused. Create learning aids. Build content and feedback into visual aids. Prepare instructor "scripts." Test out your activities on someone willing to give you good feedback before your class. Record, on audio or video tapes, a run-through of the class. Anticipate and be prepared to answer a wide range of questions about the topic.
- Arrange the classroom to most successfully stimulate learning. Arrange the physical space of the classroom furniture to best suit your target audience and to your training design. Get to the room early and welcome the learners as

they arrive. Do not have your back to them when they arrive in class. Read your class roster and visit with the learners before you start.

- Use icebreakers and openers to immediately involve your learners, put them at ease, and pique their interest. Icebreakers do not necessarily need to be related to the content. They provide a way to help the learners become acquainted and energized, set the tone for the session, and get everyone involved. Typically, openers are topic-related activities that serve the same function as icebreakers, while at the same time leading the learners gently into the topic at hand.

- Thank your learners at the beginning of the session for attending. Acknowledge that you know they are all busy, and explain how the training will help them in the long run to do their jobs in a more secure and, possibly, more efficient way.

- Consider giving the learners a quick quiz related to the content at the beginning of the session. For instance, if the topic is on information security policies, you could ask five true-or-false questions and then ask the learners to work on the questions either with a partner or alone. For some audiences, working in pairs will be less threatening and will generate interest as the pairs discuss their answers. See Appendix P and Appendix Q for examples of quizzes to use.

- Communicate what you expect of the participants. For instance, encourage them to be honest and offer their own opinions in a professional way. Ask them to keep private the confidential information that may be discussed, and to try and use the training opportunity to take risks they would normally not consider, such as role-playing. Let the participants know you expect everyone to participate. Make sure you ask them to give thoughtful feedback about the session. Ask them to be punctual when returning from breaks.

- Ask all participants to turn off the sound of their cell phones, pagers, and other potential noisemakers. Explain how disruptive such unexpected noises can be.

- Tell the participants how the session relates to them, and how they will benefit by enhancing their security and privacy knowledge, and skills, and by overcoming barriers or misconceptions that may have been making their security and privacy efforts less than effective up to this point.

- Encourage interaction during the class. Consider using group discussions. Ask relevant questions that stimulate discussion. Notice your learners' interactions and handle conflicts in a nonthreatening but effective way. Use structured interaction throughout group activities to stay on track.

- Telling stories and anecdotes can be very powerful for illustrating and demonstrating key points. Most people enjoy and are interested in hearing real-life accounts of events related to the topic they are learning.

- Before, during, and following the classroom session, assess your progress. List the activities or characteristics that the learner should demonstrate to signal that they have adequately acquired the knowledge and skills being covered.

Identify the measures that help the participant learn and the measures that help you or others evaluate the participant's potential.

■ If turning out the lights for a film or for some other reason, do not keep them off for too long. You do not want to create a dark and sleepy atmosphere.

■ Try not to teach complex or difficult-to-comprehend material immediately before or after lunch. Your learners are probably either thinking about eating or feeling the listless effect of a full stomach during this time. Another time to avoid such heavy material is right at the end of the day when your learners are thinking about leaving.

Tips for Trainers

1. Be well prepared.
2. Use language understandable by your target audience.
3. Be a good listener.
4. Do not go too fast or too slow.
5. Do not fake knowledge.
6. Involve the participants.
7. Do not make judgmental statements.
8. Do not lead with statements such as "This is easy," "This is self explanatory," "This is obvious," etc., which sound condescending.
9. Accommodate all participants as much as possible.
10. Stay focused on the task and stay within scope.
11. Be approachable; smile and look participants in the eye.
12. Know where you should be timewise and stay on your schedule as closely as possible.
13. Relate information to participants' job responsibilities.
14. Know the cultures of your participants.
15. Include everyone.
16. Avoid taking sides.
17. Give breaks when necessary, even if unplanned. Short (5 minute) hourly breaks instead of a few long breaks will help keep students alert during the actual training session.
18. Restate key points.
19. Do not dismiss questions.
20. Be aware of your voice; keep listeners interested.
21. Speak to your audience, not to the wall, monitor, projector, or screen.
22. Do not just read your slides.
23. Arrive early and make sure everything works.
24. Do not block the view.
25. Use microphones when necessary.
26. Repeat learner questions so everyone knows what was asked.
27. Present professional-looking slides.

28. Do not absentmindedly play with your clothing, hair, and so on.
29. Open with and use questions often.
30. Use games to promote interest and understanding.
31. Dress professionally and appropriately.
32. Do not wear anything distracting; for example, big dangling jewelry or shirts with political slogans will distract your learners.
33. Have good posture. Bad posture not only affects your appearance, but also makes you tire quickly and can give you aches and pains, possibly making you grumpy.
34. Be aware of your face. Do not frown. Smile and warm up to your learners. Remember, what the participants see is more powerful than what they hear.
35. Create the training language, content, examples, and case studies to fit the learners and their environment; do not create content to fit the instructor.
36. Construct and deliver the training to encourage participation and involve the learners.
37. Be aware of aligning the delivery and content to the participants' job responsibilities.
38. Use activities that are related to and aligned with the participants' job responsibilities.
39. Be punctual and start on time at the beginning of the day and after breaks.
40. Give clear and succinct instructions.
41. If possible, prepare flip charts prior to the training session. Or, consider asking a participant to write on the flip chart while you conduct the session.
42. Ensure that participants have handouts and materials prior to the session.

Visual Aids

Effective use of visual aids, in any type of training delivery, helps to reinforce the written or spoken message and, quite frankly, makes the instruction much more interesting and engaging. For example, instructors should try to move around the classroom, include some silent and group activities such as debates in addition to lecturing, along with whiteboard or flip chart work, films, audio, diagram building, or other visual aids to help engage a wide range of learners. Using multimedia training, such as group learning exercises, CBTs, films, and so on, creates the ability to be highly creative and, thus, more likely to be successful, depending on the topic. In general, a training program should include a range of delivery approaches, such as those described in Chapter 9. Some reasons to use visual aids with training methods include the ability to

■ Emphasize key points. Learners will clearly see important points and issues when they are highlighted with visual aids. Most people are better at observing than listening. Hence, the use of visual aids will emphasize important learning points.

- Reinforce key points. Visual aids can also provide diagrams, graphics, photos, and other items to reinforce the message being delivered.
- Capture and maintain the learners' attention. Visual aids do not have to be elaborate; some of the most effective visual aids are very simple. It all depends on personal choice, costs involved, topic, type of training method, target audience, and purpose of the training.
- Enhance the spoken education delivery. Visuals can support what you are describing or actually show it in graphic detail.
- Promote understanding of the topic or message. Illustrations with graphs, photos, charts, tables, etc., can make a complex topic easier to understand and remember.
- Organize information to keep the trainer or message delivery method on track. When placed strategically throughout the session, visual aids can enhance learning and provide a thread of continuity throughout the session. Also, they not only help to keep a trainer on track, but also help learners understand how and why the session was organized in the way presented.
- Do not let discussions go on too long. When starting a discussion, establish a time limit.
- Use good-natured humor. Be careful that you do not sound patronizing or sarcastic.
- Use analogies, metaphors, and comparisons. Consider creating your own information security and privacy Aesop's fables or parables.

Training in Group Settings

When delivering training in a group setting, you need to do more than just spout facts, especially when discussing topics such as information security and privacy, which can be quite complex and difficult to understand. You will usually be more effective if you view yourself as a facilitator of learning, and also as a role model for those learners in the group. As with the other topics in this chapter, entire books have been written on just how to be a good facilitator to groups in adult education situations. However, many of you will not have such books, and because the goal of this book to provide help for all aspects of awareness and training, some basic tips are presented here:

- Encourage participation. Use nonverbal communication (employ lots of eye contact, show your understanding by nodding, and smile; however, do not use body movements that are distracting), use verbal encouragement (simple words of genuine praise or encouragement can be very powerful; also, restate or clarify learner comments), and acknowledge feelings (let learners know if you sense they are frustrated, upset, or otherwise affected by something the training topic touched).
- Use questions effectively. Use open-ended questions, such as those that begin with *who, what, when, where, how,* and *why* whenever possible. These will

involve more thinking and, thus, more meaningful responses than just asking "yes" or "no" questions. Keep in mind to use "why" questions carefully; training and communications experts* indicate that such questions can easily put your learners on the defensive if not asked carefully. After asking questions, let there be silence while your learners think. Silence may feel uncomfortable at first, but give your learners 10 or so seconds to respond before expanding upon the question, or offering the answer.

■ Respond to questions thoughtfully. Understand the typical reasons why people ask questions. Of course, to obtain more information or clarify the topic at hand is one reason. But there are also other reasons that are more difficult to answer. For example, there are people who will ask questions as a way to be noticed or impress the others in the group, in addition to participants who just enjoy the opportunity to make the trainer look bad. There are also those who will really like the trainer and ask questions to make the trainer look good. And then, of course, there are the participants who just want to prolong the training as long as possible to keep from going back to work. So, to deal with these types of questioners, let them know the rules at the beginning of the session for questions. Then, when questions do occur, remember the following:

- Repeat and/or rephrase questions to ensure understanding.
- Look the questioner in the eyes when you are restating the question to make sure they indicate you have gotten the question correctly.
- Think before you answer. Choose your words carefully and anticipate the effect they will have on the learners. For example, using the words, "obviously," "apparently," "everyone knows," etc., may come across as condescending.
- Show respect to the group. Do not embarrass or belittle a participant. This means you will need to exercise patience sometimes.
- Respond appropriately to narrow or off-topic questions. If someone asks a question that just pertains to him or her, or is about something out of the scope of training, suggest that you talk about it with him or her offline, after the class, or during a break.
- Look at and include everyone. Do not look at just a few of the learners. Make an effort to look at and include everyone in the room.
- Do not fake knowledge, or make up facts to support your information. If someone asks you a question you cannot answer or do not know, be honest and say so. Be sure to offer to look up the information later, though, and get back to the group with the response. Or, tell the group where they can go to get the answer, if this is something you know.
- Be sincere and try not to sound patronizing. Be gracious. Following your answer, ask if you need to go into more detail.

---

* Karen Lawson, *The Trainer's Handbook*, Jossey-Bass/Pfeiffer, San Francisco, 1998, p. 167.

■ Overcome resistance among the learners. Did some of your participants bring work with them to do during class? Or, perhaps a newspaper or book? Do some participants look generally unhappy to be in the session? There are many signs of resistance in addition to these. Be ready to deal with resistant learners. Reasons for resistance may include that they may
  - Not want to be in the session
  - Not feel well
  - Be preoccupied with personal problems
  - Not know why they had to attend the session
  - Not be fluent in the language in which the training is being given
  - Have negative feelings about the organization, or his or her manager
  - Not want to learn about the topic
  - Feel challenged and uncomfortable with the topic
  - Have difficulty reading or using the concepts within the session
  - Have had bad training experiences prior to this session
■ Anticipate the unexpected. Even with the best planning, something unexpected will likely happen. To help avoid the unexpected:
  - Plan well and be creative. Have a backup plan for room and technical problems, changes in schedules, and unexpected participants.
  - Find out as much as possible about your participants ahead of the session. Consider using questionnaires, surveys, manager interviews, and similar techniques, or even assigning tasks for the participants to do ahead of the session and bring with them.
  - For long sessions, ask for basic items such as refreshments, pads, and pens or pencils, and other items that the participants may forget, but should have. This will keep them in the room instead of wasting time by going back to their office to get the necessary items.
  - Adapt your training style according to the learners. This is especially important if you find you have a learning-resistant group. If the group is especially rowdy, consider dividing them into smaller groups and give each a different assignment.
  - Keep your cool when personal attacks occur. Retain your composure. If someone points out an error, do not be defensive, but thank the person for pointing out the error. Acknowledge differences of opinions.
  - Deal effectively with one or a few difficult attendees. There are many types of difficult personalities, such as those who always want to talk, those who do not seem to be aware of the topic, those who tend to ramble, those who are know-it-alls, those who are openly hostile, those who refuse to consider others' points of view, those who are the group clowns, those who are negative about everything discussed, those who are completely indifferent, those who continuously start side conversations, etc. Think about how you will handle such personalities ahead of time.

■ When doing group activities, have each group write their findings on their own flip chart so the other groups can see them. When reviewing, ask each group to cover just one finding, then go to the next group, and ask them to cover a point not already covered. This will be more time efficient and eliminate redundancy.

Case Studies

Using real stories and case studies are wonderful ways to engage the participants and to obtain their participation and attention, and to enrich their learning experience. Use such activities to provide reference points and memorable images to help reinforce the topic.

You can use either real or fictional situations and accounts for your case studies. I find both to be very effective. Real stories are by default highly credible because they have actually occurred. When writing fictional situations, be sure to base the account upon an event that has occurred, which you are modifying to preserve confidentiality, or prevent liability or slander. Or, be very sure that a completely fictional account is absolutely credible.

What is nice about case studies is that you can include in them information that is normally given in a lecture format. Case studies present nice opportunities to present abstract information in concrete ways. Usually, the biggest challenge in using case studies is finding or creating the case study, or studies, to use in your training session that best fits your training program, topic, and audience. Here are some pointers for creating case studies:

■ Identify in your training session the key issues, concepts, messages, and so on, that you want to get across to the participants.
■ Interview employees at different levels in the organization prior to creating your case study. Collect "war stories" about situations and incidents related to the topic.
■ Discuss war stories and incidents at seminars and conferences with other attendees as you are networking. Get stories of real incidents from the news. I have many actual incidents I suggest to use as case studies at my blog, http://www.realtime-itcompliance. Use generic versions of these situations, to retain confidentiality as necessary, as the basis of case studies.
■ Brainstorm, either alone or in a group with some of your key contacts or teammates, the types of situations that exemplify the topics you are covering.
■ Choose one or a few of the situations that seem the most realistic and with which the target audience will identify.
■ Write a draft description of the case study scenario and ask a trusted colleague to read it, as written and without any more explanation from you, and

get feedback. Are there portions that do not make sense? Does it clearly relate to the topic you are teaching?

- Rewrite the case study based on feedback.
- Create discussion questions for your target audience based on the case study. If possible, include graphics, photos, or other types of visuals that can add to the impact of the case study experience and make it more realistic.
- It is very effective if you have the opportunity to simulate the case study on a video, an interactive CD, and so on.
- Prior to the training session, in the training announcements or invitations, ask participants to send you examples of situations they have actually experienced, and use these as the basis for case studies. Keep in mind that this will require you to be able to quickly form a case study structure to use as part of the training.

See Appendix U for some sample case studies. See Chapter 19 for case study discussions from leading information security practitioners.

Chapter 17

Launch Awareness Activities

Imagination is more important than knowledge.

—Albert Einstein

An effective information security and privacy awareness program will communicate to personnel, outside of the formal training sessions, the importance of observing and maintaining information security and privacy, as well as motivating personnel to learn and follow the organization's information security and privacy policies and procedures. The awareness program should, as often as possible, use as many methods as is possible to increase the awareness of information security and privacy issues, concerns, and the organization's efforts and procedures. Organizations have tried a variety of methods to launch awareness to ensure that their personnel receive at least the minimum amount of information necessary to help them discharge their job responsibilities in the most secure and private way possible.

Organizations have commonly launched their awareness activities with the following approaches. Pick and choose what will work best in your business environment:

- Including information security and privacy policies in employee handbooks online and in printed manuals
- Requiring personnel to take self-study courses when they have time, and sometimes prior to getting access to information resources
- Administering annual acknowledgment of understanding and committing to follow information security and privacy policies

- Annual testing of information security and privacy policies and job-related issues
- Launching awareness campaigns using posters, the Web, e-mail reminders, and a wide range of other methods, such as those listed in Chapter 14

Before skipping to the delivery of awareness, organizations need to plan how the awareness events will be launched and create a road map for their delivery.

Carefully plan your awareness deployment prior to trying to execute the content and delivery. A critical factor in the success of an awareness program is ensuring that the targeted audiences understand that awareness is an ongoing process and not a one-time event. You need to communicate the following to them within awareness communications and activities:

- The mission and goals of the information security and privacy awareness and training program
- The importance of incorporating security and privacy activities into their job functions
- The components of the information security and privacy awareness and training program
- A timeline for when they can expect to participate in awareness events and training
- The need to participate in training and observe awareness communications

Here are some steps to take to successfully launch your information security and privacy awareness program:

1. Identify areas in which you need to improve, update, or create awareness.
2. Obtain executive sponsorship.
3. Communicate the information security and privacy program overview.
4. Identify trigger events.
5. Identify target groups.
6. Identify awareness methods and messages best suited to your organization and business needs.
7. Evaluate changed behaviors.
8. Update and continue awareness messages.

Step 1: Identify Areas in Which You Need to Improve, Update, or Create Awareness

Use the suggestions in Chapter 6 and Chapter 7 to determine where to target your awareness efforts and to identify the topics you want to cover.

Step 2: Obtain Executive Sponsorship

To be effective and help ensure high participation, your security and privacy awareness program needs to be visibly sponsored and supported by a member of executive management who has the ability to influence personnel actions. It is critical to obtain executive sponsorship of your awareness program from a known and respected member of your business unit executive team. When you have your awareness plan and materials completed, have an announcement sent from your executive sponsor to personnel that they will soon be expected to participate in the awareness events. See Appendix A for a sample memo to issue from the executive information security and privacy sponsor or champion.

Step 3: Communicate the Information Security and Privacy Program Overview

Chapter 15 covers the ways to communicate the program to your various target groups.

Step 4: Identify Trigger Events

There are some common events that trigger when awareness communications and activities should be provided to the target groups. These trigger events are listed in Chapter 6.

Step 5: Identify Target Groups

The targeted awareness groups are elaborated on in Chapter 10. Before communicating with the groups, get cooperation from the departmental management. Then, send the target group communications outlining the upcoming information security and privacy awareness activities in which the target group members are expected to participate. Include a schedule of your planned awareness events, along with a list of available awareness communications and resources that the target groups will be able to request directly from the information security and privacy office.

Following the communication from the information security and privacy office, each information security and privacy advocate should send a memo outlining the awareness activities planned for the following 12 months to their respective areas.

An effective information security and privacy awareness program will communicate to personnel, outside of formal training sessions, the importance of observing and maintaining security and privacy, as well as motivate personnel to learn and follow the security and privacy policies and procedures. The awareness program should, as often as possible, use as many methods as is possible to increase the awareness of security and privacy issues, concerns, and your organization's efforts and procedures.

Chapter 14 lists many possible awareness activities. The following are some of the methods that tend to be the more popular or common ways to deliver awareness messages:

- Weekly or daily messages on intranet sites
- Awareness commercials on corporate intranet sites (like Web site banner ads)
- Scrolling marquees with links to the information security and privacy sites
- Newsletter articles
- Pop-up messages (be careful with these; they may be more annoying to your recipients than they are helpful)
- Posters
- Paycheck inserts
- Corporate publication "ads"
- Communicate updated awareness schedules monthly or quarterly
- Develop a menu of awareness activities from which the personnel can select, depending upon how their job responsibilities are related to security and privacy issues. The menu of activities could include:
  - E-mail postcards
  - Streaming video of executive security and privacy champion message to personnel
  - Security and privacy computer-based training module information
  - Prizes for participating in security and privacy "Jeopardy"-like competitions as incentives to participate
  - Voice mail messages from the executive security and privacy champion to personnel
- Personnel online security and privacy seminar
- Link to your organization's external customer privacy Web site
- Link to your organization's intranet security and privacy Web site
- Security and privacy newsletters
- Security and privacy alerts in e-mail messages
- Security and privacy announcements on your organization's Web site
- Posters and signs
- Privacy icons and taglines
- Videos
- Customer privacy day
- International security day

Step 6: Identify Your Awareness Methods and Messages

Communicate to your audiences the ways in which you will be delivering awareness messages. Engage your audiences with your methods. Consider launching awareness utilizing such methods as identified in Chapter 9. See Appendix U for examples of how to engage your audiences not only within a formal training setting, but also by providing them these scenarios through communications such as posters, Web site activities, and so on.

Step 7: Evaluate Changed Behavior

A major goal of your awareness campaign is to change the behavior of your audiences such that they become active partners in your security and privacy efforts. Chapter 18 goes into detail about evaluation methods. However, it is worth emphasizing that seeking out feedback following an awareness campaign or event can provide you with valuable, timely information about the effectiveness of your awareness communications, and help you to modify them appropriately.

By obtaining immediate feedback during or immediately after an awareness event, you can ensure that the awareness activities remain timely, useful, and relevant for supporting your organization's business goals related to security and privacy, in addition to your audiences' needs for the information necessary to help them discharge their job responsibilities in the most secure and efficient manner possible. The feedback will also help identify gaps in your awareness program, in addition to being a metric to incorporate into your formal evaluation methods. Consider using a form similar to Exhibit 1 to gather your feedback to try and determine how behaviors, attitudes, and habits have been altered as a result of your awareness efforts.

Encourage active participation in the security and privacy program by making a form similar to Exhibit 2 available to personnel. The more of these forms you receive, the more evidence you have that you have altered personnel behavior through your awareness efforts.

Step 8: Update and Perform Ongoing Awareness

Once you have set the awareness ball rolling, you must work to keeping it going. It is critical to remember that an awareness program never ends. An effective awareness program must repeat your message many times in many ways. The more important the message, the more often it should be repeated using multiple methods. Because it is an ongoing activity, it requires creativity and enthusiasm on your part to maintain the interest of all audience members. You will need to go back to Step 1 and start again. Awareness messages must demonstrate that information security and privacy are important not only to your organization, but also to each employee, customer, and business partner.

Exhibit 1   Sample Suggestion Form

Security and Privacy Awareness Program Suggestion Form

We appreciate your use of this security and privacy awareness suggestion form for to help us continuously improve upon and increase the effectiveness of our organization's security and privacy awareness efforts. By returning this form you are also participating in the design and maintenance of our security and privacy awareness program. Each month we will have a prize drawing from all those who submit this form as a token of our appreciation. Special recognition will be given to all personnel who make suggestions that are implemented. To submit a suggestion, fill out the form located at www .organization.com/securityform.htm. You may also submit this form anonymously, in which event you will not be eligible for the drawing.

Name:

Department:

Date:

E-mail:

Phone:

1. Does our organization's awareness program provide you with the information you need to perform your job in a way that reduces security risks and preserves privacy? If no, please describe what we can do to improve upon this.

2. What communications methods do you believe are most effective for security and privacy messages?

3. What awareness activity, or activities, do you believe has been most effective to date?

Exhibit 2   Sample Incident Report

Suspected Security or Privacy Incident Report

If you notice unusual or suspicious activities related to information security or privacy, please report them immediately. Promptness in reporting an event will help to mitigate the impact of verified incidents. Examples of such events include, but are not limited to, the following:

• Unknown person in area

• Caller requesting confidential information whose identity you cannot verify

• Unauthorized network access

• Persons digging through trash bins

• Persons carrying computing equipment out of the building

• Destruction of hardware or software

Exhibit 2   (continued)

- Unusual computer activity that could result from malicious code
- Messages requesting your user ID, password, credit card number, SSN, or other similar confidential information

To report an event immediately, call the information security and privacy office at 999-999-9999, or fill out the form located at www.organization.com/indicent_form.htm.

Name:

Phone number:

E-mail:

1. Describe suspicious event:

2. Date of event:

3. Location of event:

As part of your communications, let your target audience know about your plans for special days or weeks well ahead of time. Invite their participation and give them incentives, such as recognition or prizes, for participating. This way, they can arrange their schedules around the events.

Plan for Specific Events

Create planning road maps for your awareness events to ensure that you have thought of all the issues involved, and so that you can also identify potential glitches or problems, adjust accordingly, and make your event go as smoothly as possible. Here is a high-level planning and execution road map for a special awareness event such as a "Privacy Awareness Day." You will want to add more details in your plan as you start making more decisions about the event. (See Appendix M for other designated privacy and security days.)

Sample Plan for Privacy Awareness Day

1. Identify target audience.
2. Determine a day that will not conflict with another organized event. For example, if you want to celebrate Personal Information Privacy Day on April 26 (see Appendix N), check to ensure that you do not have another major event scheduled in your company for the same day. If you do, consider doing the event a day or two before or after the scheduled event.

3. Arrange publicity and event marketing.
4. Determine if you will give prizes or free trinkets.
5. Create format for the event.
6. Set time allocations.
7. Determine activities. Do not be afraid to try something new.
8. Check with HR, law department, and labor unions to ensure that your plans are acceptable from legal and contractual perspectives.
9. Communicate plans to management (approximately 1 + the number of months prior to the event).
10. Launch communications to target audiences (approximately 1 month prior to the event, then again 1 week before the event).

See Chapter 14 for activities and communications to consider for your special security and privacy day.

Chapter 18

Evaluate Education Effectiveness

Action to be effective must be directed to clearly conceived ends.

—**Jawaharlal Nehru**

When the effective leader is finished with his work, the people say it happened naturally.

—**Lao Tse**

Real knowledge is to know the extent of one's ignorance.

—**Confucius**

There are many ideas and possibilities for you to consider for evaluating the effectiveness of your education program. Many books about evaluating training have been written (see Appendix S for some). This chapter presents some methods for you to consider. Pick and choose whatever works best for your industry, organization, and location, and modify it to best meet your situation.

Evaluation Areas

The methods you use for information security and privacy evaluation and measurements are diverse. The following areas or "objects" of evaluation identified by Verduin and Clark* are useful. Tailor them to facilitate the evaluation of your

---

* John R. Verduin, Jr. and Thomas A. Clark, *Distance Learning*, Jossey Bass, San Francisco, 1991.

organizational education programs by considering the questions listed with each area.

1. *Access.* What groups are you reaching? Are there groups missing? Is everyone in the target group participating? Are you providing appropriate delivery methods for your target audiences? Can all your target audience access your training and awareness materials and participate in your delivery methods?

2. *Relevancy.* Is your education program relevant to your organization's business goals and expectations? Are your training and awareness messages and information relevant to job responsibilities? Will your education program have a noticeable impact on business practices? Was your training content appropriate for your target participants? Did your training cover regulatory and policy requirements?

3. *Quality.* Is the quality of your awareness materials adequate to get attention and effectively deliver the intended message? Does the quality of your training materials contribute to your learners' success? Do your trainers and teachers deliver quality education? Do they know how to interactively adjust to the abilities and experiences of their learners? Were the conditions right for learning and for each learner's subjective satisfaction?

4. *Learning Outcomes.* Is the amount of time allowed for learning appropriate for successfully understanding the message? What do your participants say about the usefulness and effectiveness of your training and awareness activities? Do you tell the participants the expected outcomes of your educational activities? What did the participants actually learn? Did your participants indicate they had a satisfactory learning experience?

5. *Impact.* What is the impact of your education program on your organization as a whole? Were activities and habits changed appropriately following training and awareness activities? What are the long-term impacts? Did the training methods promote the desired skills? Did job performance improve? What is the pattern of learner outcomes following each training session? Did you assist managers with determining their own workforce performance? Did you create return on investment statistics to support training and awareness funds?

6. *Cost-Effectiveness.* What time requirements are involved? What are the costs for the materials? How many people are in your targeted groups? How is training being delivered? Are you using inside and/or outside training and awareness resources? What is the value of the method of awareness activity or training session you used compared to other awareness and training options?

7. *Knowledge Generation.* Do you understand what is important for your personnel to know? For your managers to know? Do you understand what works and what does not work in your education program? Are you utilizing your evaluation results? Did you assist employees in determining their own performance success? Did you compile trend data to assist instructors in improving both learning and teaching?

8. *General to Specific.* Do your instructors tell learners enough information to allow them to self-evaluate their own success in implementing what they learn? Are learners told overall goals and the specific actions necessary to achieve them? Are goals and actions realistic and relevant? What is the necessary prerequisite general and specific knowledge?

Evaluation Methods

Consider using a combination of the following methods for determining the effectiveness of security and privacy education within your organization. Be sure to discuss the methods with your legal department and labor unions prior to implementation to make sure you are not violating any applicable laws, labor union requirements, or employee policies.

1. Videotape your training sessions. Review and critique to identify where you can improve delivery, content, organization, and so on.
2. Give quizzes immediately following training to measure comprehension.
3. Distribute a security and privacy awareness survey to all personnel, or to a representative sample. Do this prior to training to establish a baseline, then following training to help determine training effectiveness.
4. Send follow-up questionnaires to people who have attended formal training approximately 4 to 6 months following the training to determine how well they have retained the information presented.
5. Monitor the number of compliance infractions for each issue for which you provide training. Is this number decreasing or increasing? Why are they increasing or decreasing? Increased infractions may at first be a sign that the program has some weaknesses, but an increase in reporting infractions may instead be a result of increased awareness, which would be a sign of success.
6. Measure security and privacy knowledge as part of yearly job performance appraisals.
7. Place feedback and suggestion forms on an appropriate intranet Web site.
8. Track the number and type of security and privacy incidents that occur before and after the training and awareness activities.
9. Conduct spot checks of personnel behavior. For instance, walk through work areas and note if workstations are logged in while unattended or if patient information printouts are not adequately protected.
10. Record user IDs and completion status for Web- and network-based training. Send a targeted questionnaire to those who have completed the online training.
11. Have training participants fill out evaluation forms at the end of the class.
12. Identify the percentage of your target groups that participate in training.
13. Determine if you had an adequate number of instructors with the necessary level of expertise for the corresponding training topic.

14. Determine if the training materials addressed all your goals and objectives. Identify the gaps and make a plan to fill them.
15. Review training logs to see trends in attendance.
16. Tape or film participants performing their work after training to determine if they are utilizing the skills taught.
17. Administer occasional tests to personnel. Use multiple choice, short answer, essay tests or a combination. Avoid using true or false tests.
18. Perform interviews with past training participants, as well as personnel who have not yet been trained. Use structured and unstructured interview sessions.
19. Do an after-hours work-area walk through to document all the information security and privacy risks and violations that are in the area prior to giving training. Then, approximately 1 to 3 weeks following training, perform the after-hours walk through again to document how security and privacy risks have lessened, to show the effectiveness of the training or awareness activity.

Evaluating Education Effectiveness: Intangible Benefits

A successful information security and privacy awareness and training program will not only result in tangible benefits, but will also create intangible benefits as well. Intangible benefits are positive results that cannot be given monetary values, or would involve too complex calculations to create such monetary values.

However, intangible benefits have a great impact on your organization and on your bottom line. They can also be used as additional evidence of an awareness and training program's success. Different evaluation levels are described in the following pages. You can document the intangible benefits in the "Intangible Benefits" level of the effectiveness evaluation framework examples found in Exhibits 11 and 12 at the end of this chapter. Most organization leaders are interested in such measures and impacts; they are often as important to them as monetary measures. The following are common intangible benefits of corporate education programs:

- Increased job satisfaction
- Increased organizational commitment
- Improved work climate
- Fewer employee complaints
- Fewer employee grievances
- Reduction of employee stress
- Increased employee tenure
- Reduced employee lateness
- Reduced absenteeism
- Reduced employee turnover
- Increased innovation
- Increased customer satisfaction
- Decreased customer dissatisfaction

- Enhanced community image
- Enhanced investor image
- Fewer customer complaints
- Faster customer response time
- Increased customer loyalty
- Improved teamwork
- Increased cooperation
- Conflict reduction
- Improved decisiveness
- Improved communication

Exhibit 1   Job Satisfaction Levels

	Satisfied	*Dissatisfied*
No training	70%	23%
Training 6+ days/year	84%	8%

A 1998 Gallup Organization study* of 2 million employees within 700 companies, based upon a survey of all workers, concluded that employer-sponsored training and education is viewed by employees as a plus in recruitment, contributes significantly to retention, and that employees want more training particularly in technology, communications, and management. Exhibit 1 demonstrates the results of the survey.

The survey revealed that employer-provided training is a significant factor in overall employee recruiting and retention.

Other findings from this survey include the following:

- 80% indicated training is important or very important in keeping them as employees.
- Only 50% indicated the current training received from employers exceeded their expectations, indicating training and awareness quality can be improved.
- 58% of employees 32 years old and younger think training is useful or extremely useful in leading them to a higher-level job.
- 42% of employees 33 years old and older think training is useful or extremely useful in leading them to a higher-level job.

Determining Intangible Benefits of Training and Awareness

To determine the impact of information security and privacy awareness and training activities within your organization, include questions similar to those in the following subsections within your employee, training participants, manager and trainer evaluation surveys, interviews, and focus group discussions.

---

* Employees Speak Out on Job Training: Findings of a New Nationwide Study. (1998) The Gallup Organization. Survey Research Division.

Employees and Training Participants

1. Are you more satisfied with your job and support for your responsibilities as a result of this training?
2. Do you feel more committed to supporting the goals of the organization as a result of this training?
3. Do you believe the work climate is better as a result of information security and privacy awareness activities?
4. Do you feel less work-related stress as a result of the information security and privacy training?
5. Do you believe your job advancement opportunities have improved as a result of this training?
6. Do the awareness and training activities motivate you to come to work each day?
7. Has the training given you ideas for how to improve information security and privacy within your own team?
8. Do you believe better information security and privacy practices will result in increased customer satisfaction?
9. Do you believe the information security and privacy awareness and training efforts enhance the organization's community image?
10. Do you believe the information security and privacy awareness and training efforts enhance the organization's investor image?
11. Has the training resulted in better teamwork with your coworkers?
12. Has the training provided you the ability to make better decisions related to information security?

Managers, Trainers, and Human Resources

1. Do you see increased job satisfaction in your personnel as a result of information security and privacy awareness and training efforts?
2. Do you believe your personnel have increased organizational commitment as a result of information security and privacy awareness and training activities and participation?
3. Has your work climate improved as a result of information security and privacy awareness and training efforts?
4. Do you notice fewer employee complaints regarding information security?
5. Do you receive fewer employee grievances concerning information security?
6. Do you believe your personnel have reduced their stress as a result of information security and privacy awareness and training activities?
7. Do you believe employees will stay with the organization longer in part because of the information security and privacy awareness and training efforts?
8. Have your personnel improved their punctuality and absenteeism in part because of information security and privacy awareness and training activities?

9. Have you witnessed increased innovation among your team members following information security and privacy awareness and training participation?
10. Do you believe there is now increased customer satisfaction because of the changes in how your personnel communicate with them as a result of training and awareness efforts?
11. Do you believe the organization has enhanced their community image as a result of providing information security and privacy awareness and training activities?
12. Have you received fewer customer complaints following implementation of information security and privacy awareness and training activities?
13. Are customer complaints resolved more quickly since implementing awareness and training?
14. Do you believe the organization's information security and privacy efforts will result in greater customer loyalty?
15. Do you notice increased personnel cooperation following training and awareness activities?
16. Have your information security and privacy communications with personnel improved?

Evaluating the Effectiveness of Specific Awareness and Training Methods

There are many ways to evaluate the effectiveness of the wide range of training and awareness activities. Some will work better than the others depending upon your organization, situation, and regulatory requirements. The following subsections give some examples of evaluating the effectiveness of a couple of specific training and awareness methods. Modify these as necessary for your specific education and delivery methods.

Evaluating the Effectiveness of Computer-Based Training Modules

Computer-based training (CBT) modules can be very effective for some types of training, but may be inappropriate and/or ineffective for other types. Whether or not you should use CBT depends upon your target audience, the topic, and the amount of interaction, feedback, and inquiry necessary. In general, here are the benefits and drawbacks of CBT education in a corporate setting:

- Benefits
    - Can be taken by the participant at a time most convenient to him or her.
    - Does not require trainer interaction.
    - Is cost-effective.
    - Participants can work at their own pace.

- Participants do not have someone watching over them.
- No associated travel expenses for trainers.
- More interesting for some participants than classroom training.
- Takes less time for the participant than classroom training.
- The participant can retake the portions of the CBT where more instruction is necessary.
- Drawbacks
  - No human instructor interaction, so may seem too impersonal.
  - Little, if any, individualization for each person's understanding capabilities.
  - Not as interactive.
  - Trying to find human help when necessary during the training may be hard.
  - The CBT may be poorly constructed.
  - The topic may not be best taught via CBT.
  - Errors within CBT content will be communicated and propagated to the learners.
  - Technology problems can occur with CBTs because of bandwidth, network, and similar problems.

When Does CBT Training Make Sense?

A few situations when CBT training is generally more practical than classroom or lecture style training:

- Procedural or hard skills training is required.
- A "safe," or more comfortable, learning environment is needed.
- Learners are geographically dispersed.
- Quick roll-out of training is required.
- Consistency in training delivery and materials is required.
- The training topic must meet standards on an ongoing basis.
- When the training is legislated, regulated, or must be based on best practices and given to large numbers and/or geographically dispersed participants.
- Training can effectively be self-directed.
- A large number, such as more than 100 learners, must be trained.

Launching CBT Training

1. Perform a needs analysis for training requirements to determine if the learners are receiving training for informational use, where a live instructor would be more beneficial, or for skills progress, where interaction with the computer would increase learning.
2. Perform a task analysis to determine the type of information that needs to be included within the CBT.

3. Design the learning objectives for the CBT. The objectives give the learner an idea of the outcome, conditions, and how he or she will be evaluated in the CBT program. The objectives give the developer of the CBT parameters to match to cognitive skills being communicated within the material.
4. Design the CBT screen designs. Create user-friendly screens with several characteristics: they should be simple as well as informative. Ideally, the participant should be able to perform some sort of activity like playing a video, giving an answer to a question, or placing something on the screen by using the drag-and-drop on each screen.
5. Give the CBT participant some control over the learning experience as is appropriate. For example, for advanced or high-level topics, give the participant the option of choosing how many examples he or she wants to be given, or the density of the topic context. In lower-level, or basic, participant situations, the participant may grasp the knowledge better if the program is "in charge," so that it leads the participant through the module in a very structured way consistent from one person to another.
6. Feedback is a very important part of a CBT program. Thoughtful, informative feedback is an essential component of CBT programs and can be formative and/or summative feedback or evaluations. In formative evaluations, the participant's knowledge is tested on the facts that were just given, while a summative evaluation tests the participant about the complete CBT module. Feedback words can be standard such as "correct" or "incorrect." For correct answers, restate the idea to reinforce learning. For incorrect answers, provide an explanation and the correct answer. Then, place the reworded question again later in the module so the participant can be confident the concept is understood.
7. Other important considerations:
   a. Course organization
   b. Screen composition
   c. Colors and graphics
   d. Text placement
   e. Wording
   f. White space
   g. Text justification (left or center)
   h. Navigation toolbar
   i. Consistency
8. Perform a quality assurance review of the finished CBT to ensure the finished product is successfully meeting the goals of the course. Use trainers, subject matter experts (SMEs), and a target learner or two as reviewers.
9. Obtain executive sponsorship and visible support for the training. Communicate this to all your target participants. It is most effective for the communication to come from the executive sponsor.
10. Identify your primary contacts within each team/department where you are launching the training. Communicate with them your timelines for

completing the training, along with directions for how the training needs to be presented, implemented, and documented within their area.

11. Obtain feedback from the primary contacts.
12. Review quiz and CBT module results.
13. Perform business impact analysis to determine how the training affected the personnel in their daily job performance.

Managing CBT Participation

The key to ensuring high participation in a CBT is to get the support and cooperation of your identified primary contacts throughout the organization, typically managers, who will instruct their personnel to take the CBT.

1. Have your information security and privacy champion send messages to your primary contacts asking them for their cooperation.
2. Send your primary contact a CBT implementation information package, including:
   a. Overview of the CBT along with learning objectives
   b. Target audiences
   c. Timeline for completion
   d. Responsibilities for the contacts and personnel participants
   e. Data collection forms (see Exhibits 3 and 4 for example forms)
   f. Sample memos for the contact to send to the participants about the training (see Exhibit 5 for an example memo)
3. Collect data forms from contacts on date designated within the timeline.
4. Follow-up by contacting those who have not responded within a week of the target date. Give them one more week to have their personnel complete the training and for them to submit their data collection forms.
5. One month following completion of the CBT, send evaluation surveys to contacts to determine what impact the training had on their personnel.
6. Update the CBT content according to feedback, quiz and test results, and other identified factors from your six levels of evaluation forms (see Exhibit 11 at the end of this chapter).

Effectiveness Evaluation Methods

Some possibilities include the following:

- Test each participant's knowledge acquisition with an online exam following completion of the module.
- Test each participant's knowledge acquisition with an online quiz following each section of the module.
- Control access to the exam questions and exam results.

- Calculate the number of participants who completed the module.
- Calculate the high, low, mean, and mode final CBT module test results.
- Calculate the high, low, mean, and mode results for each of the quizzes.
- Identify questions that had a low success rate, review them, and determine if the question is bad, or if the concept was not clearly communicated by the CBT curriculum.
- Compile reports for all the above; monitor participation progress as well as areas of concern that may need additional training or updated content.
- Obtain feedback via surveys, interviews, and/or focus groups from the managers in the areas where the training was given.
- Obtain feedback via surveys, interviews, and/or focus groups from the CBT participants 1 to 3 months following completion of the CBT.

Evaluating the Effectiveness of Awareness Newsletters

The two methods of effectiveness evaluation that lend themselves best to determining the effectiveness of many awareness activities, such as electronic awareness newsletters, that are targeted at a large population are sampling and surveys.

Sampling

Sampling is drawing information from a subset of your target group, the people you want to read the newsletter, to estimate the characteristics of the entire target population. Sampling is a good choice for newsletter effectiveness evaluation when:

- You cannot collect data from the entire population to whom the newsletter is targeted.
- You do not have the time to interview the large number of targeted individuals.
- You do not have the travel budget to visit all the target population.
- Some people in the target group are difficult to reach or contact.
- You do not have enough qualified staff to conduct interviews or compile surveys from everyone.

Sampling Procedures

1. Identify your target population.
2. Create a list of all members within the population.
3. Determine your sampling approach.
4. Determine your sample size.
5. Identify your sample participants.

Sampling Approaches

1. *Probability sampling.* Ensures every member of the target population has an equal chance of being selected for the sample.
   a. *Simple random sampling.* Determine what percentage of the target population to contact, and then randomly choose from the entire population. This is the most straight forward, but not frequently used. It is often difficult to get a list of the entire population. Some of the employees in the list may have left the organization. The clerical effort to draw the sample may be very time-consuming if the population is large. And, it may not be more appropriate to select some individuals and not others.
   b. *Stratified random sampling.* Divide the entire target population into groups, based upon such characteristics as geographic location, personnel levels, departments, and so on. Then, choose an identified percentage from each of these groups (strata). This enables the evaluator to analyze the data of different subgroups and to compare and contrast the findings.
   c. *Cluster sampling.* First sample a large subgroup, then sample from within the subgroup. For example, select 6 out of a total of 12 field offices, and then within each of the 6 chosen offices, draw a random sample of employees to contact. This is useful for reducing costs and the time required to survey people across many groups and/or locations.
2. *Nonprobability sampling.* This method does not provide information that can be generalized with confidence to the entire population. The results may be biased and could affect the usefulness of the findings. However, it is easier than the probability sampling methods.
   a. *Convenience sampling.* Contacting personnel who are most accessible for feedback. The evaluator does not know if these people have characteristics that bias the outcome. For example, asking for volunteers to participate may result in people who have a specific motivation to give feedback that would be completely different than if others were contacted who did not have the same motivations.
   b. *Purposive sampling.* Individuals are selected because of their position, experience, knowledge, or attitudes. Because the sample is not randomly selected, the findings cannot be generalized beyond those who participated.
   c. *Snowball sampling.* Contact identified departments, individuals, etc., and ask them for suggestions for individuals to include in the sample. It is particularly useful when a list of names is difficult to obtain any other way.

When choosing your sampling method, take into consideration the following issues:

■ *Budget.* How much money is available for travel, hiring consultants, interviewers, postage, audiotapes, and other applicable materials?
■ *Size* of sample population

- *Geographical locations* of the population
- *Availability* of the list of all possible people within the population
- The data collection *methods*
- How much *variance* exists within the population

Determining Sample Size

You need to determine, "how many participants are enough?" The larger the number, the more representative the results will be for the entire population. The sample size should depend on the following factors:

- *The rarity of the event being evaluated.* If the event is rare, then a larger sample size should be used. For example, if you want feedback for an event that happens once a year, you should use a larger sample size than if you are getting feedback for an event that happens once a month.
- *Available resources.* If you have sufficient time, resources, and personnel, draw a large sample.
- *The degree of precision needed.* The impact of the evaluation must be considered. For example, if the evaluation involves whether the training led to reducing the amount of financial fraud resulting from access to customer data, then you will want a larger sample so you can be more accurate determining if the benefits of the training outweigh the side effects.
- *Whether or not the findings will be generalized.* If generalization is not a goal, then the number depends upon the key evaluation questions, how many methods are being used to collect data, and what decision makers believe is sufficient in order to use the findings. If generalization is a goal, then you will likely need a probability sampling method.

Exhibit 2 gives you an idea of how large your sample size needs to be to have a confidence level (assurance that the results represent the total target population) of 95% with a range of 5% and 10%.

Surveys Composition

Create your survey to best obtain the feedback you need for your information security and privacy newsletters, or other awareness or training activity for which you are using surveys. Solicit the opinions, beliefs and feedback from your target group. Surveys typically provide information for the Level 3 type of evaluation method, but may also provide Level 4 information (see Exhibit 11 at the end of this chapter). To improve the response rate for your surveys to determine the effectiveness of newsletters, keep the following in mind:

1. Keep the survey as short and easy to answer as possible.
2. Stick with yes/no, rating (Likert), or multiple-choice answers.

Exhibit 2 Determining Responding Sampling Size Based on a Confidence Level of 95%

Population	Required Precision + or –5%	Required Precision + or – 10%
Total # of people	Sample size	Sample size
50	44	33
75	63	42
100	80	49
150	108	59
200	132	65
300	168	73
400	196	78
500	217	81
1,000	277	88
3,000	340	93
5,000	356	94
10,000	369	95

3. Consider using a combination of questions.
4. Use terms the participants will understand.
5. Phrase items in the same manner that participants speak.
6. Do not use "and/or" in survey items.
7. Avoid using acronyms.
8. Do not use double negatives. For example, do not use a question like the following:

   "Do you believe that trainees should not have to pay for their own training? Yes or no?"

   If the participant answers "no," it actually means, "Yes, trainees should pay for their own training."
9. Avoid wording that suggests answers or biases responses in one direction. For example, do not start a question with "Isn't it true that …"
10. Avoid leading or loaded questions. These are questions that lead the respondent to answer differently if the question were worded a different way.

11. Avoid "double-barreled" questions that ask for more than one piece of information in the question. For example, do not ask, "Is this newsletter interesting and useful? Yes or no?"
12. Use plenty of white space to make the survey easy to read.
13. Group items into logical sections.
14. Provide clear, simple, and brief directions/instructions.
15. Make it easy to return the survey. For example, via online form submission, e-mail, self-addressed stamped envelope, and so on.
16. Provide advance communication, preferably from the information security and privacy sponsor, that the survey will be taking place.
17. Clearly communicate the reason for the survey. For example:
    a. To improve the applicability of the information to personnel job responsibilities
    b. To learn the topics that are of most concern to personnel
    c. To discover information security and privacy risks that were not yet known
    d. To ensure personnel are reading the newsletters
    e. To improve the quality of the newsletters
18. Indicate who will see the results of the survey.
19. Describe how the results will be used.
20. Pilot the survey before wide distribution. This will allow you to identify, remove, or revise confusing and unnecessary items.
21. Notify personnel the survey is coming within an issue or two of the newsletter and ask for their participation.
22. Estimate the time needed to complete the survey.
23. Allow participants to remain anonymous. You will likely want to attach some other type of stratification if you do this, though; such as job level, department, and so on.
24. Ask managers to support the survey and encourage participation.
25. If applicable for sampling method, communicate to the target audience that they are part of a carefully selected sample, and that their participation is very important.
26. Use one or two follow-up reminders.
27. Send the survey on behalf of executive management; including the leader's signature if possible.
28. Provide incentives for completing and returning the survey. For example, a coupon for a free personal pan pizza, a drawing from those participating for a free day of vacation, and so on.
29. Send a summary of your survey results to your participants.
30. Take advantage of including survey questions within existing surveys whenever possible, for instance, within existing HR employee satisfaction surveys.

Survey Questions

Think about the purpose and goals for the information security and privacy newsletter, or the awareness event or training offering for which you are surveying. Construct the survey questions to determine if those goals are met. For example, consider including questions similar to the following if these are some of your newsletter goals:

1. How well does the newsletter communicate recent information security and privacy incidents within the company?
2. How well does the newsletter communicate incidents outside the company that present a risk to the organization?
3. How well does the newsletter communicate the organization's information security and privacy policies?
4. How often do you read the information security and privacy newsletter?
5. What are the reasons you do not read, or rarely read, the newsletter?
6. What topics would you like to see included within the newsletter?
7. What do you feel is the most helpful information currently within the newsletters?
8. What do you feel is the least helpful information currently within the newsletters?
9. Do you feel the newsletters should be published more often, less often, or is the current publication rate just about right?
10. Which of the following types of information security and privacy newsletters do you believe is most beneficial: one that goes to all corporate personnel or newsletters that are department specific and tailored?
11. What form of newsletter do you prefer and are most likely to read: e-mail, paper, or Web-based?

Survey Administration

1. Identify and document the survey participants along with contact information.
2. Prepare the surveys for distribution.
3. For mailed surveys, prepare return envelopes.
4. Compose a cover letter to accompany each survey. It is ideal to have the executive sponsor sign the letter. The cover letter should state the purpose, give instructions, and other items as applicable from the list of 30 items earlier.
5. For mailed surveys, prepare envelopes for mailing.
6. Create a survey tracking form to record each participant's name, the date the survey was sent, and when it was received.
7. Record the receipt of surveys as they are returned. Even if they are anonymous, you can count the forms to determine how many participants have responded. You will need this to determine the response rate.
8. Follow up with those who do not return the survey to help increase your response rate.

Education Effectiveness Evaluation Framework Activities Checklist

Create a checklist (see Appendix R) to help you keep on track with establishing baseline measurements, delivery measurements, and impact measurements that you collect within the education effectiveness evaluation framework (see Appendix C). Use any of the following forms in conjunction with this checklist to help you plan and implement your own, customized information security and privacy education evaluation framework.

1. Establish the information security and privacy training and awareness schedule.
2. Identify your goals for each training and awareness activity.
3. Obtain executive support for the awareness and training program.
4. Create an inventory detailing your training and awareness activities and associated information (see Appendix J). Use this inventory to track progress with your education program. See Exhibit 3 for an example form.
5. Identify your awareness and training contacts for each location where the education activities will be given. See Exhibit 4 for an example form. Consider combining Exhibits 3 and 4 into one spreadsheet to centralize tracking, contacts, and other inventory information.
6. Send your contacts the training and awareness schedule, along with a memo from your executive education sponsor. See Exhibit 5 or Appendix A for an example memo.
7. Create an effectiveness evaluation framework for each training and awareness event/activity and fill in the information you have so far. See Exhibits 11 and 12 for training and awareness examples. A generic copy is in Appendix C.
8. Three weeks before each education activity, send your appropriate contacts the baseline preevaluation. See Exhibit 6 for an example form.
9. Two weeks before the activity, follow-up with contacts who have not yet returned their completed baseline preevaluation.
10. Take the information from the completed baseline preevaluations and put into the corresponding effectiveness evaluation framework worksheet. Use the example version of the baseline preevaluation form to help you determine within which levels to place the information. See Exhibits 11 and 12 to see how information is incorporated into the evaluation.
11. Send the appropriate contacts the information privacy and security education effectiveness evaluation at the time the activity is scheduled to occur. See Exhibits 7 and 10 for example forms. See Appendix B for a slightly different version of the form.
12. One week following the activity, follow up with contacts who have not yet returned their completed information security education effectiveness evaluation.
13. Take the information from the completed information security education effectiveness evaluations and put into the corresponding effectiveness

evaluation framework. Use Exhibits 11 and 12 to help you determine within which levels to place the information.

14. Send the appropriate contacts the information security education effectiveness follow-up evaluation 2 to 4 months following the activity, depending upon what is best for your organization. See Exhibits 8 and 9 for example forms.

15. Two weeks after sending the form, follow up with contacts who have not yet returned their completed information security education effectiveness follow-up evaluation.

16. Take the information from the completed information security education effectiveness follow-up evaluations and put into the corresponding effectiveness evaluation framework form. Use Exhibits 11 and 12 to help you determine within which levels to place the information.

17. Analyze the completed effectiveness evaluation framework and create your executive summary and reports from the information you have received.

18. Circulate the reports to your executive sponsors and contacts as appropriate.

19. Update the awareness or training activity as necessary.

20. Start the education evaluation cycle again!

Exhibit 3 Example Training and Awareness Inventory and Tracking Form

Company: *Company X*

Date:

Type of Education: *Information Privacy and Security*

Information Security Training

Topic Description	Been Given? Y/N	Baseline Measurement? Y/N	Executive Support? Y/N	Goals	Target Group	Group Size	Delivery method (e.g., CBT, Classroom, Webinar, Video, etc.)	Next Delivery Date	Local, National, or International?	Notes

Information Security Awareness

Topic Description	Been Given? Y/N	Baseline Measurement? Y/N	Executive Support? Y/N	Goals	Target Group	Group Size	Delivery method (e.g., Poster, Web site, Newsletter, Presentation, Contest, etc.)	Next Delivery Date	Local, National, or International?	Notes

Exhibit 4 Example Training and Awareness Contacts Form

Company: *Company X*

Date:

Type of Education: *Information Privacy and Security*

Information Security Training

Contact Name	Location	Training Description	Scheduled Date	Goals	Target Group	Group Size	Completed? (Y/N)	% Participation	Notes

Information Security Awareness

Contact Name	Location	Awareness Description	Scheduled Date	Goals	Target Group	Group Size	Completed? (Y/N)	% Participation	Notes

Exhibit 5   Example Executive Sponsorship Memo

Company X is a strong proponent of information security and privacy. Ensuring security and privacy is essential for customer satisfaction as well as for ensuring regulatory and legal compliance. Effective security and privacy training and awareness is critical for ensuring information assets are secured. Throughout the coming months, we will be holding a general security and privacy training sessions with all Company X personnel along with additional training sessions for groups with specific security and privacy job responsibilities.

Our goals for training and awareness are to

- Arm Company X personnel with the information necessary to incorporate information security and privacy actions within their job functions
- Heighten awareness and understanding of security and privacy fundamentals
- Enable deeper insights into consumer privacy needs, enhancing consumer confidence and more effectively meeting consumer needs across multiple points of contact with Company X, resulting in greater consumer loyalty
- Ensure everyone within Company X knows about new and emerging security and privacy requirements
- Communicate employee obligations under the organization's security and privacy policies
- Communicate Company X legal and regulatory security and privacy obligations and impact
- Comply with regulatory requirements for security and privacy training
- Keep security and privacy in the minds of personnel while they perform daily job tasks

All Company X personnel are required to participate in the general training and to observe awareness efforts. All personnel notified about the job-specific training are required to attend those sessions.

If you have any questions or concerns, please contact Alpha Omega, Information Privacy and Security Manager, alpha.omega@companyx.com, 999.999.9999.

Thank you in advance for your participation in this important endeavor.

Mary Ann Lewis, President, Company X

Exhibit 6   Baseline Preevaluation Worksheet

Name:	Department/Location:
Training or Awareness:	Planned Delivery Date:
Total Number in Target Group:	Today's Date:

Executive Listed on Communications Concerning the Awareness or Training:

Instructions:

Managers and information security and privacy contacts responsible for ensuring the personnel in their applicable area participates in information awareness activities and information training should complete this evaluation form and return to John Doe in the information privacy and security office 2 weeks before the training or awareness event.

This form will take an average of 5 to 10 minutes to complete.

Explanation of Ratings

1. Unsatisfactory: There is virtually no knowledge of the issues necessary to security business information assets.

2. Needs Improvement: There is a little knowledge of information security, but a lot of work is needed to bring knowledge to an acceptable level.

3. Satisfactory: Personnel have the knowledge necessary to perform the business activities in this area.

4. Better Than Expected: Personnel have information security and privacy knowledge for this area and to help other areas.

5. Role Model: Personnel exceed expectations for the amount of information security and privacy knowledge they possess.

Answer the Following

1. How many personnel are you responsible for managing? (Include contractors and temporary workers in your total)

2. Is information security and privacy part of your job descriptions and job appraisal process?

3. Approximately how much do you currently spend on information security and privacy in your area (round to the nearest $100)?

4. Approximately how many hours do you spend on information security and privacy activities in your area each week?

(continued)

Exhibit 6 (continued)

5. How do you rate your personnel's knowledge of information security and privacy policies, procedures, and business-related issues (check one)?

☐ Unsatisfactory

☐ Needs Improvement

☐ Satisfactory

☐ Better than other areas

☐ Role model

6. Indicate approximately which of the following is closest to your estimate of how many of your personnel have participated in each of the following:

Activity	*1* *0%*	*2* *25%*	*3* *50%*	*4* *75%*	*5* *100%*
a. Regularly view the Information Security intranet Web site	☐	☐	☐	☐	☐
b. Reported information security and privacy concerns or incidents to you	☐	☐	☐	☐	☐
c. Been infected with malicious code (virus, worm, Trojan horse, etc.)	☐	☐	☐	☐	☐
d. Attended information security and privacy training or taken an information security and privacy CBT	☐	☐	☐	☐	☐
e. Discussed information security and privacy with Company X customers or clients	☐	☐	☐	☐	☐
f. Participated in information security and privacy contests, quizzes, or special events	☐	☐	☐	☐	☐

7. List concerns you have for information security and privacy within your area, or within Company X organization-wide:

8. Which of the following awareness and training activities are most effective for your personnel (check all that apply)?

☐ Computer-based training (CBT)   ☐ Classroom training

☐ Web-based interactive training   ☐ Awareness newsletters

☐ Awareness Web sites   ☐ Awareness posters

☐ Special information security and privacy events   ☐ Information security contests

☐ Awareness pop-up messages

Exhibit 7   Sample Education Effectiveness Contact Evaluation for Managers: Sample 1

Training or Awareness Title: _____

Location: _____

Manager: _____Delivery Date_____

PART I: Demographic Information

1. How many people were asked to participate?
2. How many actually participated to completion?
3. Did you send a memo asking all target participants to attend?
4. Did you indicate participation was required?
5. Did you incorporate participation in information security and privacy training into the job appraisal process?

PART II: Your Reaction to This Training

Circle One Rating Number for Each Item.	Strongly Disagree	Disagree	Agree	Strongly Agree	Not Applicable
1. The training objectives were clear.	1	2	3	4	n/a
2. Overall, the information will be useful in my area's work.	1	2	3	4	n/a
3. The order of the training topics and activities made sense to me.	1	2	3	4	n/a
4. The pace of training was good—neither too fast nor too slow.	1	2	3	4	n/a
5. The training module was easy to use.	1	2	3	4	n/a
6. I am satisfied the information in the module is applicable to my personnel.	1	2	3	4	n/a
7. I would recommend this training to other departments.	1	2	3	4	n/a

(*continued*)

Exhibit 7   (continued)

Circle One Rating Number for Each Item.	Strongly Disagree	Disagree	Agree	Strongly Agree	Not Applicable
8. This training is a good investment for the company.	1	2	3	4	n/a
9. Examples and illustrations supported understanding the material.	1	2	3	4	n/a

The Overall Rating I Would Give This Training Module Is:	Not Useful	Useful	Very Useful	Extremely Useful
	☐	☐	☐	☐

Comments:

Job Appraisal Process

1. How often are job appraisals performed?

2. Who performs job appraisals?

3. What items are consistent for all personnel appraisals?

4. What impact do appraisals have on personnel job success (e.g., promotions, raises, demotions, terminations, etc.)?

5. When are job appraisals performed? At the same time each year for all personnel?

6. What global issues do you need to consider? In what countries do you have personnel?

7. Do you have any restrictions with regard to the job appraisal process in other countries that are different from the United States? These could be organizational restrictions, or regulatory and legal restrictions.

8. Do you need to make training and awareness available in different languages? This could impact how you can incorporate into the job appraisal process depending on how widely you can deploy your set of training and awareness curriculum.

Exhibit 8 Education Effectiveness Follow-Up Evaluation

Training Title: _____   Location: _____

Manager: _____   Beginning Date: _____

Training completion date: _____

PART I: Demographic Information

1. How many personnel do you manage?

2. To how many of your personnel did you send a CBT announcement memo?

3. How many of your personnel completed the entire CBT?

4. Do you see increased job satisfaction in your personnel as a result of information security and privacy awareness and training efforts?

5. Do you notice fewer employee complaints regarding information security?

6. Did you incorporate participation in information security and privacy training into the job appraisal process?

(continued)

Exhibit 8 **(continued)**

PART II: Your Reaction to this Training

Circle One Rating Number For Each Item.	Strongly Disagree	Disagree	Agree	Strongly Agree	Not Applicable
7. The training objectives were clear.	1	2	3	4	n/a
8. Overall, the information in the CBT will be useful in my area's work.	1	2	3	4	n/a
9. The order of the training topics and activities made sense to me.	1	2	3	4	n/a
10. The pace of training was good—neither too fast nor too slow.	1	2	3	4	n/a
11. The training module was easy to use.	1	2	3	4	n/a
12. I am satisfied the information in the module is applicable to my personnel.	1	2	3	4	n/a
13. I would recommend this training to other departments.	1	2	3	4	n/a
14. This training is a good investment for the company.	1	2	3	4	n/a
15. Examples and illustrations supported understanding the material.	1	2	3	4	n/a

The Overall Rating I Would Give This Training Module Is:

Not Useful ☐   Useful ☐   Very Useful ☐   Extremely Useful ☐

Comments:

Exhibit 9 Contact and Manager Follow-Up Worksheet

Name:_____ Department and Location: _____

Training or Awareness:_____ Today's Date: _____

Date Training or Awareness Occurred:_____

Instructions:

Managers and information security and privacy contacts responsible for ensuring the personnel in their applicable area participates in information awareness activities and information training should complete this evaluation form and return to John Doe in the information privacy and security office 2 months following the training or awareness event.

It will take, on average, 5 to 10 minutes to complete this form.

1. Did the training or awareness activity have a noticeable impact on business practices? Please check all the following that are applicable:

   ☐ The number of information security and privacy incidents has reduced since the education activity.

   ☐ There are visible indications of increased information security and privacy awareness (for example, posters, more secure work areas and desks, etc.).

   ☐ Increased personnel job satisfaction.

   ☐ Personnel understand the need for information security and privacy policies and procedures.

   ☐ Increased budget for information security and privacy activities and tools. If so, indicate by how many dollars your budget has increased:

   _____

2. Indicate approximately which of the following is closest to your estimate of how many of your personnel now do the following:

Measures	1 0%	2 25%	3 50%	4 75%	5 100%
a. Regularly view the Information Privacy & Security intranet Web site	☐	☐	☐	☐	☐
b. Report information security and privacy concerns or incidents to you	☐	☐	☐	☐	☐
c. Been infected with malicious code (virus, worm, Trojan horse, etc.) since the training or awareness event	☐	☐	☐	☐	☐
d. The level of confidence you place in the value of this activity to your area	☐	☐	☐	☐	☐
e. Discuss information security and privacy with Company X customers or clients	☐	☐	☐	☐	☐

3. Describe the impact of this awareness or training activity in your area:

**Exhibit 10   Education Effectiveness Contact Evaluation
for Managers: Sample 2**

Name:_____Department & Location:_____

Training or Awareness Activity: _____Date Given:_____

Total Number in Target Group:_____

Number of People Who Participated:_____

Today's Date:_____

Executive Who Was Listed on Communications as Supporting the Awareness or
Training:_____

Instructions:

Managers and information security and privacy contacts responsible for
ensuring the personnel in their applicable area participates in information
awareness activities and information training should complete this evaluation
form and return to Sue Jones in the information privacy and security office
within 1 week following the training or awareness event. Please send along
with any training participants evaluations.

This will take, on average, 5 to 10 minutes for you to complete.

Explanation of Ratings

1. Unsatisfactory: Was very poor and/or did not apply to business practices or
   goals at all.
2. Needs Improvement: Was relevant to business, but needs improvement.
3. Satisfactory: Adequately supported business processes and goals.
4. Better Than Expected: Provided information to allow personnel to improve
   information security and privacy in more ways than expected.
5. Role Model: Excellent information that supports business goals and will
   help my area be a role model for the entire company.

Answer the Following

1. How many people were asked to participate?
2. How many actually participated to completion?
3. Did you send a memo or message asking all target participants to attend?
4. Indicate your rating for each of the following:

Exhibit 10 (continued)

Measures	1 Unsatisfactory	2 Needs Improvement	3 Satisfactory	4 Better than Expected	5 Role Model
a. Participants indicated the activity will help them with their job responsibilities	☐	☐	☐	☐	☐
b. Participants have greater demonstrated knowledge of information security and privacy risks	☐	☐	☐	☐	☐
c. Quality of training or awareness materials	☐	☐	☐	☐	☐
d. Delivery method for the target audience was effective	☐	☐	☐	☐	☐
e. The education activity was relevant to your area's business goals and expectations	☐	☐	☐	☐	☐
f. The training and awareness messages and information were relevant to job responsibilities	☐	☐	☐	☐	☐
g. The education activity had a noticeable impact on business practices in your area	☐	☐	☐	☐	☐
h. The time it took for your personnel to participate in the training or awareness activity	☐	☐	☐	☐	☐
i. The cost in dollars to your area for your personnel to participate in the training or awareness activity.	☐	☐	☐	☐	☐
j. The activity supports applicable regulatory requirements and/or demonstration of due diligence	☐	☐	☐	☐	☐
5. Please describe what can be improved:					

Exhibit 11   Effectiveness Evaluation Framework: Training Example

Training: Information Security Fundamentals

Date: December 10, 2011

Been Given? Yes

Baseline Measurement? No

Executive Support? Yes

Target Group: All new hires globally

Group Size: Unknown

Delivery Method: CBT Module International

Next Delivery Date: Ongoing

Goals:

Notes/Observations:

General Effectiveness Indicators:

Your answers to the following questions can be incorporated into an executive summary report covering the effectiveness of your training or awareness activity. Answer by using the information from the forms on the following pages.

1. **Access.**
   a. What groups are you reaching?
   b. What groups are missing?
   c. What is the participation rate for the group?
   d. Are you providing appropriate delivery methods for your target audiences?
   e. Can all your target audiences access your training and awareness materials and participate in your delivery methods?

2. Relevancy.

   a. Is your education program relevant to your organization's business goals and expectations?

   b. Are your training and awareness messages and information relevant to job responsibilities?

   c. Will your education program have a noticeable impact on business practices?

   d. Was your training content appropriate for your target participants?

   e. Did your training cover regulatory and policy requirements?

3. Quality.

   a. Is the quality of your awareness materials adequate to get attention and effectively deliver the intended message?

   b. Does the quality of your training materials contribute to your learners' success?

   c. Do your trainers and teachers deliver quality education?

   d. Do they know how to interactively adjust to the abilities and experiences of their learners?

   e. Were the conditions right for learning and for each learner's subjective satisfaction?

4. Learning Outcomes.

   a. Is the amount of time allowed for learning appropriate for successfully understanding the message?

   b. What do your participants say about the usefulness and effectiveness of your training and awareness activities?

   c. Do you tell the participants the expected outcomes of your education activities?

   d. What did the participants actually learn?

   e. Did your participants indicate they had a satisfactory learning experience?

5. Impact.

   a. What is the impact of your education program on your organization as a whole?

   b. Were activities and habits changed appropriately following training and awareness activities?

   c. What are the long-term impacts?

   d. Did the training methods promote the desired skills?

   e. Did job performance improve?

   f. What is the pattern of learner outcomes following each training session?

   g. Did you assist managers with determining their own workforce performance?

   h. Did you create return on investment statistics to support training and awareness funds?

(continued)

Exhibit 11 (continued)

6. Cost Effectiveness.

a. What time requirements are involved?

b. What are the costs for the materials?

c. How many people are in your targeted groups?

d. How is training being delivered?

e. Are you using inside and/or outside training and awareness resources?

f. What is the value of the method of awareness activity or training session you used compared to other awareness and training options?

7. Knowledge Generation.

a. Do you understand what is important for your personnel to know?

b. For your managers to know?

c. Do you understand what works and what doesn't work in your education program?

d. Are you utilizing your evaluation results?

e. Did you assist employees in determining their own performance success?

f. Did you compile trend data to assist instructors in improving both learning and teaching?

8. General to Specific.

a. Do your instructors tell learners enough information to allow them to self-evaluate their own success in implementing what they learn?

b. Are learners told overall goals and the specific actions necessary to achieve them?

c. Are goals and actions realistic and relevant?

d. What is the necessary prerequisite general and specific knowledge?

Training Objectives

1. Reaction/Satisfaction and Planned Actions

FOCUS: *Training program, the facilitator/trainer, and how the application might occur.*

	Measures	Data Collection Method/ Instruments	Data Sources	Timing	Goals
Communicate information security and privacy fundamentals to all new staff.	Average rating of at least 4.2 on 5.0 scale.	Training evaluation questionnaire Online participation system	Participants System data Management memos	Prior to training During training Immediately following training	Communicate global information security and privacy policies, procedures, and standards to new personnel. Demonstrate management support. Ensure quality instructional material. Obtain participant view of training effectiveness and quality. Cover all necessary regulatory requirements.

(continued)

Exhibit 11   (continued)

Measures	1 Unsatisfactory	2 Needs Improvement	3 Satisfactory	4 Better than Expected	5 Role Model
1. Class attendance participation (% of expected participants)	☐	☐	☐	☐	☐
2. Support from management (visible support)	☐	☐	☐	☐	☐
3. % of quiz questions answered/attempted	☐	☐	☐	☐	☐
4. Demonstration of knowledge through quiz results	☐	☐	☐	☐	☐
5. Postclass evaluation average rating	☐	☐	☐	☐	☐
6. Quality of training materials	☐	☐	☐	☐	☐
7. Goals met	☐	☐	☐	☐	☐

Average rating: (sum of rows 1 through 7) / 7 =

Training Objectives 2. Learning Acquisition of Skills Selection of Skills	Measures	Data Collection Method/ Instruments	Data Sources	Timing	Goals
Participants will learn how to secure information on Company X networks. Participants will learn procedures applicable to their job responsibilities.	Role-play scenarios Demonstrate appropriate selection and use of controls Quiz results Participation rate	Skill practice Post training test Pre-training test Self-assessment Trainer assessment	Participants Test results Evaluations	During program Immediately following training 3 months following training.	Understand and comply with Company X security policies, procedures, and standards. Incorporate security into their job activities. Provide individual feedback to build participant confidence. Ensure individuals are learning. Evaluate trainers. Communicate regulatory requirements.

(continued)

Exhibit 11 (continued)

Measures	1 Unsatisfactory	2 Needs Improvement	3 Satisfactory	4 Better than Expected	5 Role Model
1. Role-play scenarios	☐	☐	☐	☐	☐
2. Self-assessment	☐	☐	☐	☐	☐
3. Trainer assessments of perceived learning	☐	☐	☐	☐	☐
4. Demonstration of knowledge and skills through module case studies and related quizzes	☐	☐	☐	☐	☐
5. Postclass test scores	☐	☐	☐	☐	☐
6. Improvement of postclass scores over preclass test scores	☐	☐	☐	☐	☐
7. Goals met	☐	☐	☐	☐	☐

Average rating: (sum of rows 1 through 7) / 7 =

Training Objectives 3. Application/ Implementation	*Measures*	*Data Collection Method/ Instruments*	*Data Sources*	*Timing*	*Goals*
Ensure the training methods, procedures, and security controls are being used within daily job activities. Incorporate good information security and privacy practices into job responsibilities.	Reported frequency and effectiveness of skill application Follow-up information collected Systems security data improvement	Questionnaire Follow-up survey Job performance observation Follow-up session Follow-up interview Follow-up focus groups Assignments related to the training Action planning/improvement plans Performance contracting Security logs, reports, and incidents	Participants Surveys Questionnaires Interviews Systems data	1 week following training 3 months following training 9 months following training	Obtain understanding for the need for information security and privacy in business processing. Incorporate information security and privacy into daily job activities. Be able to identify information security and privacy risks.

(continued)

Exhibit 11 (continued)

Measures	1 Unsatisfactory	2 Needs Improvement	3 Satisfactory	4 Better than Expected	5 Role Model
1. Participant opinion questionnaires	☐	☐	☐	☐	☐
2. Job site observation of security practices following training	☐	☐	☐	☐	☐
3. After-hours area reviews for security risks	☐	☐	☐	☐	☐
4. Satisfactory assignment completion	☐	☐	☐	☐	☐
5. Postclass evaluation average rating	☐	☐	☐	☐	☐
6. Quality of training materials	☐	☐	☐	☐	☐
7. Goals met	☐	☐	☐	☐	☐

Average rating: (sum of rows 1 through 7) / 7 =

Training Objectives 4. Business Impact	Measures	Data Collection Method/ Instruments	Data Sources	Timing	Goals
Improve the business process while also improving information security.	Management feedback Time to address security Identification of new information security risks	Performance monitoring Follow-up impact questionnaires Assignments related to the training Action planning/ improvement plans Performance contracting Program follow-up session Management interviews	Systems records Participant managers Participants	6 months after training 12 months after training	Reduce number of security incidents. Identify information security and privacy risks more quickly than prior to training. Resolve security incidents more quickly.

(continued)

Exhibit 11 (continued)

Measures	1 Unsatisfactory	2 Needs Improvement	3 Satisfactory	4 Better than Expected	5 Role Model
1. Management opinion questionnaires	☐	☐	☐	☐	☐
2. Job site observation of security practices	☐	☐	☐	☐	☐
3. Information security risks resolved more quickly	☐	☐	☐	☐	☐
4. Incorporated training topics into job appraisal for the participants	☐	☐	☐	☐	☐
5. Number of security incidents reduced	☐	☐	☐	☐	☐
6. Information security risks discovered more quickly	☐	☐	☐	☐	☐
7. Goals met	☐	☐	☐	☐	☐

Average rating: (sum of rows 1 through 7) / 7 =

Training Objectives	Measures	Data Collection Method/Instruments	Data Sources	Timing	Goals
5. Education Investment Analysis (EIA)					
Obtain more tangible + intangible value for the training than the total training costs.	Productivity Software costs Personnel costs Downtime efficiency Customer complaints	System availability reports Management reports Time reports Security incident reports Training costs Surveys Interviews Trend data	Managers Administrators Executives Participants Business partners Trainers Human Resources	Prior to training Immediately following training 6 months following training	25% EIA for training investment 25% reduction of losses from security incidents 25% reduction of customer security incident reports Increased job satisfaction

(continued)

Exhibit 11   (continued)

Measures	1 Unsatisfactory	2 Needs Improvement	3 Satisfactory	4 Better than Expected	5 Role Model
1. Cost of training (materials, trainers, participant time from work, etc.)	☐	☐	☐	☐	☐
2. Security incident statistics	☐	☐	☐	☐	☐
3. Customer complaints statistics	☐	☐	☐	☐	☐
4. Network availability improvement related to security incidents	☐	☐	☐	☐	☐
5. Management feedback evaluations	☐	☐	☐	☐	☐
6. Cost for training was comparable to or below trend data	☐	☐	☐	☐	☐
7. Goals met	☐	☐	☐	☐	☐

Average rating: (sum of rows 1 through 7)/7 =

Training Objectives 6. Intangible Benefits	Measures	Data Collection Method/ Instruments	Data Sources	Timing	Goals
Increase understanding of information security and privacy issues and risks. Information security practices are included in all phases of project development.	Stakeholder feedback Information Privacy and security office statistics Project participation by information security staff Communications with Information Privacy and security office	Systems monitoring Observation Impact study Data analysis Interviews Surveys Trend data	Program stakeholders Trainers Participants Managers Legal HR	Immediately following training 3 months following training 6 months following training	Address training and awareness regulatory requirements. Effectively communicate Company X policies requirements. Increase corporate-wide information security and privacy understanding. Ensure training was aligned with applicable business measures. Obtain management support for continuing information security activities.

(continued)

Exhibit 11   (continued)

Measures	1 Unsatisfactory	2 Needs Improvement	3 Satisfactory	4 Better than Expected	5 Role Model
1. Training results met the information privacy and security office expectations	☐	☐	☐	☐	☐
2. Postevaluation scores higher than baseline evaluation scores	☐	☐	☐	☐	☐
3. Training addressed current high priority risks	☐	☐	☐	☐	☐
4. Information security office contacts included in new projects to incorporate information security	☐	☐	☐	☐	☐
5. Increased communications with information security office staff	☐	☐	☐	☐	☐
6. Increased visits to information security Office Web site	☐	☐	☐	☐	☐
7. Goals met	☐	☐	☐	☐	☐

Average rating: (sum of rows 1 through 7)/7 =

Exhibit 12 Effectiveness Evaluation Framework: Awareness Example

Awareness: Worldwide Computer Security Day—awareness building

Date: December 10, 2011

Been Given? Yes

Baseline Measurement? No

Executive Support? Yes

Target Group: All personnel globally

Group Size: All personnel and partners

International? Yes

Delivery Method: Video, bulletins, contests (w/prizes), activities will vary from year to year and office to office

Next Delivery Date: November 30, 2004

Goals: Build corporate-wide awareness of chosen information security and privacy topic.

Notes/Observations:

General Effectiveness Indicators:

Your answers to the following questions can be incorporated into an executive summary report covering the effectiveness of your awareness or training activity. Answer by using the information from the forms on the following pages.

1. Access.
   a. What groups are you reaching?
   b. What groups are missing?
   c. What is the participation rate for the group?
   d. Are you providing appropriate delivery methods for your target audiences?
   e. Can all your target audiences access your awareness and training materials and participate in your delivery methods?

(continued)

Exhibit 12   (continued)

2. Relevancy.

a. Is your education program relevant to your organization's business goals and expectations?

b. Are your awareness and training messages and information relevant to job responsibilities?

c. Will your education program have a noticeable impact on business practices?

d. Was your awareness content appropriate for your target participants?

e. Did your awareness cover regulatory and policy requirements?

3. Quality.

a. Is the quality of your awareness materials adequate to get attention and effectively deliver the intended message?

b. Does the quality of your awareness materials contribute to your learners' success?

c. Do your trainers and teachers deliver quality education?

d. Do they know how to interactively adjust to the abilities and experiences of their learners?

e. Were the conditions right for learning and for each learner's subjective satisfaction?

4. Learning Outcomes.

a. Is the amount of time allowed for learning appropriate for successfully understanding the message?

b. What do your participants say about the usefulness and effectiveness of your awareness and training activities?

c. Do you tell the participants the expected outcomes of your education activities?

d. What did the participants actually learn?

e. Did your participants indicate they had a satisfactory learning experience?

5. Impact.

a. What is the impact of your education program on your organization as a whole?

b. Were activities and habits changed appropriately following awareness and training activities?

c. What are the long-term impacts?

d. Did the awareness and training methods promote the desired skills?

e. Did job performance improve?

f. What is the pattern of learner outcomes following each awareness or training session?

g. Did you assist managers with determining their own workforce performance?

h. Did you create return on investment statistics to support awareness and training funds?

6. Cost-Effectiveness.

a. What time requirements are involved?

b. What are the costs for the materials?

c. How many people are in your targeted groups?

d. How is awareness being delivered?

f. Are you using inside and/or outside awareness and training resources?

g. What is the value of the method of awareness activity or training session you used compared to other awareness and training options?

7. Knowledge Generation.

a. Do you understand what is important for your personnel to know?

b. For your managers to know?

c. Do you understand what works and what doesn't work in your education program?

d. Are you utilizing your evaluation results?

e. Did you assist employees in determining their own performance success?

f. Did you compile trend data to assist instructors in improving both learning and teaching?

8. General to Specific.

a. Do your instructors tell learners enough information to allow them to self-evaluate their own success in implementing what they learn?

b. Are learners told overall goals and the specific actions necessary to achieve them?

c. Are goals and actions realistic and relevant?

d. What is the necessary prerequisite general and specific knowledge?

(continued)

Exhibit 12 **(continued)**

Awareness Objectives	Measures	Data Collection Method/ Instruments	Data Sources	Timing	Goals
1. Reaction/Satisfaction and Planned Actions FOCUS: Awareness program, the facilitator/trainer, and how the application might occur.					
Raise global and partner awareness of information security and privacy issues and risks.	Average rating of at least 4.2 on 5.0 scale Visits to information security office Web sites Questions to information security office personnel	Employee surveys Interviews Observation Web site statistics Web site feedback forms	Employees Information security office personnel Systems data	Prior to Computer Security Day (CSD) Immediately following CSD	Communicate global IT security policies, procedures, and standards to mid-level management and senior titled IT staff. Demonstrate management support. Ensure quality instructional material. Participant view of awareness effectiveness and quality. Cover all necessary regulatory requirements.

Measures	1 Unsatisfactory	2 Needs Improvement	3 Satisfactory	4 Better than Expected	5 Role Model
1. Awareness participation (% of expected participants)	☐	☐	☐	☐	☐
2. Support from management (visible support)	☐	☐	☐	☐	☐
3. Interaction (questions, etc.)	☐	☐	☐	☐	☐
4. Ease of delivery for awareness materials	☐	☐	☐	☐	☐
5. Post-awareness evaluation average rating	☐	☐	☐	☐	☐
6. Quality of awareness materials	☐	☐	☐	☐	☐
7. Goals met	☐	☐	☐	☐	☐

Average rating: (sum of rows 1 through 7)/7 =

(continued)

Exhibit 12 (continued)

Awareness Objectives 2. Learning Acquisition of Skills Selection of Skills	Measures	Data Collection Method/Instruments	Data Sources	Timing	Goals
Participants will understand the importance of securing information for the selected CSD topic within the Company X facilities.	Number of posters created Number of participants within contests	Notes Printing and mailing statistics E-mail Baseline quizzes Post-CSD quizzes Post-CSD area reviews	Personnel Systems data Management	During program Immediately following CSD 3 months following CSD	Raise awareness of information security and privacy risks. Get a poster in each department. Improve information security practices by personnel and partners.

Measures	1 Unsatisfactory	2 Needs Improvement	3 Satisfactory	4 Better than Expected	5 Role Model
1. Number of posters distributed	☐	☐	☐	☐	☐
2. Number of participants within contests	☐	☐	☐	☐	☐
3. Participation in quizzes	☐	☐	☐	☐	☐
4. Improvement of post-CSD quiz scores over baseline quiz scores	☐	☐	☐	☐	☐
5. Feedback from management	☐	☐	☐	☐	☐
6. Area security reviews improved from previous reviews	☐	☐	☐	☐	☐
7. Goals met	☐	☐	☐	☐	☐

Average rating: (sum of rows 1 through 7)/7 =

(continued)

Exhibit 12 (continued)

Awareness Objectives 3. Application/ Implementation	Measures	Data Collection Method/ instruments	Data Sources	Timing	Goals
CSD security topic is incorporated into personnel job responsibilities. Reduce global information security and privacy risks.	Reported frequency and effectiveness of skill application Follow-up information collected Systems security data improvement	Questionnaire Follow-up survey Job performance observation Follow-up session Follow-up interview Follow-up focus groups Assignments related to the awareness Action planning/ improvement plans Performance contracting Security logs, reports, and incidents	Participants Surveys Questionnaires Interviews Systems data Trainers	1 week following awareness 3 months following awareness 9 months following awareness	Obtain understanding for the need for information security and privacy in business processing. Incorporate information security and privacy into daily job activities. Be able to identify information security and privacy risks.

Measures	1 Unsatisfactory	2 Needs Improvement	3 Satisfactory	4 Better than Expected	5 Role Model
1. Participant opinion questionnaires	☐	☐	☐	☐	☐
2. Job site observation of security practices	☐	☐	☐	☐	☐
3. After-hours area reviews for security risks	☐	☐	☐	☐	☐
4. Number of internal security incidents	☐	☐	☐	☐	☐
5. Management feedback	☐	☐	☐	☐	☐
6. Focus group feedback	☐	☐	☐	☐	☐
7. Goals met	☐	☐	☐	☐	☐

Average rating: (sum of rows 1 through 7)/7 =

(continued)

Exhibit 12 (continued)

Awareness Objectives 4. Business Impact	Measures	Data Collection Method/ Instruments	Data Sources	Timing	Goals
Improve the business process while also improving information security and privacy for the CSD topic.	Management feedback Time to address security incidents Identification of new information security risks	Performance monitoring Follow-up impact questionnaires Assignments related to the awareness Action planning/ improvement plans Performance contracting Program follow-up session Performance monitoring Management interviews	Systems records Participant managers Participants	6 months after CSD 12 months after CSD	Reduce number of security incidents. Identify information security and privacy risks more quickly than prior to CSD. Resolve security incidents more quickly.

Measures	1 Unsatisfactory	2 Needs Improvement	3 Satisfactory	4 Better than Expected	5 Role Model
1. Management opinion questionnaires	☐	☐	☐	☐	☐
2. Job site observation of security practices	☐	☐	☐	☐	☐
3. Information security risks resolved more quickly	☐	☐	☐	☐	☐
4. Incorporated CSD topics into job appraisal for the participants	☐	☐	☐	☐	☐
5. Number of CSD topic security incidents reduced	☐	☐	☐	☐	☐
6. CSD security topic risks discovered more quickly	☐	☐	☐	☐	☐
7. Goals met	☐	☐	☐	☐	☐

Average rating: (sum of rows 1 through 7)/7 =

(continued)

Exhibit 12 (continued)

Awareness Objectives	Measures	Data Collection Method/Instruments	Data Sources	Timing	Goals
5. Education Investment Analysis (EIA) Obtain more tangible and intangible value for the CSD topic than the total CSD costs. Raise global and partner awareness of the CSD topic information security and privacy issues and risks.	Productivity Software costs Personnel costs Downtime Efficiency Customer complaints	Systems availability reports Management reports Time reports Security incident reports Awareness costs Surveys Interviews Trend data	Managers Administrators Executives Participants Business partners Trainers Human Resources	Prior to CSD Immediately following CSD 6 months following CSD	25% EIA for awareness investment 25% reduction of losses from CSD-related security incidents 25% reduction of CSD-related customer security incident reports Increased job satisfaction

Measures	1 Unsatisfactory	2 Needs Improvement	3 Satisfactory	4 Better than Expected	5 Role Model
1. Cost of CSD (materials, trainers, participant time from work, etc.)	☐	☐	☐	☐	☐
2. Security incident statistics for CSD topic	☐	☐	☐	☐	☐
3. Stayed at or below CSD budget	☐	☐	☐	☐	☐
4. Improved customer feedback for the CSD topic	☐	☐	☐	☐	☐
5. Management feedback evaluations	☐	☐	☐	☐	☐
6. Job satisfaction surveys	☐	☐	☐	☐	☐
7. Goals met	☐	☐	☐	☐	☐

Average rating: (sum of rows 1 through 7)/7 =

(continued)

Exhibit 12   (continued)

Awareness Objectives 6. Intangible Benefits	Measures	Data Collection Method/ Instruments	Data Sources	Timing	Goals
Increase understanding of CSD information security and privacy issues and risks.	Stakeholder feedback	Systems monitoring	Program stakeholders	Immediately following CSD	Address awareness and awareness regulatory requirements for CSD topic.
Raise global and partner awareness of CSD topic information security and privacy issues and risks.	Information privacy and security office statistics	Observation	Trainers	3 months following CSD	Effectively communicate Company X CSD-related policies requirements.
	Project participation by information security staff	Impact study	Participants	6 months following CSD	Increase corporate-wide CSD topic information security and privacy understanding.
	Communications with Information privacy and security office	Data analysis	Managers		Ensure CSD topic was aligned with applicable business measures.
		Interviews	Legal		Obtain management support for continuing information security activities.
		Surveys	HR		
		Trend data			

Measures	1 Unsatisfactory	2 Needs Improvement	3 Satisfactory	4 Better than Expected	5 Role Model
1. Awareness participation results met the information privacy and Security office expectations	☐	☐	☐	☐	☐
2. Stakeholders support for planning next CSD event	☐	☐	☐	☐	☐
3. CSD topic addressed current high priority risks	☐	☐	☐	☐	☐
4. Information security office contacts included in new projects to incorporate information security	☐	☐	☐	☐	☐
5. Increased communications with information security office staff	☐	☐	☐	☐	☐
6. Increased visits to information security office Web site	☐	☐	☐	☐	☐
7. Goals met	☐	☐	☐	☐	☐

Average rating: (sum of rows 1 through 7)/7 =

Chapter 19

Leading Practices

The more extensive a man's knowledge of what has been done, the greater will be his power of knowing what to do.

—Benjamin Disraeli

Information security and privacy professionals can learn much from the experiences of others. Why keep reinventing the wheel, when we can share with each other, learn what has worked and has not worked in other organizations, and then apply that knowledge appropriately? With this is mind, I invited some of the most successful information security awareness and training practitioners to share some of their experiences and tips.

Many readers will find this to be one of the most useful chapters in the book. It demonstrates how practitioners have put into practice the concepts and tips discussed within this book. It contains some real-life gems that will make corporate education for security and privacy a little more successful and, possibly, less stressful. Once more, I want to give a heartfelt thanks to each of my talented, generous contributors.

Setting the Standard for Data Privacy and Awareness

By Brian Honan*

The strength of your information security program, like a chain, is only as strong as its weakest link. Very often the weakest link in an information security management program is people. People click unknowingly on e-mail attachments, they choose insecure passwords and in some cases share those passwords with colleagues, they fall victim to clever—and not-so-clever—social engineering attacks, or they simply bypass your security controls because they want to get the job done quicker.

Organizations in highly regulated industries find the challenge of educating staff about their security responsibilities a daunting one. How do you address the various requirements of the differing standards while at the same time not over-loading or alienating your staff with too much information?

Faced with ever-changing legal and regulatory requirements, many companies deal with these requirements on a case-by-case basis. However, this often leads to a piecemeal approach, with solutions being implemented to address the specific requirements for the compliance requirement being dealt with. This in turn leads to disparate systems, which can prove costly to manage and support, resulting in information security being viewed as a hindrance to the business's ability to provide effective services to customers and subsequently being ignored or bypassed by staff.

This was the challenge faced by an organization based in Ireland. The organization was subject to many industry regulations and also legal obligations under Irish law such as the Data Protection Act. Various security awareness initiatives had failed, and the newly appointed chief information security officer was tasked with developing a security awareness program that would address all the needs of each of the regulations while engaging with the staff.

A review of the various in-house programs identified a number of security awareness initiatives that had been started relating to a specific regulation or business requirement. However, the results of the review highlighted that each of these security awareness initiatives focused solely on their own individual project. This in turn led to duplication of efforts resulting in staff, and indeed management, seeing security awareness as a waste of time.

Another key element that was identified as causing the failure of these programs was the lack of senior management support for the various security awareness programs. Each of the programs was supported by the line management responsible for the business area sponsoring the project. However, outside of that business area

---

* Brian Honan is an independent security consultant based in Dublin, Ireland, who is recognized as an industry expert on information security and, in particular, the ISO 27001 Information Security standard. Brian is regularly published in various industry publications and has authored the book *Implementing ISO 27001 in a Windows Environment* (http://www.itgovernance.co.uk/products/2207). He is also the European editor for the SANS Institute's SANS NewsBites, a semi-weekly electronic newsletter. Brian also founded the Irish Reporting and Information Security Service (IRISS www.iriss.ie), which is Ireland's first national CSIRT (Computer Security Incident Response Team).

there was little or no support for the program, and while intentions were good, in many cases the security awareness programs failed due to management in other business areas not viewing the program as a high-priority issue.

The chief information security officer (CISO) for this organization faced the challenge of introducing a security awareness program into a skeptical environment. How would she be able to get senior management backing for an initiative that had failed numerous times before while at the same time getting buy-in from disillusioned staff and persuading them to engage with a new security awareness program?

Having discussed the issue, we decided the most effective way of ensuring success would be to establish an Information Security Management System (ISMS) that could address all the regulatory and legal requirements. To this end, we elected to use the International Organization for Standardization/International Electrotechnical Commission (ISO/IEC) 27001:2005 Information Security Standard.

Formerly known as BS 7799, ISO/IEC 27001:2005 is now a vendor- and technology-neutral internationally recognized standard that provides companies with a risk-based approach to securing their information. Being an international standard, ISO/IEC 27001:2005 provides organizations with independent third-party verification that their information security management system meets an internationally recognized standard. This provides a company, and its customers and partners, with the confidence that they are managing their security in accordance with recognized and audited best practices.

By adopting the risk- and standards-based approach to implementing an information security management system in accordance with ISO/IEC 27001:2005, companies can reap many advantages, not the least being better able to demonstrate compliance with legal and industry regulatory requirements.

It is important to note that ISO/IEC 27001:2005 can simply be used as a framework against which a company can implement and measure its information security management system against, without necessarily having to be accredited or registered. This is particularly useful for companies wishing to ensure they are implementing an effective ISMS but may not want the expense and overhead of being audited.

There were a number of key elements within the ISO/IEC 27001:2005 Information Security Standard that we feel are appropriate for this project.

Risk-Based Approach

One of the key success factors to any ISO/IEC 27001:2005 implementation is to have a comprehensive risk management approach to your information security management system. By identifying all the information security risks faced by the organization and the level of risk that management and the business are willing to accept, the most appropriate controls can be selected and implemented to manage those risks within acceptable risk levels.

The risk of not being compliant with the various regulatory and legal requirements was identified. Some of these regulatory and legal requirements stipulate that staff must be made aware of their obligations under those regulations.

In addition, the ISO/IEC 27001:2005 Information Security Standard requires that the risk assessment is conducted regularly so that the effectiveness of the selected controls can be measured and new risks identified and managed. This ensures that the security awareness program has to be subsequently updated when new risks are identified. This keeps the program fresh and up to date.

Senior Management Support

As the lack of training in compliance issues was a risk identified as part of the risk assessment, it had to be subsequently managed, and the identified ways of addressing the risk accepted by senior management. One way of managing this risk was the implementation of a security awareness program. As this had to be acknowledged and signed off by senior management, the CISO now had the full backing of the senior management team, something that was lacking in the previous initiatives.

With senior management supporting the security awareness program, the appropriate funding, resources, and facilities were provided to enable its success.

Continuous Improvement

One of the key advantages of implementing an information security management system based on the ISO/IEC 27001:2005 Information Security Standard is the requirement to continually improve your ISMS. Under the standard, this is known as the Plan, Do, Check, and Act cycle, otherwise known as the PDCA (see Exhibit 1).

Each step of the PDCA cycle ensures that you constantly improve your ISMS and the elements within it.

- The Plan stage ensures that you identify the appropriate controls, such as a security awareness and privacy training program, to manage the identified risks.
- The Do element of the cycle is where you implement the identified controls.

Act   Plan

Check   Do

Exhibit 1   The Plan, Do, Check, and Act (PDCA) Cycle.

■ The Check step is the process of gathering feedback on the effectiveness of the implemented controls and what improvements may be necessary. In the case of a security awareness program, this could be simple elements such as the number of people who attended the course or the number of people who passed any subsequent security awareness tests. For our program, my client used other statistics to reinforce the effectiveness of the new security awareness program such as a reduction in computer virus infections for those that attended the course against those that did not, the lowering in volume of password reset requests for those that attended the course, and the increase in the number of potential security incidents reported to the help desk after people took the course.

■ The Act part of the cycle is where the feedback gathered from the Check stage is acted upon and the security controls updated or new ones added. In relation to the security awareness and privacy training program, the CISO was able to identify weaknesses in the program that she could address in future iterations of the course or, indeed, add in new elements to the course where necessary.

Compliance

Within the ISO/IEC 27001:2005 Information Security Standard there is a complete section, Section 15 in Annex A, dedicated to the whole area of compliance. The standard has a number of controls within this section relating to areas such as

■ Identification of Applicable Legislation
■ Data Protection and Privacy of Personal Information
■ Compliance with Security Policies and Standards

Having identified all the relevant legislation and regulatory requirements facing the organization, the CISO was able to ensure that all of these requirements were included in the overall ISO/IEC 27001-based ISMS. Having all the regulatory and legal requirements managed within the one ISMS also made the task of developing the appropriate training courses much simpler. In many cases, there were similar compliance needs across each of the different legal and regulatory requirements, making the development of a single ISO/IEC 27001:2005-based security awareness and privacy program a worthwhile investment for the business.

By adopting the risk- and standards-based approach to implementing an information security management system in accordance with the ISO/IEC 27001:2005 Information Security Standard, my client gained many advantages in developing a solid information security program that was accepted and actively supported by the business and senior management. Being able to develop a security awareness and privacy training program that met the real needs of the business also ensured the success of the training program and indeed of the CISO.

It is important to note that while my client did get her ISMS system certified, or registered, against the ISO/IEC 27001:2005 Information Security Standard, it can also simply be used as a framework against which a company can implement and measure its information security management system.

As well as providing a solid foundation upon which to build the security awareness and privacy training program, my client saw other efficiencies and benefits from using the standard such as

- **Compliance with legislation:**
  Having a structured information security management system in place makes the task of identifying compliance requirements easier. It also made including new or changed compliance requirements into the security awareness and privacy training program a more efficient and effective process.
- **Improved management:**
  Having a single security awareness and privacy training program also ensured that management was confident, knowing that the key information security elements that staff should be trained in were properly identified and catered to. Senior management was also confident in knowing who had attended the training course. This enabled management to ensure only trained personnel were assigned to key tasks and maintaining the security of the information in those areas. The metrics produced to support the training program also enabled management to quickly identify where there were gaps in the training and what additional investments needed to be made to address those gaps.
- **Improved customer and partner relationships:**
  By demonstrating that the company takes information security seriously, customers and trading partners can deal with the company confidently, knowing that it has taken an independently verifiable approach to information security risk management.

  Another advantage of achieving certification or registration in the ISO/IEC 27001:2005 Information Security Standard was being able to demonstrate to compliance bodies that the company took the privacy of their client data extremely seriously. Indeed, the Irish Data Protection Commissioner has stated, "If a body is certified to be ISO/IEC 27001-compliant, it would demonstrate compliance with the security requirements of the Data Protection Acts."
- **Increased reliability and security of systems:**
  Security is often defined as protecting the confidentiality, integrity and availability of an asset. Using a standards-based approach, which ensures that adequate controls, processes, and procedures are in place and that staff have been properly trained, guarantees that the above goals are met. Meeting the Confidentiality, Integrity, and Availability (CIA) goals of security will also by default improve the reliability, availability, and stability of systems.
- **Increased profits:**
  Having stable, secure, and reliable systems ensures that interruptions to those systems are minimized, thereby increasing their availability and productivity. In addition to the above, a standards-based approach to information security demonstrates to customers that the company can be trusted with their business. This can increase profitability by retaining existing, and attracting new, customers.

■ **Reduced costs:**
A standards-based approach to information security ensures that all controls are measured and managed in a structured manner. This ensures that processes and procedures are more streamlined and effective, thus reducing costs.

My client also found that by using a central security awareness and privacy training program, as opposed to the previous individual programs, the cost of staff training was significantly reduced and the return on investment in the training was higher.

While not guaranteeing 100% security (no standard or system can), ISO/IEC 27001 allows a company to implement a qualitative approach to securing their customers' data and ultimately protecting the privacy of their customers' personal information.

Establishing a Security Culture Through Security Awareness

By Dr. Gary Hinson, PhD, MBA, CISSP, CISA, CISM*

Introduction

We are often told how important it is to "establish a security culture," a laudable objective that is easy to say yet rather difficult to put into practice. In this section I elaborate five specific design goals for a security awareness program that intends to establish a security culture, followed by some awareness techniques to help us meet the goals and hence achieve the objective.

Awareness Program Design Goals

First of all, let us examine the objective, breaking it down by addressing two key questions: What do we mean by a "security culture" and how might we "establish" it?

What Is a Security Culture?

Security culture refers to a generalized understanding and respect for information security throughout the entire organization and at all levels. Employees steeped in a security culture view security as "the way things are done here," in other words, an almost subconscious recognition that security should be taken into account in routine activities. Security is part of ongoing operations and gets duly considered in new initiatives such as new software development and business processes. In the

---

* Dr. Gary Hinson, PhD, MBA, CISSP, CISM, CISA, has more than two decades' experience as practitioner, manager, and consultant in the field of information security, risk, and IT audit, originally in Europe and later in Australasia. Gary designed the information security awareness subscription service NoticeBored in 2002 and now spends his days writing security awareness materials and managing IsecT Ltd. Gary is a passionate supporter of the ISO/IEC 27000-series information security management standards and actively contributes to the continued development of the standards through the international committee responsible.

> ### Design Goal 1
>
> The awareness program must be inclusive, covering everyone in the organization.

desired state, all employees (staff and management), contractors, consultants, and the like have at least a basic level of security awareness, with most having a more advanced appreciation and a few being "thought leaders." Therefore, an important design goal for the awareness program is to reach all of these people: the program should not be limited to, say, staff only.

> ### Design Goal 2
>
> The awareness program must be motivational, engaging, and relevant.

Cultures exist at different scales, from teams, gangs, or groups through departments and business units to corporations and even nations. At the lower end particularly, charismatic leaders often have a strong and distinct influence on the culture but at the upper end, culture tends to be a more diffuse concept, more difficult to pin down and even harder to control or direct. To a large extent, cultures emerge of their own accord, rather than being formed or directed by design; arguably, the best management can hope for is to influence corporate culture, but having an enthusiastic and motivational figurehead will surely help, along with other techniques to make it interesting and useful to the audience.

Consider the whole employee base as a population of individuals whose behavior you are trying to change. Some of your audience will be ahead of the game, most will go along with it once they understand what is required of them, and some laggards will resist and may even undermine the awareness program. This is illustrated diagrammatically below (see Exhibit 2).

Employees in the vicinity of "A" on the curve are the laggards with a limited ability to understand and/or absorb the awareness messages you are trying to put across. They may perhaps have a low IQ, short attention span, lack of interest, or may simply be too busy with other things to apply much mental effort and time to information security. Some of them may resent being "subjected to" the awareness program, and passively or actively resist by failing to attend training sessions or subversively spreading dissent.

Employees at "C" are eager to learn about security. They relish the awareness sessions and look forward to awareness events. They may even be keen to get actively involved in planning and organizing information security awareness activities. These are exactly the kinds of people you want to act as "awareness ambassadors" throughout the organization, promoting security in various ways to their colleagues.

Most employees, however, fall somewhere in the middle around "B". They are prepared to put some time and effort into security, but range from mildly averse to mildly supportive of the awareness program. Information security is probably not

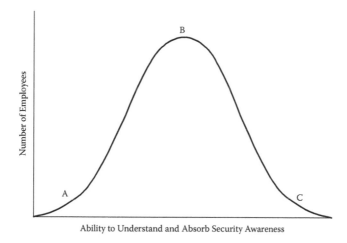

Ability to Understand and Absorb Security Awareness

Exhibit 2   Employee knowledge level.

their main concern at work but once they achieve a basic level of security awareness, they will begin to see how the subject relates to both their private and work lives.

While shown here as a bell-shaped normal curve, the distribution may well be skewed in your organization. Military people, for example, seem more likely to have an inherent interest in security, so the curve for, say, an army unit may be shifted to the right. The peak height of the curve may also vary since some proportion of the organization may have zero interest in information security, however it is put across to them. Some aspects of information security are relatively obscure, making it hard for nontechnical people to understand them. Even technical people struggle with complex modern technologies, and nobody is an expert in all fields. Effective security awareness programs need to strike a balance between glossing over important points and getting buried in the jargon, acronyms, and fine details all too common in technical manuals. It is vital that awareness materials are written in a clear yet engaging style, and that the information content is interesting, relevant, and useful.

Establishing a Culture

The word *establish* implies that the security culture should end up deeply embedded in the organization and rather permanent in nature. The instantaneous level

---

Design Goal 3

The awareness program must take account of the range of interest and competence in information security within the target audience.

Design Goal 4

The awareness program must be deeply embedded in the organization, forming an integral part of strategy and operations.

---

of security awareness may vary in response to particular threats or incidents (e.g., a state of heightened alert to the potential for industrial espionage during corporate mergers and acquisitions), but the mean level should remain sufficiently high at all times in order to counter ubiquitous information security threats such as malware, human errors, and social engineering.

If a security culture is truly established in an organization, it would take a substantial effort to displace it. Ideally, therefore, cultural change should be self-sustaining; in other words, once initiated, the culture should keep going with

---

Design Goal 5

The awareness program must be cost effective, collecting suitable metrics to justify its continuance.

---

limited further investment of time and money by management. One way to achieve this is to provide positive feedback, measuring and recording the effects of the program to help justify both the initial start-up (capital) investment and the ongoing operating costs (revenue). Naturally, keeping both capital and revenue costs under control will help sustain the business case for security awareness.

Modern Security Awareness Techniques That Help Establish a Security Culture

In this section, I explain the evolution of modern techniques for information security awareness from more traditional approaches, in order to highlight how intelligent design of the awareness program helps it meet the five design goals I have just explained.

One-Off or Sporadic Security Awareness/Training Events

From the early days of security awareness, major organization-wide security awareness or training events such as annual "security days" have been popular with management, if not necessarily with staff. Substantial effort goes into planning each event, making sure that as many employees as possible attend on the day. The costs are concentrated into a relatively short period but are inevitably quite high, taking into account lost productivity as well as the event organization and delivery. However, although a major security awareness event may reach a significant proportion of employees, their level of awareness gradually decays afterward back to more or less the same state as before the event (see Exhibit 3).

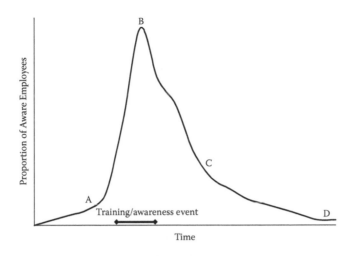

Exhibit 3   Employee knowledge retention: Traditional approach.

In the region marked A, prior to the big event, those people directly involved in planning and preparing for the event, along with their managers, are, of course, aware of its content. The height of the peak at point B reflects two factors: the reach or coverage of the event (e.g., how many employees actually attend the event, ignoring those who are not invited or fail to attend for some more or less legitimate reason) and the effectiveness or quality of the event in raising their awareness. After the event at C, the awareness level drops gradually as more and more people forget it and move on to other things, with the rate of decay again relating to the effectiveness or quality of the event itself (more effective events are more memorable). Some people can still recall the event considerably later, perhaps because they are routinely using the information they gained, and for a few at point D, the effect is essentially permanent (i.e., they have learned and changed as a result of the event—it really sank in for them).

Highly engaging and relevant awareness or training events may have a measurable effect on employees for a few weeks or months, whereas tedious, boring, or seemingly irrelevant sessions may be forgotten almost immediately. This insight often leads management to put more effort into making the awareness events exciting and memorable, but this can backfire, for instance, if the effect is achieved through games, cartoons, and the like that employees perceive as childish and condescending. There is a fine line between encouraging employees to have fun and enjoy the learning experience versus trivializing information security issues.

By the way, new employee security induction or orientation training also tends to be delivered as a single event per employee, typically a classroom-type presentation or seminar session lasting between about 10 and 90 minutes. Organizations that take on a lot of new recruits run such sessions on a daily or weekly basis; others typically run them monthly. The more frequent sessions may be delivered as part of a fairly intensive set of awareness/training activities on the employees' first day or week on site, with the risk of overwhelming them with new information. Conversely, employees who join up just after a monthly session may not receive any official information security advice or instruction for most of their first month at work. Furthermore, new employees exhibit the same knowledge decay as indicated above, so within a short period most will have forgotten the content of the induction/ orientation sessions. I am not arguing that such sessions are unnecessary—far from it—rather, that they need to lead into a more comprehensive awareness approach.

> "Repetition of information security policy ideas is essential; repetition impresses users and other audiences with the importance that management places on information security."
>
> *Charles Cresson-Wood*

Periodic, Continuous, and Rolling Security Awareness Programs

Since cultural change is not something one can achieve overnight, sporadic and infrequent security awareness or training sessions stand little chance of achieving a deep-rooted and widespread culture of security, *no matter how much impact each individual event may create.* To put it bluntly, most people forget what they have been told within a relatively short period unless they are frequently reminded, so clearly a different approach is called for.

Periodic awareness programs extend the delivery from, say, a single annual event to multiple days, for example, holding a "security day" every calendar quarter. This *can* be a more effective approach, particularly for organizations that have mature employee training and communications functions, although employees tend to become somewhat negative or cynical if forced to attend awareness events too often. Creativity in the programs for each event can help, however—for instance, covering security issues that employees are most likely to be concerned about and using motivational speakers and/or awareness activities.

Continuous awareness programs are a natural extension of the periodic approach, but there is an obvious problem with simply running major corporate events much more frequently: both the costs and employee resistance rise dramatically. Hence, continuous delivery normally involves less intensive and expensive awareness events—for example, using the corporate intranet to deliver security awareness and training materials to employees "on demand." On-demand solutions allow employees to access awareness or training materials in slack periods or work breaks, when they feel motivated to do so. This gives an immediate benefit for employees who are already sufficiently aware to seek out further security awareness and training, since nobody is forcing them to do it. However, the laggard employees noted earlier are unlikely to take up the option, thereby alienating them from the awareness program.

A practical solution uses periodic or continuous delivery, but each awareness event focuses on a different security topic. For example, March might be designated "Malware Month" with a series of coordinated mini-awareness activities explaining and

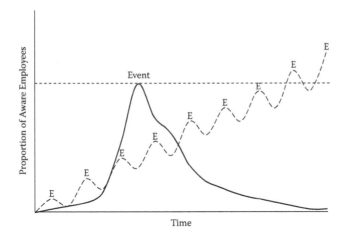

Exhibit 4   Employee knowledge retention: Rolling approach.

countering the malware threat. April might perhaps be "Network Security Month," shifting the focus of the awareness program to issues such as user authentication and the logon process, and so on. I call this the **rolling approach to security awareness.**

The rolling approach is a deceptively simple concept combining more-or-less continuous delivery with a planned succession of security awareness topics and materials. The idea is essentially to cover a sustained and coherent sequence of information security awareness topics, moving on week-by-week, month-by-month, or quarter-by-quarter, according to the overall program design (see Exhibit 4).

Contrast the one-shot major awareness event with the dashed line graph representing a rolling awareness program that delivers a whole series of smaller, discrete awareness events or episodes (the little Es), each one building on the last. As the graph indicates, a rolling program can be launched more quickly since each event is smaller and focused. The effectiveness of each event is bound to vary but frequent repetition allows those planning and delivering the awareness program to exercise and continually improve their skills. Aside from awareness metrics, this is another form of positive feedback, with learning and developing occurring in the course of delivery.

Over time the rolling approach gradually reaches a wider variety of employees than the one-off event (e.g., it picks up employees who might have missed the single event through sickness or other commitments); hence, the dashed graph extends above the peak level reached by the one-off event. Furthermore, the total area under each graph (being the product of the proportion of the organization that is security aware and the duration of that awareness) is telling: the rolling approach achieves a significantly greater coverage than a single event.

The rolling approach allows us simultaneously to broaden and deepen the coverage of the awareness program: we broaden it by covering a wider variety of topics in sequence, and deepen it by concentrating on one topic at a time, providing more focus and detailed content for those who typically need it (e.g., information technology professionals in the case of technical topics; managers in the case of strategy, governance, risk, compliance, and related topics; general employees in the case of social engineering awareness). Going into more depth per topic than one would normally consider blurs the distinction between awareness and training. This is particularly important for IT professionals in the audience, who mostly find normal security awareness content somewhat superficial or banal and hence boring.

> "After a while, a security poster, no matter how well designed, will be ignored; it will, in effect, simply blend into the environment. For this reason, awareness techniques should be creative and frequently changed."
>
> *U.S. Army security training manual*

The constant refreshing of awareness content also helps stave off boredom at a more general level. Old posters used for security awareness (or indeed health and safety awareness, corporate mission statements, etc.) tend to become virtually invisible over time as people become oblivious to them—a process known in biology as *accommodation*, something even Pavlov's dogs exhibited after a while.

Given that individuals have different interests in information security, and that each topic will only be promoted for a limited period before moving ahead to the next, the collection of topics covered by a rolling program can achieve wider appeal than a one-off event. Careful design of the materials for each topic helps, too, especially targeting particular audience groups within the overall organization. I have already mentioned staff, managers, and IT professionals, but there are often narrower audiences for certain topics (e.g., receptionists, security guards, personal assistants/secretaries, help desk personnel, and customer service agents generally have an important role to play in spotting and rebuffing common social engineering attacks).

The rolling awareness approach has another more subtle advantage over the traditional one-shot event, namely that the topics covered need not necessarily be entirely predetermined months in advance. With sufficient resources on hand (most likely assisted by functional experts from training, employee communications, human resources, legal, IT, risk, compliance, physical/site security, and other departments), it is perfectly feasible to research and develop the awareness materials for new topics one at a time, in parallel with delivery of previous topics. The program can therefore be dynamic, responding rapidly to new information security risks (such as a major worm outbreak) more or less as they emerge. Furthermore, the awareness materials on each topic can refer back to previous topics and refer forward to other exciting content planned for future topics, making the overall program more coherent. The fundamental concepts of information security and privacy (such as the need to protect information confidentiality, integrity, and availability) inevitably form longitudinal threads linking all the topics into a consistent whole, supported by branding of the program materials.

Finally, in these economically desperate times, any awareness program must justify its own existence, ideally through delivering demonstrable business benefits that clearly outweigh the costs. While the total costs of a rolling awareness program may meet and perhaps exceed those of a one-shot approach, it can achieve substantially greater benefits. The key is to be able to measure and prove this to management. Metrics is one of the most challenging areas of information security but even here the rolling approach offers a partial solution. Since all awareness topics will most likely address management, this is an opportunity for the information security professionals to propose and discuss possible metrics associated with the topic, or at least to open the dialogue as part of the awareness program itself.

Conclusion

Security awareness is the glue that binds the whole information security management system together and sticks security firmly in employees' minds. Combining innovative awareness program designs (such as the rolling approach described here) with creative and engaging awareness materials (such as those described throughout this book) allows us to establish and maintain a deep-rooted, widespread, and long-lasting culture of security in the organization. Explaining a wide variety of security issues in a consistent and engaging style, informing and encouraging everyone in the organization to take note, gradually makes information security an inherent part of the corporate culture, and best of all it can help demonstrate and indeed maximize the business value of information security.

Empirical Evaluations of Embedded Training for Antiphishing User Education

By Lorrie Faith Cranor,* Jason Hong,† Ponnurangam Kumaraguru,‡ and Alessandro Acquisti§

Introduction

Cyber security training for people who are not security experts is difficult because nonexperts are generally unfamiliar with computer security concepts and unmotivated to spend time on training. They typically view computer security

* Lorrie Faith Cranor is cofounder and chief scientist of Wombat Security Technologies, Inc. She also directs the CyLab Usable Privacy and Security Laboratory at Carnegie Mellon University. http://lorrie.cranor.org/

† Jason Hong is cofounder and CTO of Wombat Security Technologies, Inc. He is an assistant professor in the Human Computer Interaction Institute at Carnegie Mellon University. http://www.cs.cmu.edu/~jasonh/

‡ Ponnurangam Kumaraguru is a research associate in the CyLab Usable Privacy and Security Laboratory at Carnegie Mellon University. http://www.cs.cmu.edu/~ponguru/

§ Alessandro Acquisti is an associate professor of information technology and public policy at the Heinz College at Carnegie Mellon University. http://www.heinz.cmu.edu/~acquisti/

as someone else's problem and not something they feel empowered to do much about. Thus, to effectively train nonexperts, cyber security training must be both understandable and compelling, and delivered in a manner that captures people's attention. For the most part, e-mailed security messages sent by companies to their customers or employees are not effective because recipients of these messages seldom read them. On the other hand, phishers have discovered ways of crafting e-mail messages that get people to read them.

One approach to making training more compelling and relevant to people is to embed the training directly into their regular activities. Thus, we developed an embedded training system that teaches users to avoid falling for phishing attacks by sending them simulated phishing e-mails. These e-mails deliver an embedded training message when the user falls for the attack and clicks on the simulated phishing URL, thus taking advantage of a "teachable moment." The training materials present the user with a succinct and engaging comic strip that defines phishing, offers steps to follow to avoid falling for phishing attacks, and illustrates how easy it is for criminals to perpetrate such attacks.

We used learning science principles to develop antiphishing training materials as part of a research project conducted by the CyLab Usable Privacy and Security Laboratory at Carnegie Mellon University. Exhibit 5 shows an example of our training materials. We subsequently spun off a company, Wombat Security Technologies, Inc., to offer an embedded training system called PhishGuru™ to companies.

We conducted a series of laboratory and real-world studies to evaluate the effectiveness of embedded training. This paper provides an overview of the methodology and results of these studies. Further details about these studies are available in the referenced publications.

Laboratory Study 1: Evaluation of Knowledge Acquisition

Our first laboratory study was designed to compare the effectiveness of embedded training cartoons with two other types of e-mail-based training.*

Study Design

We recruited 30 participants who were not computer security experts to participate in a study at the CyLab Usable Privacy and Security Laboratory at Carnegie Mellon University. We placed each participant randomly in one of three conditions: notices, text/graphic, and comic. The user study consisted of a think-aloud session in which participants played the role of "Bobby Smith," an employee of Cognix Inc., who works

---

* P. Kumaraguru, Y. Rhee, A. Acquisti, L. Cranor, J. Hong, and E. Nunge. Protecting people from phishing: the design and evaluation of an embedded training e-mail system. In *CHI 2007: Conference on Human Factors in Computing Systems,* San Jose, California, April 28–May 3, 2007, p. 905–914. http://doi.acm.org/10.1145/1240624.1240760.

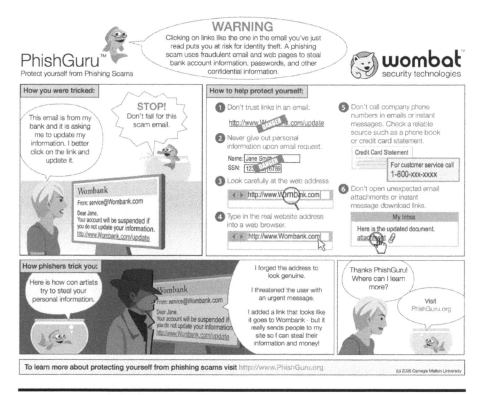

Exhibit 5   A PhishGuru™ embedded training cartoon.

in the marketing department. Participants were told that the study investigated "how people effectively manage and use e-mail." They were told that they should interact with Bobby Smith's e-mail the way they would normally interact with their own e-mail.

Each participant was shown 19 e-mail messages. Nine of these messages were legitimate e-mails (from coworkers at Cognix, friends, and family) that requested Bobby to perform simple tasks and reply by e-mail. Two messages were simulated legitimate e-mails containing links from organizations with which Bobby had an account. The mailbox also contained two spam e-mails, two fraudulent e-mails that appeared to come from organizations where Bobby had an account (which we refer to as "phishing-account" e-mails), and two fraudulent e-mails that appeared to come from a bank with which Bobby did not have an account. The mailbox also had two training e-mails. Participants in the notices condition received training in the form of a typical e-mail-based security notice sent by a major company to its customers. The training e-mails for participants in the other two conditions were phishing-account e-mails that included embedded training. When participants clicked on a link and fell for the phish they were directed to a Web site with a training intervention. In the text/graphics condition, the training intervention was a single page of text and

Exhibit 6   Conditions Method Impacts

	Comic Condition	Text/Graphics Condition	Security Notices Condition
Participants who fell for phishing-account e-mail *before* training	100%	80%	90%
Participants who fell for phishing-account e-mail *after* training	30%	70%	90%
Average time spent reading training materials	120 seconds	107 seconds	9 seconds

graphics that defined phishing and provided tips for detecting phishing messages. In the comic condition, the intervention was presented in the form of a comic strip.

Results

In this study, we measured knowledge acquisition based on whether or not users clicked on links in legitimate e-mails and phishing e-mails before and after training. We found statistically significant differences in knowledge acquisition between the three study conditions, with participants in the comic condition demonstrating the greatest knowledge acquisition (see Exhibit 6). Participants in the comic condition also spent the most time reading training materials. Average time spent reading training materials was 9 seconds for the notice condition, 107 seconds for the text/graphics condition, and 120 seconds for the comic condition.

In the security notice condition 90% of participants fell for the phishing-account e-mail before training, and we saw no improvement after training. The participants who had seen the security notices said that the information took too long to read, and they were not sure what the messages were trying to convey.

Participants in the comic condition were significantly better at recognizing phishing e-mails than those in the notices condition.* Participants in the text/graphics group also performed better than those in the notices condition, but this difference was not significant. In the text/graphic condition, 80% of the participants fell for the first phishing-account e-mail, and 70% fell for the final phishing-account e-mail after training. In the comic condition, all participants fell for the first phishing-account e-mail, and only 30% fell for the final phishing-account e-mail after training.

---

* Chi-square was used to test for statistical significance in this study. P values <0.01 are reported as significant.

Conclusions

Our results suggest that the current practice of e-mailing out security notices is ineffective because people are unwilling to spend time reading these notices. On the other hand, our comic-strip-embedded training is an effective way to teach people how to avoid falling for phishing attacks. When study participants fell for our simulated phishing attacks, they were motivated to spend time reading training materials.

Laboratory Study 2: Evaluation of Knowledge Retention

In our first laboratory study, we tested users immediately after training. In our second laboratory study, we examine (1) how well users trained with embedded training can retain and transfer knowledge, and (2) how important it is to fall for simulated phishing attacks, as opposed to simply receiving the training interventions directly as e-mail messages.*

Study Design

Our second study used a similar design as the previous study, once again asking participants to play the role of Bobby Smith. We had four conditions: embedded, nonembedded, suspicion, and control. Participants in the embedded condition received a simulated phishing e-mail and saw a revised version of the comic strip intervention when they clicked on a link in that e-mail. Participants in the nonembedded condition received the same comic strip directly as part of an e-mail message, without having to fall for a simulated phishing e-mail. Participants in the suspicion condition received a brief e-mail from a friend that mentioned phishing, without providing any information about how they could protect themselves. Participants in the control condition received an additional e-mail from a friend, but received no training.

The second study was conducted in two parts, seven days apart. In the first part, participants saw 33 e-mails in Bobby's inbox: a set of 16 e-mails, a training intervention, and a set of 16 additional e-mails shown immediately after training. In the second part, the participants saw another 16 e-mails in Bobby's inbox.

Results

Our results provide evidence that embedded training enhances knowledge acquisition, knowledge retention, and knowledge transfer, allowing learners to effectively identify phishing messages without misidentifying legitimate messages.

We measured the percentage of correct decisions that participants in each condition made for phishing and legitimate e-mails before and after the training, as shown in Exhibit 7. Our results demonstrate that participants in the embedded

---

* P. Kumaraguru, Y. Rhee, A. Acquisti, L. Cranor, J. Hong, and E. Nunge. Protecting People from Phishing: The Design and Evaluation of an Embedded Training E-mail System *In CHI 2007: Conference on Human Factors in Computing Systems*, San Jose, California, 28 April–May 3, 2007, p. 905–914. http://doi.acm.org/10.1145/1240624.1240760

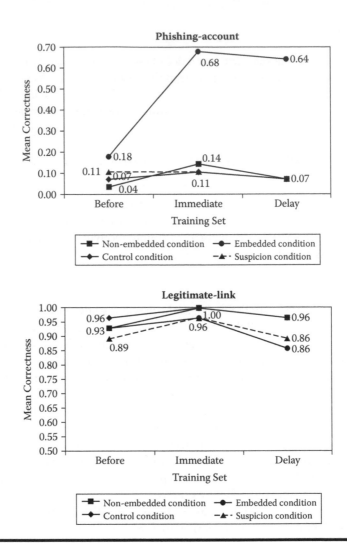

Exhibit 7 Mean correctness for identifying phishing-account and legitimate e-mails before training, immediately after training, and after a one-week delay. On the left, we can see that in the embedded condition, there is a sizeable improvement in participants' abilities to detect phishing e-mails after having been trained. In contrast, there is no statistically significant improvement in the other conditions. On the right, we see that there are no statistically significant differences in the number of people clicking on legitimate links over time or across conditions. This indicates that our embedded training does not increase false positives.

training condition learned to detect phishing-account e-mails effectively, whereas participants in the other conditions did not. While participants did not perform significantly differently in correctly identifying phishing-account e-mails before the training, those in the embedded condition performed significantly better than those in the other conditions immediately after training.* Indeed, those in the nonembedded condition did not perform significantly differently than those in the control condition immediately after training. This may be due in part to the fact that participants in the embedded condition were motivated to spend more than twice as much time reading the cartoon than those in the nonembedded condition. Participants in the embedded condition spent an average of 97 seconds reading the cartoon, while participants in the nonembedded condition spent an average of 37 seconds.

To measure knowledge retention, we compared performance on phishing-account and legitimate e-mails before, immediately after training, and after a one-week delay. Our results suggest that users in the embedded condition were able to retain the knowledge they acquired and use it to distinguish phishing and legitimate e-mails, even after a one-week delay. In all conditions there was no significant difference between mean correctness on phishing-account e-mails or legitimate e-mails immediately after the training and after a one-week delay. Participants in the embedded condition improved their performance significantly on phishing-account e-mails after the delay compared to before the training, while participants in the other conditions did not improve. While 64% of the embedded-condition participants identified the phishing-account e-mail correctly after a one-week delay, only 7% of the participants in the other conditions identified the e-mail correctly.

Conclusions

Our results reinforce and extend the findings of our previous study, which suggested that embedded training can be an effective method to train users to distinguish between legitimate and phishing e-mail messages. The fact that we saw no significant performance drop-off after one week suggests that users are likely to retain their training for longer time periods. Our observation that the suspicion condition was not significantly different from the control condition suggests that it is not helpful to tell users about phishing without providing them with information about how to identify phishing or actionable steps they can take to protect themselves.

Finally, our observation that the nonembedded condition was not significantly different from the control condition provides a strong indicator that the delivery method is an important factor in determining antiphishing training effectiveness. Indeed, we found that our revised comic strip intervention, which provided effective training when displayed at that teachable moment after participants had fallen for a simulated phishing attack, was completely ineffective when sent directly via e-mail.

---

* Two-sample and paired t-tests were used to test for statistical significance in this study. P values <0.01 are reported as significant.

Real-World Study

To evaluate our embedded training approach in the real world, we conducted a 515-participant, real-world experiment in which we measured long-term retention over a 28-day period.*

Study Design

Study participants were faculty, staff, and students from throughout the Carnegie Mellon University (CMU) community. The simulated phishing e-mails we created were all spear-phishing e-mails targeted at the CMU community.

Five hundred and fifteen participants were randomly assigned to three conditions: control, single training, and multiple training. All participants, regardless of condition, were sent a series of three legitimate and seven simulated spear-phishing e-mails over the course of 28 days (on days 0, 2, 7, 14, 16, 21, and 28). In the body of each spear-phishing e-mail was a simulated phishing URL that directed participants to a simulated phishing Web site that requested the private credentials necessary to login to CMU Web sites. Participants in the single- and multiple-training conditions who clicked the URL on Day 0 saw a training cartoon instead of a simulated phishing Web site. Participants in the multiple-training condition who clicked the URL on Day 14 also saw a training cartoon (the second cartoon contained the same training content as the first, but included different characters and a slightly different story line). Participants in the control condition did not receive any antiphishing training as part of the study.

We developed seven plain-text, spear-phishing e-mails with subject lines relating to password changes, bandwidth quota, event registration, prizes, and volunteering for community service. These were all e-mails that the CMU community might normally receive, though they were not based on any information that a phisher would not be able to obtain from public Web pages. All of our phishing messages displayed the phishing URLs in the body of the messages. We did not replicate the common phishing tactic of using HTML to hide phishing URLs from users.

To ensure that the aggregate response rates per day were not confounded by the potential difference in natural response rates for individual e-mails or by the interdependence of response rates among the e-mails, we developed a counterbalancing schedule. The counterbalancing schedule avoided these confounding issues by dividing the 515 participants randomly and equally per condition among 21 different viewing schedules for the seven e-mails.

To estimate the false positive rate, we measured the response rate to three legitimate e-mails sent to study participants by the CMU Information Security

---

* P. Kumaraguru, J. Cranshaw, A. Acquisti, L. Cranor, J. Hong, M.A. Blair, T. Pham. *School of Phish: A Real-Word Evaluation of Anti-Phishing Training.* CyLab Technical Report CMU-CyLab-09-002, 2009. http://www.cylab.cmu.edu/research/techreports/tr_cylab09002.html.

Office (ISO) on day 0, day 7, and day 28 after the test/training e-mails were sent. The three legitimate e-mails were announcements for an ongoing security-related scavenger hunt begun during Cyber Security Awareness Month that gave community members an opportunity to gain points in return for specified security-related tasks. The e-mails indicated that the recipient needed to login with their password to claim their bonus points. Clicking the link took them to a real CMU Web site where they were asked to provide their username and password.

So that we could track user responses, each participant was given a unique 4-character alpha-numeric hash that was appended as a parameter to the URL of all e-mails sent to participants. To ensure that the e-mails were not blocked by CMU spam filters, the machine from which the e-mails were sent was put on a white list.

After all real and simulated phishing e-mails were sent, another e-mail was sent to all participants asking them to complete a poststudy survey. Of our participants, 279 completed the poststudy survey. These participants were distributed nearly equally across our three conditions.

Results

Our results show that people in the single- and multiple-training conditions who fell for our first phishing message performed significantly better when they received our second phishing message than those in the control condition. In addition, we observed no significant loss in retention after 28 days. We found no significant differences among the click rate of participants across the three conditions on day 0 or in the click rate of participants in the control group across study days.*

On day 0, 48.4% of the participants in the training conditions viewed the training cartoon intervention. To determine the effectiveness of the training, we conditioned the click rates of days 2 through 28 on those participants across all conditions who clicked the links on day 0. This way we could compare the participants who actually received the training in the single- and multiple-training conditions to those in the control condition who took the analogous action on day 0. Exhibit 8 (left panel) shows the percentage of these participants who clicked on links in e-mails and gave information to the fake phishing Web sites from day 2 until day 28. There is a significant difference† between the percentage of users who clicked in the control condition (54.4%) and the percentage who clicked in the single-training condition (27.0%) on day 28. Similarly, there is a significant difference between the control and multiple-training (32.5%) conditions on day 28. We also find that, in the single-training condition, participants who gave information to fake phishing Web sites on day 2 are not significantly different than on day 28. This shows that users trained with our embedded training retain knowledge even after 28 days.

---

* ANOVA was used to test for statistical significance. P values <0.01 are reported as significant.
† Chi-square was used to test for statistical significance. P values <0.01 are reported as significant.

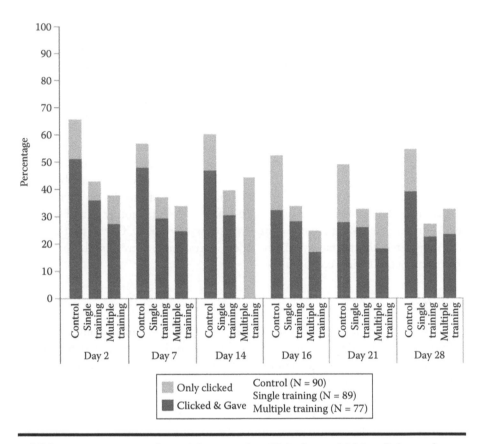

Exhibit 8   Percentage of participants who clicked on phishing links and gave information. Left: Days 2 through 28 conditioned on those participants who clicked on day 0. *N* is the number of people who clicked on day 0. There is significant difference between the control and single-training condition and between the control and multiple-training condition in the percentage of people who clicked on days 2 through 28. Nobody gave information in the multiple-training condition on day 14 because it was a training e-mail. Right: Days 16 through 28 conditioned on those participants who clicked on both day 0 and day 14. *N* is the number of people who clicked on day 0 and on day 14. There is significant difference between the single- and multiple-training conditions in the percentage of people who gave information to phishing sites on days 16 through 28.

We found that users who saw the training intervention twice were less likely to give information to the fake phishing Web sites than those who only saw the training intervention once. Exhibit 8 (right panel) shows the percentage of participants who clicked on links in e-mails from day 16 until day 28 conditioned on participants who clicked on the link on day 0 and those who clicked on day 14. There is a significant difference between the percentages of users who clicked in the

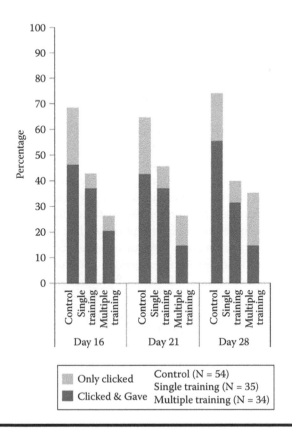

Exhibit 8 (continued)

single-training condition (42.9%) and those who clicked in the multiple-training condition (26.5%) on day 16 and a similar difference on day 21. However, we did not find a significant difference between users who clicked in the single-training and multiple-training conditions on day 28. Exhibit 8 (right panel) also shows that participants who were trained twice did significantly better than participants who were trained once when it comes to giving their personal information to fake phishing Web sites. For example, on day 28, 31.4% of the participants in the single-training condition gave information to the Web site, while only 14.7% of participants in the multiple-training condition gave information.

We also found 30 participants (17.5%) in the multiple-training condition who did not see the intervention on day 0 but saw the intervention on day 14. These people probably needed training, since they fell for the e-mail on day 14. This suggests that multiround training is useful not only for reinforcement, but also for providing an additional opportunity for people who need training.

Our results indicate that training users to recognize phishing e-mails using our embedded training cartoons does not make them more likely to identify legitimate e-mails as phishing e-mails. We found no significant difference between the three conditions in response rate to the legitimate e-mails on day 0 and on day 28.

Our results demonstrate that our embedded training system effectively trains users in the real world, and that people who received embedded training retained this knowledge for at least 28 days. Results also show that people who were trained twice were significantly less likely to provide information to the simulated phishing Web pages after training. We also found that our training did not increase the likelihood of false-positive errors (participants identifying legitimate e-mails as phishing e-mails).

The large size and duration of our real-world study also allowed us to draw some conclusions about susceptibility to phishing based on certain demographic factors. We found little or no difference in susceptibility to phishing attacks with respect to gender. However, we found that age is a factor in phishing susceptibility, as participants in the 18–25 age group were more likely to fall for phishing than those in older age groups.

In our poststudy questionnaire, 80% of participants said they would recommend that CMU continue providing embedded antiphishing training. One participant wrote, "We should have this kind of program every year to increase the awareness." Another wrote, "I really liked the idea of sending CMU students fake phishing e-mails and then saying to them, essentially, "HEY! You could've just gotten scammed! You should be more careful—here's how ... " Most participants liked the idea of multiround training. One participant wrote, "I think getting reminders once a month is a good way of helping us to remember." Participants commented that they enjoyed receiving training in cartoon form: "I think the idea of using something fun, like a cartoon, to teach people about a serious subject is awesome!"

Conclusions

The CMU study demonstrated the effectiveness of the embedded training approach of using teachable moments combined with engaging and actionable training materials. Participants who fell for a phishing e-mail and received our embedded training were 50% less likely to fall for subsequent phishing e-mails than those who fell for the first phishing e-mail but did not receive training. In addition, they were just as likely to be able to protect themselves from phishing 28 days after training as they were 2 days after training.

While there are many antiphishing education Web sites available, most users are unlikely to visit them voluntarily. Furthermore, studies have shown that while some of these Web sites successfully raise users' suspicion of all e-mail, they don't deliver techniques they can use successfully to distinguish legitimate e-mails from phishing messages.* With our embedded training approach we were able to raise user suspicion without decreasing their willingness to interact with legitimate e-mail messages.

---

* S. Sheng, B. Magnien, P. Kumaraguru, A. Acquisti, L. Cranor, J. Hong, and E. Nunge. Antiphishing phil: The design and evaluation of a game that teaches people not to fall for phish. In *Proceedings of the 2007 Symposium on Usable Privacy and Security*, Pittsburgh, PA, July 18–20, 2007. http://cups.cs.cmu.edu/soups/2007/proceedings/p88_sheng.pdf.

Our embedded training approach allows for convenient and fast ongoing training in which each simulated phishing e-mail acts both as a mechanism to deliver training and as a test of whether the recipient has learned how to distinguish legitimate from phishing messages. Our embedded training system not only trains users in about 2 minutes, but also assesses their performance at regular intervals. In this way, we can identify and present training interventions only to those users who continue to fall for simulated phishing attacks. In addition, this approach can be used to introduce recipients to new phishing threats over time and focus on those recipients who are most susceptible to the new threats.

We Are Now the Targets of Thieves!
By Brad Smith*

Yes! You, I, and everyone in the healthcare business are currently the target of data thieves. Administrators, doctors, nurses, unit secretaries, dietary, physical plant, janitorial staff, and even your garbage cans. We are all in the sights of nefarious people. People who want to make you their friend or make you scared of them or make them think they are somebody else. They only want the information in your head and what you can steal from your employer. Medical facilities have made it harder to break in from the outside, making you and I on the inside the new target.

Your facility is currently under attack by a threat that is so powerful that the federal government had to pass a law mandating training against this threat. The law is the Red Flag rule, and it is designed to lessen the threat of social engineering attacks (SEA), which contribute to identity theft. It requires organizations to train staff on how powerful SEA really is. This section will help you understand the severity of the SE threat and how you can understand and defend against these powerful attacks being unleashed against medical facilities. Better yet, you will learn something about yourself, your friends and family, and people in general.

Why Are We Targets?

We have data. Lots of data. Data on staff, on patients, on stars, on sports people, and on your facility itself. We are targets because we have data that can be easily stolen

---

* Brad ("The Nurse") Smith was the first registered nurse and Certified Information System Security Professional (CISSP) on record. He was the first RN to be certified by the National Security Agency (NSA) in information security assessment methodology. Brad's input to the HIPAA law helped rural facilities not get bound to high-priced methodology. He speaks at many security and medical conferences such as the Healthcare Information and Management Systems Society (HIMSS), the American Medical Information Association (AMIA), the American Nursing Informatives Association (ANIA), DefCon, the Computer Security Institute (CSI), and Interop, and works on staff for the BlackHat security conference series throughout the world. He is currently a private practice informatics nurse helping rural and frontier medical facilities in outer Montana, Wyoming, and the Dakotas.

and resold. Information is now $$$. What surgery did some actress just have? What about a star player who was just hurt? Is he out for the season or will he be back next week? While this may not seem valuable to us, it is highly sought after, and the pay is good for this type of data theft. There is high profit in high-profile people.

Healthcare professionals are some of the easiest people to get data from. We spend our days helping people; we went into healthcare to help people. Most of us have that "need" to help others; that is why we picked the medical profession. And that is what the professional criminals know about us. We need to help.

Medical facilities do not really seem to care. How can I say that? The federal government had to pass a law (the Health Insurance Portability and Accountability Act, or HIPAA) that brought *minimum* privacy and security requirements to healthcare. What an outcry from the medical field! Gonna put us out of business! Raise health costs! And how many CEOs have gone to jail for HIPAA violations? None, zero, zip, not one has! Healthcare can learn much from the financial industry about the value of data.

A large pharmacy chain was fined $2.25 million for disposing of documents, such as labels from prescription bottles and old prescriptions and medical records in unsecured dumpsters. This breach happened in multiple national locations, multiple times. The information in the dumpster was everything needed to steal a person's identity. The people with pill bottles already have lots of problems, so the medical industry giving away their identity is adding more gloom to their doom. I am still trying to figure out how nobody at this huge company thought throwing away medical records in the dumpster outside of the store was a bad idea?

As a healthcare security and privacy advisor, I have found that few hospitals really spent as much time and money on these critical areas as they should. The old excuse that security and privacy get in the way of patient care is just another example of not enough money and planning before both were put into place. Keeping people from losing their identity while they are in contact with the healthcare field does not seem to be out of line with our mission. I am still big on "Do no harm." The root problem is that healthcare does not really care about security and privacy, because nothing happens to the violators. Sure, you do get your name on a list of know breaches, but few know where to look for the list of medical security breaches. Do you?

Want a shock? Visit www.PrivacyRights.org, and see all the medical facilities that have been breached in the last few years. Read how healthcare facilities were breached, and you will realize what a bad job we are doing. When you start thinking we have done enough for security or enough to protect our privacy, visit the site above and get a big dose of reality.

What Do the Attackers Want?

Everything! Every bit of information from patients accounts because all their financial information is there to pay for the medical treatments. Most patients are not checking their credit card bills while they are laid up in the hospital, so they are easy targets.

Many sick are elderly, which makes the problem even worse when they get their identity stolen. The FDIC reports that 20% of all identity thefts are seniors. This group is the least technically competent, and so less likely to be aware of how to protect themselves in the electronic age.

Everything in the staff personnel files is under attack so they can borrow your identity to take out credit in your name. Doctors and nurses can easily get credit, so everything in HR is under attack. Do you use your free credit checks every year? If yes, then good for you! If no, then why don't you?

Don't We Have People to Protect This Stuff from Attack?

Sure, if you are a huge organization. What about most small facilities, doctor's offices, private practice nurses, pharmacies, free standing labs, and insurance offices? Most cannot afford to hire certified security consultants, so they get their network person to do security. Like the floor float nurse, we'd get into the unit or I'd get pulled to OB, wide-eyed and jumpy. Sure we're all RNs, but that didn't mean we knew this specialty. Security is a specialty, privacy is a specialty, just like critical care or OB, but most IT staff think they can do it without any help.

Before computers, nurses and record management specialists monitored the physical access to records (consisting mostly of "Who are you? Why are you touching that record!") Now that IT has the records, many do not seem to understand the depth or importance of information they are watching. If they truly did, we would not see so many hospitals on the breach list or I would have found more than a handful of hospitals that could pass a privacy and security assessment. Both can be transparent to the user, but until IT realizes the importance of the data they watch and management understands the bad privacy/security = bad press = people in the community do not trust the facility, the medical field will have bad security.

Test: How Is Your Facility's Security?

Try this simple test. Go to a floor where nobody knows you, sit at a terminal and say, "Hey I know we use the same password, but I seem to have forgotten it, can you tell me?" You really do not want to know how many people have given me the master password when I have done this test. Why keep it a secret? Everybody uses the same password, so it is not that important, right?

How Are They Attacking?

Social engineering attacks (SEAs) are really the new threat. These are such low-tech attacks that most businesses do not even know they are being attacked. Few businesses track the attempted SEA. Yet, this has become one of the most powerful tools in the hacker's arsenal.

Social engineering has gotten vastly more powerful for two basic reasons. The first was the science of neurolinguistic programming developed in the 1970s. This was developed by studying a successful therapist (instead of studying failures as we normally do) and developing a methodology based on that success.

The second reason is money. Now that there are more people, banks, credit card processing, and on-line purchasing on the Internet, organized crime has entered the arena. Stealing and reselling identities is now big business for organized crime.

How Exactly Do Social Engineering Attacks Work?

Let us do some simple SEA exercises so you can see how powerful and simple it is. To start, just listen. That is all. Listen to not just what people are saying but how they say it. Listen to their word choices, how fast or slow they talk, how long they talk and the pitch of their voice. Simple and hard at the same time.

Can You See What I Am Saying? Can You Hear What I Am Saying? Do You Feel My Words?

People have a dominant sense that re-presents the world to their inner self. Some people are visual, some auditory, and some feeling. Can you see/hear/feel my point? Now listen to people and try and figure out what their dominant sense is. Just listen to the person's speech patterns because it shows up in their choice of words. The hardest part for most people is to let the other person talk. Listen for words related to each sense. This is easy when people are talking about things they like, so make sure you direct the conversation to an area they like, then sit back and watch what happens (then sit back and listen to what they say).

Examples

Run it up the flag pole and see who salutes it! Who saw this coming? Something smells funny about this deal. You'd better watch out for that person!

If you do the above exercise, you'll find lots of men are visual. Women tend to be more aural. Some says it's the way we are socialized, while others contend it is nature. Be aware that not all men or women fit in one style, so no general stereotyping please. Is this why men will sit with the remote control watching stuff, just for the visual stimulus? When you look at ads in the newspaper, notice that products for men tend to have more visual stimulus while women's advertising has more word. Yes, this can help when you are doing PowerPoint for mainly men or mainly women.

Now that you know how to figure out someone's dominant sense, have you figure out yours yet? How about your family or friends? This dominant sense shows up in many ways. I used to have "friends" who were constantly fighting about everything. She would say, "He never hears what I'm saying," and he would respond, "She never sees my point." While they are still married, it does not feel like they'll make it much longer.

Here is the difficult part: Can you change your dominant sense when you are in a group conversation? Try it, you will find that it is a difficult task. I have watched several true masters of the field, and they can just smoothly talk to each person in the group utilizing their dominant sense speech pattern. Purely amazing and scary!

People also use different lengths of words and different lengths of time when they speak. Think of that someone you know who speaks few words and that person who just will not shut up. Both are using different lengths of speech. I am sure you know some sesquipedalist who uses large words when little ones will do. I found my patients crying because they were "going to die" because someone told them they were diaphoresing.*

When you listen to people in conversation, try and become aware of these small but important differences in speech. When you change these small items, it helps the other person feel that you are "like them." That is what social engineering is all about, helping people believe you are just like them. Why shouldn't I give you the information you want, after all, you are just like me and I would never do anything bad with that data, password, or medical record. Birds of a feather flock together.

Exercise: Speed Kills (Maybe)

Here is an exercise that you will find fun and difficult at the same time. People speak at different rates, some fast and some slow. When you listen to a conversation, try to match their speed. Fast or slow, it is your job to speak at their rate. While it sounds easy, you will find it is easier to either be fast or slow; it all depends on *you*.

Many people have trouble understanding overseas help centers. Why? Because speed of speech is also based on culture. Some cultures (even just different parts of the same country) have a rapid flow of words, while others are slow and deliberate. It is important to note here that speed of speech does not reflect speed of thought. Some people actually think about what they are going to say before they speak. Other people just use filler words like "um" and "ah" to fill the space where they should have been thinking before speaking.

Turning Friendship into an Attack

Now let us see how these simple techniques can cause a major security breach. While lots of books and lectures divide these into categories, I think there are only two basic types: soft and hard attacks. These two attacks can be used when on the phone, in e-mail, in person, and even in printed advertising.

Soft Attacks

These are the hardest to defend against. How do you protect yourself from nice? The classic story of the person dressed like an intern who "forgot his password"

---

* Which is to say, "profusely sweating."

and had to finish his H/P before he could go home. It was his anniversary, and he had a box of chocolates for his "wife" that he offered to a nurse in exchange for the password. You know what happened then: The hacker stole data, data, and more data. Jobs were lost, and a federal breach report had to be filed.

Soft attacks are usually the most effective because most people do not see the threat. We recently did a security assessment on a medical facility by putting flyers on the employees' cars for a new restaurant that lets you order online if you worked from the hospital. When they logged onto the site, a hidden Trojan was downloaded to their computer that would have allowed us to steal every password from every user that had ever logged onto that computer. Quick, easy, and they failed miserably.

I was sitting in the CIO's office drinking coffee. He kept looking at his watch and finally said, "Hey, aren't you going to do the penetration test," and I replied that it was currently under way. My laptop signaled "ding." They failed. That simple. (Glad it did not take longer; they made terrible coffee.)

Here is how it's done. Take a 16 GB USB drive, and put special software on it that, when plugged in, will download all password files, all Excel spreadsheets, and all Word documents, and put any type of worm, Trojan, virus, or key-logging software back on the computer it was plugged into. Put the USB back in the package so it looks new, and then drop it in the parking lot. (I like to use the executive or doctors' lots because they seem to pick it up faster than others.) Just sit and wait, because it never takes longer than 45 minutes to show up on the inside of the private network. When it gets plugged into the local computer network, it contacts me and tells me the address where it is located. This was started with iPods, so it is called Pod slurping. Soft, free, and deadly. Firewall? It totally bypassed all the external security most facilities have, making the firewall just a fat brick of technology.

There are lots of soft attack vectors because they are so deadly and easy. Does your organization track soft SE attacks?

Hard Attacks

These are the older-style attacks, but can still be used effectively. This is when someone calls up and starts yelling. "Don't you know who I am?" These seem to work well in the corporate environment, but lack effectiveness in the medical field.

This can be used effectively in conjunction with the Out of Office (OoO) message. These are great for SE attacks. When I go out to do an SE attack on a facility, I e-mail everybody in the organization (the list is easy to find using Google; check out Johnny Long's book *Google Hacking*). When I get an OoO message, I call, knowing they will not be there: "Where's that record they were supposed to send! You'll lose our business if you don't fix this MISTAKE. SEND ME THAT RECORD NOW, HOW COULD YOU BE SO SLOPPY/LAZY/IRRESPONSIBLE!" Guess what? A large percentage do send the requested data. Please specify more on your OoO message, so I can say: "How could they go on a cruise to Europe with this job undone?" Thanks for sharing your schedule with all the hackers in the world.

Garbage Out: Data In

One last area that really is a gold mine and is not actually hard or soft: the garbage. Seems simple; we know we must shred, but the shredder buy goes to the lowest bidder. When I see a straight cut shredder, all your shreds belong to me! My ops manager loves to reassemble these, sort of like a puzzle with deadlier ends. Over the years we've reassembled medical records, billing records, and even facility budgets with bank accounts on them. My hint is to call ahead and find out what is for lunch because you will be crawling through it in the garbage. Do not go on days they serve spaghetti—hard to keep the pages clean and the red sauce reminds me of trauma. Do not forget to check the trash pickup schedule, and go the day before to get the best data. Do take a stick and rubber gloves, it makes it so much cleaner.

Remember these techniques are best in a large facility where rotation is the norm. Most difficult is the small rural facility where they know everybody, and everybody's business in town. Do not try this in rural America (like Hamilton, Montana) unless you want to go to jail and have the CEO come and bail you out!

Test: Do You Have Good Garbage?

When was the last time you checked your facility's garbage? How about your home garbage?

OK, What Can We Do to Protect Ourselves and Our Facility?

A multilayered approach to privacy and security is always the best. All employees should become aware of how powerful an attack tool SE is. Every organization should have adequate policies and procedures to provide protection and discipline to those who break the rules. A tracking system for attacks should be implemented, and education for IT staff on SEA should be started.

Awareness and Training

The federal Red Flags Rule is a good start. They require training on SE, including signs and symptoms of an attack. Every facility needs to train all their staff about this problem, not just clerks, nurses, and doctors but executives, janitors, dietary—everybody! Awareness is the first step to fixing the problem.

Extra training should be given to anybody who deals with outside people in their job. Clerks at the help desk, volunteers who escort people, and executives should all get role-playing scenarios where they are attacked using hard/soft methods. Both the awareness and training can be easily incorporated into the new person orientation and the yearly employee training sessions.

Policies and Procedures (P/P)

Policies and procedures that help people become aware of what data should never be given out and how to handle request for private data should be created and enforced. These must be applied to all staff and management professionals equally to show that this is a serious area.

Tracking SEA

Most facilities can tell me how many attacks they have had on their firewall but cannot tell me how many attempts to gain a "lost password" were used against them. Since facilities have started to lock down their external access, the next attack point is the staff. Can your facility tell me how many SE attacks were used against it last year? You bet they can show some number for how many attacks the firewalls stopped, but those fancy firewalls do not stop the 16 GB USB drive in the parking lot SEA. Firewalls are old by computer time, while SEA is now. SEA can easily defeat almost any firewall!

Incorporating a P/P is a must that elevates any request for restricted information to a privacy/security person who can use SEA to try to locate the attacker and the reason for the attack. This removes the additional burden of security from the busy staff and redirects it to where it belongs: with the privacy and security professional.

Problems in Implementation

OK, IT people are not known for their high social skills. Watch ITs. Their favorite color is black, they are mostly male, and work with inanimate objects like wires, switches, and routers. Healthcare's (especially nurse's) favorite color is white; they are mostly female and work with people every day. Can you see where there might be a problem here? Some IT and management people fully understand the importance and power of SEA attacks. Then there are the rest. Many an IT specialist has bought me dinner and drinks while telling me SEA does not work. OK for me but sad for their facility.

Once you really see how badly the medical field has fared in protecting our health records, you'll change your mind.

Summary

The healthcare worker is now the target of data thieves. They use SEA techniques based on neurolinugistic programming to trick us into giving them protected information they can sell.

It is weird to think you might be under a social engineering attack if someone is too nice, too mean, or too nosey about specific information. People have been after protected information as long as information has been protected, but now the motivation is higher because of profitable identity theft.

SEA is about learning to adjust your own word length, sentence length, speed of speech, and dominant sense. Then, making up some reason to have you give them the information. Please review all the protected information that HIPAA has specified because that's what most criminals are after.

A multilayered approach to protection involves: awareness, training, policies and procedures, proper enforcement, and education for IT personnel. These will help in defeating this new form of attack. You already do awareness and training, and most facilities have those few special people who love to construct policy and procedure, so the cost for these is minimal. Education on proper security/privacy for IT professionals is available either on line or in person at conferences and can add that extra layer of protection against social engineering attacks. When you do the return on investment for protecting against this new threat, you'll see the rewards are really great! It also keeps you off PrivacyRights.org, and the people will still trust you.

Risks from Advanced Malware and Blended Threats

By Dr. Christophe Veltsos*

Privacy and security professionals have come to realize that technologies that work today to protect the company may no longer be effective tomorrow. The ever-changing security measures are due not only to the adoption of new technologies but also to the rapid pace of adaptation and innovation shown by attackers. Attackers exploit new vulnerabilities almost as soon as existing ones are being patched, creating a constant game of cat-and-mouse between security professionals and attackers. Making matters worse are various reports over the past few years about a growing underground market for stolen electronic data. This underground market has matured to the point that hackers can increase their profits by specializing in a given skill-set (e.g., browser hacks or PDF hacks). Even worse, these reports suggest that organized criminals are shifting their operations to take advantage of the global nature of the Internet. In short, the growing demand for sensitive electronic data is fueling a boom in criminal hacking activity. The failure of existing technical controls to provide adequate protection against these threats puts greater importance on appropriate coverage of such threats during information security and privacy awareness and training programs (ISPAT). Effective ISPATs need to be periodically revised in order to stay current with company policies and practices as well as the ever-changing nature of threats. Over the past decades, improvements in network defenses and operating system defenses have resulted in attackers shifting their attack strategies to exploit software applications (such as browsers, word processors, and digital formats like PDF) and social networks, often combining those attacks in a blended threat.

---

* Dr. Christophe Veltsos is a faculty member in the Department of Information Systems & Technology at Minnesota State University–Mankato, where he regularly teaches information security and information warfare classes. From 2007 to 2009, Christophe served as the president of the Mankato Chapter, Information Systems Security Association (ISSA). In addition to providing consulting services to small and mid-sized businesses, Christophe also regularly writes on security and privacy topics on his blog at www.DrInfoSec.com.

As companies embrace the benefits of Web 2.0—a term that I use broadly to include Internet-based applications, Software as a Service, and Cloud Computing—new opportunities are created for attackers to try to acquire, modify, or destroy company data. As explained in more details below, current technological controls have so far proven ineffective in countering these new and rapidly evolving threats. Existing policies must be updated (or new ones created) and practices adjusted to ensure continued safety and privacy of sensitive data. To date, a company's best asset in protecting sensitive data is a workforce that has been educated to deal with the risks associated with operating in a Web 2.0 world.

The Changing Attack Landscape: Malware and Blended Threats

While end users are often well versed with terms like *firewall* and *antivirus*, they are also often convinced that those technologies provide close to impenetrable defenses against all potential risks of attack. During several interviews with end users and management, I have often heard people indicating that they were "safe" when browsing online as they were protected by a popular antivirus program. Yet various reports* on Internet security and data breaches for 2007, 2008, and early 2009 have shown that hackers use malware to evade defenses, infect machines, and establish long-term control or surveillance of user activity and/or network traffic in spite of such "protection" from typical antivirus programs.

Due to the sensitive nature of the topic, few companies are willing to share the lessons learned from investigating a data breach. However, the investigative arm of Verizon has produced two data breach reports containing useful aggregate data. The 2009 Verizon Data Breach report shows that a majority of records breached involved the use of hacking and malware (94% and 90%, respectively). While only 17% of attacks employed "difficult" attack techniques such as malware, they resulted in over 95% of the total records breached. These attacks often use specially crafted malware that is extremely hard to detect and remove with current technological security controls. In one recent case, for example, Heartland Payment Systems was notified several times by law enforcement and payment card industry fraud departments that its computer networks were likely breached, yet the company's first two investigations failed to find a deeply rooted piece of malware hiding in unallocated sectors on a hard drive. At press time, there were over 650 banks affected by this breach.

Employees need to be aware that the current state of security technologies does not provide complete protection against the latest attacks, particularly against targeted attacks. The reason for this (usually temporary) gap in protection is simple:

---

* Verizon Data Breach report 2009 available at http://www.verizonbusiness.com/resources/ security/reports/2009_databreach_rp.pdf; Symantec Internet Security Threat Report 2008 available at http://www.symantec.com/business/theme. jsp?themeid= threatreport; McAfee Threat Report available at http://www.mcafee.com/us/threat_center/white_paper.html.

antivirus companies need to observe and collect malware samples in the wild before they are able to update their programs to properly detect and/or remove the malware. Yet the process is not perfect. The Secunia Internet Security Suite test report* released in October 2008, tested 12 leading antivirus suites against 300 vulnerabilities, including 126 deemed "important" cases due to known exploits (i.e., successful attack programs reportedly in use by hackers). The report paints a dismal picture as the highest detection rate across "important" cases was only 31%; even worse, the second-highest detected just under 4% of the cases.

Equally dangerous are blended threats, attacks that use multiple malicious techniques to achieve maximum harm and fast infection rates. As corporations experiment with moving data to the cloud or foray into social networks to tap into an expanded user base, users find themselves interacting with new environments. Yet users are often unaware of the additional threat vectors associated with these environments. When users leave the well-guarded confines of the internal company network to access Web 2.0 services, they often do so using software applications that have thus far proved quite vulnerable. Internet browsers, usually the vehicle of choice for accessing Web 2.0 services, are easily compromised and often used in the early stages of an attack. For example, in a 2009 browser hacking contest held at CanSecWest (an annual security conference in Canada), the winner was able to exploit one browser (Safari) in under 2 minutes while another contestant was able to exploit three major browsers (Internet Explorer 8, Safari, and Firefox) the same day.

This means that the primary vector of access to Web 2.0 services is fragile from a security standpoint. As the Verizon Data Breach report pointed out, "The most common malware delivery method is the scenario in which an attacker compromised a system and then installed malware on it remotely" (page 20). While some attacks require user action such as downloading, installing, or clicking on an item, there is a class of attacks termed "drive-by attacks" that will infect a machine without any user intervention beyond visiting an infected site. Out of seven infections perpetrated via Web sites, the Verizon Data Breach report listed four that employed "drive-by" downloads.

IT Controls for Protecting Users from Advanced and Blended Threats

To minimize the likelihood and damage potential of advanced malware and blended threats, IT and security departments can apply technological controls, such as the following:

- Periodically review user access privileges and remove unnecessary ones.
- Periodically review access logs for indications that shared credentials are in use.
- Provide users with "hardened" browsers (or Web 2.0 applications).
- Provide users with "sandboxed" work environments.

---

* Available at http://secunia.com/gfx/Secunia_Exploit-vs-AV_test-Oct-2008.pdf.

- Ensure patching process covers operating systems as well as installed applications.
- Provide protection for users at home or on the road. While corporate users are usually protected by several layers of security technologies, users at home or on the road are often more vulnerable. Several factors create risks for users, including but not limited to: using hostile networks (at coffee shops, at hotels, "free Wi-Fi" spots, and possibly at home), using outdated antivirus signatures or outdated software (i.e., not having patches applied).

Strategies for Educating Users about Advanced Malware and Blended Threats

In *How to Achieve 27001 Certification* (CRC Press, 2007), Arnason and Willett argue that "an effective security program promotes defining policy and implementing controls that raise awareness of malware carriers and how to address their safe use as a business tool" (page 39). In 2007, the Organization for Economic and Cooperative Development (OECD) created a special publication entitled "Malicious Software: A Security Threat to the Internet Economy."* This free publication provides detailed information about the threats that malware pose, and should be an integral part of the ISPAT development process. In particular, effective ISPAT programs should include the following characteristics.

1. *Use a consistent learning model.* One effective learning model is the Kirkpatrick Method, named after Dr. Donald L. Kirkpatrick, a former president of the American Society for Training and Development. This model proposes a four-level learning model consisting of *reaction, learning, behavior*, and *results* can help measure the effectiveness of the ISPAT program.
2. *Educate and counsel users on password management practices (especially to avoid shared credentials).* While it may be tempting to provide users with run-of-the-mill password education, simply telling users to pick good complex passwords can lead to surprises. For example, "P@$$w0rd" is technically a complex password (consisting of four character classes: upper-case, lower-case, numbers, symbols) but would be easy for a hacker to think of. A recent online survey[†] conducted by the security firm Sophos reported that one-third of respondents used the same password for all Web sites. When it comes to choosing passwords, users should be shown real-world examples of poor choices, such as the list of 200 passwords that the Conficker/Downadup worm[‡] (a type of malware) attempts to gain access into a system.
3. *Provide targeted security training to users that use Web applications frequently.* Users of Web 2.0 services are at greater risk as they need to periodically

---

* Available at http://www.oecd.org/dataoecd/53/34/40724457.pdf.
† Available at http://www.sophos.com/pressoffice/news/articles/2009/03/password-security.html.
‡ Available at http://www.sophos.com/blogs/gc/g/2009/01/16/passwords-conficker-worm/.

Exhibit 9   NoScript blocks the TrendMicro online antivirus scanner House Call.

access or update content using technologies (browsers) that are often quite vulnerable to attacks. In order to balance the inherent vulnerabilities present in Web-browsing technologies, a browser should be supplemented by being "hardened" and "sandboxed." Users should receive special training to cover the resulting small changes in the operation of the browser. One example of a hardened browser is Firefox with the NoScript plugin. Exhibit 9 shows a Web page as viewed with the default (i.e., more secure) settings with Javascript disabled. Exhibit 10 shows how one can quickly enable rich browser features like Javascript for trusted sites. Exhibit 11 shows the same Web page now reloaded and fully functional.

Exhibit 10   The NoScript dialog box.

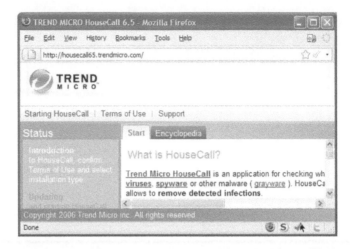

Exhibit 11   TrendMicro HouseCall after enabling scripts in the NoScript add-on.

Sandboxing a Web browser is an effective way to mitigate many of the current exploits and is often used and recommended by security professionals. Sandboxie is a low-cost program that provides a security sandbox for a browser (or any other application program) so that any changes to the drive or the registry would be wiped when the browser is closed. Exhibit 12 shows the Sandboxie desktop icon; clicking on it will open the default browser in a secure sandbox. Exhibit 13 shows

Exhibit 12   Sandboxie icon.

Exhibit 13   The sandboxed browser (note the extra "[#]" characters).

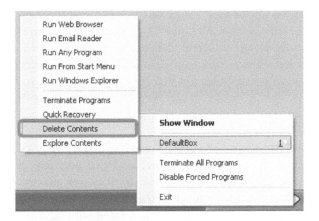

Exhibit 14   Deleting any changes to the sandboxed program(s).

the default browser loaded in the sandbox; note the extra "[#]" characters in the application window title bar. Exhibit 14 shows how one can delete any changes potentially done to the sandbox by malware.

Measuring the Effectiveness of Your Privacy and Security Program

In order to measure the effectiveness of their ISPAT programs, organizations must routinely collect data that can later be turned into useful metrics. For example, collecting data about password complexity, number of incidents reported, and number of visits to known malware-hosting sites can prove extremely useful in gauging the effectiveness of the program. Here is a list of additional measures to gather:

- *Survey employees on password management practices.* Businesses should conduct an anonymous survey of how users manage the myriad of passwords they need to perform their daily tasks.
- *Perform phishing attacks against users and management.* Several tools and services exist that allow a company to perform a mock phishing attack against its own employees. The aim is to test how likely users are to fall for a social engineering attack and adjust the next cycle of awareness, education, and training accordingly.
- *Conduct password complexity checks.* With proper backing and permission from administration, regular password audits should be conducted in order to detect poor password choices and correct the behavior. Acceptable thresholds should be determined based on the business function and the type of data that can be accessed.

■ *Assess employees on the level of risky behavior they engage in when "protected" by technical security controls.* Alexander Pope said, "A little knowledge [learning] is a dangerous thing." A survey designed to gauge how (wrongly) protected employees feel when using an antivirus could reveal that users engage in more risky behaviors because they feel that they are invulnerable to attacks.

Conclusion

The underground economy has fueled a wave of hacker activity that threatens the privacy and security of data closely guarded by corporations across the globe. Corporations must adjust their information security and privacy awareness and training programs to provide employees with the knowledge needed to maintain the safety of the data entrusted to them when faced with advanced malware and blended threats.

Case Study: 1200 Users, 11 Cities in 7 Weeks ... and They Wanted to Come to Security Awareness Training

By Todd Fitzgerald, PMP, CISSP, CISA, CISM, CGEIT*

The true barometer of a successful training program is when the attendees are talking about it in the hallways, telling their co-workers how much fun they had, providing high marks on the feedback forms, and explaining the lessons that were learned in the training to their fellow colleagues. Even more gratifying to the instructors are the comments received from the training, such as "Best training program ever offered at this company," "Absolutely entertaining and informative," "Taught a boring subject in a fun way!" "Kept you interested," "Excellent content and creative presentation," and "Fun and informative." So how was this accomplished? Great instructors? Enormous security subject? While we would like to think that all of the above were available and present, the reality is that the areas of true importance were (1) creating a singular message, (2) detailed planning, and most importantly, (3) keeping it interactive with audience participation. Let us explore the real-life specifics that were executed to achieve "strongly agree" evaluation results!

---

* Todd Fitzgerald, PMP, CISSP, CISA, CISM, CGEIT, ISO27000, and ITILV3 certified, is responsible for external IT audit and facilitating IT internal control technical compliance for National Government Services, Milwaukee, Wisconsin, one of the largest processors of Medicare claims. Todd was a 2005 Midwest Finalist for ISE Security Executive of the Year, recipient of 2009 SC Magazine Best Security Team Award, and coauthored the ISC2 Press book CISO Leadership: Essential Principles for Success. Todd earned an MBA with highest honors from Oklahoma State University. He is a frequent writer, presenter, and facilitator of modern security issues.

The Problem

The first step in embarking on any successful endeavor should be to define the problem. Where is the organizational pain? What topic area has not been fully addressed before? It is important to define a *singular* problem, or at most a few concepts that are related together. Cramming training on all of the security issues into one session will cause frustration with the users and not provide enough time to deliver enough examples. To those of us working daily in the security profession, it is easy to lose sight of the knowledge and understanding that we have around the subject, and expect others to "just get it" by saying it once. The theme selected for training was "Internet and E-Mail Security Practices." By picking a theme, other security principles can be embedded into the message. In this example, copyright issues (downloading music/software), confidentiality, identity theft (sharing logon/passwords), and securing passwords were embedded into the theme without overloading the users.

Review Videos

Once the problem was defined, eight different free demo security videos were obtained and reviewed to select one that would be most appropriate. The demo videos were all full length, with the words "Demo—not for training purposes" across the screen. Short 15–20 minute videos are an excellent way to begin the training session.

Enter Creativity, Collaboration, and Conceptualization

Once the theme had been decided, it was time to discuss some conceptual ideas, being very open at this point. The security officer and two staff members contributed ideas to develop the training program during an initial brainstorming session. In our case, the security officer had an initial vision of what was to be delivered; however, this was shaped and changed based on the input of the team. *At this stage, every idea is a good one!* The key to this stage is understanding that it may turn out completely different from that originally conceptualized, and that is OK! It was decided through this collaboration to give the security presentation the theme of "Why Gamble? Get.Net.Smart!" With this theme, the training could be developed around the appropriate use of the Internet and e-mail, and the risks to the individual and company for inappropriate use.

Toys, Toys, and More Toys!

Toys provide an excellent visual aid for training and people immediately have a perception that this is "going to be fun" when they walk in the room. The toy, game, and party stores are excellent places to roam around. It is also useful to not limit the toy selection to toys in the stores, but to also use a search engine, such as Google, to locate items in quantities that are not available locally. Dollar stores are also an excellent resources. To tie in with the theme of gambling and the Internet, six different-colored 12-sided, numbered 8-inch foam dice were ordered from an Internet company. At this point, it was unknown how they would be utilized, but that was okay! All that was known was that some sort of game would be created.

Initially, it was thought that there would be six tables of five people each (30 per session), and they would throw the dice at each other. Then, based on the number, some activity would be performed. The key point here is to build on (1) the number of people requiring training, (2) the theme, (3) the video, and (4) the toys. In keeping with the dice and gambling theme, we found while at a game store that was going out of business, some dice marked at 70% off, or 30 cents for six dice. Again, not knowing exactly how these would be used, but knowing that there would be about 60 training sessions, 600 packs of the dice were purchased as giveaways. Another toy store had some light-up dice that would also be excellent giveaways, so after purchasing one pack from the toy store, the distributor was contacted and a quantity discount price was negotiated on 1300 pair of dice (an extra 100 pair were ordered for new hires).

The video and toy ordering were among the first activities completed to support the theme of the training. Why? Because there may be longer lead time associated with acquiring the toys, depending upon the product and quantity. There also may be internal organizational lead times to getting the purchase orders and payments through the accounts payable department that had to be considered.

The Training Scenario

After much brainstorming and roaming around party and toy stores, the training scenario was developed. A video on the appropriate use of the Internet and e-mail would be watched, and then scenarios would be acted out with the use of props and 20–30-second segments of downloaded music clips. In preparation for the training, 12 scenarios of inappropriate Internet activity would be matched with a music clip and props for the presenters to act out the inappropriate activity. As the attendees entered the room, they would draw a colored number (1–24), matching the color of the dice placed at their table, from a bag that would determine their assigned table. Assigning individuals to tables separates chatty friends, reducing the anxiety of people picking a spot, and helps people meet new coworkers. For each scenario, one of the presenters would draw a matching number from another bag and call on the attendee to roll the 12-sided, numbered 8-inch dice on their table. The number shown on the top of the foam dice after the roll would be the number corresponding to one of the 12 scenarios of inappropriate Internet/e-mail activity. The instructors would then play the music clip and act out the scenario, while the person selected would have to guess the inappropriate activity. If they were unable to guess, the members of their table could help them out. After each activity was guessed, it was briefly discussed, explaining the inappropriate activity and risks to the business of the activity.

For example, the inappropriate activity may be viewing pornography, and the music clip used could be "Sexy Thing" by Hot Chocolate or "This Love" by Maroon 5, while the presenters wear purple wigs, beads, and interact with the audience, delivering the message of sexual harassment. Or a "clean" version of Eminem's song "Real Slim Shady" could be used to highlight identity theft, password sharing, and exposure to confidential information while the presenters are dressed in backwards-facing baseball caps, sunglasses, and blowup microphone's imitating the dance moves of the singer. Spreading rumors through message boards and e-mails could be highlighted through Fleetwood Mac's song "Little Lies," while the instructors' gossip with each other and the audience wearing Pinocchio noses. Use imagination and creativity to develop the scenarios in advance. The key is to interact with the audience while acting out the scenarios, as well as tying them to the business risk after each music clip. It is useful to use a variety of songs from the present and past, and related to different regions of the country where you may be training. For example, the country song "The Gambler" and playing 52-card pickup with a selected victim used to communicate Internet gambling was popular in Northern Wisconsin training, as well as in our Virginia/West Virginia offices. Alternatively, songs using the Beach Boys, such as "Little Deuce Coupe," while pretending to drive little toy cars used to communicate "surfing the net" were most popular in the California offices. Each of the songs was well received across all regions.

During the playing of each music clip, it is important for the presenters to move around the audience, visiting each table and interacting with different people. This is what makes it fun for the participants. Putting beads around someone while "You Sexy Thing" is playing, or staring at someone close-up, or better yet surprising someone with a 6-inch nose on your face usually brings laughter. If they are laughing, they are being entertained and are paying attention to the message. Sneaking up from behind people while wearing dark sunglasses and moving to the sounds of the James Bond Theme song for "007," can raise laughter while communicating the Internal hacking and electronic monitoring capabilities related to a "spying message."

Communication needs to be deliberate and in multiple forms, as different people learn differently. We communicated through written words (presentations), speech, visual effects, and our body language. This is why the video and scenarios are so effective at reinforcing the message. After the training, people will remember the visuals and music and then have a higher probability of retaining the message.

The One-Hour Agenda—Do Not PowerPoint Them to Death

The training was also limited to a 1-hour session. It is difficult to hold someone's attention to a subject that is not considered his or her primary job or interest for longer than that time. PowerPoint slides are a great visual tool, but for this type of training, they were used sparingly and only to frame the beginning and the end. The following agenda was determined:

1. Introductions: 15 seconds, keeping the training light.
2. Video: 20 minutes, but ask them if it is OK to watch an hour video and get their reaction, then tell them it is only 20 minutes.
3. Exercise recall of the video: 15–20 minutes; do not explain what they will be doing until after they have viewed the video. Keep it vague at this point. This is where the 1–12 scenarios are repeated.
4. Question and answer: 5 minutes.
5. Evaluations: 5 minutes; actually takes less time.
6. Drawing: 5 seconds.

After all of the attendees have drawn their numbers and are seated at the table with the matching colored dice, it is time to briefly go through the agenda. The agenda is intentionally 50 minutes in length, as it is a good idea to add a few minutes for scenarios that may run a little longer, or if there are questions that come up during one of the scenarios. It is also advisable to start each session 5 minutes late and to tell everyone to be prompt in attending the sessions. Why? Because there will always be a few individuals that will be late, and this minimizes any distractions; the latecomers will also be able to receive the entire presentation. As a general rule, if someone arrives more than 5–10 minutes into the video (25%–50%), it is acceptable to tell him or her to return for another session (however, in small geographic offices with only one session, they will have to get the most out of the time remaining in the session).

Logistics—Success Is in the Details

This cannot be stressed enough. To really be successful, especially across geographic locations, the program must be rigorously planned so that the proper communication, facilities, equipment, materials, and people are engaged. Multiple spreadsheets were used to manage the process.

Pretraining Planning

Be sure to plan and do all coordination activities in advance. This is necessary to conduct successful training. Coordination activities should include the following:

1. Determine number of individuals in each location, training materials needed, and order training supplies 4–6 weeks before training starts to provide ample time for receipt of materials.
2. Preparation of one page PowerPoint slide to launch training with theme. Send out 3 weeks before training.
3. Recruit coordinator in each office to help with room scheduling and times (1–2 months before training).

4. Negotiate training times with each office (1–2 months before training).
5. Negotiate special training sessions for groups with phone coverage (for example, customer service) that may limit their availability.
6. Identify hotels near each office (1 month before training).
7. Determine schedule and make flight, hotel reservations.
8. Review video and create associated spreadsheet with inappropriate activities, and the music and props that will be used for each scenario 1 month prior to training; continuously improve during training, New ideas will surface.
9. Prepare individual office signup sheets, evaluation forms, and sign-in sheets 1 month prior to training.
10. E-mail notification of training 3 weeks prior to training, with another notification reminder 1-week prior.

Class Sizes and Scheduling

With offices ranging from 15 to 600 people spread across 10 cities in 7 states, the number of sessions and attendees per session varied. The optimal class size for interactive training appeared to be in the 20–24-class range, so signup sheets were limited to 24 people. Individuals would typically add their own lines and signup if the session was full, so the rooms were setup in advance to handle 30 people (6 tables of 5) to handle this situation. This avoids moving chairs around at the last minute and after class starts. If it is known that something could happen, it is best to plan for it ahead of time.

The sessions were 1 hour in length with 30 minutes in between each session. This was necessary as 15 minutes are needed for resetting the room with evaluation forms and candy, putting the props away, and setting up the computer for the next session. Another 15 minutes were reserved so that the instructors would be ready for the early birds that get to the sessions early. There is no time to go back to your desk and look at e-mail.

Four sessions each day were scheduled for the larger locations, avoiding the lunch time period and the end of the day if possible. People get antsy around these time periods and are thinking about how hungry they are or if the session will end in time for them to pick up the kids. Optimal session times that worked were 8–9 a.m., 9:30–10:30 a.m., 11–noon, and 2–3 p.m. More than four sessions can be taxing on the instructors, while completing by 3 p.m. each day permits some time to handle e-mail and other daily activities. In locations where customer service representatives needed training and needed to be on the phones, the training was shifted to begin at 7 a.m. For the larger locations, class sessions were held across a 2-week period (preferably noncontiguous) and scheduled on different days to increase the likelihood those individuals would be able to attend.

Session Planning for Each Location

When training across multiple geographic locations, there are many details that cannot be taken care of until arrival at the location. It is important to provide plenty of time outside of the training to make this successful. Arriving at the first session in the morning at least 1 hour in advance is necessary to (1) set up the LCD projector and computer, (2) test and verify the music volume is appropriate, (3) distribute evaluation forms to the tables, (4) distribute chocolate to the tables, (5) set up the dice on the tables and any other visuals around the room, (6) double-check the props are all there and hidden from attendee view, (7) configure the room tables, and (8) check the signup sheets for attendance numbers. By ensuring these details are taken care of in advance, when the participants enter the room, the instructors are available to meet and greet each person and have them draw a number from the bag instead of trying to get setup while people arrive.

While each video was being viewed, the instructors would sit at the back of the room and match up the numbered cards (1–36) between two bags; one bag that the attendees picked from, and the other that the instructor used to draw the next number. Since there would never be exactly 24 people in a session, by matching the numbers that were left (not taken) and removing them from the instructor bag, this removed the possibility of wasting time by calling out a number that did not exist. Time is important, as there is only 1–1.5 minutes per scenario. Although the sessions were planned for 24 participants to signup, numbers 1–36 were used to be able to handle up to 36 people. Upon reviewing the signup sheets prior to each session, higher numbers were removed from the selection (for example, 31–36 or 25–30) so that when the participants chose a number, they would be evenly distributed to one of the six colored tables.

99% of Evaluations Returned

The common experience with evaluations is that few people fill these out. However, out of approximately 1200 people trained, 99% were returned! This is not by accident, but rather planning. In the beginning of the presentation, the evaluation forms are mentioned, and at the end of the presentation the instructor said "Please fill out the evaluation forms and in return we will provide you with a pack of light-up dice." Additionally, it is effective to stand at the door and hand out a plastic bag containing the dice and a card stating the inappropriate Internet activities and the associated risk to the business to each person. The participants place their evaluations on the chair next to the instructor by the door, affording them anonymity. It works. It is also important to give them a few minutes to complete the evaluation, and have it present in front of them when they sit down at their table.

Makeup Sessions

In the smaller locations where one or two sessions were held, it was not feasible to hold makeup sessions due to the interactive nature of the sessions. In the larger locations, plenty of sessions (between 20–25) were scheduled where individuals had ample opportunity to attend. For the 10% that could not attend a session, the video was placed on the server at each location, and the users were sent an e-mail containing a makeup packet that included some expanded slides to cover the interactive piece, and a quiz required to be completed within 3 weeks. License agreements were negotiated with the video vendor to remain compliant with copyright laws. This was an effective method of ensuring training was completed for everyone, while minimizing the time involvement of the instructors for creating makeup sessions.

Final Thoughts

Training the associates is arguably the best use of the information security budget. Taking time in this very important step to make it fun, deliver a focused message, and highlight the importance of information security will provide a return on investment unmatched by other efforts. Not only will the associates enjoy the training and learn, they will also be much more likely to view information security as critical to the business and be willing to be on alert for those items they see that are in conflict with the policy. This results in increased user awareness and reporting of those items as security incidents that can then be corrected. The rewards of delivering an interactive program are tremendous to the participants and the instructors. Before the training is even over, the participants are asking, "How will you top that next year?" and the instructors are already thinking, "What can we do next year?" By having fun, everyone wins.

Obtaining Executive Sponsorship for Awareness and Training

By Michael J. Corby, CCP, CISSP*

Some organizations, or better said, many *people* in some organizations, have an outstanding grasp of what information security is and what their responsibility is in preserving it. In all the instances I have come across where this has been the case,

---

* Michael J. Corby, CCP, CISSP, is Principal Advisor & Expert at Secure IT Experts. Mr. Corby has over 35 years of experience in IT strategy, operations, development, and security. Mike has successfully managed large projects, and developed flexible IT infrastructures and sound security organizations for hundreds of the world's most successful organizations. He is also the founder of (ISC)², Inc., the organization that established the CISSP credential. In 1992, Mike was named the first recipient of the Computer Security Institute's Lifetime Achievement Award. A frequent global speaker and author, he formerly held executive positions with several global consulting organizations including Netigy Corporation and QinetiQ prior to joining META Group Consulting in July 2003, and was formerly CIO for a division of Ashland Oil and for Bain & Company. A business owner for over 15 years (M Corby & Associates, Inc.) and community supporter, Mike has established a reputation for creativity and excellence in technology and its application to business needs. He holds a B.S.E.E. degree from Worcester Polytechnic Institute, is a Certified Computer Professional (CCP), and a Certified Information Systems Security Professional (CISSP).

I have discovered that support for the awareness and training program has come from the top. In some organizations, the senior executive has actually initiated the effort! The situation is almost always quite the opposite when executives do not support the effort. In those cases, (and surprisingly there are still a large percentage of companies still following this model), security is viewed as the belonging only to the data center or the technology departments.

There are certain attributes of an organization where the executive actively supports an awareness and training program. By exploring those attributes, it is possible to identify the catalyst of executive behavior, and improve the chance of successful implementation by providing that catalyst under the right conditions to generate senior level support and sponsorship.

Recognizing Business Benefit

The first attribute I have seen in successful executive sponsorship is an understanding of the *business benefit of security*. Recent compliance expectations have been seen as a driver of security programs, but if the only reason for compliance is to avoid regulatory whacks, then there is no real sponsorship. Executives who want to sponsor any aspect of a security program recognize that good ideas build good business, and effective process builds great companies. Security, when done right, is part of an effective process that is pervasive throughout the organization. The most efficient way to get something done is to get it done accurately without doubt in the data, the process, or the results. Good security fosters trust in the whole process. Some executives understand this. Many more should.

I once worked in a company that designed and built power systems. The senior executive believed that security was one of life's difficulties to be tolerated. We had a password management program, a disaster recovery plan, and a typical host of security- and behavior-related policies, which he approved because the auditors said he had to. When we went to him looking for sponsorship of a new security initiative, he seemed frustrated that we kept pushing this "security thing." His explanation was simple: "We don't have secrets here. We boil water that makes steam that drives turbines to make electricity. Everybody knows that water boils at 100 degrees centigrade (212 Fahrenheit for us in the United States). What's so secret about that?" He understood the concept of security to protect the *confidentiality* of proprietary information, but failed to recognize the *integrity* and *availability* components of security. After showing him a short internal video that we produced where a manager made a wrong decision because the accurate information was not available, he understood that security is also important for ensuring that the decisions that everyone makes in the company are based on having and *trusting* the data they have to make that decision. Once he recognized this, he was a vociferous supporter of good security policies and practices, and gave an inspired introduction to security and its importance in the company's success on the awareness video. Case closed. The program worked.

Security Metrics

A second attribute of executives that support security programs is that they apply the same success metrics to security as they do to other areas of the business. They know that any successful business operation includes a definition of how success is measured. A security program is no different, and if launched properly can show *measurable results*. There has been much talk about security *return on investment* (ROI). "Because you have to" isn't the kind of success metric that will appeal to a senior executive. Few projects are successful unless they have targets to measure their end point or expectations of benefits gained.

In the security world, several ways to establish success criteria can be measured. Recently I worked on a project to define a security "dashboard" that management could use to track how well the security program was doing. On a monthly basis, data was collected and reported on number of software patches/upgrades available, number and total time spent on the ones that were installed, and number and total time spent on the ones that had to be backed out. These figures were compared with the number of malware (viruses, Trojan horse, worms, etc.) vulnerabilities announced, number of malware vulnerabilities caught, and number of incidents reported. The obvious expectation was that the time, money, and effort spent on applying fixes was showing improved defense. It also showed that as techniques for applying patches were improved, the time spent on them was decreasing.

Similar metrics can be developed to show how well an awareness program is working by measuring the security events being reported by employees before and after an awareness program is launched. One company measures calls to the help desk to report a potential security violation: for instance, PC left logged on at the end of the day, password sharing, or "hallway talk" about unauthorized access to a protected site.

Including success metrics in a program plan results in the decision being made on the real value of the program, not on the emotional fear, uncertainty, and doubt, commonly referenced as FUD, used by many security practitioners when attempting to gain approval for a security program.

Professional Delivery

A third attribute that shows the security program has executive sponsorship is that the program deployment is a collaborative effort involving many departments. Computer people do computer things well. Financial people do financial things well. Marketing people do marketing things well. Very few people do all of these things well. By showing collaboration among several departments, the security program has much more of a chance of garnering the top level support necessary to succeed. One of the surest ways of a desired awareness program never getting launched is to have it meet with confusion or opposition before it is even started. If the financial "experts" have doubts about the program's cost or its expected savings, the chances of a ringing executive endorsement are slim.

Marketing people are experts at conveying a message that causes people to do something they might not normally do. They are great motivators. Good marketing causes people to spend all kinds of money on things that they probably don't really need and maybe can't afford. Just think how effective they can be as part of a security awareness project. One large consumer products company deployed their awareness program using techniques developed in their highly successful marketing department. The program's success was revealed when one of my colleagues was in a CIO's office and a frantic call came in from a field location. It seems they had a new employee starting the following week and just discovered they were out of security awareness materials. Could the CIO please have someone overnight them several new security awareness packages? Now that's what I call a program success!

In summary, the most successful security programs I have seen are security programs that use these techniques, and maybe several others. Keep in mind: This is business, not just a technical exercise. Help senior executives to see the full business benefit of security awareness and training. Provide metrics that will help demonstrate value, or even provide a stop-loss so that money isn't continually spent on areas that are not achieving value. Include the real experts from other business areas in your proposed plan. Showing a willingness to call upon experts and not be the "Lone Ranger" is the kind of message that many executives will want to hear.

You will no doubt call upon your own success stories to build a plan for getting executive sponsorship of your program. Whatever works for you with one executive style may not work with another. Listen to how he or she makes decisions, and respond in a way that makes sense. Be flexible and be persistent. If it's worth doing, it is worth making several tries at getting it done.

Education and Awareness for Security Personnel
By Anita Hartman, CISSP, CISM, FLMI*

Overview

In the best of all possible worlds, every security staff member would be an expert in every area conceivable and know company security policies, standards, and procedures inside and out. However, if there is much diversity in the systems implemented,

---

* Anita Hartman, CISSP, CISM, FLMI, is a security professional with 15+ years experience in the information security field. Her functions have included education and awareness for a wide variety of audiences, as well as policy development, incident response, and general security consultant. She is currently responsible for governance, risk management, and compliance for a Fortune 500 company. Her involvement in the security industry ranges from membership to the Computer Security Institute (CSI) and their working peer group program to being a founding member of the Iowa Infragard chapter. Her submission to CSI earned her company the prestigious "1998 CSI Information Security Program of the Year." She has presented numerous times on security topics at a variety of conferences and security professional meetings.

the reality is that there is too much information for anyone to know it all, so it is necessary to develop specific means of targeting the internal security staff just as you probably target audiences for other areas of your company for awareness. Once you have got a feel for the key items for the various groups in the security organization, how do you get the word out? Is it enough to just post a bunch of important information to a Web site and tell them to have at it? Probably not...

The Basics

All security department staff should have a fundamental understanding of the company's information protection policies and standards; at least enough to answer basic questions and know to whom to direct the inquiry if it is something out of the ordinary. Staff should also know what the responsibilities are for other security teams, and at least a high level of understanding of the project work being accomplished on those teams. If you have an internal Web site specific to security, this can be an ideal place to store material as reference for your staff as well as the general employee audience. As with any Web site, the information is only valuable if the viewer can find what they are looking for, so make certain to organize the material in a manner that makes sense to your coworkers. You will want to remember to secure anything that should not be seen outside of the department. Departmental meetings are also good ways of disseminating information to coworkers; choose a topic of interest and have some fun with it. Security versions of *Jeopardy!* or *Family Feud* have proved effective in my experience.

Security Administrator

Obviously, the administrative staff must understand the mechanics of access control and have set procedures to follow that, in addition to meeting business needs, must also meet applicable laws, regulatory requirements, and so on. This group of people may actually have the most face time with business people because of their job. Time spent with them explaining what red flags to keep an eye out for, and who to contact when spotted, is very helpful.

In addition to specific on-the-job training, it may be beneficial to engage this group in some role-playing, especially regarding social engineering. Computer-based training to cover policy and standard information is helpful, as well as job aids to assist in spotting those red flags. If time permits, they also have a vested interest in keeping current on access and identity management types of security issues, as well as looking for ways to improve customer service. These operations personnel, whose job allows other employees to get their work done, are at times overlooked for training outside of just keeping the wheels on. It is wise to provide those eager to move ahead in their career with some suggested reading; either periodicals or Web sites where they can pick up information that may help them in deciding what that next step will be for them.

Monitoring and Compliance

The monitoring and compliance personnel have a vested interest in understanding all security policies and standard. Keep this group in mind as any new documentation is developed; they will be the ones trying to figure out ways to check compliance on anything new that comes along. Their interests tend to be very specific, possibly narrow, and may at times seem akin to the "can't see the forest for the trees" scenario. These personnel will be the ones buying or developing tools to verify that standard "xyz" is indeed being met, or calling to say "it's impossible to check this, can the standard be changed so it's less gray and easier to monitor?"

These folks are also good to supply with job aids to assist when answering questions, but they probably do best in a situation where it's possible to focus on one policy to obtain thorough understanding from an expert on the topic at hand. You may wish to schedule regular meetings for this group to sit and visit with the subject matter expert (SME) on whatever the "policy of the day" might be. Make certain there is someone in the room that can answer questions, or immediately know to whom you need to reference these folks. Group sessions like this are valuable in that the monitoring team will receive a consistent message from the expert. The interesting thing about these discussions is that the SME may very well decide that the wording used in the policy or standard is either too narrow or too broad and wish to rework the material to better reflect the environment, based on the feedback of those monitoring for compliance. The monitoring people will expect the presenter to be able to answer all their questions; I have known some people to compare this to an interrogation, so make certain the SME is an expert or, at a minimum, not faint of heart!

The tools that a SME should bring for this type of discussion include a copy of the proposed or actual policy wording, an example or two of what this would mean in the company's environment and a thorough understanding of the topic. The more examples the better for this group, especially if the SME is already aware of quirky items (such as, this is the rule in 98% of the cases, and here's the oddball item we know will be an issue) it will spark discussion and ensure a thorough understanding when finished.

Designers and Architects

The designers and architects of security are the ones who can help shape and define policy. These folks can assist with determining consistent, repeatable, and auditable solutions. The trick with this group is to make certain lines of communication stay open and flexible on both sides. They need to be out there on the leading edge of the technologies in which your company is interested and help you determine when new or updated policies and standards become necessary. Awareness for these folks is to make certain they understand what is currently in place, and remember to keep you in the loop on what the future holds.

There need to be close ties between the designers and the consultants, as one can develop standard security solutions, and the other group can use their influence to ensure these are kept in front of project people. Then the policy developer can put the requirements into standards and make the circle complete. My recommendation for the policy writer is to schedule an hour a few times a month with the architect and work together on what are considered hot topics so there is a constantly evolving list of items that will need to be addressed in policy. At the same time, pick an existing policy and see if it appears that the current business environment has made some requirements obsolete. For example, perhaps, management has changed its viewpoint on the amount of personal use employees can have of the Internet, say from none to some. This helps keep policies current, while keeping both the architect and the policy person on the same page.

Security Consultant

The Jacks and Jills of security—these are the folks sitting in on project work and providing security requirements for vendor requests and security reviews of development work; they must understand the ins and outs of policy in order to perform their function. It helps them to have an awareness of what the designer is working on. They may be able to assist with the reality of how a solution will fit, and thus influence how policy is worded as well. Their preference is to have repeatable solutions, so the environment follows a pattern that is consistent as well as less difficult to secure.

The consultants will also do well with group discussions. Their focus will be different from the compliance staff in that they will want to see how flexible or broad coverage of policies and standards are. For example, are the mobile device standards written broadly enough to include laptops, smart phones, and cell phones? Another example would be some new application that will blatantly be in conflict with a long-held standard. They will answer questions as to whether standards should be revised to include the change, or if a formal exception needs to be documented, tying back to the specific standard in question. Consultants must provide due diligence and documentation around application implementation, and like being able to point back to something in writing that defends their position on a given topic. They may need a bit more one-on-one training or Q&A sessions than other types of security personnel given the work that they do.

Education and Awareness (E&A) Staff

The education and awareness staff require tools and resources to help them keep coworkers, as well as the rest of the company, familiar with the information handling requirements for the organization. This group needs to have a toolbox of various ways to present information, and must also be made aware of upcoming changes to ensure the message remains current. It's key for the E&A staff to stay in close contact with the policy writers to best judge ways and means of communication out to the company as things change.

Along with staying current with the requirements at the office, it is good for this group to keep an eye on what's in the security news such as in articles in business periodicals and newspapers, and reveal related questions they need to ask of other staff. The E&A staff will want to take a glance through any periodicals specific to their industry, as well as the security news lists. Senior management has a habit of finding out about the latest virus or spyware from business focused materials such as the *Wall Street Journal* or *Fortune* magazine. Trying to stay ahead of business people who catch only part of the story or focus on one piece of it can be challenging.

In Conclusion

Do not forget about internal security staff when it comes to awareness. Staff people have their own networks of contacts that can assist with getting important messages out, but make certain your information security coworkers have the right message to share!

Aetna's Award-Winning Security Awareness Program

By Donna Richmond*

Aetna's Security Awareness Program

For many organizations, the most significant information security risk to manage is not the hacker/cracker toiling away outside of the organization (although that *is* important), but rather it's an organization's own employees and contract workers (e.g., users). Companies routinely give access to information assets to many types of users so they can perform their duties. Most security breaches are not malicious; they are the result of errors, omissions, and just trying to get the work done.

The overall objective of Aetna's information security awareness program is to influence the behavior of all users who have access to our information assets by continuously training and encouraging users to follow good security practices. To

---

* Donna Richmond is the security advisor for Aetna. Aetna's information security awareness program has been referred to as "*the* model" for other organizations to emulate since 2000 by the SANS Institute (http://www.sans.org/) and was a distinguishing factor in Computer Security Institute's (http://www.gocsi.com/) presenting the Information Security Program of the Year Award to Aetna in 2002. Donna has provided briefings to over 70 organizations of all sizes—public and private, for profit and not for profit, as well as state and federal government organizations that are beginning security awareness programs. Also, Donna has presented at nearly 30 conferences and seminars on what Aetna has learned and achieved, including techniques that worked well, and those you should avoid in your programs. Currently, Donna is also involved with local community colleges in Connecticut, assisting in the development of undergraduate information security degree programs.

effectively influence user behavior, we use a number of mediums and disciplines on a regular basis. For example, one technique, borrowed from the marketing discipline, is to broadcast key messages repeatedly in many ways. Most people will follow the rules and not circumvent your controls once they understand them and see the value, from continuous reinforcement, that their employer is serious about compliance. By minimizing incidents, you will expend fewer resources to recover from problems and your bottom line will be positively affected. You will have greater resources to go after individuals who intend to do you harm.

An information security education effort is not disconnected from other mechanisms to control a business environment; it is an essential component. At Aetna, I developed a control framework called the PIMA model (see Exhibit 15), which is an information security framework comprised of four key segments working in concert to create and maintain a reliable and controlled environment. These segments are Policy, Implementation, Monitoring, and Awareness.

Exhibit 15   The Policy, Implementation, Monitoring, and Awareness (PIMA) Model

Policy	Establish the baseline rules under which controls must operate.	
Implementation	Implement an appropriate combination of controls to minimize security risk and enforce policy. Any appropriate, cost-effective combination of controls can be used: technical, physical, or social.	
Monitoring	Ensure that the control environment is working as expected, to the level that is appropriate.	
Awareness	Educate the appropriate user population to enlighten users as to the value of controls; lower the probability that users will circumvent the control environment; and achieve InfoSec goals in an efficient and effective manner (ROI).	

Four Basic Concepts

Aetna's Information Security Awareness Program is based on the following four basic concepts: user life-cycle, audience targeting, multiple delivery mediums, and message balancing:

1. *User Life-Cycle.* Aetna considers the entire life-cycle of a user beginning with initial access, continuing through the ongoing company/user relationship and then, finally, to termination or expiration of the relationship (voluntarily or not). For an overview of the three stages of a User Life-Cycle, see Exhibit 16.

2. *Audience Targeting.* Consider crafting messages for key audiences and their specific roles and responsibilities for ensuring confidentiality, integrity, and availability of information and systems. As a starting point, begin with the highest risk audience to kick-off your program, and then progress to other target audiences over time. Feature the user behavior you want to reinforce, then cross-reference the supporting policy. Avoid forcing users to read every single policy and call that "training." For examples of typical audience groupings, see Exhibit 17.

3. *Multiple Delivery Mediums.* Depending on the size of the user population to be addressed, you can decide what combination of media is most effective and efficient to communicate good security practices. As a general guideline, organizations under 1000 users can effectively leverage face-to-face group meetings (brown bag lunches, round tables, etc.) along with print media (posters, table tents, flyers, etc.) to convey a consistent message and track compliance, while organizations with greater populations will find that electronic means to convey the message will be needed, along with face-to-face meetings and print media as supporting tools. This solves the one-to-many ratio where there may be only one full-time position responsible for the entire security awareness program. Also, consider delivery solutions that address the needs of sight-, hearing-, and other physically impaired users.

4. *Message Balancing.* When crafting your message, it doesn't hurt to be engaging or somewhat entertaining, but don't undermine the seriousness of your topic. This is a subjective and difficult balance to achieve. It needs to be entertaining in order to hold the user's attention, but cannot be too "cute" or you risk the message not being taken seriously. Test-drive your ideas with colleagues beforehand to gauge what is acceptable in your organization's culture, and refine your message based on the feedback. We have generally found that stock photos, graphics, and company-specific images are sufficient to craft engaging materials that appeal to a broad user base. Usually, avoiding a "cartoon" look is recommended.

Exhibit 16 Overview of a User Life-Cycle

Stage		Print media	Electronic media	Personal contact
1. Orientation	Employee	N/A	• New Employee Orientation on first day via Web-based InfoSec Orientation streamed video • Web-based InfoSec Exam (within 30 days)	Direct manager: • Enforces message of mandatory training requirement • Supplements general awareness program with specific information security processes that apply uniquely to that business area
	Contract Workers	Pre-engagement orientation package	Web-based for application development workers	
2. Retained Workers	Employee	• Posters • InfoSec promotional give-aways • Flyers	• Topical reminders (Web-based and e-mail) • Internal security portal (InfoSec policies, training, and reporting)	Direct manager: • Provide management with tools to monitor compliance such as forms and log sheets • Customer service fairs (or periodic contract face-to-face activity)
	Contract Workers			
3. Termination	Employee	• Obtain signed agreement to return off-site company assets within 10 business days (hardware, software, files, etc.)	• Terminate electronic access (network, e-mail, etc.) • Reassign data used by individual • Return all company property onsite (PC, laptop, hand-held devices, etc.)	Direct manager: • Provides exit interview and collects access assets: keys; photo ID badge, etc. • Addresses special procedures for involuntary and job elimination situations
	Contract Workers			

Exhibit 17   Examples of Audience Groupings

Audience	Key Message	Delivery Mechanism
General User	Directed to *all* users in organization (*very* few exceptions) Understanding of all InfoSec policies, but focus on several per release Exposure to pertinent legislation affecting the industry Knowledge of how to apply certain security needs that apply to *all* users	Employees: Web-based exam and monitoring Contingent workers: combo of manual (CD, paper distribution), Web-based exam, and monitoring
Application Developers (onshore and offshore)	Directed to *all* users involved in application development Understanding of key InfoSec policies Understanding of organization's SDLC (leverage prerequisite training) Knowledge of checkpoints in SDLC for security requirements	Employees: Web-based exam and monitoring Contingent workers: combo of manual (CD, paper distribution), Web-based exam, and monitoring
Management	Directed to all users who have direct reports (e.g., staff) Understanding of key InfoSec policies Understanding their role in restricting access to a need-to-know basis Knowledge of need to supplement general awareness programs with details of their own business segments	Web-based exam and monitoring
Executives	Directed to all users within three levels of the president of organization. Understanding of key InfoSec policies Understanding legal drivers, and the true costs to the organization of poor security Knowledge of information security concepts and the importance of executive support	Face-to-face presentation with Web-based support of information

User Life-Cycle and Delivery Mechanisms Expanded

In my many years of developing and delivering a quality information security awareness program, I have learned a few lessons. In the beginning, I did not have other security awareness programs in private industry to reference. We started from scratch, thought about our objectives, and developed it from there. For the most part, our decisions brought us good outcomes—some that even exceeded our expectations. I will share several things I would recommend for you to try, and some that you should avoid, based on our experiences and those of other organizations with whom we have spoken over the years. Even when the anticipated results are not achieved completely, you are still serving the main purpose of raising the awareness of your user community to good information security practices. Keep in mind that you do not have to start from scratch on everything. Look around your organization for other elements or programs to build on or leverage.

1. Orientation

New users are introduced to Aetna's information security program via the New Employee Orientation Program. This is an entirely Web-based program. New users receive an e-mail on their first day of employment welcoming them and providing them with a link to the New Employee Orientation Program. This includes a briefing on information security, a 6-minute information security orientation streamed video, and the link to our InfoSec exam. Each user is asked to satisfy Aetna's Information Security Exam within 30 days of hire, and is contacted by e-mail with a reminder after that.

This originally began as a face-to-face presentation given in the home office auditorium, supplemented with a PowerPoint presentation. (This is an example of finding an existing process to leverage.) Once that message was refined, we realized that it could be made more consistent if we developed a video version of the presentation. This required that the key messages (as indicated by answers to the questions, What is information security; What are some of the basic rules of information security; and How can individuals promote good information security practices?) be reformatted somewhat for a new communication medium. We utilized Aetna's corporate communications resources (another existing operation) and employed an actor's voice-over to read the presentation, accompanied by appropriate images (such as company office images, screen scrapes, etc.) that supported the content. Now, we could provide the InfoSec orientation video to each centralized location around the country where larger weekly orientations were conducted, as well as to each manager who provided this to new staff directly throughout all U.S. field offices. The final improvement was to have the video cassette version converted for play on each user's desktop as a streamed video, and eliminate the need to distribute physical tapes.

Orientation Lesson Learned: Here is one practice that I have observed and that I would recommend you not follow: another organization that developed a video decided to use the head of that particular organization as the spokesperson. Within a year that person left the company and the video was instantly obsolete.

Lesson: Avoid using the voices or faces of real staff to convey your key message; the risk of a short shelf life is high.

2. Retained Users

Many mechanisms have been developed to reinforce the information security message, including the following:

Security Portal — The best tool for conveying a consistent message over time is having an internal security portal, or Web site. This does not replace entirely the need for face-to-face activities, but it is the backbone of ongoing communications. It will always beneficial to gain candid feedback to adjust various approaches on. At Aetna, this security portal is called SecurNet, a site which has six sections (see Exhibit 18).

Security Portal Lesson Learned: Don't be alarmed if you are not a Web developer – neither was I. There are several good end-user products for Web development which

Exhibit 18   SecurNet Security Portal

Home	States the purpose of the site, and the mission of the organization responsible for it, including a message from the CIO.
Policies	Retains all information security policies and supporting materials.
Learning Resources	Provides all Web-based information security learning tools, such as annual role-based exams; quarterly newsletter, and video library.
Incident Reporting	Provides descriptive information on information security incidents from the user's perspective and what to do when incidents occur. Differentiates between people and property security incidents.
Contacts	Provides a listing of each security-related organization and its objectives, contact information (site address, e-mail service account names, head of organization), and several FAQs.
Links	Provides a quick reference for malicious code activity pertaining to virus, hoax and scam activities.

you can find supplemental training locally for very reasonable fees. Part of my Web development learning curve was understanding how a user interacts with the Web medium. Users do not read for comprehension as with print media—they scan the content. The most important material must be displayed in the window with as little scrolling down as possible. This means that the content you may have in a memo or a report must be repackaged into key concepts, bulleted points with white space, and link to another small window or pages for more detail. Users are quick to note that if the scroll bar to the right of the page is very small, that means there is a lot of text below "the fold" (an old reference to the newspaper print media). In monitoring Web metrics of activity, I have found that the further down the Web page the material goes, the lower the rate of click-ability it has. No one reads it!

Branding — Consider developing an information security logo for use with all awareness initiatives. In our case, we used a lighthouse theme (a guiding light for good security practices, see Exhibit 19). Branding your campaign in this way gives your message instant context and provides a unifying theme for the variety of activities and media that you use to convey that message.

Branding Lesson Learned: One of the first things we did once our SecurNet portal was up and running was launch a Web-based contest inviting employees across the enterprise to make recommendations for a logo image and name. The total cost was for the prizes: two $50 gift certificates to a national home improvement store. The site allowed us to define the three concepts of information security: Confidentiality, Integrity, and Availability. This in itself became a security awareness activity.

Lesson: Choose your logo carefully. There may be an unanticipated downside. A cosmetics company developed an InfoSec logo without feedback from their organizational community and selected a shark as their mascot. They purchased squeeze toys and launched an awareness campaign based on the shark concept. Employees, though, did not warm to the mascot because it brought to mind the company's previous public relations difficulties resulting from the company's perceived (albeit, untrue) testing on animals. Inanimate objects seem to avoid best the problem of the unanticipated downside.

Exhibit 19   Example of a logo used for branding.

Newsletter — Our internally developed newsletter (also called *The Beacon*, see Exhibit 20) is issued quarterly and is available on SecurNet. Each issue contains a selection of articles from the *SECURITYsense* subscription service provided by the National Security Institute (nsi.org/SECURITYsense.html), and from other sources available on the Internet. Each issue of *The Beacon* uses a security policy from the theme of the quarter. We select the featured policy based on its relevance to our organization and the topics we feel need focus at that particular time. The cost of a *SECURITYsense* subscription depends on the size of your organization. Be sure you have permission from the authors and publishers before publishing a full article in your newsletter from the Internet! Paraphrase information security articles from the Internet, or use a subscription service. Always list credit to the source publication with a link to the full article, as applicable.

Exhibit 20   *The Beacon* Newsletter

Main Page
Policy of the Quarter
In The News
Real InfoSec War Stories
Legislative Spotlight
Cheers and Jeers
Scams, Hoaxes, and Hacks
Education

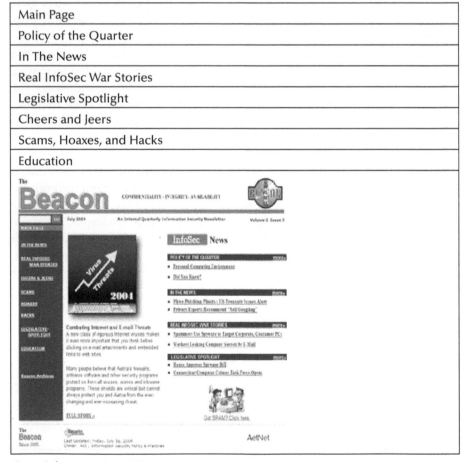

Copyright Aetna Inc. 2004

Exhibit 21   Example of branded promotional giveaways.

Each issue of *The Beacon* features eight segments, with no more than three short articles within the segment.

Promotional Giveaways — Giveaways are a lot of fun; however, you should consider the probability of the marketing value of the item in making your selection. The best candidates for giveaways are items that workers will use daily. For example, items on which you can print reminders, logos, and/or pertinent phrases. Building on the branding concept, Aetna purchases a supply "barrel-type" pens with a rolling message window on which we imprint our Beacon InfoSec logo (see Exhibit 21). Each time the pen is clicked, one of six messages rotates into view on the window in the side of the pen.

Face-to-Face Activities — Interaction directly with users can improve your program by their feedback, and the PR efforts you can perform by putting a "face" on your security organization. We have recently launched a brown-bag lunch series on a quarterly basis in Aetna's headquarters office, but we have participated in an annual customer service fair (CSF) for seven years. This event is focused on providing good internal customer service, and many internal organizations participate just to bring awareness to their purpose and services. Since we have established brand recognition, we leverage that by raffling several lighthouse-themed prizes, such as lamps, artwork, and other functional items.

CSF Lesson Learned. Slow down attendees for a brief interaction with your display. We observed in our very first CSF that attendees roamed from display to display. They quickly took each give-away and hardly found out anything about that display. The person running the booth couldn't promote their services very well. We introduced the Beacon InfoSec Raffle as a means to engage the participant in a brief exchange while they completed the entry ballot. Of course, each person who completed a ballot received one of our Beacon InfoSec pens. The ballot posed three very short pertinent information security true/false questions (for which we promptly provided the answers). Often attendees knew the correct responses, but when they did not, an opportunity to exchange information is created and we can get feedback on our other efforts.

Posters — At Aetna, we have not focused a great deal on placing posters throughout all office facilities. We feel that an organization of our size benefits much more by electronic means of communication. However, we have tapped into our advertising design resources to develop creative designs for recurring events such as the brown-bag lunch series, and the customer service fairs. These posters are more sturdy and reusable than merely paper sheets. Once the design is complete, we leverage Aetna's relationship with a print services vendor to have the actual poster printed.

Spam "InfoSec-Mercial" — We, like many other organizations, have experienced a tremendous increase in spam volume. Much of it was due to users providing their work e-mail address when registering for various online resources. Once submitted, these internal addresses proliferated across the Internet, contributing to the rising tide of spam. We worked with our eLearning vendor to create a spam InfoSec-mercial with a total seat time of 60 seconds. It is a simple Web-based animated graphic developed in Flash that shows a woman seated at a work station who is clearly overwhelmed by the spam coming across her computer screen. The learning material is presented in brief text balloons accompanied by a voice-over of the same text about what spam is and how, as a user, you can take certain steps to minimize or avoid spam. The final screen provides a link to SecurNet with more printable details on what you can do about spam.

Mandatory Information Security Exam — Users are required to take an annual Web-based interactive Information Security Exam (the same application referenced in the new employee orientation discussion) and receive their own personalized certificate of completion when they are done. Providing users with the option to print a certificate of completion was an afterthought for us. Completion statistics are tracked and stored on-line, so hard-copy certificates served no administrative purpose. But we found that users were proud of their accomplishment, and many users chose not only to print their certificates, but also posted them in their cubicles and offices. Some executives would post them on the doors to their offices as examples and reminders to their staff of the importance of this training. Once we observed this behavior, we capitalized on it by adding key security messages to the certificate. The certificates now serve double duty as information security posters that reinforce the InfoSec message.

Electronic registration for the exam requires each user to read an abbreviated version of the company's IT Security Statement of Policy, and electronically agree to abide by the policy. This creates a very useful electronic evidentiary record of employee awareness and acceptance of the policy. Other compliance reporting tools allow management to monitor who has completed the training. All of the monitoring tools (e.g., status queries at the enterprise, cost center, and individual levels) are available in an administrator's center. This is useful in measuring compliance, as well as in development of the communications plan (e.g., to determine when to issue periodic reminders to management)

The cost to have an eLearning vendor develop an online exam will range from approximately $14,000 to $55,000, depending on the volume of content to be developed. At Aetna, we found that an investment of $1 to $2 per user was adequate to produce a good product. I have compared costs of our custom-developed program to that of several off-the-shelf security awareness solution providers and have found that the custom solution provides the best value for a company the size of Aetna (currently 23,000 employees). Our estimate of the cost of off-the-shelf solutions ranged from $4–$12 per user, not including package licensing fees.

InfoSec Exam Lesson Learned #1: I would like to caution you against focusing your security awareness program efforts primarily on reaching 100% compliance for any given delivery mechanism. While deep penetration is important, it should not be your primary goal. I have observed that too much emphasis on participation rate translates into a less effective program that does not focus on influencing user behavior.

Lesson #1: The first objective of an information security awareness program is to get as many users as possible to follow good security practices. You *can* reach 100% compliance, and still not affect the behavior of your users. Unless your learning application addresses issues around what is best for users to accept key concepts, then the effort will likely fall short of your main goal. See Exhibit 22 for examples what a Web-based e-Learning application should and should not do.

Exhibit 22   What a Web-Based e-Learning Application Should and Should Not Do

A Web-based e-Learning application **should**	A Web-based e-Learning application **should not**
• Repackage material into key concepts, shored up by bulleted support material, and provide links to even more detail, if desired	• Dump print medium material into a series of slides
• Provide a glossary of terms, and cross reference to supporting InfoSec policies	• Use unreferenecable, new, or unfamiliar terms
• Provide training within modules, so that a user can exit/return as needed, and not have to begin all over again	• Require a forced one-time completion pass that does not allow the learner to go outside of the module (this would not address the business need of allowing for an interruption)
• Be highly interactive to keep a user engaged mentally; create activities for the user to auto-tailor the pace of the training	• Merely display text line after text line in a CBT-style training model
• Include quiz questions within the subject modules to perform a skill check that reinforces material	• Provide a test outside the subject modules to "grade" their retention level

InfoSec Exam Lesson Learned #2: The first release of Aetna's Information Security Exam is sometimes remembered as the "punitive" exam. We had originally created the learning content in a series of topics, which was followed by a 20-question exam. A user had to get 100% of the questions correct in order to "pass" and satisfy the training requirement. Here's where it gets ugly. When a user did not "pass," they were provided with a summary of the sections that required "more study." When the user returned to complete the training requirement, the program did not retain any credits earned on the segments they had previously passed! Somehow, we still managed to achieve a respectable 85% compliance level for that first year effort.

Lesson #2: Recognizing that it can be demeaning to users to be required to reach a "'passing grade," we incorporated into our next release some new design enhancements, including quiz questions embedded within each module. Moreover, after a user submitted two incorrect answers, the exam automatically provided the correct answer, accompanied by a short explanation. Users were much less irritated and more likely to continue with the training in an engaged manner. This format allowed users to complete segments of no longer than 10 minutes, achieve a sense of accomplishment, and absorb information in reasonable chunks—a true exchange of knowledge. The application stored user credit for each segment, so there was no unnecessary repetition. Total seat time was no longer than 60 minutes. Administrative tools were developed such as a cost center query listing users who had *not* finished the training for managers to follow-up. Each exam released after this has resulted in 100% compliance.

3. Exiting Users

In every case, a user's employment status will eventually come to end, either voluntarily or involuntarily. It will be the responsibility of that individual's management to cancel all access and have all company property returned. In work-at-home arrangements, this can be a more difficult issue. At Aetna, once a user's human resources record is electronically cancelled, then all system access company-wide is automatically terminated.

Closing Comments

Aetna's security awareness program is administered by the information security policy and practices group. The program itself requires approximately one full-time employee to manage it, with supplemental support from other staff from time to time.

Many of the program elements that I have described in this paper were established over a 2-year period, with new elements being introduced and existing elements continuously being refined or redesigned. Two thoughts I would like to leave you with (just in case you are feeling somewhat overwhelmed at this juncture):

■ Be creative; use or piggy-back on what is already in place around your organization. You don't necessarily have to have a big budget. Be resourceful; find and leverage what you can.
■ The critical skills needed to build and manage an information security awareness program include project management and interpersonal communications. Project management skills are important because it is essential for you to always be focused on the "big picture" and the goal you are trying to reach, while having a handle on all the details that need to get done in order to get you there. Also, if you are like most of us, you probably do not have direct reports allocated to security awareness. It is likely that you will be matrix-managing multiple teams of up to 20 resources (occasionally simultaneously!), most of whom have other pressing responsibilities. The ability to motivate these resources to achieve *your* goals will be indispensable.

Security awareness has been an extremely interesting, sometimes exhausting, and often exhilarating experience for me, and I hope you will find the experience as rewarding, as well. You can help your organizations and have a positive impact on its bottom line.

Security Awareness Case Study

By Charles R. Hudson, Jr., CISSP, CISM*

When looking at developing a security awareness program in an organization, one of the first questions that will arise is the amount of budget that is needed to implement the program. Often this question limits, if not eliminates, a successful program from being deployed within an organization.

The use of external resources, such as professional firms and commercial products, can enhance a program but will also significantly increase the cost of the program. An effective security awareness program can be done without a large budget. As I titled a presentation I have given in the past, security awareness can be done on a shoestring!

---

* Charles R. Hudson, Jr., CISSP, CISM, is an information security manager and assistant vice president at Wilmington Trust Company. All of his tenure has been in the financial industry. Mr. Hudson obtained the Certified Information Systems Security Professional (CISSP) designation in 2000 and the Certified Information Security Manager (CISM) designation in 2003. He is a regular presenter at national conferences, speaking at over 20 conferences in the last 5 years as a subject matter expert. Mr. Hudson has been involved in numerous security magazine articles and recently was a contributing author for the 2005 *Information Security Handbook*.

Although I will concentrate on explaining how we have deployed successful security awareness programs with a minimal budget, to have a level mindset, I will briefly describe the fundamental aspects of a program. This basic understanding will assist in understanding why we implemented the programs we did.

After establishing the framework, I will describe general techniques that can be used and outline a successful program we have done.

Security Awareness Framework

Having a successful security awareness program starts with the foundation upon which it is built. This foundation can be broken down into four major areas:

- Corporate culture
- Current corporate awareness
- The information security policy
- Support from senior leadership

It is extremely difficult to implement a successful program without knowledge of this information. This framework is not static and is subject to change at anytime.

Imagine if you reviewed the culture of a company and determined that most of the business the client had was from the National Football League (NFL). As a promotion you had decided to give away small footballs with security awareness messages on them. If the company had recently lost their contract with the NFL, how well do you think this would have been received?

The football example may seem obvious, but many programs are static and focused on just doing the program instead of adapting to the current situation.

Security Awareness Techniques

Once you have determined the foundation for your program, you need to develop the program you are going to deliver. Programs can be from one presentation to a multiple-year plan. There is not a magic number to use; it is basically up to you. Personally, I prefer to use reoccurring 1-year programs. Having annual dates has helped us keep a fresh outlook on training and requires us to revamp our program periodically.

Unless your program is only one event, you will need to develop a way to tie all of the activities of the program together. The best way I have found to do this is by the use of themes and slogans. These themes and slogans can be reinforced by the use of a particular image that represents the program.

The one aspect of your program that should remain constant is the theme and slogan. Determining what to use will require you to think through all of the delivery mechanisms you want to use and the messages you want to get across with the program.

Examples of themes and slogans that can be used include:

Program #1

- Theme: Mission Impossible
- Slogan: It's Not Mission Impossible. It's Mission Critical!

Program #2

- Theme: Key theme
- Slogan: YOU are the Key to Information Security

Program #3

- Theme: Security Election 2004
- Slogan: Get Out the Security Vote!

If you are still uncomfortable with the use of themes and slogans, it will be shown in more detail with the outline of an entire program in the next section.

There are numerous techniques that can be used to deliver your program. I am not going to cover these techniques in detail, but it is important to remember to use mechanisms that work with the theme of your program and the framework you have examined.

Here is a list of some techniques I have successfully used in the past:

- Company-wide seminars
- Expos (in high traffic areas such as lunch rooms)
- Lunch-and-learn sessions
- Company newsletters
- Intranet sites
- Posters/flyers
- Daily reports on recent security events in the news

A Complete Security Awareness Program

Program Summary

- Theme: Game shows
- Slogan: Information Protection—It's Not a Game!
- Total expenditures: Under $1,000
- Work hours: 400

It is very common that it may take several brainstorming sessions before a theme and slogan for a program can be finalized. Usually we may have as many as 10 themes and slogans to start with. In 2000, this was exactly what happened to us while trying to develop our annual program.

With the popularity of *Who Wants to Be a Millionaire?* at that time, there was a significant buzz about game shows. Ultimately we decided to use a theme around game shows and a slogan of "Information Protection—It's Not a Game!"

To kick off development of the program, we did a security walkthrough of two of our buildings. The walkthrough was used to collect statistics on workstations left on, laptops left unsecured, and media left out. The information was used to determine the areas we needed to address and the mechanisms we should use to do that.

Results from the walkthrough were presented to senior management with the announcement of our security awareness program. During the program, we also published the results of the walkthrough in our monthly company magazine.

The major delivery mechanism for the program was focused on expos outside of the lunch areas. When staff entered and left the lunch rooms they could stop at the expos, but they were not required to.

The expos were geared around game shows such as *Wheel of Fortune.* In that particular expo, each staff member went through three stations. The stations discussed three unique security points. After finishing all three stations the user took a chance at spinning the wheel (about 6 feet high) to win a prize.

The stations for this expo were focused around three points: data classification, laptop security, and physically securing data (both electronic and paper). Specifically, one station showed a picture of an internal office, and we asked the participants to point out the six security violations in the picture. The second station let participants try security cables and other techniques to secure a computer, such as locking your workstation before you leave. The last station had a printer with several documents on it not classified. The point of the station was to show the importance in denoting classifications and securing the information appropriately.

Prizes and giveaways are important to our programs. Although we would all like to think that every staff member would want to attend security awareness training, we know this is not realistic. The gifts we give away act as an incentive for staff to come. Besides picking the theme of our programs, the second most discussed aspect is the gifts and prizes we will give away. This may seem somewhat odd, but a great program with only 25% of the staff participating will not be a successful program.

Giving away gifts with your program does not necessarily mean a large expense to your program budget. Most of the prizes we gave away during the program were less than $5 and geared toward the game theme.

With the Wheel of Fortune Expo the top prize was $10 cash. As people entered and left the lunch room, one of our security staff members was asking them if they wanted to play with a handful of $10s. This technique is usually very effective and not expensive.

Some of the other gifts we gave away with this program included a bendable stick that could be used as a stress reliever, a Slinky®, and playing cards. All the material had either the logo of the program or security tips on it.

Besides using expos as delivery mechanisms, we also used traditional games like word finds that consisted of security terms such as classification, encryption, and password that were sent to all staff members. A glossary with definitions for all the words was also provided.

Crossword puzzles were also sent out; they asked basic questions around our three key points. Sample questions would include

1. Before leaving at night you should always _____ the information you were working with.
2. Documentation containing personal client information is considered _____.

Other types of games were used with the program too. Staff members were asked to return the completed game forms to the information security office, and we randomly picked winners from the responses we received.

Answers to the games were provided on the security awareness intranet site. When staff went to the site it did have the answers, but it was also populated with more security training material and pictures.

I believe minor changes to programs are healthy, and usually needed to make a program successful. With this particular program, like others, we were making small changes constantly as it progressed. One presentation we did was changed just a few hours before it was delivered!

These types of changes cannot be made without feedback. It is essential to any program to have feedback. With this game show program we gave out surveys, questionnaires, and solicited personal feedback with every event we did. Usually when we finish an event, the first thing I do is read the feedback forms and assess that session.

One popular technique that we use with most of our programs is to coordinate events around specific occasions. For example, on Halloween we usually give out candy bars with security messages on them as staff members enter the building.

The timeliness of the information you use in your program is also important. Using a security video that was produced 20 years ago can be viewed negatively by your audience. In our programs we always try to find current information in media outlets our audience will recognize.

I cannot express enough how powerful it can be to start a information session with a 20-minute clip from *60 Minutes*, your local news station, or other new outlets. These are media outlets that are commonly recognized and respected. Most of the clips we have purchased have been well under $100.

Besides videos, we have also incorporated recent articles in periodicals and newspapers. There are numerous sources where you can find a summary of security articles in the news. On a daily basis we sent out a security update to senior leadership with current events around security and the financial industry. These updates are also published on our intranet site and sometimes in our monthly company magazine. Here is an example of a story we have used in the past:

> **June 8, Finextra Research**—*Financial details for sale on online auction site. [The current access codes and admin rights to the secure Intranet of one of Europe's largest financial services group was purchased on a hard drive over e-Bay for just under $10 by U.K. security specialist Pointsec Mobile Technologies. It was the first of 100 drives and laptops purchased as spare and used parts over Internet auction sites and other public auctions by the firm. Pointsec found it was able to read 7 out of 10 harddrives bought in this way ...]*

In the end, the entire game show program cost less than $1000. It took approximately 400 hours to create and deploy the program. The key to its success, in my opinion, was the creativity of the information and the delivery of it, not the cost.

Conclusion

I have attempted to show in this documentation that an effective and successful security awareness program is not directly related to the amount of money that you have to spend on it. Usually the creativity of the program is the deciding factor in its success.

No matter what technique you ultimately decide to use, or the amount of money you decide to spend, the most important aspect to remember is that security awareness is ongoing and not just an event to do once.

There are numerous sources on the Internet that discuss security awareness techniques and ideas. In my opinion, one of the best sources of information is your fellow colleagues at the companies in your geographic region or industry. Ultimately, security awareness training benefits everyone, and companies should readily share this type of information. As our security awareness slogan in 2002 said, "We are only as strong as our weakest link."

Appendix A: Sample Executive Education Sponsorship Memo

Sample Memo

Send a memo similar to the following from your executive sponsor as an e-mail communication and on the information security and privacy intranet Web site:

Company X is a strong proponent of information security and preserving privacy. Ensuring information security is essential for protecting our valuable information assets, as well as for ensuring employee and customer satisfaction—in addition to ensuring regulatory and legal compliance. Effective information security and privacy training and awareness are critical for ensuring information security and privacy. Throughout the coming months we will provide information security and privacy training for all Company X personnel, along with additional training sessions for groups with specific information security and privacy job responsibilities.

Our goals for information security and privacy training are to

- Arm Company X personnel with the information necessary to incorporate information security and privacy actions within their job functions.
- Heighten awareness and understanding of information security and privacy fundamentals.

- Enable deeper insights into information security needs, enhancing consumer confidence and more effectively meeting consumer needs across multiple points of contact with Company X, resulting in greater consumer loyalty.
- Ensure everyone in Company X knows about new and emerging information security and privacy requirements.
- Communicate employee obligations under the organization's information security and privacy policies.
- Communicate Company X legal and regulatory information security and privacy obligations and impacts.
- Comply with regulatory, contractual, and industry standards requirements for information security and privacy training.
- Keep security and privacy in the minds of personnel and business partners while they perform daily job tasks.

All Company X personnel are required to participate within the training sessions to which they are invited. All personnel notified about job-specific training are also required to attend those sessions.

If you have any questions or concerns, contact Chris Doe, Company X information security and privacy education manager, chris.doe@companyx.com, 999.999.9999.

Thank you in advance for your participation in this important endeavor.
Rebecca Flint, Chief Executive Officer, Company X.

Appendix B: Training Contact Training Data Collection Form

Training TITLE: _____ Location: _____

Manager: _____ BEGINNING DATE: _____

Training completion date: _____

PART I: Demographic Information

1. How many personnel do you manage?

2. To how many of your personnel did you send a training announcement memo?

3. How many of your personnel completed the training session?

4. Do you see increased job satisfaction in your personnel as a result of information security awareness and training efforts? If yes, please give examples.

5. Do you notice fewer employee complaints regarding information security? If yes, please give examples.

6. Did you incorporate participation in information security training into the job appraisal process? If yes, please give examples.

PART II: Your Reaction to This Training

Circle one rating number for each item.	Strongly Disagree	Disagree	Agree	Strongly Agree	Not Applicable
1. The training objectives were clear.	1	2	3	4	N/A
2. Overall, the information in the training will be useful in my area's work.	1	2	3	4	N/A
3. The order of the training topics and activities made sense to me.	1	2	3	4	N/A
4. The pace of training was good—neither too fast nor too slow	1	2	3	4	N/A
5. The training delivery method was easy to use.	1	2	3	4	N/A
6. I am satisfied the information provided in the training is applicable to my personnel.	1	2	3	4	N/A
7. I would recommend this training to other departments.	1	2	3	4	N/A
8. This training is a good investment for the company.	1	2	3	4	N/A
9. Examples and illustrations supported understanding the material.	1	2	3	4	N/A
The overall rating I would give this training module is:	Not useful ☐	Useful ☐	Very useful ☐	Extremely useful ☐	

COMMENTS:

Appendix C: Effectiveness Evaluation Framework

Training or Awareness: Date:

Been Given?   Baseline Measurement?

Executive Support?   Target Group:

Group Size: Delivery Method:

Next Delivery Date: International?

Goals:

Notes:

General Effectiveness Indicators and Measures:

1. **Access.**
   a. What groups are you reaching?
   b. What groups are missing?
   c. What is the participation rate for the group?
   d. Are you providing appropriate delivery methods for your target audiences?
   e. Can all your target audiences access your training and awareness materials and participate in your delivery methods?

2. **Relevancy.**
   a. Is your education program relevant to your organization's business goals and expectations?
   b. Are your training and awareness messages and information relevant to job responsibilities?
   c. Will your education program have a noticeable impact on business practices?
   d. Was your training content appropriate for your target participants?
   e. Did your training cover regulatory and policy requirements?

3. **Quality.**
   a. Is the quality of your awareness materials adequate to get attention and effectively deliver the intended message?
   b. Does the quality of your training materials contribute to your students' success?
   c. Do your trainers and teachers deliver quality education?
   d. Do they know how to interactively adjust to the abilities and experiences of their students?
   e. Were the conditions right for learning and for each learner's subjective satisfaction?

4. **Learning Outcomes.**
   a. Is the amount of time allowed for learning appropriate for successfully understanding the message?
   b. What do your participants say about the usefulness and effectiveness of your training and awareness activities?
   c. Do you tell the participants the expected outcomes of your education activities?
   d. What did the participants actually learn?
   e. Did your participants indicate they had a satisfactory learning experience?

5. **Impact.**
   a. What is the impact of your education program on your organization as a whole?
   b. Were activities and habits changed appropriately following training and awareness activities?
   c. What are the long-term impacts?
   d. Did the training methods promote the desired skills?
   e. Did job performance improve?
   f. What is the pattern of student outcomes following each training session?
   g. Did you assist managers with determining their own workforce performance?
   h. Did you create return on investment statistics to support training and awareness funds?
6. **Cost Effectiveness.**
   a. What time requirements are involved?
   b. What are the costs for the materials?
   c. How many people are in your targeted groups?
   d. How is training being delivered?
   e. Are you using inside and/or outside training and awareness resources?
   f. What is the value of the method of awareness activity or training session you used compared to other awareness and training options?
7. **Knowledge Generation.**
   a. Do you understand what is important for your personnel to know?
   b. For your managers to know?
   c. Do you understand what works and what does not work in your education program?
   d. Are you utilizing your evaluation results?
   e. Did you assist employees in determining their own performance success?
   f. Did you compile trend data to assist instructors in improving both learning and teaching?
8. **General to Specific.**
   a. Do your instructors tell students enough information to allow them to self-evaluate their own success in implementing what they learn?
   b. Are students told overall goals and the specific actions necessary to achieve them?
   c. Are goals and actions realistic and relevant?
   d. What is the necessary prerequisite general and specific knowledge?

BROAD PROGRAM OBJECTIVE(S) 1. Reaction/Satisfaction and Planned Actions FOCUS: Training Program, the Facilitator/Trainer, and How the Application Might Occur.	MEASURES	DATA COLLECTION METHOD/INSTRUMENTS	DATA SOURCES	TIMING	GOALS

Measures (Note: These are examples; replace with what is appropriate for the training or awareness)	1 Unsatisfactory	2 Needs Improvement	3 Satisfactory	4 Better than Expected	5 Role Model
1. Class attendance participation (% of expected participants)	☐	☐	☐	☐	☐
2. Support from management (visible support)	☐	☐	☐	☐	☐
3. Class interaction (questions, etc.)	☐	☐	☐	☐	☐
4. Demonstration of knowledge through case studies	☐	☐	☐	☐	☐
5. Postclass evaluation average rating	☐	☐	☐	☐	☐
6. Quality of training materials	☐	☐	☐	☐	☐
7. Goals met	☐	☐	☐	☐	☐

Average rating: (sum of rows 1 through 7)/7 =

BROAD PROGRAM OBJECTIVE(S)
2. Learning
Acquisition of Skills
Selection of Skills

	MEASURES	DATA COLLECTION METHOD/INSTRUMENTS	DATA SOURCES	TIMING	GOALS

Measures (Note: These are examples; replace with what is appropriate for the training or awareness)	1 Unsatisfactory	2 Needs Improvement	3 Satisfactory	4 Better than Expected	5 Role Model
1. Role-play scenarios	☐	☐	☐	☐	☐
2. Self-assessment	☐	☐	☐	☐	☐
3. Trainer assessments of perceived learning	☐	☐	☐	☐	☐
4. Demonstration of knowledge and skills through case studies	☐	☐	☐	☐	☐
5. Postclass test scores	☐	☐	☐	☐	☐
6. Improvement of postclass scores over preclass test scores	☐	☐	☐	☐	☐
7. Goals met	☐	☐	☐	☐	☐

Average rating: (sum of rows 1 through 7)/7 =

BROAD PROGRAM OBJECTIVE(S) 3. Application/Implementation	MEASURES	DATA COLLECTION METHOD/INSTRUMENTS	DATA SOURCES	TIMING	GOALS

Measures (Note: These are examples; replace with what is appropriate for the training or awareness)	1 Unsatisfactory	2 Needs Improvement	3 Satisfactory	4 Better than Expected	5 Role Model
1. Participant opinion questionnaires	☐	☐	☐	☐	☐
2. Observation of skills within job activities	☐	☐	☐	☐	☐
3. Number of security incidents lowered	☐	☐	☐	☐	☐
4. Satisfactory assignment completion	☐	☐	☐	☐	☐
5. Postclass evaluation average rating	☐	☐	☐	☐	☐
6. Quality of training materials	☐	☐	☐	☐	☐
7. Goals met	☐	☐	☐	☐	☐

Average rating: (sum of rows 1 through 7)/7 =

BROAD PROGRAM OBJECTIVE(S) 4. Business Impact	MEASURES	DATA COLLECTION METHOD/INSTRUMENTS	DATA SOURCES	TIMING	GOALS

Measures (Note: These are examples; replace with what is appropriate for the training or awareness)	1 Unsatisfactory	2 Needs Improvement	3 Satisfactory	4 Better than Expected	5 Role Model
1. Management opinion questionnaires	☐	☐	☐	☐	☐
2. Job site observation of security practices	☐	☐	☐	☐	☐
3. Security and privacy incidents resolved more quickly	☐	☐	☐	☐	☐
4. Incorporated training topics into job appraisal for the participants	☐	☐	☐	☐	☐
5. Number of security incidents reduced	☐	☐	☐	☐	☐
6. Number of customer privacy complaints reduced	☐	☐	☐	☐	☐
7. Goals met	☐	☐	☐	☐	☐

Average rating: (sum of rows 1 through 7)/7 =

BROAD PROGRAM OBJECTIVE(S)	MEASURES	DATA COLLECTION METHOD/INSTRUMENTS	DATA SOURCES	TIMING	GOALS
5. Return on Investment (ROI)					25% ROI

Measures (*Note: These are examples; replace with what is appropriate for the training or awareness*)	1 Unsatisfactory	2 Needs Improvement	3 Satisfactory	4 Better than Expected	5 Role Model
1. Cost of training (materials, trainers, participant time from work, etc.)	☐	☐	☐	☐	☐
2. Security incident statistics	☐	☐	☐	☐	☐
3. Customer complaints statistics	☐	☐	☐	☐	☐
4. Network availability improvement related to security incidents	☐	☐	☐	☐	☐
5. Management feedback evaluations	☐	☐	☐	☐	☐
6. Cost for training was comparable to or below trend data	☐	☐	☐	☐	☐
7. Goals met	☐	☐	☐	☐	☐

Average rating: (sum of rows 1 through 7)/7 =

BROAD PROGRAM OBJECTIVE(S) 6. Intangible Benefits	MEASURES	DATA COLLECTION METHOD/INSTRUMENTS	DATA SOURCES	TIMING	GOALS
Measures (Note: These are examples; replace with what is appropriate for the training or awareness)	*1 Unsatisfactory*	*2 Needs Improvement*	*3 Satisfactory*	*4 Better than Expected*	*5 Role Model*
1. Education results met the expectations of the executive sponsor	☐	☐	☐	☐	☐
2. Postevaluation scores higher than baseline evaluation scores	☐	☐	☐	☐	☐
3. Training addressed current high-priority risks	☐	☐	☐	☐	☐
4. Education contacts were included in new projects to incorporate security and privacy	☐	☐	☐	☐	☐
5. Increased communications with security and privacy office	☐	☐	☐	☐	☐
6. Increased visits to the security and privacy Web site	☐	☐	☐	☐	☐
7. Goals met	☐	☐	☐	☐	☐

Average rating: (sum of rows 1 through 7)/7 =

Appendix D: Sample Privacy Roles Definitions

Privacy Advocate

Mission

The privacy advocate will help the security and privacy office manage specific business unit (BU) requirements and concerns. The privacy advocate will also provide feedback and information to the security and privacy office to help address new and emerging privacy concerns, and to help facilitate management of the corporate privacy program. Additionally, the privacy advocate will assist the BU privacy manager and BU regional privacy manager in performing privacy activities and implementing policies and procedures.

Communications with the Security and Privacy Office

- Provide a communications connection between the security and privacy office and the BU personnel.
- Provide feedback, advice, and input regarding general and function-specific privacy training content and development.
- Attend quarterly privacy advocate meetings.
- Communicate with the security and privacy office about new information privacy materials, procedures, support, policies, tools, and training.
- Notify the security and privacy office of privacy procedures, policies and tools implementation concerns, difficulties, and other related issues.
- Communicate privacy complaints to the security and privacy office
- Communicate privacy policies and procedure implementation issues, concerns, and difficulties to the security and privacy office.

Training and Awareness

- Perform and arrange actions and activities to raise BU awareness of privacy policies, procedures, training requirements, and other related issues.
- Arrange and oversee participation for BU personnel privacy training.
- Ensure that company business partners and appropriate third parties receive information about company privacy policies and procedures.
- Track privacy training participation and follow up with applicable management to ensure all personnel participate according to their job responsibilities.
- Ensure available privacy training content is applicable to the area and up to date.
- Implement the portions of the BU privacy training and awareness strategy applicable for their role.
- Ensure awareness of privacy issues related to or impacted by planned business process changes.
- Keep BU personnel updated on privacy incidents and news outside of the company.

Privacy Incidents

- Act as a local field resource and first point of contact for privacy concerns, incidents, and investigations.
- Notify the security and privacy office, BU privacy manager, and BU regional privacy manager about newly discovered privacy complaints.
- Escalate privacy incident investigations and give early warnings appropriately, for example, to the BU privacy manager, the security and privacy office, etc.
- Help to identify, track, and document the areas where privacy incidents and concerns occur, where they originated, and how they were resolved.
- Provide advice and support for escalation resolution and ensuring the implementation of appropriate actions and fixes.
- Provide privacy incident resolution reports to the BU privacy manager and BU regional privacy manager.
- Communicate to the security and privacy office, BU privacy manager, and BU regional privacy manager about privacy incident resolution progress as appropriate.
- Provide advice and support for escalation investigation.

Communications with the BU

- Keep the BU privacy manager and BU regional privacy manager updated on new and emerging privacy incidents and activities.
- Communicate privacy policies and procedure implementation issues, concerns, and difficulties to the BU privacy manager and BU regional privacy manager.

- Work with and influence developers, development managers, technology peers, and business contacts with regard to privacy technology and administrative controls, privacy risk mitigation techniques, and standardized information privacy solutions for your company and third-party applications.
- Participate in project development teams for new applications, systems, products, and services to determine how they can or will impact privacy.
- Regularly communicate privacy issues and requirements to the BU.
- Track BU privacy policies implementation and daily use of privacy processes and procedures.
- Act as the first point of contact for BU personnel with privacy questions and concerns.
- Communicate new privacy material, processes, and other related items that come from the security and privacy office to BU personnel.

Role Requirements

- Good understanding of your company privacy policies and procedures and leading privacy practices.
- Keep up to date with privacy news, inside and outside your company.
- Effective written and verbal communications skills.
- Experienced with, and having a good understanding of, the BU services and products.
- Ability to dedicate 10%–15% of work time to the privacy advocate responsibilities.
- Participate in required privacy training and awareness activities.

Executive Customer Privacy Champion

Mission

The executive BU privacy champion is the local executive management sponsor for the BU. This role is closely linked to the regional BU executive management as well as to your company corporate executive management. The BU privacy champion visibly supports and is involved in implementation of the company and BU-specific privacy initiatives, policies, procedures, and training. The BU privacy champion works with the BU privacy manager, BU regional privacy manager, and BU privacy advocate to create applicable privacy strategies.

Communications with the BU

- Advise and support the regional privacy manager and BU privacy manager in building the privacy advocates network.

- Provide help and support for communication with region general management and staff.
- Provide executive support and approval of privacy policy and process changes requested by the BU privacy manager and BU regional privacy manager, and as required by changes in the company privacy policies and applicable privacy-related regulations.
- Interact as necessary with the BU privacy manager and regional privacy manager in negotiation of large deals to ensure that privacy issues are comprehensively and appropriately addressed as part of the negotiation and decision process.

Training and Awareness

- Support and endorse applicable BU privacy awareness and training strategies.
- Review privacy training and awareness activity reports, and provide feedback to the BU privacy manager and BU regional privacy manager.

Privacy Breaches

- Be involved as necessary in critical privacy breach escalations, negotiations, and resolutions.
- Provide executive backing for privacy efforts to facilitate and hasten the approval and implementation of necessary actions, updates, fixes, and monitoring following privacy incidents and escalations.

Role Requirements

- Should be an executive business unit manager.
- Should plan to dedicate approximately 3%–5% of time to fulfilling role requirements.
- Must have a good understanding and support of privacy issues.
- Must be visibly supportive of privacy policies and procedures.
- Must participate in required privacy training and awareness activities.

Appendix E: Suggested Privacy Awareness and Training Strategy Announcement as Voice Mail Message

Audience: All your company personnel.

Sample Voice Mail Message

The privacy champion, or better yet the CEO, could record a message similar to the following:

> *Ensuring organizational awareness of privacy policies and practices is a requirement of effective privacy policy and practice compliance. You are the foundation of ensuring privacy policy compliance. I am counting on you to know and understand what we expect of you with regard to meeting privacy requirements. To help you understand your privacy responsibilities, you will be asked to participate in privacy training. Depending upon your job responsibilities, you may be asked to participate in one or more additional training sessions covering specific privacy implementation, facilitation, and support issues. Your participation is required and will be a factor in your job performance review. Your manager knows that you are being*

asked to participate in the training and must allow you time to attend. If you have any concerns with getting the time to participate in the training, please contact the security and privacy manager. Thank you for helping the company meet its privacy goals.

Most enterprise phone systems can be configured to automatically deliver the recorded message to all personnel voice mailboxes.

Appendix F: Privacy Icon or Mascot

Background

Privacy and secure computing need to be routine and second nature, just like the habits learned as children. Your company will establish a culture of security and privacy when personnel perform job responsibilities with security and privacy in mind and automatically follow security and privacy practices and procedures. Personnel must reach the point where they intuitively think about security privacy when handling information and working on computer systems and networks.

The first step to a culture of security and privacy involves awareness and education. Personnel must believe that security and privacy are important. To help accomplish this goal, a security and privacy icon or mascot can be created. Such awareness symbols have been used with success for many years in many industries for information security awareness, and they can work equally well for privacy awareness.

A successful implementation of a security and privacy icon will become immediately associated with your company security and privacy practices and can be used to promote security and privacy policies and practices, as well as demonstrate appropriate actions with regard to security and privacy.

A security and privacy icon or mascot can promote and instill commonsense and appropriate actions that will go far to help the company meet security and privacy goals and compliance. A mascot can help create a new way of thinking and promote security and privacy compliance habits.

Icon and Mascot Use in Organizations

One example of a hugely successful icon and mascot campaign in the United States is that of Smokey the Bear. Some critics initially panned the idea of Smokey the Bear; however, his character became, and still is, incredibly effective and universally known.

Examples of Icons and Mascots from Various Organizations

Dewie the e-Turtle

The Federal Trade Commission (FTC) introduced its own awareness mascot. All over the FTC Web site is Dewie the e-Turtle, their security and privacy mascot for consumers and businesses (see Exhibits 1 & 2). Dewie posts information and materials on the FTC site with useful information for computer users, from kids to business professionals. Dewey is a long-term investment the FTC made to raise awareness and educate people about how to practice safe computing.

We created Dewie as our FTC mascot to promote good online security.

Dewie will help us educate consumers of all ages, and he reminds us of the story of the tortoise and the hare, where knowledge, experience, and persistent effort win the race—a good theme for us today because we are in this for the long haul.

Dewie's shell shields him from harm. Although we cannot carry a shell around with us like Dewie, we can follow some of his practical tips for computer users of all ages.

http://www.ftc.gov/bcp/conline/edcams/infosecurity/popups/cleveland-speech_swindle.htm.

Exhibit 1   Dewie the e-Turtle.

Exhibit 2   Join Team Dewie.

SAM (Security Awareness Mouse)

SAM is the mascot for the Information Security Awareness Program at the University of Texas–El Paso. The University Security Committee wanted a mascot to make information security awareness a friendlier concept.

Exhibit 3   SAM (Security Awareness Mouse).

Roary Pride

Roary Pride from Columbia University (see Exhibit 4):

Security Awareness Week

September 23–25 on Hamilton Lawn
To mark the first annual Columbia University Security Awareness Week, the security department will sponsor a three-day event on Hamilton Lawn from September 23 to 25.

Specialists from the New York City Police Department will hold discussions on prevention in the lounges of Hartley and Wallach, and security equipment vendors will display locks and other prevention products.

An $800 Raleigh 21-speed mountain bike will be raffled off, with raffle chances increasing for those who participate in several events.

http://www.columbia.edu/cu/record/archives/vol23/vol23_iss3/17.html

---

Exhibit 4   Roary Pride.

Cyber Tiger

Cyber Tiger from the Nuclear Regulatory Commission (NRC) (see Exhibit 5):

Our giveaway item included a picture of NRC's computer security mascot (CyberTiger) dressed in a football uniform and included slogans like: "Kick SPAM into the Trash," "Block Viruses by Keeping Definitions Updated," "Don't Pass Your Password Around, and "Hoax Messages Should Take a Hike.

http://www.nrc.gov/

Exhibit 5   CyberTiger.

Keyboardillo

Keyboardillo, the information security mascot for Arhont, Ltd, from the firm's Web site, http://www.behance.net/Gallery/Arhont-Corporate-Identity/83951 (see Exhibit 6).

Exhibit 6   Keyboardillo.

Global Security Week

The icon for Global Security Week from its Web site, http://www. globalsecurity-week.com (see Exhibit 7).

Exhibit 7   Global Security Week Icon.

Choosing an Icon or Mascot

Icons and mascots can be useful tools for enabling staff to quickly associate a message, policy, procedure, or other type of communication with information security and privacy. Icons and mascots can take one of unlimited possible forms. Possibilities include the following:

- *A human or cartoon character.* For example, use a person dressed as half a burglar and half a police officer to symbolize stealing privacy and maintaining privacy. Or, use as a person dressed in something associated with your company and who looks very unique or distinctive.
- *An animal character.* For example, use an owl to remind everyone to keep their eyes open for privacy breaches, or an eagle as a sign of protecting privacy.
- *A mythical character.* For example, use a dragon to guard the privacy of your company's personally identifiable information (PII).
- *An object.* For example, use a padlock or bank vault/safe to indicate the privacy and security of information, or use a hat to symbolize staff putting on their privacy hat when working with PII.
- *A symbol.* Consider showing a padlock attached to your company symbol. Or, perhaps use, if possible, one of the privacy organization symbols that your company uses on its Web site. For example, perhaps you could use the Better Bussiness Bureau (BBB) privacy symbol linked to the your company symbol with wedding rings to show your company's "commitment" to privacy, or the "marriage" of privacy and your company, or a similar variation.

Instead of having one team choose the security and privacy icon or mascot, consider holding an "Identify the Security and Privacy Mascot" competition to solicit creative ideas from personnel. This would also build a sense of ownership for the icon, as well as creating opportunities for staff to think about security and privacy.

Choose the icon or mascot carefully. Be sensitive to political, religious, race, and ethnic references or potential associations. Culture, geographic location, and type of business are important factors in the selection criteria. For example, Chinese dragons may symbolize doom and death in the Western culture or a bear may signify the downside of the investment cycle in the banking industry.

Icon and Mascot Use

A security and privacy mascot or icon can be used in multiple ways. Examples include the following:

- Memos
- Newsletters

- Security and privacy messages
- Security and privacy rule book
- Security and privacy intranet site
- Customer communications
- Contests
- Videos
- Computer-based training (CBT)
- Classroom training
- Web-based training
- E-mails; allow personnel to send the mascot or icon security and privacy questions
- Desk items, such as memo pads and folders

You can also use security and privacy icons and mascots to indicate security and privacy certification; a visible indication that a person has participated in security and privacy training, did an outstanding job of managing a security or privacy incident, and so on.

Establishing a Security and Privacy Mascot or Icon

To successfully launch a security and privacy mascot or icon, you will need to establish and document:

- Who "owns" (controls the use of) the mascot or icon
- Who can use the mascot or icon
- When the mascot or icon can be used
- If the mascot or icon will be used externally as well as internally
- If the mascot or icon will be used to "brand" certain processes, products, or services as being privacy certified
- Security and privacy topics you want to emphasize
- Where the mascot or icon will be used, such as
  - on corporate Web site security and privacy policies,
  - within documented security and privacy procedures,
  - when discussing or identifying security and privacy risks,
  - when communicating about recent security and privacy incidents in your company,
  - when reporting recent security and privacy incidents outside your company,
  - when sending customers information for marketing,
  - on corporate social media sites.
- On caller identity authentication procedure documentation

Appendix G: Sample Privacy Training Survey

Company X is a strong proponent of customer privacy. Ensuring customer privacy is essential for customer satisfaction as well as for ensuring regulatory and legal compliance. Effective privacy training and awareness is essential for ensuring privacy. To help ensure that our privacy training program is effective and to identify areas where we can improve our program, take a few minutes and complete this survey sponsored by Sue Smith, CEO. The results will not only help us improve our privacy training program but will also help the company reach privacy compliance goals and regulatory requirements, while helping us to identify how to further address privacy risks. Your individual responses will be kept confidential and will be incorporated into the complete response results.

Please complete and return to Rebecca Herold, rebecca.herold@companyx .com, by Friday, May 30.

1. Please indicate which of the following apply to you. Check all that apply.

   ☐ People manager   ☐ Individual contributor
   ☐ Customer contact representative   ☐ Collect customer information
   ☐ Use personally identifiable information   ☐ Company employee
   ☐ Company contractor/business partner   ☐ Marketer or sales
   ☐ Product development   ☐ Applications or systems development

2. Did you take the "Basic Privacy at Company X" privacy and security training session?

   ☐ I have never taken the training; I have never heard of it
   ☐ I have never taken the training; I did not know I had to take it
   ☐ Yes, within the past 3 months   ☐ Yes, 3–6 months ago
   ☐ Yes, 6–9 months ago   ☐ Yes, 9–12 months ago

3. Did you take the "Company X Respects Privacy" training?
   ☐ I have never taken the training; I have never heard of it
   ☐ I have never taken the training; I did not know I had to take it
   ☐ Yes, within the past 3 months   ☐ Yes, 3–6 months ago
   ☐ Yes, 6–9 months ago   ☐ Yes, 9–12 months ago

4. Please indicate your overall evaluation of the training session(s) you took

☐ Excellent   ☐ Good   ☐ Average   ☐ Poor   ☐ Ineffective   ☐ Not Applicable

Comments: _____

5. Which area(s) do you feel are the most helpful for fulfilling your job responsibilities at your company? Please check all that apply.
   ☐ Privacy from a consumer's   ☐ Privacy from a business
       perspective   perspective
   ☐ Privacy laws around the world   ☐ Privacy fundamentals
   ☐ Company X's commitment to privacy   ☐ Implementing privacy
   ☐ Privacy resources   ☐ Other _____

6. Which area(s) do you feel are least relevant for fulfilling your job responsibilities at Company X? Please check all that apply.
   ☐ Privacy from a consumer's   ☐ Privacy from a business
       perspective   perspective
   ☐ Privacy laws around the world   ☐ Privacy fundamentals
   ☐ Company X's commitment to privacy   ☐ Implementing privacy
   ☐ Privacy resources   ☐ Other _____

7. Is your management visibly supportive of Company X privacy policies, procedures, and training?
   ☐ Yes   ☐ No   ☐ Don't know

8. Which area(s) within the computer-based training do you feel need improvement?
   ☐ Privacy from a consumer's   ☐ Privacy from a business
       perspective   perspective
   ☐ Privacy laws around the world   ☐ Privacy fundamentals
   ☐ Company X's commitment to privacy   ☐ Implementing privacy
   ☐ Privacy resources   ☐ None

Comments:_____

9. In what ways can these topics be improved?
☐ Include more technical information.
☐ Include more business examples.
☐ Give classroom training on this topic.
☐ Give training in a Web-based format (such as a webinar).
☐ Provide business-unit-specific information.
☐ Bring in a guest speaker on the topic.
☐ Provide areas with posters covering the topics.
☐ Include more interactive exercises directly related to your job.
☐ Provide information on the intranet privacy Web site on this topic.
☐ Provide ongoing information in newsletters and/or e-mail messages.
☐ Include more information and make it longer.
☐ Include information about related procedures.
☐ Other _____

10. What additional privacy-related topics would be helpful for you to perform your job responsibilities? Please check all that apply.
☐ Privacy laws and regulations ☐ Spam
☐ The company's privacy policies ☐ Marketing and privacy
☐ Customer care and privacy ☐ Company X privacy procedures
☐ The company's privacy incident response plans
☐ The company's privacy contacts and resources ☐ Privacy-related news
☐ Privacy and customer relationship management ☐ Privacy and IT/product development
☐ Safe harbor and international privacy requirements
☐ Privacy incident response information and procedures
☐ Other _____

11. Which single privacy topic is most important for helping you to perform your job responsibilities?

☐ Privacy from a consumer's perspective

☐ Company X privacy policies

☐ Privacy laws around the world

☐ Customer contact management rules

☐ Company X's commitment to privacy

☐ Privacy fundamentals

☐ Privacy resources

☐ Implementing privacy

☐ The company privacy incident information

☐ Current news on privacy

☐ Business unit privacy procedures

☐ Privacy technology implementation

☐ Privacy from a business perspective

☐ Other _____

12. What suggestions or ideas do you have for improving the Company X privacy policies, procedures, training, and awareness activities?

Thank you for your time and participation in the survey!

Appendix H: Privacy Sample Training Plans

Privacy Training: Interactive Group Learning

Purpose: To provide a group learning activity to foster discussion, active decision making, and provide actionable results for improving security and privacy within the areas where the learning groups are located.

Target audiences include
  a. All employees
  b. Marketing and sales
  c. Customer support
  d. Executive management and privacy champions
  e. Contractors
  f. Third parties
  g. Privacy advocates
  h. Trainers
  i. Legal and HR
  j. IT
  k. Internal audit

Description: Provide a visual representation of information security and privacy risks covering
  ■ Desk areas
    – Public areas, such as lobbies and restaurants
    – Computer rooms
    – Meeting rooms
    – Building and facilities security
    – Lost and stolen computer items, etc.

- Perform a pretraining evaluation to determine awareness levels.
- Establish a tracking system to determine those taking the test.
- Include participation as a job appraisal requirement.
- Survey and get feedback following the training activity.
- Perform a posttraining evaluation to determine the impact of the training activities.
- Review issues and comments and, where required, recommend changes.

Planning:
- Identify areas participating and determine learning team members.
- Determine the dates when the learning activity will occur, so that it is not held when another company event is held.
- Obtain and communicate executive management sponsorship and support.
- Send memo from executive management to managers with instructions and dates for holding the learning event.
- Send the learning event materials.

For an example of this type of effective and engaging learning activity, see my Security Search learning package at http://www.privacyguidance.com.

Privacy Training: Classroom

Purpose: To provide face-to-face training and active participation to personnel who deal most directly with privacy issues.

Target audiences include
    a. Marketing and sales
    b. Customer support
    c. Privacy advocates
    d. Trainers
    e. Legal and HR

Description:
- Create specialized group-targeted classroom privacy training and materials.
- Include case studies, role playing, and other interactive learning methods.
- Approximately 2–3 hours.

Planning:
- Address international issues in class content.
- Ensure that the class length is feasible for the topics to be covered, in addition to attendee time availability.
- Simplify and clearly communicate sign-up process.

- Is participation via satellite possible (cost-effective, technically feasible)?
- Obtain and communicate executive management sponsorship and support.

Privacy Training: Computer-Based Training (CBT)

Purpose: To provide self-paced desk-located training to personnel.

Target audiences include
a. All employees
b. Marketing and sales
c. Customer support
d. Executive management and privacy champions
e. Contractors
f. Third parties
g. Privacy advocates
h. Trainers
i. Legal and HR

Description:
- Communicate privacy CBT modules to
  - Leadership
  - Country managers
  - Functional managers
  - Privacy advocates
- Localize as much as possible.
- Establish tracking system to determine those taking the test.
- Include participation as a job appraisal requirement.
- Survey and get feedback at end of each CBT.
- Review issues and comments and, where required, recommend changes.

Planning:
- Address international issues within CBT content.
- Make sure CBT length will not discourage participation.
- Simplify and clearly communicate CBT sign-up process.
- Obtain and communicate executive management sponsorship and support.

Privacy Training: Briefings

Purpose: To provide face-to-face presentation to personnel who have a vested interest in addressing privacy issues.

Target audiences include
   a. Marketing and sales
   b. Customer support
   c. Privacy advocates
   d. Trainers
   e. Legal and HR
   f. Executive management and champions
   g. Research and development

Description:
   ■ Create specialized group-targeted presentations to discuss privacy points, impacts, and action items.
   ■ Approximately 15–30 minutes.

Planning:
   ■ Address international issues within briefings.
   ■ Make content very specific to audience and how the issues relate to them.
   ■ Is participation via satellite possible (cost-effective, technically feasible)?

Privacy Training: Voice Mail

Purpose: To provide a personal voice message from business unit leaders and the customer privacy champions to personnel who need to address customer privacy issues.

Target audiences include
   a. Marketing and sales
   b. Customer support
   c. Customer privacy advocates
   d. Trainers
   e. Legal and HR
   f. Executive management and champions
   g. Research and development
   h. New employees
   i. All employees

Description:
   ■ Create general and specialized group-targeted messages to deliver directly to personnel to discuss recent customer privacy incidents, new privacy policies, privacy laws, impacts, and action items.
   ■ About 2–3 minutes.

Planning:
- Address international issues within the messages.
- Make content very specific to audience and how the issues relate to them.
- Ensure delivery is conversational and not overly managerial or condescending in tone.
- For all-employee messages, clearly communicate the importance and impact to the company.
- Deliver in language appropriate to the geographic area of the office.

Appendix I: Advocate and SME Interview Questions to Assist with Privacy Training Development

These questions will help guide the interviews with the functional area subject matter experts (SMEs) and identified security and privacy advocates, and to identify privacy needs and concerns.

- It is not expected that all questions will necessarily be asked; the conversation during the course of the interview will determine this.
- Several issues related to customer privacy training and awareness that are not on this list are likely to be brought up during the course of the conversations.
- If it is available, review the existing or proposed training content during the interview. If this is not available, then the following questions will still provide valuable feedback.
- Ask interviewees if they will be able to review (vet) the training content following incorporation of their suggestions.
- Use this list for guidance in order to ensure all issues are covered, but do not just go through the list question after question because many of them may not be appropriate for the meeting, depending on how it goes. Listen closely to what the interviewee says.

General Questions

1. What is your (the interviewee's) background?
2. What is important to you with regard to privacy in your area?
3. What training methods work best for your functional area?

4. Has upper management communicated their support for privacy training and related privacy issues?
5. What training methods work best for the various levels in your area, such as executives, middle management, and staff?
6. Does your area have a clear understanding of the types of information considered to be personally identifiable information?
7. What does your area do with personally identifiable information? How is it used, handled, etc.?
8. What current projects involve the use of personally identifiable information?

For Sales and Marketing

1. What rules/procedures do you follow for sending e-mail to consumers, customers, and others outside of the organization?
2. What customer relationship management (CRM), knowledge acquisition, etc., projects do you currently have going on?
3. What type of training and communications do sales and marketing staff currently receive regarding customer communications and information management?
4. What types of sales and marketing privacy incidents have occurred? How were they resolved? What was the incidents' impact, especially financial loss?
5. Does your functional area have direct verbal contact with consumers, or is it primarily through e-mail, postal mailings, etc.?
6. Does your functional area understand spam, what it is, how to avoid creating it, etc.?
7. Has your area been told how to handle customer complaints about privacy and marketing?
8. What kind of training occurs regarding no-call/contact lists?
9. What types of awareness messages—e.g., e-mails, Web sites, posters, etc.—work best for this area?

For Customer Service and Call Centers

1. What rules and procedures do you follow for responding to calls from customers regarding privacy issues?
2. Do the customer service representatives go through formal classroom training to learn how to address customer calls? If not, what type of training occurs?
3. Where are call center staff located? Geographically in the same location? Is classroom training feasible?
4. What current projects do you have related to customer information and privacy concerns?
5. What are the most common questions you get from customers regarding privacy?

6. Are customer service representatives your company employees, or is this function outsourced to some extent?
7. What communications have occurred from your senior management regarding the handling of customer-privacy-related calls?
8. What types of awareness messages— e.g., e-mails, Web sites, posters, memos, and so on—work best for this functional area?

For Partners and Vendors

1. How are partners and vendors told about your company's privacy policies?
2. Are partners and vendors required to take any privacy-related training or any other training prior to getting access to your company resources?
3. What is the best way to ensure training, in addition to requiring it contractually? Is it ever verified that they actually participated in training, or that the training material was effective?
4. How do partners and vendors know what their company is contractually bound to do regarding privacy?
5. Do you know of all the individuals from partners and vendors who have access to customer and other personally identifiable information? How is this documentation maintained?
6. What incidents related to privacy have occurred with partners and vendors? What were the incidents' impacts, especially financial loss?
7. What sanctions are enforced for noncompliance with your company privacy requirements?
8. What types of ongoing messages regarding privacy are communicated to partners and vendors? How do the communications occur?

For Procurement and Contracts

1. Are information security and privacy requirements included in all contracts?
2. Are limits placed on the value of a contract based on how the person who creates the contract understands privacy and information security?
3. Who determines the requirements?
4. How often are these requirements updated?
5. Are the requirements different depending on region and country? Do personnel creating contracts know how the laws and requirements differ from country to country and how they must be handled within the contractual requirements?
6. What types of awareness messages—e.g., e-mails, Web sites, posters, etc.—work best for this functional area?

For IT and Application Development

1. What types of privacy-impacting technologies—such as clear GIFs, cookies, and so on—do applications programming staff use? What guidelines do they follow for their use?
2. What types of privacy-enhancing technologies—such as encryption methods, digital signatures, and so on—do applications development and programming staff use? What guidelines do they follow for their use?
3. What types of training do staff currently receive related to coding with information security and privacy in mind?
4. What types of training methods work best for IT and applications staff?
5. Are staff located together geographically or are they spread out?
6. How much of the IT and applications development activities is outsourced? What types of training are provided for outsourced staff?
7. What processes are followed to ensure applications are created to be compliant with customer privacy policies?
8. What types of awareness messages—such as e-mails, Web sites, posters, newsletters, and so on—work best for this functional area?

For E-Business

1. How are e-business staff trained for information security and privacy issues?
2. How do you ensure privacy issues are considered when creating e-business initiatives?
3. What types of awareness messages—such as e-mails, Web sites, posters, podcasts, and so on—work best for this functional area?

For Product Development

1. What types of customer privacy issues are considered when developing new products? Is this a formal process?
2. What types of training related to customer privacy and product development do staff currently receive?
3. What types of training methods work best for product development staff?
4. Are staff located together geographically or are they spread out?
5. How much of the product development activities is outsourced?
6. What processes are followed to ensure that new products are created to be compliant with customer privacy policies?
7. What types of awareness messages—e.g., e-mails, Web sites, posters, etc.—work best for this area?

Appendix J: Training and Awareness Inventory

Company:

Date:

Type of education:

Information Security Training

Topic Description	Been Given? Y/N	Baseline Measurement? Y/N	Exec Support? Y/N	Goals	Target Group	Group Size	Delivery Method (e.g., CBT, Classroom, Webinar, Video, etc.)	Next Delivery Date	Local, National, or International?	Notes

Appendix K: Incorporating Training and Awareness into the Job Appraisal Process Interview/Questionnaire

1	How often are job appraisals performed?	
2	Who performs job appraisals?	
3	What appraisal items are consistent for all personnel appraisals?	
4	What impact do appraisals have on personnel job success? E.g., promotions, raises, demotions, terminations, etc.	
5	When are job appraisals performed? At the same time each year for all personnel?	
6	What global issues do you need to consider? In what countries do you have personnel?	
7	Do you have any restrictions with regard to the job appraisal process in other countries that are different from the United States? These could be organizational restrictions, or regulatory and legal restrictions.	

8	Do you need to make training and awareness available in different languages? This could impact how you can incorporate into the job appraisal process depending upon how widely you can deploy your set of training and awareness curriculum.	
9	Do you include information security considerations and activities within the job appraisal process?	
10	Do you include privacy considerations and activities within the job appraisal process?	
11	Do personnel consider the organization's methods of evaluating privacy and security in appraisals fair?	

Appendix L: Sample Customer Privacy Awareness and Training Presentation

Slide 1

Company X Privacy
Awareness & Training
Program

Overview Presentation
January, 2012

Rebecca Herold, CIPP CISSP, CISM, CISA, FLMI

Slide 2

Objectives (1)

The objective of the Company X Privacy Training & Awareness program is to provide core communication, content standardization and training infrastructure in accordance with the Company X information privacy policies and applicable leading practices, laws and regulations to enable security and privacy deployment efforts within all offices, regions, countries and business units.

Slide 3

Objectives (2)

In particular the privacy training and awareness objectives are to:

- Motivate change within personnel to improve and ensure information privacy awareness and compliance
- Comply with applicable laws and regulations requiring such education
- Identify core and function-specific training content and applicable delivery methods
- Track training metrics globally and at the local levels
- Communicate privacy related information and policies, procedures and standards to corporate and BU areas, such as training offerings, material availability, and so on
- Represent the corporate privacy perspective within the regional and BU deployment efforts
- Maintain content and version control for information privacy training materials

Slide 4

Privacy Training & Awareness Components (1)

A. **Content:**
  - Privacy Overview
  - In-Depth Training and Awareness Specific to a Privacy Issue/Process/Topic/Implementation

B. **Audience:**
  - Customer Privacy Advocates
  - Executive Management & Privacy Champions
  - Company X Indirect Personnel
  - IT Personnel
  - Marketers and Sales
  - Agents and Resellers
  - Research & Development
  - Facilities Management & Physical Security
  - All Employees
  - New Employees
  - Legal & HR
  - Third Parties
  - Customer Services and Call Centers
  - Trainers
  - Regional Management
  - International Personnel

Slide 5

Privacy Training & Awareness Components (2)

C. **Geography:**
  - Applicable Laws and Regulations
  - Regional Hot Issues
  - Regional History of Incidents and Related Activities
  - Language
  - Culture and Customs

D. **Delivery:**
  - Communication Methods
  - Timing
  - Length
  - Audiences

Slide 6

Core Privacy Training Deliverables
Content

A. CONTENT

Four Levels		Definitions
(Corp)	**High Level**	Conceptual overview; Need for information security and privacy; everyone's obligations; how business benefits; fundamentals, legal, policies, and so on
(Corp)	**Topic-Specific Modules**	Legal review, privacy processes and framework, terms/definitions, technologies, customer interactions, marketing, and so on
(Corp)	**Process Specific**	Unknowns, third party, incident response, escalation process, procedures, leading practices, recent events, and so on
(BU)	**Audience Specific**	Executives, BU, call center, marketing, sales, IT, HR, research and development, brokers and agents, outsourced IT vendors, and so on

Slide 7

Core Privacy Training Deliverables
Audience

B. Audience

16 Group Levels

1. Customer Privacy Advocates
2. Executive Management & Privacy Champions
3. Company X Indirect Personnel
4. IT Personnel
5. Marketers and Sales
6. Agents and Resellers
7. Research & Development
8. Facilities Management & Physical Security
9. All Employees
10. New Employees
11. Legal & HR
12. Third Parties
13. Customer Services and Call Centers
14. Trainers
15. Regional Management
16. International Personnel

Slide 8

Core Privacy Training Deliverables Geography

C. GEOGRAPHY

Five Levels		Definitions
(Corp)	**Laws & Regulations**	Must ensure topics address the laws and regulations applicable to each location. Identify where the laws and regulations may be in conflict.
(Corp)	**Regional Issues**	Determine what situations and issues exist that must be addressed for specific locations.
(Corp)	**Regional History**	What have been the past experiences involved with training, as well as doing business, with each region/location?
(Corp)	**Language**	What languages will need to be used in each location? How will the translations be created and tested to ensure they are true to the message?
(Corp)	**Culture & Customs**	Does the content observe and adhere to the customs and culture for each of the locations?

Slide 9

Core Privacy Training & Awareness Delivery

D. DELIVERY

Six Levels		Owner	Definitions
(Corp)	**CBT**	Corp	General purpose overview
(Corp)	**Audio/Visual**	Corp	Check out to BU privacy champions, and other resources inside BU
(Corp)	**Classroom**	Corp	Face to face highly interactive training with target groups who need immediate feedback, practice and role playing.
(BU)	**Self-Paced Slide Set**	Corp	Make notes and comments available through BU contacts and through centralized locations
(DU)	**Remote**	DU	Virtual class, net meeting, ad hoc training, Q&A
(BU)	**Face to Face**	BU/Corp	Major event opportunity, task force, hands-on, role-play, apprenticeship, classroom, and so on

Slide 10

Slide 11

Slide 12

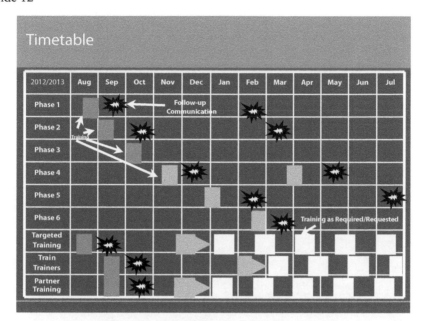

Slide 13

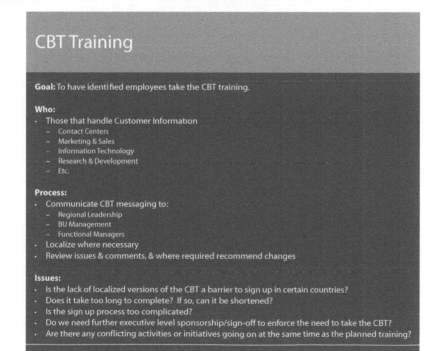

Slide 14

Targeted Training

Goal: Conduct functional target group training

Who:
- Customer and Consumer Contact Centers
- Marketing & Sales
- Information Technology
- Legal and Human Resources
- Executives
- BU Management
- Research & Development
- Business Partners

Process:
- Work with BU Contacts and Training Manager to identify groups
- Develop appropriate training material
- Conduct training according to appropriate time table

Issues:
- Lack of material and need to develop appropriate content
- Communications to target groups about training

Slide 15

Train the Trainer

Goal: Establish a network of "trainers" able to conduct information security & privacy training.

Who:
- Marketing
- Country Contacts
- Customer Service Centers
- Global Sales
- Partner Contracts

Process:
- Identify functions
- Identify suitable individuals in each
- Develop training material to train trainers
- Ensure they have access to training material that is suitable to train their staff

Issues:
- Identify candidates
- Develop training material

Slide 16

Partner & Vendor Training

Goal: Have vendors train their staff adequately for Company X information security and privacy policies and procedures

Who:
- Vendor A
- Partner B
- Marketing Service Providers (across all direct marketing groups)
- Security Service Providers (across all regions)
- Resellers/Channels
- Etc.

Process:
- Develop suitable training material
- Determine regional and contractual obligations to train personnel
- Train appropriate trainers
- Ensure that training is conducted (audits)

Issues:
- Identify vendors & partners
- Create list of requirements to which third parties must comply

Slide 17

Priorities

Priority	Who	Status
1	Senior Management	In Progress
2	BU and Country Managers	Completed

3	High Risk Groups
	   • Customer Contact Centers
	   • Direct Marketing
	   • IT
	   • Etc.
		Not Started

4	Identify Trainers	Not Started
5	Vendors and Partners	Not Started
6	General Employee Population	Not Started

Slide 18

BU	Teams				
Marketing	E-Marketing	Partners	Direct & Web	BU Marketing	Telemarketing
Sales	Contact Centers	Presales	CRM	BU Sales	Channel & Partner Mgt
Customer Support and Contact	Contact Centers	E-Business	Channel & Partner Mgt	Order Fulfillment	
Administration & Other	Contract Admin	Region & Country Mgrs	Legal	Customer Education	Human Resources

High-Risk Groups

Slide 19

Training & Awareness Materials

Information Security & Privacy Office "Information Security and Privacy Overview" CBT
- Localized where possible (Spanish, French, German, Irish, Japanese, Cantonese, Korean, etc.)
- How many have started? How many have finished? If the percentage is less than 95%, how can we improve participation?

Targeted Groups and Functional Training & Awareness
- Executive Level Briefing & Training
- Contact Centers
- Marketing and Sales
- Customer Education
- IT Presentation
- Partners & Vendors
- Contracts/Agreements
- Privacy Laws & International Standards
- Information Security Policies & Procedures

Training Methods
- Classroom
- Online Audio/Video
- DVD/Film
- Satellite

- CBT
- Slideshow
- Audio
- Workbook

- Team Learning
- Webcasts
- Podcasts

Awareness Messages (sent through BU Management, Employee Communications, Distribution Lists, and so on)
- Newsletters
- Alerts
- E-mail Announcements

- Website
- Posters
- Events

Appendix M: Designated Security- and Privacy-Related Days

There have been a number of special security- and privacy-related days, weeks, and months designated over the past few decades. Some have been launched on an international level, some on the national level, some at the state level, and some have been designated just within a specific organization. It is worth considering your goals for such a day, week, or month and whether it would be more effective for you to participate with a widely observed day or pick one that best fits your business schedule. The following will give you an idea of some of these days that have been celebrated at multiple levels.

Privacy and/or Security Day	Details
January 28: International Data Privacy Day	http://www.intel.com/policy/dataprivacy.htm Designed to raise awareness and generate discussion about data privacy practices and rights, Data Privacy Day activities in the United States have included privacy professionals, corporations, government officials, and representatives, academics, and students across the country.
February 10: Safer Internet Day	http://www.saferinternet.org/ww/en/pub/insafe/sid.htm Safer Internet Day is organized by INSAFE each year in February to promote safer and more responsible use of online technology and mobile phones, especially among children and young people across the world.

Privacy and/or Security Day	*Details*
February 19: Web Awareness Day; Media Awareness Network	http://www.cla.ca/webaware/programming.htm Media Awareness Network produces *Web Awareness Day* with sponsorship from Bell Canada.
March 7–13: Global Business Continuity Awareness Week	http://www.ccep.ca/bcaweek.html Global Business Continuity Awareness Week is an international initiative to promote the awareness of and need for Business Continuity in the business community and beyond.
April 12–18: Health Information Privacy and Security Week	http://www.ahima.org/hipsweek/ Health information is vital to the delivery of care, and so is keeping it secure. Health information management and technology professionals work diligently throughout the year to ensure valuable information is only available to those who need it and to no one else. It is a cause we celebrate and reconfirm each year during Health Information Privacy and Security Week.
April 26: Personal Information Privacy Day	http://www.armachicago.org/personal_info_privacy_day.html ARMA International and the National Association for Information Destruction (NAID)
Last week in April: Information Security Awareness Week	http://isaf.brighttalk.com/node An initiative that has been organized by the Information Security Awareness Forum. The forum comprises industry bodies that have a common interest and desire to increase security awareness.
April 30: Disaster Recovery Day	http://www.logix.be/temp/disaster_recov_reseller.htm A vendor-sponsored event.
May 8: World Information Security Day	http://w.ecademy.com/module.php?mod=meeting&mid=27917 Participate for better future of secured information.
First week in May: Privacy Awareness Week	http://www.privacyawarenessweek.org/paw/ Privacy Awareness Week is an annual promotion by the Asia Pacific Privacy Authorities (APPA) group.

Privacy and/or Security Day	*Details*
First full week in May: Choose Privacy Week	http://www.privacyrevolution.org/index.php/privacy_week/ Choose Privacy Week is an initiative sponsored by the American Library Asoociation (ALA) that invites library users into a national conversation about privacy rights in a digital age. The compaign gives libraries the tools they need to educated and engage users, and gives citizens the resources to think critically and make more informed choices about their privacy.
May 30: Security and Privacy Day	http://web.crypto.cs.sunysb.edu/spday/ The Security and Privacy Day is a biannual workshop sponsored by the greater New York City area computer security research community for bringing area researchers together, fostering multi-institutional collaborations, and discussing and exchanging our ideas and experiences with security and privacy research.
Various times in June: National E-security Awareness Week	http://www.staysmartonline.gov.au/awareness-week/ The annual National E-security Awareness Week aims to raise awareness about the importance of e-security among Australians.
First Thursday of August: Information Security Day	http://www.informationsecurityday.com/ Information Security Day was started to spread the awareness of information security issues. Information Security, also known as Information Systems Security (INFOSec), deals with the different aspects of information and its protection. Information Security Day aims at reducing the risk associated with the information systems by increasing the awareness of user community. The INFOSec Day aims at increasing the awareness in the following areas:
	>> Understanding the various information system components
	>> Security Management Principles
	>> Risk Assessment, Sensitivity, and Criticality
	>> Disaster Recover and Emergency Procedures
	>> Logical Security
	>> Physical Security
	>> Managerial Security Measures

Privacy and/or Security Day	*Details*
August 25–29: NSW Privacy Awareness Week; Australia	http://www.lawlink.nsw.gov.au/lawlink/privacynsw/ll_pnsw.nsf/ Privacy NSW Office of the NSW Privacy Commissioner Sydney South NSW 1235
First full week in September: Global Security Week	http://www.globalsecurityweek.com/ Global Security Week is an opportunity to join forces with other security professionals worldwide to raise awareness of security issues and techniques.
September 10: U.S. National Security Awareness Day—Physical, Information, and Personal Security	http://www.Securityawarenessday.org The concept of NSAD differs in that it tries to establish a culture of security without focusing solely on computers. It also seeks the validation of a government proclamation so that less effort can go into attracting attention to the event each year, leaving more energy devoted to supporting it.
September 25: Privacy Awareness Day; Tomah, WI VA.	http://www1.va.gov/tomahvamc/ Tomah, WI Veteran's Administration.
Last week in September or first week in October: Cyber-Security Awareness Week at University of Louisville, Kentucky, USA	http://security.louisville.edu/iso/CyberSecWeek "We want to increase the cyber security awareness of all university faculty, staff and students in a fun way. Instead of always reading about the scary incidents occurring throughout the world or sitting through more on-line training, we hope the events we have scheduled will allow people to come together and learn from the volunteers who are generously sharing their expertise at these events, have fun, meet people, get a free bite to eat and maybe even win a door prize." This demonstrates how some organizations choose different days (from the internationally- or nationally-observed events) each year on which to hold their security and/or privacy awareness days, weeks, or months.
October: U.S. National Cyber Security Awareness Month	http://www.staysafeonline.info/content/national-cyber-security-awareness-month The goal of National Cyber Security Awareness Month is to increase awareness about cyber security issues and engage users in implementing additional security measures to protect their computers.

Privacy and/or Security Day	*Details*
October: Information Security Awareness Month	http://infosat.tamu.edu/securitymonth/ Texas A&M University activities to increase awareness of information security. This demonstrates how some organizations choose different days (from the internationally- or nationally-observed events) each year on which to hold their security and/or privacy awareness days, weeks, or months.
First week in November: Security Awareness Week	http://uanews.org/node/22249 The Information Security Office sponsors a series of events marking Security Awareness Week. This demonstrates how some organizations choose different days (from the internationally- or nationally-observed events) each year on which to hold their security and/or privacy awareness days, weeks, or months.
November 18: Cybersecurity Awareness Day; Los Alamos National Laboratory	http://www.lanl.gov/orgs/pa/newsbulletin/2003/11/17/text04.shtml This demonstrates a type of event some organizations do to raise awareness of information security and privacy issues.
November 30: International Computer Security Day	http://www.computersecurityday.org/ Sponsored by the Association for Computer Security Day. Computer Security Day is an annual event, started in 1988, that is observed worldwide to help raise awareness of computer related security issues.
December 2: Information Security Awareness Day; University of Arizona:	http://security.arizona.edu/awarenessday.html/ Security Awareness Day is designed to promote information security and privacy among all members of the University of Arizona students, staff, and faculty.
Various times throughout the year: Shred Day	http://www.shred-day.com/ Shred Day's goal is to promote the protection of confidential data through the proper use of document shredding and the shredding of other types of data media.

Appendix N: Education Costs Worksheet

	ITEMIZED	TOTAL
Awareness/Training Program _____ Date: _____ Education Contact: _____		
Analysis Costs		
Salaries & Employee Benefits—Staff (Number of People × Average Salary × Employee Benefits Factor × Number of Projected Hours on Project)		
Meals, Travel, and Incidental Expenses		
Office Supplies and Expenses		
Printing and Reproduction		
Outside Services		
Equipment Expense		
Registration Fees		
Software		
Other Miscellaneous Expenses		
(A) Total Analysis Cost		

	ITEMIZED	TOTAL
Development Costs		
Salaries & Employee Benefits—Training Staff (Number of People × Average Salary × Employee Benefits Factor × Number of Projected Hours on Project)		
Meals, Travel, and Incidental Expenses		
Office Supplies and Expenses		
Program Materials and Supplies		
Film or Videotape		
Audio Tapes		
35-mm Slides		
CDs/Diskettes		
Overhead Transparencies		
Software		
Artwork		
Poster Boards		
Memo Pads		
"Trinkets"		
Manuals and Materials		
USB Thumb Drives		
Other		
Printing and Reproduction		
Outside Services		
Equipment Expense		
Rent		
Registration Fees		
Other Miscellaneous Expenses		
(B) Total Development Cost		

	ITEMIZED	*TOTAL*
Delivery Costs		
Participant Costs		
Salaries & Employee Benefits—Participants (Number of Participants × Average Salary × Employee Benefits Factor × Number of Hours or Days of Training Time)		
Meals, Travel, and Accommodations (Number of Participants × Average Daily Expenses × Days of Training)		
Participant Replacement Costs		
Lost Production (explain basis)		
Program Materials and Supplies		
Instructor Costs		
Salaries and Benefits		
Meals, Travel, and Incidental Expense		
Outside Services		
Facility Costs (distance learning, traditional classroom, lab, hotel, conference room, other)		
Facilities Rental		
Facilities Expense Allocation		
Snacks and Lunch Breaks		
Equipment Expense		
Other Miscellaneous Expenses		
(C) Total Delivery Costs		

	ITEMIZED	*TOTAL*
Evaluation Costs		
Salaries & Employee Benefits—Staff (Number of People × Average Salary × Employee Benefits Factor × Number of Hours on Project)		
Meals, Travel, and Incidental Expenses		
Participants Costs (interviews, focus groups, questionnaires, surveys, online feedback, etc.)		
Office Supplies and Expenses		
Printing and Reproduction		
Outside Services		
Equipment Expense		
Other Miscellaneous Expenses		
(D) Total Evaluation Costs for Project		
TOTAL PROJECT COSTS (A+B+C+D)		

Appendix O: Sample Pretraining/Awareness Questionnaire

Modify the following as applicable to your particular situation, environment, and education topic.

The purpose of this questionnaire is to help us understand your current skills in and knowledge about the upcoming information security and/or privacy training and/or awareness topic. It will help us to better meet your job responsibilities and needs to know the skills and knowledge you want to get out of our education program.
Name: Current Position: Location:
Please let us know your previous positions and responsibilities:
Please list your education (e.g., high school, bachelor's degree and major, master's degree and major, and so on):
What information security and/or privacy courses, workshops, or seminars have you attended? Include those outside of this organization.

Briefly describe your current job responsibilities:
What are the most difficult or challenging information security and privacy issues you face in your department, and for your job responsibilities?
What specific thing(s) do you want to learn about information security and privacy?
What concerns do you have about participating in information security and privacy training and awareness activities?
With what kind of training do you feel comfortable? For example, classroom, group learning activities, case studies, online webinars, computer-based training modules, etc.

Appendix P: Security Awareness Quiz Questions

The following is an example of a very basic type of quiz to give to all personnel to determine a baseline of information security and privacy awareness and understanding.

Category	Question	Answers
Instructions: For each question, pick all the answers that are correct.		
Disaster Recovery & Business Continuity	1. Why is it important to make backups of data?	A. To ensure information you need is available when you need it B. To have copies of valuable data that may be lost, stolen, or erased C. To be able to recover damaged data files D. To keep personnel busy E. To allow the business to continue to operate F. To be in compliance with multiple laws and regulations

Privacy	2. What can you do to help prevent privacy breaches?	A. Encrypt personally identifiable information sent through public networks
		B. Buy identity theft insurance
		C. Encrypt personally identifiable information stored on mobile computers and storage devices
		D. Do not give out personally identifiable information to callers without verifying their identity and determining they are authorized to have such information
		E. Do not work with personally identifiable information
		F. Put your old credit card statements in securely tied trash bags before putting out on the curb
Information Security	3. Choose the information security practices everyone should follow in their work areas.	A. Lock the computer screen and keyboard when stepping away from the desk
		B. Give passwords to managers
		C. Lock documents containing confidential information securely in drawers, cabinets, or comparable storage locations
		D. Report unfamiliar individuals not wearing name badges immediately to the security area
		E. Escort visitors to departments; do not let them wander around
		F. Do not leave printed confidential documents at printers, in fax machines, or any other open, unsecured area
Passwords	4. Which of these are good passwords?	A. QWERTY
		B. AiwfX247
		C. SueJones
		D. Ineed27Zs!
		E. 12345678
		F. Skip2ML0

Messaging	5. When sending electronic messages, which of the following actions are desirable for security and privacy reasons?	A. Never send confidential information in clear text B. When sending to many recipients from different organizations, put all their e-mail addresses in the CC line so that they can get to know each other C. Always double-check the e-mail addresses before hitting "Send" D. Never forward a message without first getting the consent of the message originator E. Spell-check your message F. Always encrypt messages containing personally identifiable information
Messaging	6. When receiving electronic messages, which of the following actions are desirable for security and privacy reasons?	A. Open attachments before scanning them for viruses and other malware B. Never click on links within messages from senders you do not know C. Forward suspicious-looking messages to everyone in the company to warn them to watch out for the message D. Scan messages for malware before opening attachments E. Click the "unsubscribe" reply link in spam messages to unsubscribe to being included in their future mailings F. Call the phone numbers provided within messages from senders with whom you are not familiar

The correct answers to the quiz are

- Question 1: A, B, E, F
- Question 2: A, C, D
- Question 3: A, C, D, E, F
- Question 4: B, D, F
- Question 5: A, C, D, F
- Question 6: B, D

Appendix Q: Social Engineering Quiz

Crooks are increasingly using social engineering tactics to get to information and data in all forms. Give this quiz to your personnel to find out how easily they could succumb to a social engineering attempt. The good thing about this type of quiz is that it gives the quiz-taker credit for being partially right. Few things in information security and privacy practices are completely right or completely wrong, and giving a quiz with weighted answers helps demonstrate this to your personnel.

Do NOT give the information in the italicized "FEEDBACK" sections to the learners if you are giving this on paper, or do not have a system to give feedback after the learner has entered his/her answer! This is for you, as the quiz administrator, to use to grade the quiz results. You can also put this quiz into a learning management system (LMS), weight the answers as shown, and then give the feedback information to the learners only after they have answered the questions.

See how well you can spot the social engineering attempts in the following scenario.

Scenario

Mary is at her desk when an unfamiliar service man approaches her. He is wearing uniform with an ID tag on his shirt that has his photo, name (Gary), and a company name (Comp-U-Tech). He informs Mary that he was hired to research why the network has been slowing down. Subsequently, he visits each machine and documents some preliminary results to identify the issues. As such, he asks Mary to login in to the computer and give him 5 minutes to use her computer to run a few tests and document their results. Mary knows the network has been slow and remembers hearing that "something was going to be done."

1. **What is the likelihood that this is a potential con? (10 points)**
    a. There is a small chance; but Mary needs to use her computer for work, so he could be genuine.

FEEDBACK (2 pts.): No. Watch out! This is likely a con. It is common for in-person social engineering crooks to try and look official and talk with technical babble to get you to believe them. The easiest way for crooks to get the information to use to commit their crimes is to just ask for it!

b. This is absolutely a social engineering attempt!

FEEDBACK (10 pts.): Yes. This is likely a con. It is common for in-person social engineering crooks to try and look official and talk with technical babble to get you to believe them. The easiest way for crooks to get the information to use to commit their crimes is to just ask for it!

c. Zero percent. Gary is a legitimate computer repair person.

FEEDBACK (0 pts.): No. Watch out! This is likely a con. It is common for in-person social engineering crooks to try and look official and talk with technical babble to get you to believe them. The easiest way for crooks to get the information to use to commit their crimes is to just ask for it!

d. There is a chance this is a con.

FEEDBACK (8 pts.): Yes. This is strongly most likely a con, making choice (b) a better answer. It is common for in-person social engineering crooks to try and look official and talk with technical babble to get you to believe them. The easiest way for crooks to get the information to use to commit their crimes is to just ask for it!

2. **What aspect of the situation most strongly suggests that this is a con? (10 points)**

a. Mary had heard of the problem, but was not previously informed of a potential tech visit.

FEEDBACK (8 pts.): Yes. Employees usually are informed of upcoming tech visits; however, the big tip-off was that Gary asked Mary to sign on with HER user id. Most legitimate repair techs have their own user IDs, so why didn't this one? Because he was a con. Cons like to get their hands on the information employees are authorized to access.

b. Gary rattled off more technical jargon than needed.

FEEDBACK (5 pts.): Well, this is not the best choice. Folks in technical jobs often use technical jargon but so do cons, so this could have been a clue. However, the big tip-off was that Gary asked Mary to sign on with HER user id. Most legitimate repair techs have their own user IDs, so why didn't this one? Because he was a con. Cons like to get their hands on the information employees are authorized to access.

c. Gary did not have his own sign-on. He asked Mary to use her own sign-on to access the system.

FEEDBACK (10 pts.): Good! Most legitimate repair techs have their own user IDs, so why didn't this one? Because he was a con. Cons like to get their hands on the information employees are authorized to access.

d. Gary was unfamiliar to Mary.

FEEDBACK (2 pts.): No. This may be true in some organizations, but in most, the folks who fix the computers are not known to all the employees. However, the big tip-off was that Gary asked Mary to sign on with HER user id. Most legitimate repair techs have their own user IDs, so why didn't this one? Because he was a con. Cons like to get their hands on the information employees are authorized to access.

3. **What would you do if Mary worked in your office and you witnessed this? (10 points)**

a. I would call the area responsible for information security as soon as possible and give them the details.

FEEDBACK (10 pts.): Yes. This is the best choice. Report the situation to the area responsible for information security right away.

b. I would wait until the Gary left, and then I'd talk to Mary about it and ask if she thought it was an actual scam.

FEEDBACK (3 pts.): No. Don't wait until Gary is gone; he could have done some real damage. Report the situation to the area responsible for information security right away.

c. I would go over and confront Gary and ask him for his ID badge and for the name of the person who sent him to do the work.

FEEDBACK (8 pts.): Your instinct to interrupt the situation is right, but there is an even better choice. This really should be handled by the area responsible for information security. Report the situation to the area responsible for information security right away.

d. I would continue with my work; it is Mary's responsibility to deal with this situation, not mine.

FEEDBACK (0 pts.): Oh, no! Don't turn a blind eye to this probable scam! Report the situation to the area responsible for information security right away.

Appendix R: Information Security and Privacy Awareness and Training Checklist

Use the following chart, or one similar, to keep track of all the tasks you have done, need to do, and when you did them, relating to your education program. Modify the activities to meet your specific situation. I find it helps to post this type of chart at my desk to help keep me on track with all the actions I need to do and also to easily see at a glance when I last performed a specific action.

Place a ✓ in the appropriate box to indicate the date on which you performed the associated activity. Modify this form to meet your particular education program.

Month (circle one)	Jan	Feb	Mar	Apr	May	Jun	Jul	Aug	Sep	Oct	Nov	Dec
Year (circle one)	2010	2011	2012	2013	2014	2015	2016	2017	2018	2019	2020	

Activity	1	2	3	4	5	6	7	8	9	10	11	12	13	14	15	16	17	18	19	20	21	22	23	24	25	26	27	28	29	30	31	NOTES
Check for new security and privacy impacting laws																																
Meet with legal counsel to discuss new laws																																
Meet with IT management to discuss impact of new laws																																
Review customer security and privacy complaints																																
Answer personnel security and privacy questions																																
Update Web site privacy policy																																
Security and privacy awareness activities: e-mails																																

Security and privacy awareness activities: intranet										
Security and privacy awareness activities: posters										
Security and privacy awareness activities: newsletters										
Security and privacy awareness activities: blogs										
Security and privacy awareness activities: podcasts										
Security and privacy awareness activities: videos										
Security and privacy awareness activities: text messages										
Security and privacy awareness activities: contests										
Security and privacy training for all employees										
Security and privacy training for IT										

(Continued)

Month (circle one)	Jan	Feb	Mar	Apr	May	Jun	Jul	Aug	Sep	Oct	Nov	Dec
Year (circle one)	2010	2011	2012	2013	2014	2015	2016	2017	2018	2019	2020	

Activity	1	2	3	4	5	6	7	8	9	10	11	12	13	14	15	16	17	18	19	20	21	22	23	24	25	26	27	28	29	30	31	NOTES
Security and privacy training for customer service																																
Security and privacy training for HR																																
Security and privacy training for marketing and sales																																
Security and privacy training for business partners																																
Security and privacy training for contracted and temporary workers																																
Security and privacy training for customers																																
Research security- and privacy-related incidents at other companies																																

Check security and privacy alerts from CERT and other organizations																									
Check recent headlines for security and privacy incidents																									
Update employee security and privacy policies																									
Meet with IT to discuss new projects																									
Quarterly security and privacy report to the board																									
Review third-party contracts to ensure security and privacy protections																									
Review evaluation forms for training																									
Review evaluation forms for awareness																									
Send pre-training questionnaire																									
Update education inventory																									
Meet with education contacts																									
Update training content																									

(Continued)

Month (circle one)	Jan	Feb	Mar	Apr	May	Jun	Jul	Aug	Sep	Oct	Nov	Dec
Year (circle one)	2010	2011	2012	2013	2014	2015	2016	2017	2018	2019	2020	

Activity	1	2	3	4	5	6	7	8	9	10	11	12	13	14	15	16	17	18	19	20	21	22	23	24	25	26	27	28	29	30	31	NOTES
Complete education costs worksheet for upcoming training or awareness																																
Create education summary and progress report for board and executive sponsor																																
Perform after-hours work area security and privacy walkthroughs																																

Appendix S: Awareness and Training Resources

Not only did many of the following sources help my research for this book, they also may provide you with some good additional information and insights into creating your own information security and privacy awareness and training program, or give you inspiration for training activities and awareness events. These are not meant to be exhaustive lists, but should offer you a good starting point for your own education program efforts. (Inclusion within any of these lists does not necessarily represent a recommendation or endorsement of the item or site. I leave it to my readers to make value determinations for themselves.)

Resources by Rebecca Herold

Here are some of my books, publications, and resources:

- Compliance Helper; complete set of information security and privacy policies, procedures, forms and work plans for program management; http://www.compliancehelper.com
- *Protecting Information* quarterly employee multimedia awareness journal; The Privacy Professor; http://www.privacyguidance.com/
- The Privacy Professor Blog; http://www.provacyguidance.com/myblog.html
- *The Privacy Management Toolkit*; Information Shield; http://www.informationshield.com/privacy_main.html
- *The Privacy Papers*; Auerbach
- *The Practical Guide to HIPAA Privacy and Security Compliance*; with Kevin Beaver; Auerbach
- *Say What You Do*; with Dorian Cougias and Marcelo Halpern; Shaser-Vartan
- *Understanding Data Protection from Four Critical Perspectives*; free e-book from http://nexus.realtimepublishers.com/sgudp.php

- *The Definitive Guide to Security Inside the Perimeter*; Realtime Publishers
- *The Business Executive Practical Guides to Compliance and Security Risks* book series; Realtime Publishers
- *IT Compliance in Realtime* monthly e-Journals; http://www.realtime-itcompliance.com/digital_library.asp
- *The Essentials Series: PCI Compliance*; http://www.realtime-itcompliance.com/digital_library.asp
- *The Essentials Series: IT Compliance-Volume II*; http://www.realtime-itcompliance.com/digital_library.asp
- *The Essentials Series: IT Compliance*; http://www.realtime-itcompliance.com/digital_library.asp
- *The Shortcut Guide to Improving IT Service Support through ITIL*; http://www.realtime-itcompliance.com/digital_library.asp

Books

In recent years there has been a virtual explosion of information security, privacy, and compliance books! Here is a short list of some of them:

- *101 Things You Need to Know About Internet Law*; Jonathan Bick; Three Rivers Press
- *A Guide to Forensic Testimony*; Fred Chris Smith and Rebecca Gurley Bace; Addison Wesley
- *Active Training*; Mel Silberman; Jossey-Bass/Pfeiffer
- *Ben Franklin's Web Site*; Robert Ellis Smith; Sheridan Books
- *Beyond Fear*; Bruce Schneier; Copernicus Books
- *Building an Information Security Awareness Program*; Mark B. Desman; Auerbach
- *Compilation of State and Federal Privacy Laws*; Robert Ellis Smith; Privacy Journal
- *Computer Security*; Ben Rothke; McGraw-Hill
- *CyberRegs*; Bill Zoellick; Addison Wesley
- *Database Nation*; Simpson Garfinkel; O'Reilly
- *Developing Trust: Online Privacy and Security*; Matt Curtin; Apress
- *E-Business Privacy and Trust*; Paul Shaw; Wiley
- *E-Policy*; Michael Overly; Amacom
- *Evaluation in Organizations*; Darlene Russ-Eft and Hallie Preskill; Perseus Publishing
- *Evaluation Strategies for Communicating and Reporting*; Rosalie T. Torres, Hallie S. Preskill, and Mary E. Piontek; Sage Publications
- *Evaluative Inquiry for Learning in Organizations*; Hallie Preskill and Rosalie T. Torres; Sage Publications

- *Fighting Computer Crime*; Donn B. Parker; Wiley
- *Hacking for Dummies*; Kevin Beaver; Wiley
- *How to Measure Training Results*; Jack J. Phillips and Ron Drewstone; McGraw-Hill
- *Identity Theft*; Robert Hammond; Career Press
- *Information Privacy Law*; Daniel Solove and Marc Rotenberg; Aspen
- *Information Security Management Handbook*; Harold F. Tipton and Micki Krause; Auerbach
- *Information Security Management Metrics: A Definitive Guide to Effective Security Monitoring and Measurement*; W. Krag Brotby; Auerbach
- *Information Security Policies and Procedures*; Thomas R. Peltier; Auerbach
- *Internet Privacy for Dummies*; John Levine, Ray Everett-Church; Gregg Stebben; Wiley
- *Net Privacy*; Michael Erbschloe and John Vacca; McGraw Hill
- *Oracle Privacy Security Auditing*; Arup Nanda and Donald Burleson; Rampant
- *Privacy for Business: Web Sites and Email*; Stephen Cobb; Dreva Hill
- *Privacy Handbook*; Albert Marcella Jr. and Carol Stucki; Wiley
- *Privacy Law*; Richard Turkington and Anita Allen; West Group
- *Say What You Do*; Rebecca Herold, Dorian Cougias, and Marcelo Halpern; Shaser-Vartan
- *Security Metrics: Replacing Fear*; Andrew Jaquith; Addison-Wesley
- *Tangled Web*; Richard Power; Que
- *Telling Ain't Training*; Harold D. Stolovitch and Erica J. Keeps; ASTD Press
- *Ten Steps to a Learning Organization*; Peter Kline and Bernard Saunders; Great Ocean Publishers
- *The Art of Deception*; Kevin Mitnick and William L. Simon; Wiley
- *The ASTD Handbook of Training Design and Delivery*; George M. Piskurich, Peter Beckschi, and Brandon Hall; McGraw-Hill
- *The ASTD Training & Development Handbook*; Robert L. Craig; McGraw-Hill
- *The Digital Person: Technology And Privacy In The Information Age (Ex Machina: Law, Technology, and Society);* Daniel J. Solove; New York University Press
- *The Electronic Privacy Papers*; Bruce Schneier and David Banisar; Wiley
- *The Gigalaw Guide to Internet Law*; Doug Isenberg; Random House
- *The Practical Guide to HIPAA Privacy and Security Compliance*; Rebecca Herold and Kevin Beaver; Auerbach
- *The Privacy Papers*; Rebecca Herold; Auerbach
- *The Privacy Payoff*; Ann Cavoukian and Tyler Hamilton; McGraw Hill
- *The Right to Privacy;* Caroline Kennedy and Ellen Alderman; Diane Publishing Co.
- *The Trainer's Handbook*; Karen Lawson; Jossey-Bass/Pfeiffer
- *The Transparent Society*; David Brin; Perseus Books
- *The Unwanted Gaze*; Jeffrey Rosen; Vintage

E-Mail Lists (listservs) and Magazines

- E-Commerce Law Week; subscribe at http://www.steptoe.com
- GCN Update; subscribe at http://www.gcn.com/profile
- Gigalaw; subscribe at http://www.gigalaw.com/newsletters/dailynews.html
- GPO Publications Lists; subscribe at http://www.gpoaccess.gov
- Health Privacy News; subscribe at http://www.healthprivacy.org/
- *Information Security* magazine; http://www.infosecuritymag.com/
- Infosecurity News: *SC Magazine*; http://www.infosecnews.com/
- *Journal of Information, Law, and Technology*; http://elj.warwick.ac.uk/jilt/
- Privacy and Information Security News; subscribe at http://www.colliershannon.com/
- Privacy Digest; subscribe at http://PrivacyDigest.com/
- Privacy Forum; subscribe at http://groups.yahoo.com/group/privacy-forum/
- Privacy Tip Sheet; subscribe at http://www.privacyfoundation.org/
- Privacy Weekly; purchase subscription at http://privacyweekly.com/purchase/pd_ purchase.asp.
- Security-Awareness; subscribe at http://groups.yahoo.com/group/security-awareness/
- The PRIVACY Forum; http://www.vortex.com/privacy.html

Membership Organizations

- American Society for Training & Development (ASTD); http://www.astd.org/astd
- Computer Security Institute (CSI); http://www.gocsi.com
- Electronic Freedom Frontier; http://www.eff.org/
- Federal Information Systems Security Educators' Association (FISSEA); http://csrc.nist.gov/organizations/fissea/
- Institute of Internal Auditors (IIA); http://www.theiia.org
- Infragard; http://www.infragard.net
- International Association of Privacy Professionals (IAPP); http://www.privacyassociation.org
- Information Systems Audit and Control Association (ISACA); http://www.isaca.org
- Information Systems Security Association (ISSA); http://www.issa.org/

Web Sites

Rebecca Herold's Web sites:

- http://www.privacyguidance.com
- http://www.realtime-itcompliance.com
- http://www.compliancehelper.com

Other Web sites:

- Auerbach Books; http://www.auerbach.com
- Bureau of National Affairs (BNA); http://www.bna.com
- California Central Coast American Society for Industrial Security (ASIS), Society of Industrial Security Professionals (NCMS, Inc.), and Vandenburg Security Awareness Council (VSAC); http://members.impulse.net/~sate/index.html
- CERT; http://www.cert.org
- COAST; http://www.cs.purdue.edu/coast
- Compseconline; *http://www.compseconline.com/compsec/show/*
- DefCon; http://www.defcon.org
- Department of Health and Human Services (HHS) Indian Health Service Information Security Awareness; http://www.ihs.gov/CIO/SecurityAwareness/index.cfm
- Incidents; http://www.incidents.org
- Information Shield; http://www.informationshield.com
- Insecure; http://www.insecure.org
- National Cyber Security Alliance; http://www.staysafeonline.info/
- National Infrastructure Protection Center; http://www.nipc.gov
- National Security Institute; http://nsi.org/SECURITYsense.html
- National Institute of Standards and Technology (NIST) Computer Security Resource Center; http://csrc.nist.gov/index.html
- NT Bugtraq; http://www.ntbugtraq.com
- Packetstorm Security; http://www.packetstormsecurity.com
- PrivaPlan HIPAA compliance information; http://www.privaplan.com
- Sandstorm; http://www.sandstorm.com
- System Administration, Networking, and Security Institute (SANS); http://www.sans.org
- SANS Info Sec Reading Room; http://www.sans.org/rr/catindex.php?cat_id=47
- Security Awareness Toolbox; http://www.iwar.org.uk/comsec/resources/ sa-tools/index.htm
- Security Wizards; http://www.secwiz.com
- The Center for Education and Research in Information Assurance and Security (CERIAS); http://www.cerias.purdue.edu/
- The Computer Underground Digest; http://sun.soci.niu.edu/~cudigest/
- The RISKS Forum; http://catless.ncl.ac.uk/Risks/
- U.S. Department of Justice—Computer Crime and Intellectual Property Section; http://www.usdoj.gov/criminal/cybercrime/

Movies and Television

Some movies, including popular box office hits, and television programs, contain story lines and details that you will find helpful for your information security and privacy education efforts, in addition to providing an entertaining alternative to other forms of training and awareness. Some of these may work well within an organization, while others may not be at all suitable for your business environment; for example, explicit language and visuals may be present in some of these. Also, some of these movies were widely panned by security critics as not representing reality well at all. In such cases, it may be a good awareness tool to view such a movie with your target audience and analyze what information is good, and what information would not be feasible in the real world. Use care and caution when considering which films to show. A few for you to consider include the following:

- Information and computer security films by Commonwealth; http://www.commonwealthfilms.com/infosec.htm
- *Burn After Reading*; Brad Pitt, George Clooney (computer security, the insider threat)
- *Dream Hackers*; David Andriole
- *Enemy of the State*; Will Smith
- *Firewall*; Harrison Ford
- *G-Force*; Nicolas Cage, Penelope Cruz (shows malware scenario)
- *Hackers Are People Too*; Documentary
- *Hackers*; Johnny Lee Miller, Angelina Jolie
- *Home Alone*; Macaulay Culkin, Joe Pesci (to teach about in-person social engineering)
- *In the Realm of the Hackers*; Ernie Gray
- *Independence Day*; Will Smith
- *Information Security Principles: An Overview*; Tim Robbins; produced by CERIAS Anti-Trust
- *Johnny Mnemonic*; Keanu Reaves
- *Sneakers*; Robert Redford, Sidney Poitier
- *Swordfish*; Hugh Jackman, John Travolta
- *Take Down*; Skeet Ulrich (movie version of the hunt for Kevin Mitnick)
- *The Billion Dollar Bubble*; James Wood
- *The Final Cut*; Robin Williams (privacy after death)
- *The Lawnmower Man*; Pierce Brosnan
- The *Matrix* series; Keanu Reaves
- *The Net*; Sandra Bullock
- *The Right to Privacy*; Lansdowne Productions and the Scottish Documentary Institute.
- *Titanic*; Leonardo DiCaprio (risk management, planning, and disaster recovery)
- *Transformers*; Shia LaBeouf

- *Tron*; Jeff Bridges, Bruce Boxleitner
- *Wargames*; Matthew Broderick
- PBS documentaries, many from the FRONTLINE series (such as *The Cuckoo's Egg* and *Cyber War!*) and also Online NewsHour features (such as *Regulating Internet Privacy* and *Conversation on Privacy*)
- Discovery Channel documentaries, such as *Project Security: Wireless Security System* and *Hackers: Methods of Attack and Defense*
- Reports from news programs such as *60 Minutes, 48 Hours, Nightline,* and so on

Other Resources (Games, Activities, etc.)

- Numerous activities and games from the U.S. Federal Trade Commission for information security and privacy; http://www.ftc.gov/bcp/consumer.shtm
- Information security and privacy awareness raising online games from the U.S. government; http://www.onguardonline.gov/games/overview.aspx
- *Jeopardy!* using LearningWare software
- Activities and games from NoticeBored; http://www.noticebored.com
- Security awareness posters; http://members.impulse.net/~sate/posters.html
- Security awareness posters; http://www.iwar.org.uk/comsec/resources/ia-awareness-posters
- Awareness tips; http://www.ussecurityawareness.org/highres/security-tips.html

Appendix T: Awareness and Training Glossary

You will find a collection of different glossaries within this appendix. I provide these to show the wide range of terms that you may want to use within your education efforts. If you cannot find a term in one glossary, look in another to see if you can find it there! You can also compare the definitions for the same term between glossaries; this provides a very good way to highlight to personnel and executive leaders how inconsistent definitions of the same terms are, even within the U.S. federal government! This demonstrates how very important it is for organizations to establish their own definitions of terms, and then make all personnel aware of these definitions.

NIST created a nice glossary for its Special Publication 800-122, "Guide to Protecting the Confidentiality of Personally Identifiable Information (PII) (DRAFT)." The following is a copy of that glossary. You can also find it online in Appendix F of Special Publication 800-122 at http://csrc.nist.gov/publications/drafts/800-122/Draft-SP800-122.pdf.

NIST Special Publication 800-122 Glossary

Aggregated Elements: Information elements collated on a number of individuals, typically used for the purposes of making comparisons or identifying patterns.

Anonymized Information: Previously identifiable information that has been de-identified and for which a code or other link no longer exists.

Confidentiality: "Preserving authorized restrictions on information access and disclosure, including means for protecting personal privacy and proprietary information." [44 U.S.C., Sec. 3542, http://uscode.house.gov/download/pls/44C35.txt].

Context of Use: The purpose for which PII is collected, stored, used, processed, disclosed, or disseminated.

De-identified Information: Records that have had enough PII removed or obscured such that the remaining information does not identify an individual and there is no reasonable basis to believe that the information alone can be used to identify an individual.

Distinguishable Information: Information that can be used to identify an individual.

Harm: Any negative or unwanted effects that would be experienced by an individual (i.e., that may be socially, physically, or financially damaging) or an organization if the confidentiality of PII were breached.

Linkable Information: Information that is not sufficient to allow the recipient to distinguish any individual, but that may be matched or compared to information from a secondary data source that is available to the general public or can be otherwise obtained, in order to link together information and potentially distinguish individuals.

Linked Information: Information that is not sufficient to distinguish an individual when considered separately, but which could distinguish an individual when taken collectively or if considered in conjunction with other data elements in the same system or in a closely related system.

Obscured Data: Data that has been distorted by cryptographic or other means to hide information. It is also referred to as being masked or obfuscated.

Personally Identifiable Information (PII): "Information which can be used to distinguish or trace an individual's identity, such as their name, social security number, biometric records, etc., alone, or when combined with other personal or identifying information which is linked or linkable to a specific individual, such as date and place of birth, mother's maiden name, etc." [OMB Memorandum 07-16].

PII Confidentiality Impact Level: The level of impact on organizations and individuals should there be a breach of confidentiality involving PII. The possible levels are low, moderate, and high.

Privacy Impact Assessment (PIA): An analysis of how information is handled that ensures handling conforms to applicable legal, regulatory, and policy requirements regarding privacy; determines the risks and effects of collecting, maintaining, and disseminating information in identifiable form in an electronic information system; and examines and evaluates protections and alternative processes for handling information to mitigate potential privacy risks.

System of Records: A group of any records under the control of any agency from which information is retrieved by the name of the individual or by some identifying number, symbol, or other identifying particular assigned to the individual.

NIST has another nice glossary in its Special Publication SP 800-115, "Technical Guide to Information Security Testing and Assessment." The following is a copy of that glossary. You can also find it online in Appendix F of Special Publication 800-115 at http://csrc.nist.gov/publications/nistpubs/800-115/SP800-115.pdf.

NIST Special Publication 800-115 Glossary

Active Security Testing: Security testing that involves direct interaction with a target, such as sending packets to a target.

Banner Grabbing: The process of capturing banner information—such as application type and version—that is transmitted by a remote port when a connection is initiated.

Covert Testing: Testing performed using covert methods and without the knowledge of the organization's IT staff, but with full knowledge and permission of upper management.

External Security Testing: Security testing conducted from outside the organization's security perimeter.

False Positive: An alert that incorrectly indicates that a vulnerability is present.

File Integrity Checking: Software that generates, stores, and compares message digests for files to detect changes made to the files.

Information Security Testing: The process of validating the effective implementation of security controls for information systems and networks, based on the organization's security requirements.

Internal Security Testing: Security testing conducted from inside the organization's security perimeter.

Network Discovery: The process of discovering active and responding hosts on a network, identifying weaknesses, and learning how the network operates.

Network Sniffing: A passive technique that monitors network communication, decodes protocols, and examines headers and payloads for information of interest. It is both a review technique and a target identification and analysis technique.

Operating System (OS) Fingerprinting: Analyzing characteristics of packets sent by a target, such as packet headers or listening ports, to identify the operating system in use on the target.

Overt Testing: Security testing performed with the knowledge and consent of the organization's IT staff.

Passive Security Testing: Security testing that does not involve any direct interaction with the targets, such as sending packets to a target.

Password Cracking: The process of recovering secret passwords stored in a computer system or transmitted over a network.

Penetration Testing: Security testing in which evaluators mimic real-world attacks in an attempt to identify ways to circumvent the security features of an application, system, or network. Penetration testing often involves issuing real attacks on real systems and data, using the same tools and techniques used by actual attackers. Most penetration tests involve looking for combinations of vulnerabilities on a single system or multiple systems that can be used to gain more access than could be achieved through a single vulnerability.

Phishing: A digital form of social engineering that uses authentic-looking—but bogus—e-mails to request information from users or direct them to a fake Web site that requests information.

Plan of Actions and Milestones (POA&M): A document that identifies tasks needing to be accomplished. It details resources required to accomplish the elements of the plan, any milestones for meeting the tasks, and scheduled milestone completion dates.

Port Scanner: A program that can remotely determine which ports on a system are open (e.g., whether systems allow connections through those ports).

Review Techniques: Passive information security testing techniques, generally conducted manually, that are used to evaluate systems, applications, networks, policies, and procedures to discover vulnerabilities. They include documentation, log, ruleset, and system configuration review; network sniffing; and file integrity checking.

Rogue Device: An unauthorized node on a network.

Rules of Engagement (ROE): Detailed guidelines and constraints regarding the execution of information security testing. The ROE is established before the start of a security test, and gives the test team authority to conduct defined activities without the need for additional permissions.

Ruleset: A collection of rules or signatures that network traffic or system activity is compared against to determine an action to take—such as forwarding or rejecting a packet, creating an alert, or allowing a system event.

Social Engineering: The process of attempting to trick someone into revealing information (e.g., a password).

Target Identification and Analysis Techniques: Information security testing techniques, mostly active and generally conducted using automated tools, that are used to identify systems, ports, services, and potential vulnerabilities. Target identification and analysis techniques include network discovery, network port and service identification, vulnerability scanning, wireless scanning, and application security testing.

Target Vulnerability Validation Techniques: Active information security testing techniques that corroborate the existence of vulnerabilities. They include password cracking, remote access testing, penetration testing, social engineering, and physical security testing.

Version Scanning: The process of identifying the service application and application version currently in use.

Virtual Machine (VM): Software that allows a single host to run one or more guest operating systems.

Vulnerability: Weakness in an information system, or in system security procedures, internal controls, or implementation, that could be exploited or triggered by a threat source.

Vulnerability Scanning: A technique used to identify hosts/host attributes and associated vulnerabilities.

And for comparison's sake, here is yet one more NIST glossary, found in NIST SP 800-66, "An Introductory Resource Guide for Implementing the Health Insurance Portability and Accountability Act (HIPAA) Security Rule." The following is a copy of that glossary. You can also find it online in Appendix A of Special Publication 800-66 at http://csrc.nist.gov/publications/nistpubs/800-66-Rev1/SP-800-66-Revision1.pdf.

NIST Special Publication 800-66 Glossary

Availability [45 C.F.R. Sec. 164.304]
The property that data or information is accessible and usable upon demand by an authorized person.

Business Associate [45 C.F.R. Sec. 160.103]
(1) Except as provided in paragraph (2) of this definition, "business associate" means, with respect to a covered entity, a person who:

(i) On behalf of such covered entity or of an organized healthcare arrangement (as defined at 45 C.F.R. Sec. 164.501) in which the covered entity participates, but other than in the capacity of a member of the workforce of such covered entity or arrangement, performs, or assists in the performance of:

(A) A function or activity involving the use or disclosure of individually identifiable health information, including claims processing or administration, data analysis, processing or administration, utilization review, quality assurance, billing, benefit management, practice management, and repricing; or

(B) Any other function or activity regulated by this subchapter; or

(ii) Provides, other than in the capacity of a member of the workforce of such covered entity, legal, actuarial, accounting, consulting, data aggregation (as defined in Sec. 164.501 of this subchapter), management, administrative, accreditation, or financial services to or for such covered entity, or to or for an organized healthcare arrangement in which the covered entity participates, where the provision of the service involves the disclosure of individually identifiable health information from such covered entity or arrangement, or from another business associate of such covered entity or arrangement, to the person.

(2) A covered entity participating in an organized healthcare arrangement that performs a function or activity as described by paragraph (1)(i) of this

definition for or on behalf of such organized healthcare arrangement, or that provides a service as described in paragraph (1)(ii) of this definition to or for such organized healthcare arrangement, does not, simply through the performance of such function or activity or the provision of such service, become a business associate of other covered entities participating in such organized healthcare arrangement.

(3) A covered entity may be a business associate of another covered entity.

Confidentiality [45 C.F.R. Sec. 164.304]

The property that data or information is not made available or disclosed to unauthorized persons or processes.

Covered Entities [45 C.F.R. Sec.160.103]

Covered entity means: (1) A health plan. (2) A healthcare clearinghouse. (3) A healthcare provider who transmits any health information in electronic form in connection with a transaction covered by this subchapter. (4) Medicare Prescription Drug Card Sponsors.

Electronic Protected Health Information (electronic PHI, or EPHI) [45 C.F.R. Sec.160.n103]

Information that comes within paragraphs (1)(i) or (1)(ii) of the definition of protected health information (see "protected health information").

Healthcare Clearinghouse [45 C.F.R. Sec.160.103]

A public or private entity, including a billing service, repricing company, community health management information system or community health information system, and "value-added" networks and switches, that does either of the following functions:

(1) Processes or facilitates the processing of health information received from another entity in a nonstandard format or containing nonstandard data content into standard data elements or a standard transaction.

(2) Receives a standard transaction from another entity and processes or facilitates the processing of health information into nonstandard format or nonstandard data content for the receiving entity.

Healthcare Provider [45 C.F.R. Sec. 160.103]

A provider of services (as defined in section 1861(u) of the Social Security Act, 42 U.S.C. 1395x(u)), a provider of medical or health services (as defined in section 1861(s) of the Social Security Act, 42 U.S.C. 1395x(s)), and any other person or organization who furnishes, bills, or is paid for healthcare in the normal course of business.

Health Information [45 C.F.R. Sec. 160.103]

Any information, whether oral or recorded in any form or medium, that:

(1) Is created or received by a healthcare provider, health plan, public health authority, employer, life insurer, school or university, or healthcare clearinghouse; and

(2) Relates to the past, present, or future physical or mental health or condition of an individual; the provision of healthcare to an individual; or the

past, present, or future payment for the provision of healthcare to an individual.

Health Plan [45 C.F.R. Sec.160.103]

(1) Health plan includes the following, singly or in combination:

(i) A group health plan, as defined in this section.

(ii) A health insurance issuer, as defined in this section.

(iii) An HMO, as defined in this section.

(iv) Part A or Part B of the Medicare program under title XVIII of the Social Security Act.

(v) The Medicaid program under title XIX of the Social Security Act, 42 U.S.C. 1396, et seq.

(vi) An issuer of a Medicare supplemental policy (as defined in section 1882(g)(1) of the Social Security Act, 42 U.S.C. 1395ss(g)(1)).

(vii) An issuer of a long-term care policy, excluding a nursing home fixed-indemnity policy.

(viii) An employee welfare benefit plan or any other arrangement that is established or maintained for the purpose of offering or providing health benefits to the employees of two or more employers.

(ix) The healthcare program for active military personnel under title 10 of the United States Code.

(x) The veterans' healthcare program under 38 U.S.C. chapter 17.

(xi) The Civilian Health and Medical Program of the Uniformed Services (CHAMPUS) (as defined in 10 U.S.C. 1072(4)).

(xii) The Indian Health Service program under the Indian Healthcare Improvement Act, 25 U.S.C. 1601, et seq.

(xiii) The Federal Employees Health Benefits Program under 5 U.S.C. 8902, et seq.

(xiv) An approved State child health plan under title XXI of the Social Security Act, providing benefits for child health assistance that meet the requirements of section 2103 of the Social Security Act, 42 U.S.C. 1397, et seq.

(xv) The Medicare + Choice program under Part C of title XVIII of the Social Security Act, 42 U.S.C. 1395w-21 through 1395w-28.

(xvi) A high-risk pool that is a mechanism established under State law to provide health insurance coverage or comparable coverage to eligible individuals.

(xvii) Any other individual or group plan, or combination of individual or group plans, that provides or pays for the cost of medical care (as defined in section 2791(a)(2) of the PHS Social Security Act, 42 U.S.C. 300gg-91(a)(2)).

(2) Health plan excludes:

(i) Any policy, plan, or program to the extent that it provides, or pays for the cost of, excepted benefits that are listed in section 2791(c)(1) of the PHS Act, 42 U.S.C. 300gg-91(c)(1); and

(ii) A government-funded program (other than one listed in paragraph (1)(i)–(xvi) of this definition):

    (A) Whose principal purpose is other than providing, or paying the cost of, healthcare; or

    (B) Whose principal activity is

        (1) The direct provision of healthcare to persons; or

        (2) The making of grants to fund the direct provision of healthcare to persons.

Hybrid Entity [45 C.F.R. Sec.164.103]

A single legal entity:

(1) That is a covered entity;

(2) Whose business activities include both covered and non-covered functions; and

(3) That designates healthcare components in accordance with paragraph § 164.105(a)(2)(iii)(C).

Implementation Specification [45 C.F.R. Sec. 160.103]

Specific requirements or instructions for implementing a standard.

Individually Identifiable Health Information (IIHI) [45 C.F.R. Sec. 160.103]

Information that is a subset of health information, including demographic information collected from an individual, and:

(1) Is created or received by a healthcare provider, health plan, employer, or healthcare clearinghouse; and

(2) Relates to the past, present, or future physical or mental health or condition of an individual; the provision of healthcare to an individual; or the past, present, or future payment for the provision of healthcare to an individual; and

    (i) That identifies the individual; or

    (ii) With respect to which there is a reasonable basis to believe the information can be used to identify the individual.

Information System [45 C.F.R. Sec. 164.304]

An interconnected set of information resources under the same direct management control that shares common functionality. A system normally includes hardware, software, information, data, applications, communications, and people. (FISMA defines "information system" as "a discrete set of information resources organized for the collection, processing, maintenance, use, sharing, dissemination, or disposition of information." 44 U.S.C., Sec. 3502.)

Integrity [45 C.F.R. Sec. 164.304]

The property that data or information have not been altered or destroyed in an unauthorized manner.

Medicare Prescription Drug Card Sponsors [Pub. L. 108–173]

A nongovernmental entity that offers an endorsed discount drug program under the Medicare Modernization Act.

Physical Safeguards [45 C.F.R. Sec. 164.304]

Physical measures, policies, and procedures to protect a covered entity's electronic information systems and related buildings and equipment from natural and environmental hazards, and unauthorized intrusion.

Protected Health Information (PHI)

Individually identifiable health information:

(1) Except as provided in paragraph (2) of this definition, that [45 C.F.R., Sec. 160.103] is:

    (i) Transmitted by electronic media;

    (ii) Maintained in electronic media; or

    (iii) Transmitted or maintained in any other form or medium.

(2) Protected health information excludes individually identifiable health information in:

    (i) Education records covered by the Family Educational Rights and Privacy Act, as amended, 20 U.S.C. 1232g;

    (ii) Records described at 20 U.S.C. 1232g(a)(4)(B)(iv); and

    (iii) Employment records held by a covered entity in its role as employer.

Required [45 C.F.R. Sec. 164.306(d)(2]

As applied to an implementation specification (see implementation specification, above], indicating an implementation specification that a covered entity must implement. All implementation specifications are either required or addressable.

Security [44 U.S.C., Sec. 3542]

Protecting information and information systems from unauthorized access, use, disclosure, disruption, modification, or destruction in order to provide:

    (A) Integrity, which means guarding against improper information modification or destruction, and includes ensuring information non-repudiation and authenticity;

    (B) Confidentiality, which means preserving authorized restrictions on access and disclosure, including means for protecting personal privacy and proprietary information; and

    (C) Availability, which means ensuring timely and reliable access to and use of information.

Standard [45 C.F.R., Sec. 160.103]

A rule, condition, or requirement:

(1) Describing the following information for products, systems, services or practices:

    (i) Classification of components.

    (ii) Specification of materials, performance, or operations; or

    (iii) Delineation of procedures; or

(2) With respect to the privacy of individually identifiable health information.

Technical Safeguards [45 C.F.R., Sec. 164.304]
The technology and the policy and procedures for its use that protect electronic-
protected health information and control access to it.
User [45 C.F.R., Sec. 164.304]
A person or entity with authorized access.

The following terms are used commonly when discussing privacy issues in business
that I have accumulated over the years. The definitions are taken from a variety of
sources, and in some cases there are two definitions from different sources for the
same term provided to allow you to see how the same concept or word can sometimes be interpreted differently by varying groups.

Definitions from Miscellaneous Sources

Access. In respect to privacy, an individual's ability to view, modify, and contest
the accuracy and completeness of "personally identifiable information" (see definition below) collected about him or her. Access is an element of the Fair Information
Practices.—Microsoft http://www.microsoft.com/security/glossary/.
ActiveX. A set of technologies that enables software components to interact with
one another in a networked environment, regardless of the language in which the
components were created. ActiveX, which was developed as a proposed standard
by Microsoft in the mid-1990s and is currently administered by the Open Group,
is built on Microsoft's Component Object Model (COM). Currently, ActiveX is
used primarily to develop interactive content for the World Wide Web, although it
can be used in desktop applications and other programs. ActiveX controls can be
embedded in Web pages to produce animation and other multimedia effects, interactive objects, and sophisticated applications.—Microsoft http://support.microsoft.
com/default.aspx?scid=/support/glossary/default.asp.
Ad Blocker. Software placed on a user's personal computer that prevents advertisements from being displayed on the Web. Benefits of an ad blocker include the ability
of Web pages to load faster and the prevention of user tracking by ad networks.—
BBBOnline http://www.bbbonline.org/UnderstandingPrivacy/PMRC/glossary.asp.
Aggregate Information. Information that may be collected by a Web site but is not
"personally identifiable" to you (see definition below). Aggregate information includes
demographic data, domain names, Internet provider addresses, and Web site traffic. As
long as none of these fields is linked to a user's personal information, the data is considered aggregate.—TRUSTe http://www.truste.org/partners/users_glossary.html.
Anonymizer. A service that prevents Web sites from seeing a user's Internet
protocol (IP) address. The service operates as an intermediary to protect the
user's identity.—BBBOnline http://www.bbbonline.org/Understanding Privacy/
PMRC/glossary.asp.

Attribute. An attribute describes a property associated with an individual.—Center for Democracy and Technology http://csrc.nist.gov/kba/Presentations/Day%201/Schwartz-Attachment.pdf.

Attribute Authentication. Attribute authentication is the process of establishing an understood level of confidence that an attribute applies to a specific individual.—Computer Science and Telecommunications Board, National Research Council, *Who Goes There? Authentication Through the Lens of Privacy* (Washington, DC: National Academy Press, 2003).

Authentication. (1) The process for verifying that someone or something is who or what it claims to be. In private and public computer networks (including the Internet), authentication is commonly performed through the use of logon passwords.—Microsoft http://www.microsoft.com/security/glossary/. (2) The process of establishing confidence in the truth of some claim.—Computer Science and Telecommunications Board, National Research Council, *Who Goes There? Authentication Through the Lens of Privacy* (Washington, DC: National Academy Press, 2003).

Authenticator. An authenticator is evidence that is presented to support the authentication of a claim. It increases confidence in the truth of the claim.—Computer Science and Telecommunications Board, National Research Council, *Who Goes There? Authentication Through the Lens of Privacy* (Washington, DC: National Academy Press, 2003).

Authorization. Authorization is the process of deciding what an individual ought to be allowed to do. Computer Science and Telecommunications Board, National Research Council, *Who Goes There? Authentication Through the Lens of Privacy* (Washington, DC: National Academy Press, 2003).

Banner Ad. A section of a Web page containing an advertisement that is usually an inch or less tall and spans the width of the Web page. The banner contains a link to the advertiser's own Web site.—Microsoft http://support.microsoft.com/default.aspx?scid=/support/glossary/default.asp.

Biometrics. The science of biometrics concerns the reading of the measurable, biological characteristics of an individual in order to identify them to a computer or other electronic system. Biological characteristics normally measured include fingerprints, voice patterns, retinal and iris scans, faces, and even the chemical composition of an individual's perspiration. For the effective "two-factor" security authorization of an individual to a computer system, normally a biometric measure is used in conjunction with a token (such as a smartcard) or an item of knowledge (such as a password).—Cyber Business Center http://www.nottingham.ac.uk/cyber/Gloss.html.

Biometrics. Biometrics is the automatic identification or identity verification of individuals on the basis of behavioral or physiological characteristics. Computer Science and Telecommunications Board, National Research Council, *Who Goes There? Authentication Through the Lens of Privacy* (Washington, DC: National Academy Press, 2003).

Blog. (1) A contraction of weblog, a form of online writing characterized in format by a single column of chronological text, usually with a sidebar, and frequently updated. As of mid-2002, the vast majority of blogs are non-professional (with only a few experimental exceptions) and are run by a single writer. (2) To write an article on a blog.—Samizdata.net http://www.samizdata.net/blog/glossary .html.

Browser. Also called a Web browser. Software that enables you to search and or navigate through Web sites or "browse" parts of the Internet, especially the World Wide Web. Examples: Mozilla Firefox, Google Chrome, and Microsoft Internet Explorer.—TRUSTe http://www.truste.org/partners/users_glossary.html.

Browser Cache. A memory file in your Web browser that stores the Internet addresses of sites you've recently visited. This capability allows you to access sites quicker.—TRUSTe http://www.truste.org/partners/users_glossary.html.

Buffer Overrun. A condition that results from adding more information to a buffer than it was designed to hold. An attacker may exploit this vulnerability to take over a system.—Microsoft http://www.microsoft.com/security/glossary/.

Bulletin Board. A public area online where you can post a message for everyone else to read. If you post a message to a bulletin board, in nearly all cases, other member participants will be able to contact you by e-mail.—TRUSTe http://www.truste.org/ partners/users_glossary.html.

Chat. A function that allows a group of people to communicate simultaneously by typing messages to one another online. Typically, everyone participating in the chat sees your message as soon as you send it. Designated chat areas are often referred to as "chat rooms," and any individual or group of individuals you respond to in the room will be able to contact you by e-mail.—TRUSTe http://www.truste.org/ partners/users_glossary.html.

Children's Online Privacy Protection Act (COPPA). Often considered the first widespread government regulation of privacy on the Internet, this act went into effect on April 21, 2000. COPPA sets restrictions for Web sites that communicate with children under 13. One of these restrictions mandates that Web sites obtain "verifiable parental consent" before engaging in ongoing communications with a child.—TRUSTe http://www.truste.org/partners/users_glossary.html.

Cipher. An encryption method, typically using a predefined key and an algorithm to transform plaintext into ciphertext.—Microsoft http://www.microsoft.com/ security/glossary/.

Click Trail. A record of all the Web page addresses you have visited during a specific online session. Click trails tell not just what Web site you visited, but which pages inside that site.—TRUSTe http://www.truste.org/partners/users_glossary .html.

Code of Fair Information Practices. The basis for privacy best practices, both online and offline. The Practices originated in the Privacy Act of 1974, the legislation that protects personal information collected and maintained by the U.S. government. In 1980, these principles were adopted by the Organization for

Economic Cooperation and Development and incorporated in its Guidelines for the Protection of Personal Data and Transborder Data Flows. They were adopted later in the EU Data Protection Directive of 1995, with modifications. The Fair Information Practices include notice, choice, access, onward transfer, security, data integrity, and remedy.—Microsoft http://www.microsoft.com/security/glossary/.

Collaborative Filtering. A means of predicting the interests and needs of a specific customer based on previously collected data from a larger group of customers.—TRUSTe http://www.truste.org/partners/users_glossary.html.

Consent. Explicit permission, given to a Web site by a visitor, to handle his or her personal information in specified ways. Web sites that ask users to provide personally identifiable information should be required to obtain "informed consent," which implies that the company fully discloses its information practices prior to obtaining personal data or permission to use it.—Center for Democracy and Technology (CDT) http://www.cdt.org/privacy/guide/terms/.

Cookie. A block of text placed in a file on your computer's hard drive by a Web site you've visited. A cookie is used to identify you the next time you access the site. Cookies cannot identify an individual user specifically unless the cookie data is attached to personally identifiable information collected some other way, such as via an online registration form.—TRUSTe http://www.truste.org/partners/users_glossary.html.

Credential. Credentials are objects that are verified when presented to the verifier in an authentication transaction. Credentials may be bound in some way to the individual to whom they were issued, or they may be bearer credentials. The former are necessary for identification, while the latter may be acceptable for some forms of authorization. Computer Science and Telecommunications Board, National Research Council, *Who Goes There? Authentication Through the Lens of Privacy* (Washington, DC: National Academy Press, 2003).

Cryptography. The use of codes to convert data by using a key so that only a specific recipient will be able to read it. Cryptography is used to enable authentication and non-repudiation, and to help preserve confidentiality and data integrity.—Microsoft http://www.microsoft.com/security/glossary/.

Customer Relationship Management (CRM). CRM entails all aspects of service and sales interactions a company has with its customer. CRM often involves personalizing online experiences, help-desk software, and e-mail organizers.—e-Future http://www.e-future.ca/pdf/efc_e-business_glossary.pdf.

Data Grids. Grids that provide shared data storage. Based on a Catalog where Logical File Names are associated to Physical File Names.—CMS Monitoring with Web Services http://www.ba.infn.it/ zito/xml/rems.html.

Data Mining (Online Profiling). The practice of compiling information about Internet users by tracking their motions through Web sites, recording the time they spend there, what links they clink on and other details that the company desires, usually for marketing purposes.—Center for Democracy & Technology (CDT) http://www.cdt.org/privacy/guide/terms/.

Data Profiling. The use of information about your lifestyle and habits to provide a descriptive profile of your life. At its simplest, data profiling is used by marketing companies to identify you as a possible customer. At its most complex, data profiling can be used by security services to identify potential suspects for unlawful activity, or to highlight parts of a person's life where other forms of surveillance may reveal something about their activities. In those states where the European Directive on Data Protection is in force, you have rights of access to any data held about you for the purposes of data processing or profiling.—GreenNet http://www.fraw.org.uk/ resources/gn-irt/glossary.html.

Data Spills. The result of a poorly designed form on a Web site. The information may leak to Web servers of other companies, perhaps an ad network or advertising agency.—BBBOnline http://www.bbbonline.org/Understanding Privacy/PMRC/ glossary.asp.

Data Warehousing. The process of visioning, planning, building, using, managing, maintaining, and enhancing data warehouses and/or data marts.—SDG Computing http://www.sdgcomputing.com/glossary.htm.

Deceptive Trade Practices. Misleading or misrepresenting products or services to consumers and customers. In the United States, these practices are regulated by the Federal Trade Commission at the federal level and typically by the Attorney General's Office of Consumer Protection at the state level.—Microsoft http://www.microsoft .com/security/glossary/.

Digital Certificate. Using encryption technology, a document can be digitally stamped or certified as to its place of origin. A certification authority supports/legitimizes the certificates.—BBBOnline http://www.bbbonline.org/UnderstandingPrivacy/ PMRC/glossary.asp.

Digital Signature. Data that is bundled with a message or transmitted separately and is used to identify and authenticate the sender and message data. A valid digital signature also confirms that the message has not been tampered with.—Microsoft http://www.microsoft.com/security/glossary/.

Domain Name. The company, individual, or organization "name" you use to access a Web site (e.g., www.truste.org).—TRUSTe http://www.truste.org/partners/users_ glossary.html.

Electronic Mail. Commonly referred to as e-mail, this form of communication enables you to send messages and files from your computer through an online service or the Internet to one or more e-mail addresses.—TRUSTe http://www.truste.org/ partners/users_glossary.html.

E-mail. See **Electronic Mail**.

E-mail Address. The computer version of a postal address. Like a postal address, it contains information about who the e-mail recipient is and where he or she resides on the Internet.—TRUSTe http://www.truste.org/partners/users_glossary.html.

Encryption. Data that is scrambled into a private code for secure transmission.— TRUSTe http://www.truste.org/partners/users_glossary.html.

Enrollment. Enrollment is the process by which an individual person, corporation, or device is issued a credential for an authentication system.—Center for Democracy and Technology http://csrc.nist.gov/kba/Presentations/Day%201/Schwartz-Attachment.pdf.

EU Data Protection Directive. A European Union (EU) law stating that personal data from EU countries can only be transferred to non-EU countries that provide an acceptable level of privacy protection. An organization must inform individuals why information about them is collected, how to contact the organization with inquiries and complaints, the types of third parties to which the organization will disclose, and the options an organization provides to limit the disclosure of certain information. Proper notice and choice must be offered to allow an individual to opt-in or opt-out of providing specific information the organization plans on tracking.—Microsoft http://www.microsoft.com/security/glossary/.

File Transfer Protocol (FTP). A software protocol used to transfer files from a remote host over a network to another computer; also used as a command to execute the file transfer. Many systems support "anonymous FTP," which lets you access a remote host without having to provide your password or user ID on the receiving system.—TRUSTe http://www.truste.org/partners/users_glossary.html.

Firewall. A combination of hardware and software that provides a security system, usually to help prevent unauthorized access from outside to an internal network or intranet.—Microsoft http://www.microsoft.com/security/glossary/.

Form. (1) A structured document with spaces reserved for entering information and often containing special coding as well. (2) In some applications (especially databases), a structured window, box, or other self-contained presentation element with predefined areas for entering or changing information. A form is a visual "filter" for the underlying data it is presenting, generally offering the advantages of better data organization and greater ease of viewing. (3) In optical media, a data storage format used in compact disc technology. (4) In programming, a metalanguage (such as Backus-Naur form) used to describe the syntax of a language.—Microsoft http://support.microsoft.com/default.aspx?scid=/support/glossary/default.asp.

Globally Unique Identifier (GUID). This unique code is used to identify a computer, user, file, etc., for tracking purposes.—BBBOnline http://www.bbbonline.org/UnderstandingPrivacy/PMRC/glossary.asp.

Identification. Identification is the process of using claimed or observed attributes of an individual to infer who the individual is. Computer Science and Telecommunications Board, National Research Council, *Who Goes There? Authentication Through the Lens of Privacy* (Washington, DC: National Academy Press, 2003).

Identifier. An identifier points to an individual. An identifier could be a name, a serial number, or some other pointer to the entity being identified. Computer Science and Telecommunications Board, National Research Council, *Who Goes There? Authentication Through the Lens of Privacy* (Washington, DC: National Academy Press, 2003).

Identity Authentication. Identity authentication is the process of establishing an understood level of confidence that an identifier refers to an identity. It may or may not be possible to link the authenticated identity to an individual. Computer Science and Telecommunications Board, National Research Council, *Who Goes There? Authentication Through the Lens of Privacy* (Washington, DC: National Academy Press, 2003).

Identity Theft. The use of personal information to falsely assume your identity.—TRUSTe http://www.truste.org/partners/users_glossary.html.

Identity. The identity of X is the set of information about an individual X, which is associated with that individual in a particular identity system Y. However, Y is not always named explicitly. Computer Science and Telecommunications Board, National Research Council, *Who Goes There? Authentication Through the Lens of Privacy* (Washington, DC: National Academy Press, 2003).

Individual. A citizen of the United States or an alien lawfully admitted for permanent residence.—Office of Management and Budget (OMB) Web site http://www.whitehouse.gov/omb/.

Individual Authentication. Individual authentication is the process of establishing an understood level of confidence that an identifier refers to a specific individual. Computer Science and Telecommunications Board, National Research Council, *Who Goes There? Authentication Through the Lens of Privacy* (Washington, DC: National Academy Press, 2003).

Infomediaries. Persons or organizations that specialize in personal information management for individual Internet users.—TRUSTe http://www.truste.org/partners/users_glossary.html.

Information in Identifiable Form. This is information in an IT system or online collection (i) that directly identifies an individual (e.g., name, address, social security number or other identifying number or code, telephone number, e-mail address, etc.) or (ii) by which an agency intends to identify specific individuals in conjunction with other data elements, that is, indirect identification. (These data elements may include a combination of gender, race, birth date, geographic indicator, and other descriptors).—Office of Management and Budget (OMB) Web site http://www.whitehouse.gov/omb/.

Information Privacy. Information privacy protects the individual's interest in controlling the flow of information about the self to others. Computer Science and Telecommunications Board, National Research Council, *Who Goes There? Authentication Through the Lens of Privacy* (Washington, DC: National Academy Press, 2003).

Information Technology (IT). This means, as defined in the Clinger–Cohen Act, any equipment, software, or interconnected system or subsystem that is used in the automatic acquisition, storage, manipulation, management, movement, control, display, switching, interchange, transmission, or reception of data or information.—Office of Management and Budget (OMB) Web site http://www.whitehouse.gov/omb/.

Informed Consent. This consent is an agreement made by an individual with the legal capacity to do so; who is so situated as to be able to exercise free power of choice, without the intervention of any element of force, fraud, deceit, duress, over-reaching, or other form of constraint or coercion; and given sufficient information of the subject matter and the elements of the transaction involved as to enable him or her to make an informed and enlightened decision.—Center for Democracy and Technology http://csrc.nist.gov/kba/Presentations/Day%201/Schwartz-Attachment.pdf.

Internet. A worldwide system of interconnected computer networks, whose use is not controlled by any government agency or central authority.—TRUSTe http://www.truste.org/partners/users_glossary.html.

Internet Access Provider. See **Internet Service Provider**.

Internet Service Provider (ISP). Also called an Internet access provider. A company that provides direct access to the Internet for individuals, companies, and institutions. Unlike commercial online service providers, ISPs usually do not provide their own content but may offer e-mail capability, browser software, and direct links to sites on the World Wide Web.—TRUSTe http://www.truste.org/partners/users_glossary.html.

Invisible GIFs (Tracker GIF, Clear GIF). Electronic images, usually not visible to site visitors, that allow a Web site to count those who have visited that page or to access certain cookies.—BBBOnline http://www.bbbonline.org/Understanding Privacy/PMRC/glossary.asp.

IP Address. Short for Internet protocol address. A 32-bit (4-byte) binary number that uniquely identifies a host (computer) connected to the Internet to other Internet hosts, for the purposes of communication through the transfer of packets. An IP address is expressed in "dotted quad" format, consisting of the decimal values of its four bytes, separated with periods; for example, 127.0.0.1. The first one, two, or three bytes of the IP address, assigned by InterNIC Registration Services, identify the network the host is connected to; the remaining bits identify the host itself. The 32 bits of all four bytes together can signify almost 2^{32}, or roughly 4 billion, hosts. (A few small ranges within that set of numbers are not used).—Microsoft http://support.microsoft.com/default.aspx?scid=/support/glossary/default.asp.

Java Applet. Java class that is loaded and run by an already-running Java application such as a Web browser or an applet viewer. Java applets can be downloaded and run by any Web browser capable of interpreting Java, such as Internet Explorer, Firefox, and Chrome Java applets are frequently used to add multimedia effects and interactivity to Web pages, such as background music, real-time video displays, animations, calculators, and interactive games. Applets can be activated automatically when a user views a page, or they may require some action on the part of the user, such as clicking on an icon in the Web page.—Microsoft http://support.microsoft.com/default.aspx?scid=/support/glossary/default.asp.

JavaScript. A scripting language developed by Netscape Communications and Sun Microsystems, Inc., that is loosely related to Java. JavaScript, however, is not a true object-oriented language, and it is limited in performance compared with Java because it is not compiled. Basic online applications and functions can be added to Web pages with JavaScript, but the number and complexity of available application programming interface functions are fewer than those available with Java. JavaScript code, which is included in a Web page along with the HTML code, is generally considered easier to write than Java, especially for novice programmers. A JavaScript-compliant Web browser, such as Internet Explorer or Firefox, is necessary to run JavaScript code.—Microsoft http://support.microsoft.com/default.aspx?scid=/ support/glossary/default.asp.

MAC Address. Acronym for media access control. It is the unique Ethernet card ID number found in network computers. These addresses are necessary in local area network (LAN) computers in order for them to communicate. The addresses are unrelated to the Macintosh computer.—BBBOnline http://www.bbbonline.org/UnderstandingPrivacy/PMRC/glossary.asp.

Major Information System. It embraces "large" and "sensitive" information systems and means, as defined in OMB Circular A-130 (Section 6.u.) and annually in OMB Circular A-11 (section 300-4 (2003)), a system or project that requires special management attention because of its (i) importance to the agency mission, (ii) high development, operating and maintenance costs, (iii) high risk, (iv) high return, (v) significant role in the administration of an agency's programs, finances, property, or other resources. — Office of Management and Budget (OMB) Web site http://www.whitehouse.gov/omb/.

National Security System. As defined in the Clinger–Cohen Act, an information system operated by the federal government, the function, operation, or use of which involves: (a) intelligence activities, (b) cryptologic activities related to national security, (c) command and control of military forces, (d) equipment that is an integral part of a weapon or weapons systems, or (e) systems critical to the direct fulfillment of military or intelligence missions, but does not include systems used for routine administrative and business applications, such as payroll, finance, logistics, and personnel management.—Office of Management and Budget (OMB) Web site http://www.whitehouse.gov/omb/.

Newsgroup. Topic groupings for articles and information posted by readers of that group. If you post a message to a newsgroup, other participants of the group will know your e-mail address.—TRUSTe http://www.truste.org/partners/users_glossary.html.

Notice. A privacy principle that requires reasonable disclosure to a consumer of an entity's personally identifiable information (PII) collection and use practices. This disclosure information is typically conveyed in a privacy notice or privacy policy.—Microsoft http://www.microsoft.com/security/glossary/.

Online Service. A proprietary, commercial network that provides a variety of information and other services to its subscribers. Commercial online services typically provide their own content, forums (e.g., chat rooms, bulletin boards), e-mail capability, and information available only to subscribers.—TRUSTe http://www.truste.org/partners/users_glossary.html.

Onward Transfer. The transfer of personally identifiable information (PII) by the recipient of the original data to a second recipient. For example, the transfer of PII from an entity in Germany to an entity in the United States constitutes onward transfer of that data.—Microsoft http://www.microsoft.com/security/glossary/.

Opt-In. An option that gives you complete control over the collection and dissemination of your personal information. A site that provides this option is stating that it will not gather or track information about you unless you knowingly provide such information and consent to the site.—TRUSTe http://www.truste.org/partners/users_glossary.html.

Opt-Out. An option that gives you the choice to prevent personally identifiable information from being used by a particular Web site or shared with third parties.—TRUSTe http://www.truste.org/partners/users_glossary.html.

P3P (Platform for Privacy Preferences Project). An open privacy specification developed and administered by the World Wide Web Consortium (W3C) that, when implemented, enables people to make informed decisions about how they want to share personal information with Web sites.—Microsoft http://www.microsoft.com/security/glossary/.

Packet Sniffer. A software tool used to track the packets of information sent to and from a computer. Programmers generally use this tool.—BBBOnline http://www.bbbonline.org/UnderstandingPrivacy/PMRC/glossary.asp.

Password. A private, unique series of letters and/or numbers that you create and must use to gain access to an online service or the Internet, specific data available online, or to make modifications to restricted-access software (e.g., parental control software).—TRUSTe http://www.truste.org/partners/users_glossary.html.

Personal Information Protection and Electronic Documents Act (PIPEDA). Privacy legislation that governs the collection, use, and disclosure of personal information by organizations in a manner that recognizes both the right of an individual to have his or her personal information protected and the need of organizations to collect, use, or disclose personal information for purposes that are reasonable. Under the act, companies' responsibilities are to be accountable; identify the purpose; limit collection; limit use, disclosure, and retention; be accurate; use appropriate safeguards; be open; give access; and challenge.—eFuture http://www.e-future.ca/pdf/efc_e-business_glossary.pdf.

Personally Identifiable Information. Information that can be traced back to an individual user (e.g., your name, postal address, or e-mail address). Personal user preferences tracked by a Web site via a "cookie" (see definition above) is also considered personally identifiable when linked to other personally identifiable information provided by you online.—TRUSTe http://www.truste.org/partners/users_glossary.html.

Pop-Up Ads. An ad that appears in its own window when a user opens or closes a Web page.—eFuture http://www.e-future.ca/pdf/efc_e-business_glossary.pdf.

Pop-Up Blockers. A utility that prevent Web site pop-ups from displaying. The challenge with this software is to distinguish a valid pop-up from an advertisement. There are an enormous number of Web pages that launch legitimate browser windows to display additional information, and pop-up is a small browser window. — *PC Magazine* http://www.pcmag.com/encyclopedia_term/0,2542,t=popup+blocker&i=49499,00.asp

Privacy Impact Assessment (PIA). It is an analysis of how information is handled (i) to ensure handling conforms to applicable legal, regulatory, and policy requirements regarding privacy, (ii) to determine the risks and effects of collecting, maintaining, and disseminating information in identifiable form in an electronic information system, and (iii) to examine and evaluate protections and alternative processes for handling information to mitigate potential privacy risks.—Office of Management and Budget (OMB) Web site http://www.whitehouse.gov/omb/.

Privacy Invasive Technologies (PITs). This term usefully describes the many technologies that intrude into privacy. Among the host of examples are data-trail generation through the denial of anonymity, data-trail intensification (e.g., identified phones, stored-value cards, and intelligent transportation systems), data warehousing and data mining, stored biometrics, and imposed biometrics.—Privacy advocate Roger Clarke http://www.anu.edu.au/people/Roger.Clarke/DV/PITsPETs.html#PITs.

Privacy Policy. An organization's requirements for complying with privacy regulations and directives.—Microsoft http://www.microsoft.com/security/glossary/.

Privacy Policy in Standardized Machine-Readable Format. It means a statement about site privacy practices written in a standard computer language (not English text) that can be read automatically by a Web browser. Office of Management and Budget (OMB) Web site http://www.whitehouse.gov/omb/.

Privacy Seal. Also referred to as a "Trustmark." An online seal awarded by TRUSTe to Web sites that agree to post their privacy practices openly via privacy statements, as well as adhere to enforcement procedures that ensure that their privacy promises are met. When you click on the TRUSTe Privacy Seal, you're taken directly to the privacy statement of the licensed Web site.—TRUSTe http://www.truste.org/partners/users_glossary.html.

Privacy Statement. A page or pages on a Web site that lay out its privacy policies (i.e., what personal information is collected by the site, how it will be used, whom it will be shared with, and whether you have the option to exercise control over how your information will be used). All TRUSTe Web site licensees are required to post comprehensive privacy statements.—TRUSTe http://www.truste.org/partners/users_glossary.html.

Profiling. Analyzing a program to determine how much time is spent in different parts of the program during execution.—Microsoft http://support.microsoft.com/default.aspx?scid=/support/glossary/default.asp.

Pseudonymity. A condition in which you have taken on an assumed identity.—Center for Democracy and Technology (CDT) http://www.cdt.org/privacy/guide/terms/.

Pseudonymous Identifiers. A pseudonymous identifier is an identifier that cannot, in the normal course of events, be associated with a particular individual. Center for Democracy and Technology. http://csrc.nist.gov/kba/Presentations/Day%201/Schwartz-Attachment.pdf.

Referrer Field. The referrer header field (mistakenly spelled referrer in the HTTP standard) is a unit of information that contains the URL of the site you are currently in. The referrer header field is sent automatically to any site you are about to visit, when clicking a link. Referrer headers allow reading patterns to be studied and reverse links drawn. The address of the page might contain privacy information (such as your name or e-mail address), or might reveal personal interests that you would rather keep private (e.g., http://www.examplesite. com/Health/Medicine/Dermatology/).—IDcide http://www.idcide.com/pages/ res_term.htm.

RFID (Radio Frequency Identification System). An automatic identification and data capture system comprising one or more readers and one or more tags in which data transfer is achieved by means of suitable modulated inductive or radiating electromagnetic carriers.—TAGSYS http://www.tagsys.net/.

Secure Sockets Layer (SSL). A protocol for establishing an encrypted communications channel to help prevent the interception of critical information, such as credit card numbers on the World Wide Web and other Internet services.—Microsoft http://www.microsoft.com/security/glossary/.

Spam. Also called junk e-mail. Unsolicited, unwanted e-mail usually sent by advertisers. Spam is usually sent out to thousands of unwilling recipients at once.—TRUSTe http://www.truste.org/partners/users_glossary.html.

Spam Filters. Programs that detect and reject spam by looking for certain keywords, phrases, or Internet addresses.—TRUSTe http://www.truste.org/partners/ users_glossary.html.

Spoof. To make a transmission appear to come from a user other than the user who performed the action.—Microsoft http://www.microsoft.com/security/glossary/.

Third-Party Ad Servers. Companies that display banner advertisements on Web sites that you visit. These companies are often not the ones that own the Web site.—TRUSTe http://www.truste.org/partners/users_glossary.html.

TRUSTe Watchdog. An easy-to-use consumer alternative dispute resolution mechanism that allows you to bring your privacy-related complaints about a TRUSTe-certified Web site. TRUSTe serves as a liaison between you and the Web site to reach an appropriate resolution to your privacy dispute.—TRUSTe http://www. truste.org/partners/users_glossary.html.

Trustmark. An online seal awarded by TRUSTe to Web sites that agree to post their privacy practices openly via privacy statements, as well as adhere to enforcement procedures that ensure that their privacy promises are met. When you click on the TRUSTe trustmark, you're taken directly to the privacy statement of the licensed Web site.—TRUSTe http://www.truste.org/partners/users_glossary.html.

Verification. Verification is any procedure in which a set of authentication credentials are validated using internal standards or third-party confirmation.—Center for Democracy and Technology http://csrc.nist.gov/kba/Presentations/Day%201/ Schwartz-Attachment.pdf.

Vetting. Vetting is any process of examining and evaluating information or data provided for the purposes of the issuance of credentials.—Center for Democracy and Technology http://csrc.nist.gov/kba/Presentations/Day%201/Schwartz-Attachment.pdf.

Web Beacon. Web Beacons are images that are placed in HTML documents (Web pages, HTML e-mail) to facilitate user activity tracking. Web Beacons are usually used in conjunction with cookies and are often used to track visitors across multiple internet domains. Web Beacon images are usually, but not always, small and "invisible."—Upright Communications http://www.walkupright.com/privacy/pglossary.html.

Web Browser. See **Browser**.

Web Bugs. Small image in a HTML page with all dimensions set to 1 pixel. Because of its insignificant size, it is not visible; but it is used to pass certain information anonymously to third-party sites. Mainly used by advertisers. Can also be referred to as a Web Beacon or Invisible GIF.—Bextra http://www.bextra.com/privacy_policy_glossary-1012.asp.

Web Log. Most Web servers produce "log files," time-stamped lists of every request that the server receives. For each request, the log file contains anonymous information such as date and time, the IP address of the browser making the request, the document or action that's being requested, the location of the document from which the request was made, and the type of browser that was being used. Log files are usually used to ensure quality of service. They also can be used in a limited way to analyze visitor activity.—Upright Communications http://www.walkupright.com/privacy/pglossary.html.

Web Site. A collection of "pages" or files on the World Wide Web that are linked together and maintained by a company, organization, or individual. Anyone with a Web site may be considered a content provider or a publisher.—TRUSTe http://www.truste.org/partners/users_glossary.html.

Webmaster. Typically, an individual or an individual within a company or organization assigned with the task of updating and maintaining an individual Web site. The Webmaster's e-mail address is often listed on the Web site as the contact person for queries and questions related specifically to the site's content and/or format.—TRUSTe http://www.truste.org/partners/users_glossary.html.

World Wide Web (WWW). A part of the Internet that links text, sound, and images in the form of Web pages and sites.—TRUSTe http://www.truste.org/partners/users_glossary.html.

Appendix U: Sample Case Studies

Here are some sample case studies for privacy breach response training that I have used with great success. Modify as necessary for your own organization.

Instructor Notes

1. Tell the class that something serious has occurred that they need to address.
2. Divide class into six groups of 8–10 people each.
3. Ask each group to choose 1 PR spokesperson/scribe.
4. Give each group the Background Information and Incident pages.
5. Tell the groups to read through the incident description, and then discuss as a group.
6. Have each group write their actions, notes, and flowcharts onto a flip chart.
7. Ten minutes later, give them page 2 of their assigned incident.
8. Have each group continue to write their actions onto a flip chart.
9. Ten minutes later, have each of the group spokespersons describe how they would respond to the incident and their other accompanying actions. Ask them to answer the questions provided on their sheets. Ask them to provide reasons for making their decisions.
10. Discuss for 30 minutes.

Incident #1: Notebook computer theft
Incident #2: Accidental e-mail incident
Incident #3: Papers with sensitive information become public
Incident #4: Programming error puts PII on Web site
Incident #5: Executive falls for spear phishing message
Incident #6: Employee sabotage of computer system

Questions Applicable to All Incidents (These Will Be Given on Paper to All Students)

1. What are the primary concerns related to this incident?
2. What positions within the company should be on the incident response team that resolves this breach?
3. Describe the incident and breach response actions that should occur. Each group should flowchart its actions to help it determine and document what it will do and what its decisions will be.
4. What information should you provide to your company leaders about the incident, and at what times? Hint: Put into the flowchart to help you with this.
5. What information, if any, should you provide to your customers, the public, business partners, etc., and at what times?
6. What laws would cover this type of breach?
7. Will the individuals to whom the data applies need to be notified? Why or why not?
8. What are the possible consequences of the incident? What are the impacts on the organization? What are the impacts on the individuals whose PII was involved?
9. What type of damage control should you do?
10. What should be done by the organization to help prevent a similar type of breach from occurring?
11. Should anyone be penalized for any of the activities described? If so, who, and what sanctions would be appropriate?

We suggest that each team assign responsibilities for different questions to make this process as effective and efficient as possible.

Case Study #1

BACKGROUND FACTS

- Your organization is a midsized (~8,000 employees) retailer with physical stores in four U.S. states (North Carolina, South Carolina, Tennessee, and Kentucky), but sells products online everywhere in the world.
- A large number of your personnel have laptops that they use on docking stations to connect to your network while within your facilities, and also to work outside the facilities.
- You also have many contractors to whom you have assigned laptops that can be used on docking stations.
- You have had information security policies implemented for the past 10 years.

- You have had privacy policies implemented for 2 years.
- The last time there was information security or privacy training was given was 2 years ago, right after the privacy policies were implemented.
- Six months ago, your organization implemented a policy requiring the data on all mobile computing devices to be encrypted within 2 months of policy implementation.
- A group of contractors has authorized access to the consumer database to perform maintenance and often performs work from remote locations on their assigned notebook computers.
- The database contains customer names, address, credit card numbers, phone numbers, purchase history, including items, dates, and locations of purchase.
- You are responsible for information security and privacy for your organization.

Incident: Notebook computer theft

- It is Wednesday, 3 p.m.
- You receive the following e-mail from Physical Security

> Hi,
> Just thought you might like to know that sometime between 11:30 a.m. and 12:30 p.m. last Friday a notebook computer used by one of our contractors, Chris Ray, was stolen from his car while he was parked by the Outback Steakhouse in Atlanta, Georgia. It had a value of $2300, but our risk insurance covers it.
> I'm not sure if this is of concern to you or not.
> Let me know if you need more information.
> Riley

FOLLOW-UP CASE STUDY #1 INCIDENT INFORMATION

- It is now Friday, 8:30 a.m.
- You have since discovered the contractor's notebook contained a database with customer information about the residents of the states where you have stores.
- The database, within an Excel spreadsheet, included the following information about 75,000 customers:
  - Name
  - Mailing address
  - Credit card number

- Phone number
- Purchased items
- Purchase prices for the items
- Transaction dates

■ The notebook also contained all the contractor's e-mail that had accumulated on it since he was assigned the notebook 11 months ago.

■ The e-mail system is Outlook.

■ The data on the notebook was not encrypted.

■ There was a login password required on the notebook.

■ The notebook was on the front passenger seat of the car, visible through the window.

■ The contractor's car was locked.

■ Nothing else was taken from the car.

■ A police report was filed for the stolen notebook on Friday when the incident occurred.

■ No individuals from within the database have been notified.

■ There was a surveillance camera on the outside of the restaurant.

■ The contractor has provided the following additional information:
  - His SecurID card, which allows access to your organization's network via VPN, was in the notebook carrying case.
  - He had a sticky note on the SecurID card that contained the PIN.

■ The incident was communicated to the local newspaper, along with the other entire police blotter about incidents and arrests in the area, and was published in Thursday morning's paper.

■ Regional television Thursday evening news reported the notebook theft. They reported the following, some of which is incorrect:
  - A notebook containing information about all 3 million customers of your organization was stolen last week.
  - No individuals have yet been notified.
  - The information included names, SSNs, birthdates, credit card number, medical information, and other personal information.
  - The notebook computer was not encrypted or password protected.

■ Your organization's call center has received calls from 205 individuals asking about the incident since the news stories broke on television.

- Chris Ray just called and said news reporters were at the facility asking him questions about the incident.

Case Study #2

BACKGROUND FACTS

- Your organization is a large (~100,000 employees) multinational financial company.
- You have customers in 35 countries including the United States, Canada, and throughout South America, Europe, and Asia.
- A large number of your personnel have mobile computers they use to work while traveling and from their homes.
- Around 3000 contractors work for your organization, to whom you have assigned laptops that can be used on docking stations.
- Your help desk function is outsourced to a company based in India.
- You have had information security policies implemented for the past 15 years.
- You have had privacy policies implemented for 5 years.
- The last time you provided information security or privacy training to your personnel was right after the privacy policies were implemented 5 years ago.
- Roy, an employee of the outsourced help desk company, has authorized access to the customer database to perform his job and answer customer questions.
- The database contains such information as name, address, credit history and score, social security number, phone number, payment information, and history.
- You are responsible for information security and privacy for your organization.

Incident: Accidental e-mail incident

- It is Friday, 8 a.m. You receive a call from your Communications VP, and he gives you the following information:
  - On this past Monday afternoon, just before leaving the work office, one of the personnel from the help desk company, Roy, tried to send a file containing the customer information to his personal e-mail address so he

could work from home on Tuesday, but he accidentally sent it to a similar e-mail group address, we will reference as Competitor E-mail, for another financial company that, yes, also happens to be a competitor of your company.
- Roy did not realize he sent the message to the wrong address until he saw the reply back from one of the recipients when he returned to the office and logged into the corporate e-mail system Wednesday morning.
- The Competitor E-mail group contained 35 individual e-mail addresses.
- The data within the file mistakenly sent to the Competitor E-mail includes the data for 20,000 customers of one of your mortgage products.
- The message had a clear-text attachment containing a spreadsheet with a list of all the customers that included their name, address, credit history and score, social security number, phone number, payment information, and history.
- The message from one of the IDs within the Competitor E-mail simply stated, "You probably sent this to the wrong e-mail address."
- Roy told his manager, Eran, about the mistake.
- Eran called the Competitor E-mail manager, and the manager assured him that the e-mail message was deleted by everyone who received it.
- On Thursday at 2 p.m. your Communications VP got a call from one of his staff indicating she found a blog posting that contained derogatory statements about your company, along with a copy of the customer spreadsheet.
■ The Communications VP wants to know (1) how this happened, and (2) what you are going to do for damage control.

FOLLOW-UP CASE STUDY #2
INCIDENT INFORMATION

■ At 9 a.m. Friday you get another call from the Communications VP. He indicates:
- He got a message from a *Wall Street Journal* reporter; it included the original message that had been forwarded to him from an anonymous e-mail address.
- The reporter has requested an interview with the VP and is asking how such sensitive information got posted to the Internet.

- Eran, the manager for the outsourced help desk service in India, calls you right after the Communications VP and says their lines are flooded with angry calls from your customers saying they have heard that their sensitive information has been posted on the Internet. He wants to know what to tell them.
- You check the Internet, and you find that the customer list that was attached to the e-mail has been posted on at least two sites that you can find.

Case Study #3

BACKGROUND FACTS

- Your organization is a small (~100 employees) background screening firm that does business within all the 50 U.S. states, but not outside the United States.
- You perform the full range of background checks, including employer confirmations, education verification, felony checks, credit checks, and reference verifications.
- You are located in Charlotte, North Carolina.
- A group of employees has authorized access to the customer database to perform maintenance.
- The database contains for each individual being investigated: his or her name, current and past addresses, SSN, phone number, birth date, credit history, police record, education transcripts, past employers, SSN benefits, family members, birth country, and birth city.
- You are responsible for information security and privacy for your organization.

Incident #3: Papers with sensitive information become public.

- It is Wednesday, 7 a.m.
- You get a call from the company operator.
- The operator indicates she got an outside call at 6:30 a.m. from someone saying "hundreds" of papers with your company's letterhead were found blowing around the street with what looked to be many other companies' names, along with background reports containing what look to be individuals' names, current and past addresses, SSNs, phone numbers, birth dates, credit histories, police records,

education transcripts, past employers, SSN benefits, family members, birth countries, and birth cities.
■ You get a call from the physical security manager, who has the local news on a monitor 24 × 7 in his office, and he says a report just was broadcast on all the morning news shows about sensitive information on papers blowing throughout the streets of Charlotte that appear to come from your company.

FOLLOW-UP CASE STUDY #3
INCIDENT INFORMATION

■ It is Wednesday, 9 a.m.
■ You have received a call from the physical security manager. The company used to take your recyclable papers away called and said that when they arrived at their recycling center, their truck was empty. Apparently, the driver did not secure the doors well, and as the driver drove through downtown Charlotte, the papers all blew out along the way.
■ You then receive a call from the receptionist indicating that there are reporters in the lobby who want to speak with you about the incident.

Case Study #4

BACKGROUND FACTS

■ Your organization is a large (~70,000 employees) technology company.
■ You have 100 million customers who purchase your products and services in locations throughout 60 different countries.
■ You sell products in stores as well as online, directly and through resellers.
■ You are located in Houston, Texas.
■ One of the Web site applications programmers mistakenly put a preproduction application, which provides customers access to their own account data, on the Internet production Web server, but did not realize he did so.
■ The application code as currently written allows anyone using the application to see a listing of all customers

and their associated data, including name, address, credit card number, phone number, account number, purchase details, and serials numbers for the purchased products.

■ The application was put on the Web server on February 1 of this year, and the quality assurance staff has been testing it and requesting changes since then.

■ You are responsible for information security and privacy for your organization.

Incident: Programming error puts PII on Web site

■ It is Wednesday, 8 a.m.

■ You receive a call from the CEO telling you about the *Wall Street Journal* article with the following headlines that appeared today: "YOUR ORGANIZATION Makes Personal Information on 100 Million Customers Available On Their Web Site." You were not aware of the application being on the Internet before getting his call. The CEO asks you to resolve the situation as quickly as possible and keep him updated.

■ No one in your organization realized that the application was on the Internet until the *Wall Street Journal* story.

FOLLOW-UP CASE STUDY #4
INCIDENT INFORMATION

■ It is Wednesday, 5 p.m.

■ The story about the application being on the Internet has been reported on all the local television stations during the noon news.

■ Reporters are asking to speak with you about the situation.

■ The reporters are asking if your organization will provide credit monitoring for all the impacted individuals.

■ The reporters are asking when your organization will notify the individuals, and why the PII was put on the Internet in the first place.

■ A member of your team has found the application site mirrored on at least two other Internet sites, in addition to finding copies of the database on at least two Internet sites.

■ Reporters are asking for more information.

■ Your CEO wants a report of the status.

Case Study #5

BACKGROUND FACTS

- Your organization is a medium-sized (~3000 employees) company that provides health insurance.
- You have 8 million customers in four U.S. states that access their account information through your online Web portal.
- You are located in Raleigh, North Carolina.
- Your organization uses a highly rated malware prevention system that studies have shown prevents 95% of spam and malware from entering your network.
- You are responsible for information security and privacy for your organization.

Incident: Executive falls for spear phishing message

- You arrive at the office on Friday morning at 8:30 a.m.
- You find a paper on your desk chair from your CTO that says, "Pat, I sent you an e-mail about a problem we have; please read it and respond as soon as possible!"
- You check your e-mail and find the following:

Pat, I got a phone call from our CEO, Mr. Enrique, this past Monday. He received an alarming e-mail message while he was working on Monday; the message included Mr. Enrique's name, our company name, phone number, and company address. The message read:

Mr. Enrique, you are hereby notified that you must appear before a grand jury on May 19, 2008, for the civil case filed by Jon Bronstein. Go to the following URL to get the details of the case and full instructions regarding your required appearance, along with a description of the penalties for not complying with this federal order.

Mr. Enrique clicked on the URL that appeared within the message. However, the site he went to was blank. After clicking the URL a few more times, Mr. Enrique called me. I told him that we had effective malware that prevents bogus messages from entering the company, and I suggested he forward the message to the corporate counsel, which he did. Mr. Enrique then continued working, but said he noticed that his computer seemed a little slower throughout the week. He said that Ms. Stone, the lawyer he forwarded the message to, also clicked on the URL, and told Mr. Enrique that a subpoena would not be delivered in this manner, and that he should just ignore it. Ms. Stone forwarded the message to the rest of the legal staff so they would be aware of it.

What I want to know from you is, are we in position to stop these e-mails? If not, what do we need to do?

- You discover that all 21 members of the legal staff have also clicked on the URL, and that the message has also been forwarded to the 35 business unit managers so they are aware of the situation, many of whom have also clicked on the URL.
- The lawyers and business unit managers collectively have access to all the customer files.
- You call the CTO and discover that network performance has increasingly degraded throughout the week.

FOLLOW-UP CASE STUDY #5
INCIDENT INFORMATION

- It is the following Wednesday.
- You are notified from the service center that there are growing numbers of customers who have reported that they have received identity theft warnings from their credit card companies.
- You have one of your team members check the Internet, and they find a large amount of your customer data files are posted on a file server located in China.

Case Study #6

BACKGROUND FACTS

- Your organization is a small (25 employees) architectural firm located in Tampa, Florida, with 100 customers, primarily residential individuals for whom you have built homes or did remodeling, within Florida.
- You have a small computer network attached to the Internet. All the architectural drawings are stored on it.
- You do not have a single person whose sole responsibility is network management or security; network administration and security is performed by five of the administrative staff members, and everyone basically has access to all the resources on the network.

Incident: Employee sabotage of computer system

■ You arrive at the office on Monday morning at 7:30 a.m.
■ You log on to your network and try to access the architectural drawings database, but there are no files within it.
■ The other people in the office also indicate that they cannot find any files.
■ Martha White, an administrative assistant who has been with the firm for 3 years, did not show up to work.
■ After a call to her, you discover, through a very heated conversation, that she read in the Sunday morning paper what she thought was a help wanted ad for her job, so, thinking she was going to be fired, she went to the office Sunday afternoon, got into the building using her key and deleted, using her authorized access, 7 years worth of the architect firm's files, valued at $3 million.
■ Your company does not have backups for any of the files.

FOLLOW-UP CASE STUDY #6
INCIDENT INFORMATION

■ It is now Tuesday morning, and you learn from the police investigators that prior to deleting the files, Martha White copied the customer files, including names, payment information, addresses, and phone numbers, to an Internet site.
■ Martha also sent an e-mail message, from one of the other employee's e-mail addresses, to all 100 customers stating:

Dear customers,
I believe it is my moral responsibility to let you know that the ABC Architect Company is not only unfair to its employees, but you should also know it sells your personal information to any marketing company willing to pay for it. Does it seem like you have been getting a lot of junk mail, spam, and phone solicitations lately? Well, you can thank Mr. Tsongas, the owner of the company! The company also has nonexistent security over its information. It would probably be a good idea to check your credit reports to see if you have been a victim of identity theft as a result. You may also want to engage the services of a lawyer!

Appendix V: Sample Awareness Activity

Here is a great example of an engaging and educational activity for personnel: an information security puzzle from the State of Virginia (see http://www.vita.virginia.gov/uploadedFiles/Security/Information_Security_Awareness_Month/2008/InformationSecurityAwarenessPuzzle.pdf).

1	Across	You can turn the pages in a ____ in your hand or read one on-line.
2	Down	When creating a Password, do not use words from your favorite _<2>_, _<28 Down>_, hobby, recording artist, or _<29 Across>_.
3	Across	Before you throw something in the _____, ask yourself, "Is this something I would give to an unauthorized person or want to become publicly available?"
4	Across	Don't transmit any __ letters via email.
5	Across	___ , Peer-to-Peer, is an informal network that allows users to share music, games, software, or other files with other users online.
5	Down	Don't share your user_<5>_ or __<15 Across>__.
6	Down	Criminals sometimes use _____ - programs like viruses and spyware– to get into your computer. Once there, they can steal information, send spam, and commit fraud.
7	Down	How to keep your laptop safe: Keep it _____ . . . use a security cable.
8	Across	A ___ [abbreviation] is a means of accessing the Internet at high speed using standard phone lines.
9	Across	Specific categories of web sites are blocked for one or more of the following reasons: _<19 Across>_Risk, _<20 Down>_Risk, or_<9>_Risk.
10	Down	How to keep your laptop safe: Treat it like ____.
11	Down	A Complex Password must be at least ____ characters long.
12	Across	A _____ is a program that can sneak onto your computer – often through an email attachment – and then make copies of itself, quickly using up all available memory.
13	Across	A _____ is a segment of Internet space denoted by the function or type of information it includes. Current ones include ".com" for commercial sites, ".gov" for governmental ones, and ".org" for non-commercial organizations.
14	Down	A _____ is hardware or software that helps keep hackers from using your computer to send out your personal information without your permission. It watches for outside attempts to access your system and block communications to and from sources you don't permit.
15	Across	Don't share your user _<5 Down>_or __<15>__.
16	Across	_____ is the scrambling of data into a secret code that can be read only by software set to decode the information.
17	Across	_____is a software program that may be installed on your computer without your consent to monitor your use, send pop-up ads, redirect your computer to certain websites, or record keystrokes, which could lead to identity theft.
17	Down	Always include a clear and specific _____ line in your email.

18	Across	____ is a method of writing, sending, receiving and saving messages over an electronic communication system such as the Internet.
19	Across	Specific categories of web sites are blocked for one or more of the following reasons: _<19 >_Risk, _<20 Down>_Risk, or_<9 Across>_Risk.
20	Down	Specific categories of web sites are blocked for one or more of the following reasons: _<19 Across >_Risk, _<20>_Risk, or_<9 Across>_Risk.
21	Down	_<22 Across>_ web sites provide an easy method for the "_<21>_" of email addresses – which leads to more spam in our mailboxes.
22	Across	_<22>_ web sites provide an easy method for the "_<21 Down>_" of email addresses – which leads to more spam in our mailboxes.
23	Down	Software _____ is the theft of software through illegal copying of genuine programs or through counterfeiting and distribution of imitation software products or unauthorized versions of software products.
24	Down	A computer ____ can be considered as the modern counterpart of a paper document which traditionally was kept in offices.
25	Down	A ____ Room is a place or page in a website or online service where people can type messages which are displayed almost instantly on the screens of others who are in the room.
26	Across	A computer _____ is a group of interconnected computers.
27	Across	A _____ is a program that allows a user to find, view, hear, and interact with material on the Internet.
28	Down	When creating a Password, do not use words from your favorite _<2 Down>_, _<28>_, hobby, recording artist, or _<29 Across>_.
29	Across	When creating a Password, do not use words from your favorite _<2 Down>_, _<28 Down>_, hobby, recording artist, or _<29>_.
30	Down	_____ is a type of software that often comes with free downloads. Sometimes it displays ads on your computer, while some monitors your computer use (including websites visited) and displays targeted ads based on your use.
31	Down	How to keep your laptop safe: Keep it off the ____ . . . or at least between your feet.
32	Down	The __ Address is a computer's "address" and consists of a series of numbers separated by periods.
33	Across	_____ is a scam that involves Internet fraudsters who send spam or pop-up messages to lure personal information (credit card numbers, bank account information, Social Security number, passwords, or other sensitive information) from unsuspecting victims.
34	Across	Never use email for any _____ or unethical purpose.

35	Across	_____ Profiling is the compiling information about consumers' preferences and interests by tracking their online movements and actions in order to create targeted ads.
36	Down	_____ engineering is referred to as an approach to gain access to information, primarily through misrepresentation, and often relies on the trusting nature of most individuals.
37	Across	Email ____, also known as unsolicited bulk email (UBE) or unsolicited commercial email (UCE), is the practice of sending unwanted email messages, frequently with commercial content, in large quantities to an indiscriminate set of recipients.
37	Down	Always check your _<37>_ and _<41 Down>_ in your email before sending it.
38	Across	A ____ is a program that reproduces itself over a network and can use up your computer's resources and possibly shut your system down.
39	Across	Only _____ invalid login attempts are permitted before the account is locked.
40	Down	Your Password is like a _____; use it regularly, change it often, and do not share it with anyone else.
41	Down	Always check your _<37 Down>_ and _<41>_ in your email before sending it.
42	Across	Last Name of the DMV IT Security Director (ISO) and the name of a truck-manufacturing company located in Allentown, Pennsylvania.
43	Down	A _____ Password contains at least 3 of the 4 following characters: Lowercase Alpha (e.g. abc), Uppercase Alpha (e.g. ABC), Numeric (e.g. 123), Special/Non-Alphanumeric (e.g. ! $ # %).
44	Down	To _____ the amount of spam you receive, be careful who you give your email address to.

Index